A Personal Note from Harley

The Internet is a vast information system that, in less than a genera... become the most important invention in the history of mankind. In a very rea... sense, the Internet reflects our destiny as a species.

Although the Internet is built upon a platform of computers, programs and communication lines, it is actually a system for people and for information. As human beings, we have created the Internet to fulfill our biological needs to communicate and to learn.

At first, such ideas may seem grandiose and exaggerated, so I don't want you to believe me—not yet. All I want you to do is read this book, and join me as we explore the various parts of the Internet.

If you do, you can count on me in several important ways:

- I promise to discuss everything you need to get started: how to choose a computer, how to connect to the Net, and how to find the programs you will want to use.
- I promise to introduce you to the words and technical terms you will encounter as you read about the Internet. I will explain each of these words to you and show you how to use them well.
- I promise to explain the important ideas you need to use the Internet, and how to use your programs well in harmony with these ideas.
- Most important, I promise to teach you how to understand what you are doing and how it fits into the Internet as a whole. I will show you the ideas behind the ideas, and help you appreciate the power and beauty that I see every day.

All I ask of you are two things.

First, read the entire book.

Although you can look up a particular topic and read it in isolation, I wrote this book for you to read from cover to cover—from start to finish. Please do so. You will not only enjoy yourself; you will find a lot more than you expect. (As I am sure you realize by now, this is not an ordinary computer book.)

Second, as you read, I want you to think about an important idea. As a human being, you are blessed with intelligence, creativity and curiosity. Many people never live up to their potential because they allow themselves to become lazy or discouraged. Along the way, such people lose (or never develop) self-confidence. They are afraid of new ideas, and they are scared that they will not be able to understand and master new technology.

I want to make sure this does not happen to you. I want to make sure you understand that *everyone* has trouble learning how to use complicated tools and understanding complicated ideas. The world is full of people who will promise to teach you quickly and simply, but don't be fooled. Learning well takes time and mental effort.

You and I are going to spend many hours together, and my job is to make sure that time is well spent. I said earlier that the Internet helps us communicate and learn. I wrote this book in the same spirit. As you read, I will be by your side: explaining, teaching and (at times) entertaining you.

Throughout this book, I will show you a lot more than how to use the Internet. I will show you how to work and how to think with elegance and style. I will show you how to open doors that you may not even know exist. You and I will walk through those doors together, and, in the weeks and months that follow, you will find that our world is a lot more exciting and wonderful than you ever dreamed.

The Internet is important, and I want you to be able to use it well.

More than that, I want you to be able to understand the Internet: what it does, how it works, and *why* it is so important to us. And, above all, I want you to enjoy using the Internet, secure in the knowledge that you know what you are doing, that you understand what is going on, and that you *belong*.

Becoming part of the Internet is our biological destiny. As I said earlier, I don't expect you to believe this now. All I ask from you now is that you read this book and spend some time with me.

Buy this book. I am on your side.

HARLEY HAHN

TEACHES

the INTERNET

About the Author

Harley Hahn is an internationally recognized writer, analyst and consultant. He is the author of twenty-one books on various topics, including the best-selling *Harley Hahn's Internet & Web Yellow Pages*, *Harley Hahn Teaches the Internet*, *The Internet Complete Reference*, and the highly regarded *Assembler Inside & Out*. His Unix books include *Unix Unbound* and *Harley Hahn's Student Guide to Unix*.

Hahn has a degree in mathematics and computer science from the University of Waterloo, Canada, and a graduate degree in computer science from the University of California at San Diego. Before becoming a professional writer, he studied medicine at the University of Toronto Medical School.

Hahn enjoys writing computer books because "I get to sleep in, and I like telling people what to do."

Hahn does not live in a converted farmhouse in Connecticut with his wife, three children, and a Labrador retriever named Rolf. Nor does he commute frequently to New York.

His favorite pajamas are red.

HARLEY HAHN® TEACHES

the INTERNET

Harley Hahn

201 West 103rd Street,
Indianapolis, Indiana 46290

que®

Harley Hahn Teaches the Internet

Copyright © 1999 by Harley Hahn

International Standard Book Number: 0-7897-1615-1

Library of Congress Catalog Card Number: 97-81381

Printed in the United States of America

First Printing: November, 1998

00 99 98   4   3   2   1

The name "Harley Hahn", the stylized Harley Hahn signature *Harley Hahn* ® and the Unisphere logo ® are all registered trademarks of Harley Hahn.

Trademarks

All terms mentioned in this book that are known to be trademarks or service marks have been appropriately capitalized. *Que Corporation* cannot attest to the accuracy of this information. Use of a term in this book should not be regarded as affecting the validity of any trademark or service mark.

NOTICE: No animals were harmed in the making of this book. (But three of them got sick and threw up.)

Executive Editor
John Pierce

Acquisitions Editor
Don Essig

Managing Editor
Thomas F. Hayes

Project Editor
Sossity Smith

Copy Editor
Lunaea Hougland

Indexer
Cheryl Jackson

Book Designer
Ruth Lewis

Layout
Eric S. Miller

Proofreader
Maribeth Echard

Back Cover Photo
Wendy Murdock

Cover Designer
Dan Armstrong

To Wendy

List of Chapters

1   Understanding the Internet 1

2   An Overview of the Internet 17

3   Everything You Need to Connect to the Net 37

4   Internet Addresses 67

5   Mail 95

6   Using Mail Well 121

7   The Web 143

8   Safety, Security and Privacy 179

9   Finding Stuff on the Internet 201

10 Plug-Ins and Controls 219

11 Downloading and Installing Sofware 233

12 Usenet 243

13 Mailing Lists 275

14 Talking on the Net 293

15 Creating Your Own Web Site 323

16 Getting Your Own Domain Name 347

A   List of Top-Level Internet Domains 355

B   Time Zones on the Internet 365

C   Abbreviations Used When Talking on the Net 369

    Glossary 375

    Index 397

List of Figures

FIGURE 1–1: List of important Internet (TCP/IP) protocols 8

FIGURE 2–1: Important clients and servers used on the Internet 35

FIGURE 3–1: Microsoft's and Netscape's suites of Internet software 45
FIGURE 3–2: Various ways to connect to an ISP 49
FIGURE 3–3: Relative speeds of dialup connections 54

FIGURE 4–1: Organizational top-level domains 69
FIGURE 4–2: Examples of geographical top-level domains 70
FIGURE 4–3: The most common schemes used within URLs 83
FIGURE 4–4: The most common file extensions used on the Internet 86

FIGURE 5–1: A typical mail message 104
FIGURE 5-2: A typical mail message showing the full header 106
FIGURE 5-3: The life cycle of a mail message 112

FIGURE 6–1: An example of a good mail message 123
FIGURE 6–2: An example of a bad mail message 124
FIGURE 6–3: Common abbreviations used in mail messages 127

FIGURE 7–1: A typical Web page within Internet Explorer 148
FIGURE 7–2: A typical Web page within Netscape 149
FIGURE 7–3: A Web page with frames 157
FIGURE 7–4: A typical Favorites list within Internet Explorer 168
FIGURE 7–5: A typical Bookmarks list within Netscape 170

FIGURE 8–1: Security warning when sending data with Internet Explorer 182
FIGURE 8–2: Security warning when sending data with Netscape 183

FIGURE 9–1: Custom buttons for accessing search engines with Internet Explorer 209
FIGURE 9–2: Custom buttons for accessing search engines with Netscape 209
FIGURE 9–3: Entering a search request into the address bar 209
FIGURE 9–4: Entering a search request into an address window 211

FIGURE 10–1: The most common file extensions used on the Web 221
FIGURE 10–2: A typical message telling you to get a plug-in 225
FIGURE 10–3: Dialog box asking to download an ActiveX control 227

FIGURE 11–1: Beginning a download with Internet Explorer 236
FIGURE 11–2: Specifying where to save a downloaded file 237

FIGURE 12–1: The seven original Usenet hierarchies 250
FIGURE 12–2: Mainstream and alternative Usenet hierarchies 251
FIGURE 12–3: The most important Usenet hierarchies 252
FIGURE 12–4: Examples of regional and organizational hierarchies 253
FIGURE 12–5: Sample Usenet newsgroups 254
FIGURE 12–6: Reading a Usenet article with Collabra (Netscape) 258
FIGURE 12–7: Reading a Usenet article with Outlook Express (Internet Explorer) 259
FIGURE 12–8: Newsgroups to which FAQs are posted 261
FIGURE 12–9: Some of the abbreviations commonly used on Usenet 263
FIGURE 12–10: Related Usenet newsgroups, including a .misc group 265
FIGURE 12–11: Examples of Usenet newsgroups that contain pictures 266

FIGURE 13–1: Examples of mailing lists 280
FIGURE 13–2: Subscribing and unsubscribing to a mailing list 283
FIGURE 13–3: Summary of important Listserv commands 286
FIGURE 13–4: Summary of important Listproc commands 287
FIGURE 13–5: Summary of important Majordomo commands 288
FIGURE 13–6: Examples of gatewayed Bitnet mailing lists 290

FIGURE 14-1: A Web chat room using a Java talk client 297
FIGURE 14–2: A Web chat room using a browser as a talk client 297
FIGURE 14–3: A Web chat room with avatars 298
FIGURE 14–4: A direct connection using ICQ 301
FIGURE 14–5: Abbreviations used while talking on the Net 303
FIGURE 14–6: A typical IRC session 309
FIGURE 14–7: Important IRC commands 311
FIGURE 14–8: An imaginary setting within a mud 314
FIGURE 14–9: Standard port numbers used on the Internet 316

FIGURE 15–1: HTML for a simple Web page 328
FIGURE 15–2: A simple Web page 329
FIGURE 15–3: The most important HTML tags 330
FIGURE 15–4: A Web page containing a table 333
FIGURE 15–5: A Web page containing a form 333
FIGURE 15–6: A Web page containing frames 334

FIGURE 16–1: Whois information for a typical domain name 352

FIGURE B–1: The 24-hour time system compared to the AM/PM system 366
FIGURE B–2: U.S. Time Zones compared to GMT 367

FIGURE C–1: Abbreviations used while talking on the Net 371

List of Internet Resources

Chapter 3:   Lists of Internet Service Providers (ISPs)   63

Chapter 5:   Web-Based Mail Services   100
Chapter 5:   Mail Programs   102

Chapter 6:   Mail Address Directories   135

Chapter 7:   Browsers   147
Chapter 7:   Ad-Blocking Software   150
Chapter 7:   Daily Comics   162
Chapter 7:   Default Home Pages   175
Chapter 7:   Push Clients for Using Channels   177
Chapter 7:   Channel Guides   177

Chapter 8:   Movie Information   185
Chapter 8:   Antivirus Programs   194
Chapter 8:   Virus Hoaxes and Myths   195
Chapter 8:   Collections of Web Sites for Children   197
Chapter 8:   Web Site Rating Systems   199

Chapter 9:   Search Engines   204
Chapter 9:   Usenet Search Engines   208
Chapter 9:   FAQs (Frequently Asked Question Lists)   215
Chapter 9:   Web Rings   216

Chapter 10:   Streaming Audio/Video Plug-Ins   229
Chapter 10:   VRML Plug-Ins   229
Chapter 10:   Multimedia Plug-Ins   230
Chapter 10:   Music Plug-Ins   230
Chapter 10:   360-Degree Photo Plug-Ins   230
Chapter 10:   Places to Look for Plug-Ins   231

Chapter 11:   Software Repositories: Windows 95/98   235
Chapter 11:   Software Repositories: Windows CE   235
Chapter 11:   Zip File Programs   240

Chapter 12:   Newsreaders   247
Chapter 12:   Web-Based Usenet Access   247
Chapter 12:   Commercial News Feeds   249
Chapter 12:   Lists of Organizational and Regional Hierarchies   253
Chapter 12:   Programs to Download Usenet Binaries   267
Chapter 12:   Harley Hahn's Master List of Usenet Newsgroups   271
Chapter 12:   Places to Search for Usenet Newsgroups   271
Chapter 12:   Creating a Mainstream Newsgroup   274
Chapter 12:   Creating an alt Newsgroup   274

Chapter 13:   Lists of Mailing Lists   288
Chapter 13:   Web-Based Mailing Lists   289

Chapter 14:   Web Chat Rooms   299
Chapter 14:   Avatar-Based Chat Rooms   299
Chapter 14:   Direct Connection Talk Facilities: Part of a Larger System   301
Chapter 14:   Direct Connection Talk Facilities: Independent   301
Chapter 14:   Voice and Video Communication   306
Chapter 14:   IRC Clients   312
Chapter 14:   IRC Help Information   313
Chapter 14:   Mud Clients   317
Chapter 14:   Mud FAQs and Tutorials   317
Chapter 14:   Lists of Muds   317

Chapter 15:   HTML Tutorials   327
Chapter 15:   Free Web Page Editors   336
Chapter 15:   Web Page Editors   336
Chapter 15:   FTP Client Programs   337
Chapter 15:   Photographs   338
Chapter 15:   Buttons, Graphics and Backgrounds   339
Chapter 15:   Clip Art   339
Chapter 15:   Image Editors   339
Chapter 15:   Sounds   340
Chapter 15:   Free Web Site Hosting   344
Chapter 15:   Promoting Your Web Site   345

Chapter C: Lists of Smileys   373

Table of Contents

A Personal Note From Harley Hahn   i

About the Author   iv

Dedication   vii

List of Chapters   viii

List of Figures   ix

List of Internet Resources   xii

Table of Contents   xiv

Acknowledgments   xxi

1: UNDERSTANDING THE INTERNET   1

What Is the Internet?   2

What Is It Like to Use the Net?   3

The Secret of the Internet: Clients and Servers   4

How TCP/IP Makes the Internet Work   6

Talking About the Net   9

Words to Avoid   10

Who Runs the Internet?   11

Where Is the Center of the Net?   13

Pornography, Bad People, and Other Evil Things Hastening the Downfall of Civilization   14

2: AN OVERVIEW OF THE INTERNET   17

What Can You Do on the Net?   18

Mail   19

The Web   20

The Parts of the Web   21

Channels   23

Usenet   24

Mailing Lists   25

Advertising and Spam   26

Anonymous FTP and Downloading   28

Talk Facilities (Including IRC)   30

Imaginary Environments (Including Muds and VRML Worlds)   32

Telnet   34

Making Sense of It All   35

3: EVERYTHING YOU NEED TO CONNECT TO THE NET   37

The Summary in Advance   38

Processors   38

Memory   39

Disks   41

Operating Systems (Windows)   42

Software   43

What Type of Computer Should You Buy?   45

How Much Should You Pay for a Computer?   46

Alternatives to Regular PCs (Such as WebTV)   47

Types of Internet Connections   48

The Speed of an Internet Connection   49

Analog and Digital   51

Modems   52

Dialup Connections   53

ISDN   55

Upstream and Downstream   56

DSL   57

Cable   58

What Type of Internet Services Are Available?   59

Why You Might Want Two Internet Accounts   60

Finding Internet Service Providers (ISPs)   61

Choosing an ISP   62

Does It Matter Whether Your Dialup ISP Has Lots of POPs?   64

What About AOL?   64

The Summary Once Again   65

4: INTERNET ADDRESSES   67

Hostnames and Top-Level Domains   68

Why Are There Two Types of Top-Level Domains?   70

Exceptions to the Rules   71

Understanding Hostnames   72

Domains   74

IP Addresses   75

DNS   77

How DNS Works for You   78

Mail Addresses   80

URLs   82

File Names and Extensions   85

Directories and Subdirectories   87

Pathnames   88

URL Abbreviations   89

One More URL Abbreviation   91

Case Sensitive Pathnames   91

What a ~ (Tilde) Means in a Pathname   92

Putting It All Together   93

5: MAIL   95

The Basic Ideas   96

SMTP Servers and POP Servers   97

IMAP Servers   98

Which Mail Program Should You Use?   100

The Most Important Header Lines   103

A Few More Header Lines   105

The Body of a Message   108

Attachments   109

Signatures   109

vCards   110

How Mail Is Stored (Folders)   111

Address Lines Within the Header (To, Cc, Bcc)   112

Address Lines Within the Header (To, Cc, Bcc)   113

Using an Address Book   114

Replying   115

Forwarding   118

Understanding Mail Error Messages   119

6: USING MAIL WELL   121

Email Conventions   122
Make Sure Your Messages Look Nice   123
Thank-You Notes   124
Smileys and Other Communication Conventions   125
Be Careful What You Write   127
Is It Okay to Use Rich Text?   129
Putting URLs in Messages   130
Using the Windows Clipboard   131
Sending Mail to a Group of People   133
Finding Someone's Mail Address   134
Spam and Privacy   137
Harley Hahn's List of Seven Ways to Keep Your Email Address Private   138
Filters   140

7: THE WEB   143

The Basic Ideas   145
Options and Preferences   147
Blocking Advertisements   149
Where to Get Help   151
Entering a URL   151
Shortcuts When Typing URLs   152
Navigating   153
Reading a Web Page   155
Right-Clicking   157
What to Do When a URL Doesn't Work   159
Managing Your Browser Window   160
Opening a New Browser Window   162
Reloading a Web Page (the Cache)   164
Creating a Shortcut to a Web Page   164
Saving URLs in a List (Favorites and Bookmarks)   166
Internet Explorer: Using the Favorites List   168
Netscape: Using the Bookmarks List   170
Sending a URL or a Web Page to Someone   173
Setting Your Home Page   174

Channels   176
The Active Desktop   178

8: SAFETY, SECURITY AND PRIVACY   179

Is It Safe to Send Personal Information over the Web?   180
Unnecessary Security Warnings   182
Secure Connections   183
Cookies   184
Controlling Cookies with Internet Explorer   186
Controlling Cookies with Netscape   187
Java and ActiveX   188
Security Settings in Your Browser   190
Computer Viruses   192
Virus Hoaxes   194
Children and the Internet   195
Filtering Software and Rating Systems   198

9: FINDING STUFF ON THE INTERNET   201

Starting a Search   202
Search Engines   202
Techniques for Using a Search Engine   204
Usenet Search Engines   206
Accessing Your Favorite Search Engines Quickly   208
Cool Browser Tricks   209
FAQs (Frequently Asked Question Lists)   212
Web Rings   216
An Approach to Searching the Net   217

10: PLUG-INS AND CONTROLS   219

File Types and Extensions   220
Plug-Ins   222
ActiveX Controls   224
Installing Plug-Ins and ActiveX Controls   225
Cool Things to Do with Plug-Ins   228

11: DOWNLOADING AND INSTALLING SOFTWARE   233

Overview of the Download Process   234
Downloading a Program   236
Anonymous FTP   237
Installing a Program   238
Installing a Program Automatically   240
Uninstalling a Program   241

12: USENET   243

The Basic Ideas   244
How Does Usenet Work?   244
The Usenet Tradition of Freedom   245
What Newsreader Should You Use?   246
News Servers   247
Newsgroups and Hierarchies   249
Configuring Your Newsreader   255
Reading Usenet Articles   256
The Format of a Usenet Article   258
Moderated Newsgroups   260
FAQs (Frequently Asked Question Lists)   261
Usenet Slang   262
Pictures (Binaries)   266
Posting an Article   267
Finding What You Want on Usenet   270
How Are Newsgroups Created?   271

13: MAILING LISTS   275

The Basic Ideas   276
How Are Mailing Lists Different from Usenet Newsgroups?   277
Mailing List Programs: Listserv, Listproc and Majordomo   279
Subscribing and Unsubscribing to a Mailing List   281
Keeping the Addresses Straight   284
Mailing List Commands   284
Finding Mailing Lists   288
Starting Your Own Mailing List   289
Mailing List Gateways   290

14: TALKING ON THE NET   293

The Basic Ideas   294
Web Chat Rooms   296
Direct Connections   299
Abbreviations Used While Talking   302
Voice and Video on the Net   304
IRC (Internet Relay Chat)   307
Muds   313
Expectations and Reality   318
Net Sex   320

15: CREATING YOUR OWN WEB SITE   323

HTML   324
The Components of a Web Page   327
Web Page Editors   335
Pictures and Sounds   337
Web Page Design Tips   340
Finding a Server to Host Your Web Site   342
Promoting Your Web Site   345

16: GETTING YOUR OWN DOMAIN NAME   347

How to Get Your Own Domain Name   348
Registering a Domain Name   349
Choosing a Domain Name   350
Using Whois to Check a Domain Name   351
Specifying Contact Names When You Register a Domain Name   352

APPENDIX A: LIST OF TOP-LEVEL INTERNET DOMAINS   355

APPENDIX B: TIME ZONES ON THE INTERNET   365

APPENDIX C: ABBREVIATIONS USED WHEN TALKING ON THE NET   369

GLOSSARY   375

INDEX   397

Acknowledgments

This is the part of the book where I thank all the people who have helped me. I realize, of course, that you probably don't care one way or the other about these people. After all, why should you? They didn't help you, and you will probably never meet them.

Still, I want you to read this section, and I would like to make it as meaningful as possible. For this reason I have set up these acknowledgments as an interesting learning experience. Here is how it works.

Before we start, I am going to show you a list of quotes. All of the quotes come from people who I will mention in the acknowledgments (one quote per person). Look at the quotes now. Then, as you read through this section, see if you can match up each quote with the person who said it. At the end of the section, I will tell you who said what. You can then grade yourself, thereby achieving significant personal insight.

Ready to start? Here are the quotes:

1: "I don't have all the answers, but the answers I have, I give freely."

2: "Since the best things in life are free, and there's no such thing as a free lunch, that means lunch cannot be one of the best things in life."

3: "It's the end of the day on a Friday, and you're asking me to be philosophical?"

4: "My philosophy is to watch as many basketball games as often as I can. It's tons of fun, and I get to yell and scream without looking like an idiot."

5. "In the end, you are what you do, not what you say."

6: "Being consistent and looking intelligent is better than trying to match whatever editorial trend is popular in the moment."

7: "When you treat people the way you want to be treated, it comes back to you."

8: "The whole education system is a government conspiracy—at least that's what they want you to think."

9: "You are more of an individual if you don't buy into the easy clichés."

10: "I'm usually the guy who writes down the good quotes—not the guy who says them."

11: "Those who want to succeed will find a way. Those who don't will find an excuse."

12: "All publishing companies run at some sort of deficit somewhere."

13: "Almost everything I say is clever, witty and fun. Can't you just remember something I said?"

14: "When you teach someone, remember that your student may be smarter than you."

15: "I can't do this now; I have rehearsal."

Now that you have seen the quotes, let's push on to the acknowledgements.

To start, I thank Wendy Murdock. Wendy is my chief researcher and knows more about what is on the Internet than anyone I know. Wendy, actually, has been using the Internet long before most people even knew it existed. She is not only skilled, talented and knowledgeable, she is fun to work with. I suppose it is possible to write a book without Wendy's help, but I wouldn't want to do so. If you'd like to find out more about Wendy and what she does, take a look at her Web site at:

`http://www.wendy.com/`

Next, I thank my editor, Lunaea Hougland. The word editor is an amorphous term that can mean many things, and such is the case for Lunaea. For years, Lunaea has been my copy editor, which means that she reads everything I write and makes sure it is perfect. In addition, Lunaea is the expert on the "Harley Hahn" style, and she ensures that everything that is printed works well and is up to the high standards we set for ourselves. She is a fountain of good advice and as valuable an editor as exists.

If you'd like to find out more about Lunaea and what she does, take a look at her Web site at:

`http://www.lunaea.com/`

(Just so you aren't confused, her work on the Web is done under the name Lunaea Weatherstone.)

The next people I would like to thank are my technical reviewers: Eli, James, Len, Mart, Ron and Zbigniew. These are experts whose job it is to read everything I write, looking for mistakes. I have known all these people for years, and they are a formidable group.

Isidor Elias (Eli) is a scholar who has been teaching science for many years. I first met him when I took a physics course from him ("The History and Philosophy of Physical Thought"). Eli is a remarkable individual who is able to do what so few of us can: light a spark of understanding and curiosity in other people.

James Brady is an accomplished programmer, as well as an actor and a writer. I have spent a lot of time working with James (he has done a great deal of programming for me), and have always been impressed by his intelligence, his quick grasp of complex details, and his willingness to accept responsibility and do what is necessary to get the job done well.

Len Babin is an Inspector in the RCMP (Royal Canadian Mounted Police), the national police force of Canada. Among his other duties, Len has acquired the expertise to be considered an international authority on Internet crime. During the time Len was helping me with this book, he was in Guatemala, working as a United Nations law enforcement expert (on loan from the RCMP), helping to train the Guatemalan police force.

Martin Rivers is a fifteen-year-old Internet savant who lives with his family in London and goes to an exclusive private school. Mart is an expert in many areas of life: inline skating, the Simpsons, ancient Roman poets, exploiting ICQ (an Internet chat system), waking up early every morning to deliver newspapers, palmtop computers, and interpreting the nuances of South Park. Mostly, though, Mart is known for being the coolest guy in the neighborhood.

Ron Dragushan is an old friend I have known for more than 25 years. In fact, 25 years ago, Ron and I worked together to start the first PIRG (Public Interest Research Group) in Canada, at the University of Waterloo where we were undergraduates. Aside from being a computer expert in many different areas, Ron has the distinction of being the wisest person I know (and I know a lot of people).

Zbigniew Jurkowski is a hard worker who has assisted me on a number of books. He is a programmer and computer aficionado who knows a great deal about Internet software. Zbigniew has the uncanny ability to find and test the newest programs before anyone else has even heard of them.

The people I just mentioned read and commented on every chapter of the book as I wrote it. However, I also had the help of other people, each of whom is an expert in his or her own area. Here are the names of these people along with the topics they discussed with me:

- Carrie Campbell [the Internet Queen of Gothic]: IRC
- Gil Leon [from GTE]: Modems, ISDN and DSL
- Jean Armor Polly: Kids' stuff
- Kenn Nesbitt: ActiveX controls
- Marlene Garstang: More kids' stuff
- Molly Holzschlag: New Web technology
- Terry Keramaris: Talking on the Internet

For important equipment and support, I thank James Adkins of the IBM Product Reviews Lab, along with the members of his team: Eldrice Murphy, James Lumpkin, Keith Snyder, Michael Red, Rich Russo, Rob Armbruster and Scott Kennedy.

For Internet access, I thank Timothy Tyndall, Marcy Montgomery and Sylvia Tyndall of RAIN (Regional Alliance for Information Networking), and Michael Ghens, their system administrator.

For Web and mail support, I thank Patrick Linstruth and Chris Linstruth, the proprietors of Qnet, the friendliest ISP (Internet service provider) on earth.

For technical assistance of the highest caliber, I thank Noel Cragg, an honest-to-goodness renaissance man of networks, computers and programming.

Finally, I would like to thank the various people at Macmillan Computer Publishing (my publisher) who worked on this book. Let's start with John Pierce. His title is "publisher", which means he is in charge. John is a visionary with a comprehensive grasp of the publishing industry and a fund of good stories.

Working with John are Don Essig (acquisitions editor), who worked with me day after day for several months, Karen Reinisch (executive editor), who managed the initial phases of the project, and John's assistant Lori Morgan, who is especially important because she knows the secret of how to control John's schedule.

Once a book is written, several things start to happen.

First, someone starts to index the book. In this case, I demanded the very best indexers in the entire company, and my request was granted. The index for this book was prepared by Cheryl Jackson (indexer)—the biggest sports fan in the entire company— under the guidance of Ginny Bess (the manager of indexers). These two wonderful young women bring indexing to the heights it rightly deserves. Along the way, they worked with me to develop a new style, just for this book, called "Jackson Double Post Topical Indexing".

At the same time as the book is being indexed, someone is figuring out what the book should look like. That someone was Ruth Lewis (book designer). My idea was that the book should be plain, straightforward and easy to read, and this is where Ruth came in. She designed the overall look of the book, and then spent lots of time with me, changing various details until everything was perfect.

Once the book design is done, the book is laid out. This is an arduous task requiring each and every page to be visually formatted to look as good as possible. I mentioned earlier that, before the index was created, I asked for the very best indexers in the company. Well, I did the same for the page layout. The skill of the person who actually creates the pages makes a huge difference to the quality of a book. For that reason, I asked Macmillan for the best layout person they had. As a result, they gave me Eric Miller (layout tech), who, like all the other people at Macmillan, was willing to keep working until I was satisfied. The proof of his skill is visible on every page of this book.

When the book is finished, the last person to work on it is the proofreader, in this case, Maribeth Echard. Maribeth's job was to compare the final book to the original files I submitted. She read every word on every page, looking for discrepancies. (What a job!)

The last two editorial people I would like to thank are Tom Hayes (managing editor) and Sossity Smith (project editor). These two people oversaw the entire production of the book and followed it, step by step, as it made its way, on time, to the printer. During this process, Tom spent hours with me on the telephone going over each and every tiny change that I needed in order to make this book into the archetype of perfection you now hold in your hands. Truly, big-time publishing is a glamorous business.

To move on, let's discuss the cover. As you know, the artist who creates the outside of a book is an important person. In this case, the important person is Dan Armstrong (cover designer), who patiently made change after change until the cover was just right. Helping with the final design was Greg Wiegand (brand manager). Greg is the person within Macmillan who worked with me on issues related to the Harley Hahn brand name.

Finally, once the book is printed and in the bookstores, someone has to publicize it. For doing this important job so well, I thank Julie Bowen (publicist).

So now that we have made it to the end of the acknowledgments, take a moment and reread the quotations at the beginning of this section. Now, see if you can figure out who said each quotation. (Don't look at the answers until you have made your choices.)

Check your choices against the answers below:

1: Don Essig
2: Ron Dragushan
3: Julie Bowen
4: Cheryl Jackson
5: Len Babin
6: Lunaea Hougland
7: Lori Morgan
8: Martin Rivers
9: Ginny Bess
10: Tom Hayes
11: Zbigniew Jurkowski
12: John Pierce
13: Wendy Murdock
14: Isidor Elias
15: James Brady

You can now grade yourself as follows:

If you scored 11-15 correct, congratulations. You are a shrewd student of human nature with a rare insight into other people. You are universally admired as someone who understands life and its nuances, with a degree of wisdom that is obvious to all who know you.

If you scored 6-10, you are a solid, middle of the road person, with both feet firmly planted on the ground. You have a strong appreciation for the thoughts of other people, but your intuition is tempered by experience, which keeps you from jumping into a new situation until you have analyzed it properly. Other people depend on you to keep an even keel when the going gets rough.

If you scored 0-5, you are a hard-working, creative person, not easily distracted by the actions of the people around you. You live in a world of your own, filled with enormous integrity and self-worth. For you, there is no higher calling than to set and achieve your goals based on what makes sense to you, as long as it is in harmony with your ideals.

Understanding
the Internet

The INTERNET—often referred to as the NET—is a general-purpose, international communication and information system. Once you have access to the Net, there are many things you can do. You can send and receive messages, access a great deal of information, and participate in ongoing discussions with people all over the world. You can also play games, look at pictures, listen to music, watch videos, chat with people, go shopping, and find lots and lots of free programs for your computer.

So what is the Internet? It's really not one simple thing, but, rather, a complex collection of resources. To understand the Internet and what it means to us today, let's take a few moments and start at the beginning.

What Is the Internet?

The roots of the Internet go back to the late 1960s. At the time, a project called the ARPANET was funded by the U.S. Department of Defense (ARPA was the Advanced Research Projects Agency). The goal of the Arpanet was to connect a number of computing facilities around the country.

In general, we connect computers together to share information and resources. When we do so, it is called a computer NETWORK. The Arpanet was a long distance computer network with a special requirement, one that would later turn out to be very important to the Internet.

The late 1960s was during the Cold War, and the U.S. Department of Defense was particularly concerned with the possibility of nuclear attack. For this reason, the Arpanet was designed to keep working even if someone dropped a bomb on part of the network. If some of the communication links were destroyed, the rest of the network would still function.

The project to create such technology was successful, and throughout the 1970s and 1980s, the network expanded and became the Internet. At first, the Internet connected only military and university computers, but, gradually, more and more companies and then individuals joined. Today, millions of people around the world have access to the Internet—what we now call the Net.

Thus, in a single generation, the Internet grew from an experimental project to a global network that has permanently changed our culture. By any standard, the Net has been fabulously successful. But why did this happen, and how did it happen so quickly? The answer is twofold.

First, the original technology developed for the U.S. Department of Defense has proven to be highly reliable. Although no one has ever dropped a bomb on the Internet, it is common for computers and communication lines to stop working temporarily. When this happens, the computers that run the Internet automatically re-route the flow of information around the broken links until they start working again. So one reason the Internet has grown so large is that it is so resilient.

When a computer or a communication line stops working, we say that the computer (or line) is DOWN. Similarly, when a computer or a line is working, we say that it is UP. The Internet is vast, and, at any time, there are bound to be some computers that are down. Regardless, the Internet as a whole is robust enough that it never goes down.

Think about that. For the rest of your life—and for many years to follow—there will be an Internet and it will always be up. In fact, the Internet is so large and so complex that there is really no way to turn it off.

The second reason the Net grew so quickly has to do with the nature of human beings. We are a species that loves to communicate. To participate in the Internet you need a computer, but it was not until the mid-1990s that personal computers became both powerful and inexpensive. However, once the average person could afford a PC, it didn't take long for tens of millions of people to buy a computer and join the Net. The history of the 20th century shows us that people have always used new technologies to communicate faster and better. There is something in our biological blueprint that makes us want to talk to one another and to share information.

To be sure, everything is not perfect on the Net. There are dishonest people who are glad to cheat you out of your money or lie to get what they want. And there are individuals who are willing to use the Internet for anything—legal or not—in order to make a buck.

But this is life, and any group of people is going to have its share of dishonesty and deceit. However, as you learn more about the Internet and how it works, you will come to a marvelous realization. The Internet is a safe place for people to gather, and, when people feel safe, they have a natural tendency to share and to help one another.

The Internet is a wonderful place, and in a very real sense, it reflects our biological destiny as a species.

What Is It Like to Use the Net?

Using the Internet is a lot like using a computer for anything. You sit in front of the monitor (computer screen) and look at words and pictures; you use the keyboard to type words, commands and other information; and you use the mouse to click on particular objects and to make selections.

However, there are two important considerations when you use the Net. First, you can't use any Internet resources until your computer connects to the Internet. There are a variety of ways to do this. For home users, the most common way to access the Internet is to have your computer connect to another computer over a telephone line.

The second consideration is that it takes longer to access information from the Internet than it does to access information from your own computer. For example, when you use a word processor to write a letter, the information you type is saved to a file on your computer. You can access that file whenever you want, usually within a few seconds. When you access information over the Internet, you must wait for a request to be transmitted from your computer to a remote computer, and then for the information to be sent from the remote computer back to you.

Sometimes this happens quickly, but often you will find yourself waiting for a minute or two. This doesn't seem like much, but your brain works quickly and waiting even a few seconds can be boring and aggravating. For this reason, I suggest that you get yourself as fast an Internet connection as possible. (We will talk about Internet connections in more detail in Chapter 3.)

I'll tell you something interesting, though. Once you have access to the Internet, the distinction between your personal computer and the rest of the world begins to blur. Within a short time, you will become so used to accessing information from around the world that you will take your position in the global community for granted.

You will be *connected*.

The Secret of the Internet: Clients and Servers

The Internet is a vast network involving millions and millions of computers all over the world. So how is it that you can connect to the Net whenever you want and just start using it? And how can it be that you can sit in front of your computer, typing and mouse clicking, and have the Internet respond to what you are doing? The secret is a system based on programs called "clients" and "servers". However, before we discuss clients and servers, I want to take a moment to talk about computers in general.

When we talk about a computer, we are really talking about three completely different systems working together. First, there is the HARDWARE, the physical parts of the computer (the machinery, so to speak). Second, there is the SOFTWARE, programs that control the operation of the computer. Finally, there is DATA, all the information that is stored in the computer.

What is a program? Most machines in our lives are designed for specific purposes. An oven heats food. A telephone lets us talk to another person. A car moves us from place to place. Computers are different in that they are designed as general-purpose machines capable of doing many, many things. A PROGRAM is a long list of instructions that, when carried out by a computer, make the computer act in a certain way. The reason a computer is so versatile is that there are many programs, each of which can make a computer act differently.

When a computer follows the instructions in a program, we say that the computer RUNS or EXECUTES the program. For example, to make your computer act like a word processor, you tell your computer to run a word processing program.

Now let's relate this to the Internet.

Think about the telephone system for a moment. The telephone system is designed to be used by people. You pick up a phone and call another person who talks to you. The Internet is different in that it is not designed for human beings—it is designed for computer programs. On the Internet, it is the computer programs—not the people—that communicate with one another. If you want something, you need to use a program to do it on your behalf. Even when you send messages to another person, you need a program to carry the messages back and forth.

Just think for a second how totally cool this is. We (the human race) have created a huge, global information network in which computer programs—like trained robots—are constantly running around doing things for us.

Broadly speaking, there are two types of programs used on the Internet: those that provide a service and those that request a service. A program that provides a service is called a SERVER. A program that requests a service is called a CLIENT.

Here is an example. Say that you want to use electronic mail to send a message to someone. You use a mail client program that runs on your computer. Once you have composed the message, your mail client uses the Internet to contact a mail server program on a remote computer. Your client sends the message to the server which makes sure it is delivered. (Don't worry about the details for now.)

Similarly, you can use your mail client to check for messages that have been sent to you. Your client contacts the mail server and requests any messages that have been sent to your electronic mail address. The server sends the messages to your client, which then displays them on your computer.

Much of learning how to use the Internet involves learning how to use the various client programs. In Chapter 2, I will discuss many of the resources that are available on the Net, for example, electronic mail, the Web, and Usenet discussion groups. To use an Internet resource, all you need is an Internet connection, the appropriate client program (running on your computer), and a knowledge of how to use that program to get what you want. For example, to send and receive electronic mail, you use a mail client; to access the Web, you use a Web client; and to participate in a Usenet discussion group, you use a Usenet client.

So that is the secret of the Internet: The whole network is one large client/server system. The Internet was built to provide a reliable way to pass data between clients and servers. To access the Internet, you use client programs that run on your computer. Your clients carry out your commands by passing data back and forth to server programs. A server program might be in the next room, across the country, or on the other side of the world. It's all the same to the client. And *that* is what makes the Internet so powerful.

hint

A server is a program that offers a service, but we often use the word "server" to refer to the computer itself.

For example, say you are being given a tour of a company. As you pass a room full of computers, the tour guide points to one of the machines and says, "That's our Web server." What he really means is, "That's the computer that runs our Web server program."

How TCP/IP Makes the Internet Work

To make the Internet function, computers connect to one another in order to pass data (information) back and forth. In fact, one might characterize the Internet as millions of interconnected computers constantly passing data back and forth. To make such communication efficient and reliable, the Internet uses a system in which data is sent in chunks. Here is how it works.

When a computer needs to send data to another computer, it divides the data into electronic PACKETS. The packets are numbered and marked with the address of the destination computer. They are then sent out over the Net to be delivered. At the other end, the destination computer collects the packets and reassembles them into the original data.

For example, say you use electronic mail to send a picture of yourself to your mother. The actual picture is stored in a file on your computer. That file is broken into packets and sent to your mother's computer, where they are automatically reassembled into a copy of the original file. The beauty of the Internet is that your mother doesn't have to worry about the details. As far as she is concerned, the file was sent intact from your computer to hers. All she has to do is look at the picture and send you a message back asking when you are going to get a haircut.

This system has two important advantages. First, it is efficient. No matter how much information is sent from one computer to another, the data is always broken up into packets that are the same size, and the Internet is fine-tuned to transport such packets as quickly as possible.

Moreover, it doesn't matter how the packets are sent to the destination or in what order they arrive. The Net can route each packet using whatever connections are available at that moment. Because the packets are numbered, it is no problem to reconstruct the original data once all the packets reach the destination, even if they did not all follow the same route. This flexibility allows the Internet to operate as efficiently as possible.

The second advantage to this system is reliability. The destination computer has a way to test each packet as it arrives to see whether it contains transmission errors. If a packet has errors, the destination computer will send a message to the source computer for the packet to be re-sent. In this way, all the data does not need to be re-sent, only those packets that arrived with errors. This system makes the Internet reliable without slowing things down unacceptably.

When computers send data back and forth, we say they TALK to one another. Of course, this is only a metaphor. Computers don't talk to each other the way people do. What is really happening is that a program running on one computer sends data to a program running on another computer. (Still, it's fun to imagine millions of computers on the Internet, connecting and talking to each other without any help from us humans.)

For this system to work, the various computer programs that run the Internet must be able to send and receive data according to standard specifications. These guidelines are called PROTOCOLS. There are well over a hundred different protocols used on the Net, each for a specific purpose. For example, there are different protocols used to transport electronic mail, to distribute Web-based information, to copy files from one place to another, and so on. The Internet protocols are highly technical, and you certainly don't have to understand them to use the Net.

Still, some of them are used a lot, and you will see their names, so, for reference, I have listed the most important Internet protocols in Figure 1-1. Don't worry about understanding what they all mean for now. I just want you to see the list so you will recognize the various names when you see them.

The various Internet protocols are developed and approved by an organization called the INTERNET ENGINEERING TASK FORCE (IETF). The IETF forms working groups to study problems and to create solutions. This allows the Internet to function smoothly and to evolve as conditions change.

Earlier, I explained that all data on the Internet is transported as packets. The two most important protocols are the ones that provide this basic transport. IP (Internet Protocol) is used to move data packets from one place to another. TCP (Transmission Control Protocol) manages the flow of packets and ensures that the data arrives intact without errors.

These two protocols are so important that the family of all the Internet protocols is called TCP/IP. Thus, what keeps the Internet running is millions of computers running millions of programs, all talking to one another by using the TCP/IP set of protocols.

Figure 1-1: List of important Internet (TCP/IP) protocols

Name	Full Name	Purpose
DNS	Domain Name System	Translate domain names to IP numbers
FTP	File Transfer Protocol	Copy files between computers
HTTP	Hypertext Transfer Protocol	Distribute Web data (hypertext)
IMAP	Internet Message Access Protocol	Access mail and other messages
IP	Internet Protocol	Transport raw data packets
LDAP	Lightweight Directory Access Protocol	Search a directory of email addresses
MIME	Multipurpose Internet Mail Extensions	Encode different types of data
NNTP	Network News Transfer Protocol	Distribute Usenet news articles
POP	Post Office Protocol	Get messages from a mail server
PPP	Point-to-Point Protocol	Connect a computer to the Internet
S/MIME	Secure MIME	Encode data securely
SMTP	Simple Mail Transfer Protocol	Send messages to a mail server
TCP	Transmission Control Protocol	Manage the flow of data packets
TELNET	Telnet	Log on to a remote computer

hint

If you want to sound like a real pro when you talk about TCP/IP, don't pronounce the slash. Just say the five separate letters real fast.

For example, "Of course, I know all about T-C-P-I-P. It's the family of protocols that is used to run the Internet."

Talking About the Net

We all identify with our computers, much more than we like to admit. Perhaps this is because computers are brain tools: We use them to gather information, to help our thinking, and to aid our creativity. You can see just how close we have become to the machines by noticing how we talk about them.

When you use a computer, it is common to talk as if you and the computer form one indivisible unit. For example, say you are in a bookstore—looking for new Harley Hahn books—and you run into a nerd (computer expert) who asks whether you have any Internet problems.

"Well," you say, "I've been hearing about computer viruses. Do I need to do anything to protect myself against them?"

"Most of the time," replies the nerd, "viruses aren't much of a problem. However, if you are worried, you can always use an antivirus program."

Notice that the nerd talks as if *you* would use the program, even though programs are run by computers, not people. Notice also that you used the expression "protect myself" when you really meant "protect my computer".

This sort of talk is so common that we take it for granted, especially when we talk about the Internet. For instance, it is common to hear people say things like, "I went crazy during my vacation. I couldn't connect to the Net for a whole week."

Similarly, we use the word ON to describe being connected to the Net. ("Shirley spent so much time on the Net, she didn't even notice that her husband had run off to Venezuela with the cleaning lady.")

However, in one sense, using words in this way *is* accurate. The Internet is much more than computers and information and wires. A big part of the Internet—perhaps the major part—is the people who use it. When you use the Net, your mind connects to something a lot larger than yourself. As you will come to realize, the power of the Internet lies in its ability to connect millions of human minds into one gigantic, global organism.

Thus, you will see the word ONLINE used to describe anything that is connected to the Net: people, computers or services. ("Shirley spent a lot of time using the Net, but her husband was rarely online, and she didn't get a chance to talk to him very often. Fortunately, she found a brand new Web site that had just come online, where people talked about relationships.")

Since people are so important to the Net, I would like to finish this section by discussing a couple of words that are used on the Net to describe special types of people.

I have already referred to a nerd. A NERD is someone who spends large amounts of time engaged in an activity in which he is particularly knowledgeable.

As a general term, "nerd" refers to a person who knows a lot about computers and the Net. ("Philbert knows everything there is to know about designing Web sites. He's a real nerd.") However, "nerd" can also refer to someone who has a particular type of esoteric knowledge. ("Martin is the Simpsons nerd around here, so he's the one to ask if you have any questions about Krusty the Clown.")

A GEEK is a nerd who is cool. ("I wish I had the nerve to ask Barbara out on a date. She's such an X-Files geek.")

hint

If you spend a lot of time on the Net, try to become a geek rather than a nerd.

Words to Avoid

As you learn to use the Net, you will encounter a great deal of Internet terminology, and throughout this book I will be teaching you a lot of new words. However, there are a few words I want you to avoid, so let's talk about them now.

First, never, ever use the word SURF to refer to using the Internet. This word is so overused as to instantly mark you as a person who doesn't know what he is talking about. This is fine if you are a politician giving a speech about "Communication in the 21st Century", but for everyone else, "surfing" is out.

Similarly, never use the words CYBERSPACE or INFORMATION SUPERHIGHWAY to refer to the Net. If there was ever a time when these words were cool, it passed a long time ago.

WHAT'S IN A NAME?

surf
cyberspace
information superhighway

Using the word "surf" in relation to the Internet comes from an article entitled "Surfing the Internet", written for a librarian's journal by Jean Armour Polly in 1992. After the journal was published, Polly used the Internet to make the article available for free, and it soon became enormously popular. By the mid-1990s, people all over the world were using the word "surf" to refer to cruising around within a big system, for example, "surfing the Internet" or "channel surfing" (jumping from one TV channel to another).

The word "cyberspace" comes from a 1982 book called *Neuromancer*, written by William Gibson. In the book, cyberspace was a futuristic computer-mediated environment. As the Internet became popular, the word "cyberspace"—and then the prefix "cyber"—was used to refer to anything having to do with computer networks.

The term "information superhighway" was created around the same time by the American news media, and popularized by American politician Al Gore (who was a U.S. senator at the time).

My advice is to never use any of these words. "Surf" and "cyber"-anything haven't been cool for years, and basic common sense should tell you to avoid expressions used by any politician who actually thinks he understands technical issues.

Finally, I want to mention the word NEWBIE. A newbie is a person who is a newcomer to the Net, but the only people who use this word are newbies, so, please, leave it out of your vocabulary.

The Internet is a place where how you talk and how you act is much more important than what you look like, where you live, or how much money you have. People on the Net will judge you by the words you use, and I want you to look good. You are one of my readers, and it is important to me that people see you as the intelligent, discriminating and thoughtful human being you are—not a clueless goober.

(After all, if you were a dummy you wouldn't be reading *this* book.)

Who Runs the Internet?

Nobody runs the Internet. This is because the Internet is not one big network. It is actually a collection of many, many smaller networks, computers and data communication lines. Each of these pieces is administered by some person or organization, but no one manages the Internet as a whole.

For example, say that a company has 100 computers connected into a local network. This network connects to the Net, providing Internet access to each of the 100 people who use those computers. The company is responsible for managing its part of the Net: the 100 computers, the local network, and the link to the Internet.

Here is another example. Consider a large university that has thousands of computers. These computers are organized into many small networks that connect to a larger, campuswide network. The campuswide network connects to the Net, giving everyone at the university Internet access. The university as a whole manages the campuswide network and the main Internet connection. Each individual department manages its own local computers and networks.

This sense of responsibility scales down as well. You are responsible for your own part of the Net: your computer. It is only a small part, but it is yours and you are in charge of it.

So that is how the Internet is administered. Each person or organization is responsible for their own part and nothing more. Although every part of the Internet is managed by somebody, no one is in charge of the whole thing.

One great thing about the Net is that, because no one is in charge, you have a great deal of freedom. For example, you can say whatever you want, and you can offer whatever information you want to the world at large. Remember, though, other people have the same freedom, so you need to be careful. No one regulates the Net and if something bad happens to you, or someone offends you, there is no one to whom you can complain. It is up to *you* to keep yourself out of trouble (but it is also up to you to have fun).

An interesting question is why is the Internet organized this way? Human beings do not generally set up organizations without putting somebody in charge. The answer is that the Internet was not developed to reflect human nature. The Internet was developed to offer reliable connections between *computers*.

Earlier in the chapter, I explained that the technology that drives the Net was originally developed by an agency of the U.S. Department of Defense. Their goal was to create a network that would keep functioning when parts of the network went down. To achieve this goal, the creators of the Internet came up with a design in which each part of the Net has its own independent existence, and a computer can access the Net simply by connecting to any computer that is already on the Net.

As human beings started to use the Internet, they created a strange mixture of human/computer collaboration in which intelligence and power are distributed throughout the Net and not centralized. What makes this even more remarkable is that virtually all of this creation was done without conscious thought on our part. Each of us just does what comes naturally, not really thinking about what the whole thing means on a global scale.

Thus, as we approach the end of the 20th century, we find ourselves with the Internet— a marvelous communication and information system that is large enough to span the globe and small enough to connect to a single personal computer—all without having anyone in charge.

No one runs the Net and no one owns the Net, but don't let this bother you. No one owns the sun and the stars, and no one runs the air, the water and the land, but somehow everything works just fine.

The Net is relatively new, but it is going to be here for the rest of your life (and it will be around long after you and I are gone).

Where Is the Center of the Net?

On the Internet, the lines of communication stretch out indefinitely in every direction. The reason is that TCP/IP—the family of protocols used to run the Net—was designed to transport data packets between any two specific computers. Still, there is no way to send data to everyone at the same time. This is fortunate, because if the Net did have universal broadcasting capabilities, it wouldn't be long before the entire network would become completely clogged to the point of uselessness. (Just imagine, for example, what the Internet would be like if companies could broadcast commercials.)

This gives rise to an interesting phenomenon. In theory, having Internet access allows you to reach millions of people. In practice, since there is no way to broadcast to everyone, you can't really reach people unless they want to reach you, or unless you have their electronic mail addresses.

For instance, say you put up some information on your own personal Web site. (We'll talk about the Web later.) That's fine, and, in theory, millions of people around the world can now access that information. The thing is, there is no way to compel anyone to look at your site, and the chances of millions of people visiting are remote.

However, the Net is a funny place. Once you put up some information on your Web site, people who are interested in that type of information will find it. As strange as it seems, on the Net, information has a life of its own. If you offer something that is important or useful or interesting or fun, the word will spread and the right people will find you.

Let's say, for example, that you enjoy model railroads, so you create an interesting Web site devoted to your hobby. It won't be long before the model railroad enthusiasts find you. Word will spread in various ways: by electronic mail, within various discussion groups, and on the Web itself. Pretty soon, other model railroad buffs will start to make links from their Web sites to your Web site.

There are other ways in which information spreads on the Net (including the so-called "search engines"), and we will talk about them throughout the book. For now, all I want is for you to begin to appreciate the power of the Net and why it is so good for humanity. The Net helps people find what they want when they want it, and it brings like-minded people together to share and to collaborate.

hint

Wherever you are is the center of the Net.

Pornography, Bad People, and Other Evil Things Hastening the Downfall of Civilization

Since no one runs the Internet, there are no Net police, and people can pretty much do what they want. Of course, you still have to follow the laws where you live. For example, if you make money on the Net, you do have to pay taxes, and if you break the law, you can be arrested.

Humans do not function well in anarchy, and, through the years, a great many customs have developed to make the Net a tolerable place. The most important custom is that you are responsible for your own actions. You are not responsible for the actions of other people. If you disagree with what someone is doing, ignore it; if you don't like certain people, avoid them; and if you are bothered by the information or pictures that someone has put on their Web site, don't look at it.

This isn't as harsh as it sounds. The Net is used by millions of people from many different cultures, and there is no possible way to devise laws—or even guidelines—that would be acceptable to everyone. From the beginning, the custom has been to live and let live, and, as a result, the Net has become our primary vehicle for free speech and dissemination of information.

When you first start using the Net, this may bother you. I guarantee that, with only a little effort, you will be able to find a great deal of material that will offend you. For example, no matter what beliefs you hold sacred, there are Web sites accessible to anyone in the world that ridicule and criticize your beliefs, and there's not much you can do about it.

Let's take an example. In the United States, there are many people who are offended by the fact that there is pornography on the Net. If you are such a person, I understand how you feel (although I don't agree with you). In the U.S., this issue is aggravated by the fact that Americans (as compared to, say, Europeans) are particularly troubled by displays of sexuality and naked bodies.

Thus, many people are bothered by the fact that anyone with an Internet connection can access pictures of all the naked bodies he or she wants. Will this not corrupt our youth, they ask? Do we not have an obligation to protect the moral fiber of our nation and teach enduring values to our children?

The answer is, yes, we do have those obligations, but the way to fulfill them is not by censorship—not on the Net, anyway. The Internet is important to everyone, and to restrict access to anyone because of the fear of what he or she will see or do is not only a bad idea, it is shortsighted.

The Internet is still a new part of our culture and, as such, it demands a new approach to how we think about the rest of the world. We need to teach our children—and ourselves—how to understand and use this wonderful communication and information system. In particular, we need to develop our judgment, our tolerance, and our self-control.

I don't mean to preach (well... yes, I do, but I care about you, and I know what I am talking about, so listen to what I have to say).

Judgment: Just because you read something on the Net doesn't mean you should believe it. Before you accept anything as fact, ask yourself, "Does it make sense? Is it likely to be true?" Do your own research; ask tough questions and look for corroboration. On the Internet, you must be extra careful not to pay too much attention to appearances: Some of the most despicable organizations have the most beautiful Web sites. You must learn to judge information on its own merits, and you must be skeptical of anything that doesn't look right.

Tolerance: No matter what you believe, no matter what you hold sacred, there are many, many people in the world who disagree, and a lot of them are on the Net. Don't let it get to you. If you really don't want to look at something, you don't have to look; if you really don't want to hear something, you don't have to listen. However, it isn't inherently bad to read or listen to things that are antithetical to what you believe. Tolerance not only makes you easier to get along with, it can open doors you don't even know exist. The Internet is a safe place to explore ideas that are strange to you and to meet people with different values. If you give the Net a chance, it will bring out the best in you.

Self-control: Not everything on the Net is good for you. In fact, there is probably a lot that is bad for you. The Internet is a wonderful source of stimulation, but there are times when we all need to exercise self-control. For example, there are various games and activities that can become addictive, especially for certain types of people. This is important for children to learn as they use the Net. If you are a parent, there are computer programs you can use to limit what your kids can and cannot look at, but no program is perfect. Nothing can take the place of a parent who takes the time to teach his or her children what is right and what is good. I think you'll find that the best way to teach is by setting a good example.

So what about all the pornography? The Internet has shown us that looking at pictures of naked men and women has an enormous universal appeal, and that's not going to change. Moreover, pornography isn't the only thing to worry about: The Net has its share of dishonest people, misleading information, harmful activities, and ways to waste your money. Should we be concerned?

Of course we should, but on the Net, censoring the activities of other people doesn't work. What does work is to spend some time and effort developing your judgment, tolerance and self-control. In my book, anyone who tells you differently is trying to sell you something. (This is my book.)

2

An Overview of the Internet

The Internet is a global information and communication system that is used by millions of people all over the world. Once you start to use the Net, you will be astonished by the amount of imagination and creativity you will find. In this chapter, I will take you on a guided tour of the Net. Along the way, I will introduce you to some of the important words and terms we use to talk about the Internet and its resources.

If you are new to the Net, you may be wondering what everyone is talking about. Let's start by talking about what the Net has to offer to you.

What Can You Do on the Net?

I explained in Chapter 1 that the Internet is based on technology developed in the late 1960s by ARPA, an agency of the U.S. Department of Defense. The original network (which later became the Internet) offered a single service: You could use the network to run programs on a remote computer. Soon after, two more services were added: You could copy files from one computer to another, and you could send messages by electronic mail.

Over the years, the Internet has expanded enormously, and you can now use the Net for many different things. Here are some examples:

- Send and receive electronic mail
- Access information on just about any topic you can imagine
- Talk with other people
- Play games (by yourself or with other people on the Net)
- Read the daily news (and the comics, weather and sports)
- Take part in ongoing discussions
- Do research
- Get free software for your computer
- Shop for just about anything
- Listen to music, radio, concerts and other live events
- Study, learn and take classes
- Watch video
- Buy and sell stocks
- Visit imaginary environments
- Gamble
- Display maps and driving instructions
- Look up someone's address and telephone number

All the activities I mentioned above are built on just a few basic Internet services. In this chapter, I will explain these services and teach you the most important words and technical terms you need to know to use the Net well.

hint

When it comes to the Net, just about anything you can think of is out there somewhere.

Mail

ELECTRONIC MAIL is a facility that allows you to send messages to anyone on the Internet. In addition, once you are on the Net, anyone else can send messages to you. Electronic mail is usually referred to as EMAIL or, more plainly, MAIL. Both words are also used as verbs; for example, "Would you like me to mail you an invitation to my party?"

Everyone on the Internet has an email ADDRESS. In order to send mail to someone, you must have his address. Similarly, if you want someone to be able to send you mail, you must give him your address.

Standard messages consist of regular text you type by using your keyboard. However, you can also ATTACH a file of data to a message, and the file will be delivered along with the message. (The file is referred to as an ATTACHMENT.) For example, you can send someone a word processing document by saving it in a file and attaching it to a message. In general, you can attach anything that can be stored in a file: a picture, a program, a voice message, and so on.

To have mail service, you arrange for an account on a MAIL SERVER. This is a computer that acts as a local email post office for a group of people. When someone sends you a message, it is stored on the mail server until you pick it up. In most cases, the company that provides you with Internet access will also provide you with mail service (including an email address).

As I explained in Chapter 1, you access Internet facilities by running client programs on your computer. For email, you use a mail client, commonly referred to as a MAIL PROGRAM.

The job of your mail program is to send and receive messages on your behalf. When you send a message, your mail program looks at the address and then delivers the message to the mail server that accepts mail for that address. To accept incoming messages, your mail program contacts your mail server and checks to see whether any messages are waiting for you.

On the Internet, when people use the word "mail", they always mean email. When it is necessary to talk about post office mail, people will sometimes refer to it as

SNAIL MAIL (the implication being that post office mail is slow compared to email). For example, you might tell someone, "I'll mail you the proposal, and if you like it, I'll send you the final copy by snail mail."

In everyday conversation, we use the word "email" (or "mail") in two different ways. First, to refer to the idea of electronic mail in general:

- "Now that Mary has email, you can send her messages whenever you want."

Second, to refer to actual messages:

- "Sammy's mother wouldn't let him see the movie until he had answered all his email."

hint

Never refer to messages as "emails". For example, do not say, "I received several emails yesterday," or "Please send me an email." Only beginners talk like this. Instead, say, "I received several messages," or "Please send me email." Here is a real-life example to show you what I mean.

(Overheard in the fruit and vegetable section of a grocery store):

Mr. Wrong: Excuse me, ma'am.

Beautiful Woman: Yes?

Mr. Wrong: If you give me your Internet address, I would be glad to send you an email.

Mr. Right: Excuse me, ma'am, but I, too, would like your address, so I can send you email.

Beautiful Woman: I am sorry, Mr. Wrong, but I do not give my email address to people who obviously don't know the first thing about the Net. Mr. Right, I would be glad to give you my address, because you are such a cool dude. Also, you may carry my pomegranates.

The Web

The WEB is an information delivery system that can display many different types of data and allow you to access a variety of services. The Web is unlike anything that has ever existed, and is the most powerful and most popular part of the Internet—so much so that beginners sometimes think the Web *is* the Net. Actually, the Web is only one part of the Internet, but, as you will see, the lines that separate the Web from the rest of the Net are somewhat blurry.

The Web is based on the concept of HYPERTEXT, data that contains LINKS to other data or to resources. As you look at hypertext, you can use the links to jump from one place to another. All you have to do is use your mouse to click on a link, and the data you are looking at will be replaced by new data. When this happens, we say that you are FOLLOWING the link. Here is an example to show you how it works.

Let's say you are using the Web to read a hypertext article about gardening. Throughout the article, the author has placed links to related information, such as plant care, pest control, growing seasons, choosing new plants, and so on. Within the hypertext, the links are displayed in a special way so they will stand out. Links that are words are commonly underlined or displayed in a particular color. Sometimes links are pictures or small images.

Regardless of what a link looks like, you can follow it just by clicking your mouse. In our example, you might click on the "plant care" link. When you do, the article you are reading will be replaced on your screen by a new article. If, instead, you click on the "pest control" link, you will jump to an article about pest control. And within these new articles, there will be more information containing more links.

Thus, the basic experience of using the Web is read, click, read, click, read, click. As you use the Web, you get a definite impression of jumping from one place to another.

WHAT'S IN A NAME?

hypertext
Web

In science fiction, spaceships need to travel vast distances in a short time. To make this possible, science fiction authors commonly have the ships travel through something called "hyperspace". Traveling in hyperspace allows a ship to magically jump from one side of the galaxy to another in a brief instant. (Actually, it's not a bad way to travel, except there's usually a 30-minute wait for luggage.)

When you use the Web, you have a similar experience. Click on a link and, within a few moments, you will jump from one Web page to another. Back in 1981, a fellow named Ted Nelson wrote a book called *Literary Machines* in which he coined the word "hypertext" to describe the type of data that might make this possible (that is, data containing links to other data).

In 1989, two scientists, Tim Berners-Lee and Robert Caillau, started work on a project to provide access to hypertext over a computer network. They conceived of their system as a large "web" of information. When the first version was ready, in May 1991, they decided to call it the WORLD WIDE WEB. Over time, as the system evolved, the name World Wide Web was shortened to the "Web".

The Parts of the Web

When we talk about computers, we use the word "data" to refer to all the various types of information. In broad terms, there are three types of data:

- TEXT consists of characters: the letters of the alphabet, numbers, punctuation, and so on.
- GRAPHICS refers to pictures, such as drawings, photographs and illustrations, as well as other visual elements.
- MULTIMEDIA refers to things that move or make sounds, such as animation, video and audio.

Information on the Web is organized into files called WEB PAGES. Web pages can contain not only data (such as text, graphics, and multimedia), but programs as well. Thus, where some Web pages are simple, containing only plain text with perhaps a few pictures, other pages are sophisticated productions with graphics, sound and animation, all tied together with programs that run automatically, doing wondrous things.

hint

When you see the word "hypertext" used to describe the content of Web pages, remember that it can contain graphics and multimedia, not just plain text.

Throughout the Internet, there are a vast number of computers called WEB SERVERS that store Web pages and make them available to anyone. There are literally hundreds of millions of Web pages available on the Net, with more being created all the time.

A collection of related Web pages created by a particular person or organization is called a WEB SITE (sometimes spelled WEBSITE). Many companies and individuals have their own Web sites, and once you get some experience, you will be able to create your own. All you need to do is create some Web pages and put them on a Web server somewhere on the Net. Once you do, anyone in the world will be able to look at your Web site.

hint

On the Net, anyone can be a publisher.

To access the Web, you use a program called a BROWSER to act as your Web client. Whenever you request a Web page (say, by clicking on a link), your browser contacts the appropriate Web server and asks for a copy of that page. Once the information arrives, your browser displays it for you. (You may have to wait a few moments, especially if you have a slow Internet connection.)

There are many browsers available for free on the Net. However, by far, the two most popular are INTERNET EXPLORER, created by Microsoft, and NETSCAPE, created by Netscape Communications.

WHAT'S IN A NAME?

Netscape

The Netscape browser is part of a collection of software called Netscape Communicator. Within this collection, the browser is actually named Netscape Navigator. However, when we talk about the browser as a separate tool, we generally refer to it as Netscape, not Navigator.

Thus, if you are talking to someone about the Internet, he might ask you, "Which browser do you use, Internet Explorer or Netscape?"

Browsers are designed to perform several different jobs. The basic job of a browser is to act as a Web client. As such, your browser displays Web pages for you and follows whatever links you click on with your mouse.

In addition, most browsers are integrated with mail clients and Usenet clients. That means you can use your browser not only to access the Web, but to send and receive mail, and participate in Usenet discussion groups (see the following).

The Internet Explorer browser has a fourth function: It can also act as a file manager, allowing you to access all the information and programs on your computer. This is part of Microsoft's plan to make their browser an integral part of the overall Windows working environment.

Channels

When you use a browser to look at a Web site, you will see text, graphics and (perhaps) multimedia. This content is sent to your computer by the Web server when you visit the Web site. But what if there were a way for a server to send you content automatically?

That is what channels do. A CHANNEL is an information source, usually a Web server, that can send data to your computer automatically. Both Internet Explorer and Netscape come with the software you need to access channels (although they use two different incompatible systems). With Internet Explorer, the channel facility is built into the browser. With Netscape, you use a separate program called NETCASTER.

One nice thing about a channel is you can have it send a whole lot of content to be stored on your computer. You can then view the channel without being connected to the Internet. For example, say you are preparing to go on a business trip. Ahead of time, you load information from a variety of channels (including the latest news) onto your portable computer. Later, while you are on the plane or in your hotel, you can enjoy looking at the channels at your leisure.

It is important to understand that Internet channels have the same type of information you might see with your browser in the regular manner, and virtually all channels— and there are many—are free. Thus, although we call them "channels", Web channels are *not* at all like television channels (except that many of them have advertising).

Usenet

Human beings love to communicate. We love to talk, argue, share information, complain, gossip, solve problems, tell jokes, spread rumors, ask questions, and help one other. In my years of using computers, I have noticed an enduring principle that I believe is a part of human nature. Whenever a new technology arises, people will find a way to use it to talk to one another. Nowhere is this better illustrated than with Usenet.

USENET is a system of discussion groups in which people all over the Net participate in ongoing discussion. There are thousands of different Usenet groups. Each group is devoted to a particular topic, and you can join the discussion for free. In its infancy, Usenet was originally designed for the posting of news articles, so you will often see the discussion groups referred to as NEWSGROUPS. Usenet itself is often referred to the NEWS, or sometimes NETNEWS.

? WHAT'S IN A NAME?

Usenet

When Usenet was first started, the Internet had not yet developed. The people who started Usenet used computers that ran an operating system (master control program) called Unix, which had been developed by AT&T.

At the time, there was a Unix users group called the Usenix Association (which still exists). This group had originally been called the Unix Users Group. However, the word "Unix" was a trademark of AT&T, and their lawyers were very picky about who could use the name, so the group decided to change their name to Usenix.

The inventors of Usenet chose the name "Usenet" to sound like Usenix, because they hoped that the Usenix Association would help organize the new discussion group system (they didn't). In retrospect, the name was a good one for two reasons. First, it sounds like the word "Internet", and, second, it looks like an abbreviation for "user's network".

Within the various Usenet newsgroups, people discuss every topic imaginable in perfect freedom with no censorship. The topics include serious discussions of science, health, politics and culture; less serious chat about movies, music, sex and television; and lots of jokes, humor, complaining and debate. Literally, any topic you can think of is discussed somewhere on Usenet.

In addition to public newsgroups, Usenet can also be used for discussions within an organization or group. For example, I have a friend who is a professor of mathematics at Cornell University. His classes use local Usenet groups to discuss questions and answers for the course. Usenet is used in this way in many schools.

To access Usenet, you use a client program called a NEWSREADER. Both of the popular browsers (Internet Explorer and Netscape) can act as newsreaders. So to access Usenet, you can either use your browser or get a special-purpose newsreader program. (Serious Usenet people often prefer the special-purpose newsreaders.)

People participate in Usenet by sending messages, called ARTICLES or POSTINGS, to the newsgroups. Using your newsreader, you can read the articles in any group. You can also send in articles of your own which can then be read by anyone on the Net. Articles are stored on computers called NEWS SERVERS and are preserved for at least several days. Thus, at any time, you can use your newsreader to see what people are currently talking about in a particular group.

If you want to use Usenet, your newsreader must have access to a news server, and it is up to you to find such a service. However, most companies that provide an Internet connection maintain a news server as a service to their customers, so Usenet access usually comes free with an Internet account.

Although we talk a lot about the Web, it is not the only important part of the Internet. Throughout this book, I will teach you about the Web, but I also want to make sure that you appreciate Usenet and learn how to use it well. You will find Usenet to be especially useful when you have a question or when you need to find out some information. Just send a message to the appropriate discussion group and, more than likely, someone will read your request and post an answer.

People love to talk, and, on the Net, people have been talking on Usenet for almost two decades.

Mailing Lists

MAILING LISTS, like Usenet, are used for ongoing discussions among people all over the Net. With a mailing list, all the messages are sent via email. Instead of having to use a newsreader client program to access a Usenet news server, you simply read the messages that appear in your incoming mailbox.

There are many thousands of mailing lists that cover just about any topic you can imagine. Like Usenet, mailing lists are free. However, you do need to join a list in order to participate. When you want to stop receiving mail from the list, you need to remove yourself from the distribution.

How do mailing lists compare to Usenet? Both Usenet and mailing lists are used for public and private discussions. In the same way that there are local Usenet groups, there are a great many private mailing lists that are set up for a select group of people.

However, there are some differences. Mailing lists tend to have more serious, longer lasting discussions, while Usenet newsgroups are like open forums where anybody can show up and say whatever they want. On the other hand, Usenet is better for browsing. You can check a newsgroup and see what articles happen to be there whenever you feel like it. With a mailing list, you have to join the list and wait for messages to arrive in your mailbox.

Finally, mailing lists have much less trouble with unsolicited advertisements, called spam (see the following), than Usenet newsgroups. This can be an important consideration.

Advertising and Spam

As you use the Net, you are going to have a huge amount of in-your-face advertising forced upon you, particularly on the Web. Personally, I don't like it one bit (and I hope you don't, either), but the economics that drive the Net are based in large part on advertising revenues, and there's not much anyone can do to change that. From time to time, people do come up with programs to filter out the ads, and I will discuss such programs in Chapter 7. Still, for the foreseeable future, advertising on the Web is here to stay.

However, there is another type of advertising, called spam, that people are doing something about. SPAM refers to unsolicited advertisements that are sent to people's personal email accounts and to Usenet newsgroups. The people who send such ads are called SPAMMERS.

As an Internet user, you will notice spam in two important ways. First, if your email address gets on a spammer's address list, you will begin to see advertisements in your mailbox. As time passes, this will get worse and worse, as your address is passed around and sold from one spammer to another.

Eventually, you will find that you are receiving a great deal of unsolicited advertising. Whether or not this bothers you depends on your temperament. It doesn't seem to cost you anything to receive email, and it is simple to delete any unwanted messages. Still, no matter how genial your personality, I predict that, when the spam gets bad enough, you will start to complain. By then it will be too late. There are brokers who sell lists of addresses, and once your name is on a list your privacy is gone for good.

The second way in which you will notice spam is on Usenet. As I explained earlier, Usenet consists of a great many discussion groups (called newsgroups). Traditionally, Usenet has afforded people as much freedom as possible. In particular, anyone is allowed to send an article to any newsgroup, and some people send a lot of articles.

But this is nothing compared to the spammers who will use automated programs to send advertisement after advertisement to every Usenet newsgroup. This means, for example, that if you want to read the articles in a newsgroup devoted to pets, you may have to wade through a lot of advertisements offering ways to "make money fast".

Spam is bad for the Internet (and for you) in two ways. First, unsolicited messages are irritating, whether you find them in your mailbox, in a Usenet newsgroup, or on a mailing list.

Second, when the spam count gets high enough, the junk really starts to get in the way. A lot of spam is carefully crafted by experts to look like important mail (just like postal junk mail), and you may have to look at many bogus messages to make sure you do not accidentally delete a real one. However, unlike postal junk mail—which requires paper, printing, envelopes and postage—spam is electronic and costs very little per message. Thus, spammers have no economic motivation to remove you from their mailing lists or to target their advertising to only those people who want it.

This problem has choked many Usenet newsgroups to death. As part of my work, I maintain a master list of Usenet newsgroups. From time to time, I go through all the groups bringing the list up to date. I have seen many groups that have been rendered unusable by high amounts of spam. In fact, more than any single thing I can think of, spam has really hurt the Usenet community.

Fortunately, there are a lot of anti-spam nerds on the Net who have developed two types of anti-spam software. One type, used for email, filters messages as they arrive in your mailbox. Messages that look like spam are thrown away automatically. The second type of software is used on Usenet to eliminate spam before it gets into the newsgroups. The Usenet software has worked particularly well, helping to make Usenet a lot more pleasant to use.

WHAT'S IN A NAME?

spam

Spam is a canned meat containing pork shoulder and ham, first produced in 1937 by the George A. Hormel Food Company (now Hormel Foods). The name Spam was chosen to mean "spiced ham".

On December 15, 1970, the Monty Python's Flying Circus television show had a skit in which a woman and man in a restaurant find that every dish contains Spam, Spam, and more Spam.

Some years later—because of this skit—the word "spam" was adopted on Usenet to refer to articles that were sent to many different newsgroups. The idea is that, no matter which newsgroup you choose to read, you will have spam forced upon you, just like the people in the Monty Python skit.

Anonymous FTP and Downloading

There is an enormous amount of free software available on the Net. Most of this software is made available via a system called Anonymous FTP. Although you don't hear people talk much about Anonymous FTP, it is one of the most important services on the Internet because it allows reliable, worldwide distribution of software and other data. However, before I explain how it works, we need to go over some basic terminology.

Let's start with the idea of a file. On a computer, a FILE is a collection of data (information), that is stored under a particular name. Files can contain any type of data, such as word processing documents, pictures, email messages, Web pages, computer programs, and so on. If you have a PC, you already have many files stored on your hard drive (a storage device inside the main box). Files are also stored on other types of media, such as CDs, floppy disks, removable disk cartridges and tapes.

One of the basic services offered by the Internet is the capability of copying files from one computer to another. This is important because it allows you to get programs from other computers to use on your own computer.

When you copy a file from a remote computer to your computer, we say you DOWNLOAD the file. When you copy a file from your computer to a remote computer, we say you UPLOAD the file.

hint

Here is an easy way to remember the difference between download and upload. Imagine the Internet is floating above you in the sky. When you copy a file from the Internet to your computer, you bring the file "down". When you copy a file from your computer to the Internet, you send the file "up".

The service that provides a lot of the file transfer on the Net is called FTP (the name stands for "file transfer protocol"). FTP can be used in two ways. First, if you have permission to use a particular computer, you can use FTP to copy files to or from that computer. In such cases, you will need a user name and a password to access the remote computer.

An example of when you might use FTP in this way is when you create your own Web site. As I explained earlier in the chapter, to make your own Web site, you create some Web pages and then copy them to a Web server. You design the Web pages on your own computer and store them in files. Once they are ready, you can use FTP to upload the files to the Web server. In other words, you "publish" your Web pages by using FTP to copy them to a Web server where they can be accessed by anyone on the Net.

WHAT'S IN A NAME?

FTP

FTP—file transfer protocol—is the name of the service that allows you to copy files from one Internet computer to another. On the Net, we also use the word "FTP" as a verb. For example:

Jack: "When is the new Web site going to be ready?"
Jill: "Well, I've made all the final changes. All I have to do is FTP the files to the Web server."
Jack (who grew up in the Sixties): "Far out!"

There is a great need on the Net to be able to distribute programs and other files to the general public. All over the Net, there are many computers, called FTP SERVERS, that store files for public downloading via FTP. However, FTP requires that you have a user name and password in order to be able to access the files on a remote computer.

Clearly, it is not feasible to give each person in the world a user name and password for every FTP server. Instead, we use a system called ANONYMOUS FTP that allows anyone, anywhere, to access particular files on an FTP server. This is the second way in which FTP can be used. Here is how it works.

The people running the FTP server set aside a special area to hold files for the general public to download. To access these files, you use FTP to connect to the computer and then specify a user name of **anonymous** with any password that you want. (The custom is to use your email address as a password. This allows the people running the FTP server to see who is using it.) Once you connect to an FTP server in this way, you are allowed to download any of the files that have been placed in the public Anonymous FTP area. However, you are not allowed to access files in the nonpublic areas.

The power of Anonymous FTP is that it can allow anyone to download anything. In particular, Anonymous FTP is used to distribute the software that runs the Net. This is one of the most important reasons why the Internet was able to grow so quickly. On a more personal level, Anonymous FTP provides you and me with free access to a massive amount of software and information.

To use FTP, you need an FTP CLIENT program. All browsers can act as FTP clients for Anonymous FTP. In fact, when you download software or other files from a Web site, you are often using Anonymous FTP without even knowing it. The browser will take care of all the details automatically (such as specifying the user name of **anonymous** and a password). All you will have to do is tell the browser where you want to store the downloaded file.

If you need more than Anonymous FTP—for example, if you need to upload files—you need a more powerful FTP client. There are many such programs available on the Net.

hint

There are many programs you can use to design Web pages. Some of these programs are able to upload the finished pages right to your Web server. Although you may not realize it, these programs are using FTP behind the scenes.

Talk Facilities (Including IRC)

The Net is a great place to talk to people. You can keep in touch with friends, or talk to people you don't know and make new friends. There are lots of ways to talk on the Net, but before we get into the details, I want to discuss a basic idea: What do we mean by the word "talk"?

In regular life (off the Net), we talk by speaking, whether in person or on the phone. On the Net, it is possible to have voice communication, but much of the time we communicate by typing what we want to say. Thus, when we say TALK, we refer to typing messages back and forth, as well as regular speech.

There are many different ways to talk on the Net. You can have a private conversation with one person at a time; you can have a meeting with a group of people so that everyone can see what the others are typing; or you can talk in a public area, where anyone who wants can join the conversation. Some public discussions are devoted to particular topics; others are for general conversation. You can choose whatever you feel like at the moment.

hint

Taking part in public conversations on the Internet is a good way to meet people and make new friends.

Like everything you do on the Net, talking uses clients and servers. The client you use depends upon which talk facility you are using. On the Web, there are a great many public talk areas called CHAT ROOMS. To participate in a Web chat room, you can use your browser as a client.

There are also talk facilities that are completely separate from the Web and require special client programs. The largest such facility is IRC or INTERNET RELAY CHAT. To participate in IRC, you use a program called an IRC CLIENT. Using this client, you connect to an IRC SERVER. Once you do, you will find a large number of conversations in progress on separate CHANNELS. You can join any channel you want and be part of the conversation, and you can start your own channels. If you like a lot of stimulation, you can join more than one channel at the same time and try to follow several conversations at once.

hint

Do not confuse IRC channels with Web channels. IRC channels are used within IRC for conversation. Web channels (explained earlier in the chapter) are used to send content from a Web site automatically. We use the same word (channel) for both facilities, but they have nothing to do with each other.

hint

When it's late at night and you have nothing to do, there are always lots of people to talk to on IRC.

Web chat rooms and IRC are similar in that they use central servers. Everything you type is sent to a server, where it is relayed to the other people in the conversation. Other types of talk facilities establish direct connections between the people who are talking. There are a variety of such direct-connect facilities available on the Net, the most important being ICQ. (The name is a pun: ICQ = "I seek you".)

All of these systems require special client programs, which you can download for free from the Net. These clients provide a variety of useful services. Not only can you talk to someone—or a group of people—you can send notes back and forth (similar to email), as well as transfer files from one person to another. You can also have your program keep an address book of the various people you talk to and let you know whenever they come online. Some programs have another useful feature. They allow two or more people to use their browsers to look at the same Web sites at the same time. One person can act as a tour guide, taking everyone else from one Web site to another.

Aside from chat rooms, IRC and ICQ, there are also talk facilities within imaginary environments (see the following). When you visit such places, you not only talk, you assume the role of a character, explore, have adventures, and a lot more.

I mentioned earlier that most talking on the Net is by typing messages back and forth. This is true, but it is also possible to talk by using speech, just like a telephone. Talking in this way can be a lot of fun because you can hear people's voices from all over the world, and you talk as long as you want without having to pay long distance bills. Of course, if you want to talk in this way, your computer will have to have a microphone and speakers. (Most new PCs come with such hardware.)

In addition, there are video conferencing systems that let you see live images as you speak and type. Again, you need the appropriate equipment. Aside from a microphone and speakers, you also need a special video camera to connect to your computer.

hint

On the Net, you never need to be alone. There is always someone to talk to.

Imaginary Environments (Including Muds and VRML Worlds)

Real life is fine when it's time to balance your checkbook or go to the dentist, but once in a while we can all use a break. When the time comes to escape reality, there are many imaginary environments on the Net where you can go to explore, have adventures, meet people, or indulge in good, old-fashioned make-believe.

MUDS are text-based worlds in which you adopt the role of a specific character. To use a mud, you need a MUD CLIENT (which you can download for free from the Net). Many people find one mud they really like and visit often, using the same character each time. Muds are places of the imagination, devoted to particular themes, such as fantasy, gothic, or science fiction. I myself sponsor a mud called Zhing which is an imaginary fantasy world. Zhing has five continents to explore, quests to complete, magic spells, monsters, and lots more.

Since muds are text-based, you don't see any pictures. Instead, you read descriptions of places, people and events, and build your own vision using your imagination (just like when you read a book). But unlike a book, muds are interactive: What you experience depends on what you do.

Muds are also multiuser. This means that many people can use the mud at the same time. Whenever you are on a mud, you will be able to see and talk to anyone else who is there. Some muds are devoted mainly to conversation and are highly social places. Other muds are designed more for adventures: killing monsters, going on quests, accumulating points, and so on. Adventure muds can be complex places, and it may take you weeks or months to explore everywhere and become a master.

hint

The word "mud" is also used as a verb; for example, "Mudding can be addictive, so make sure you have your homework done before you start."

WHAT'S IN A NAME?

mud

The first mud was developed in 1978 as a computerized game based on Dungeons and Dragons. At the time, the name MUD was chosen as an acronym meaning "multiuser dungeons". Within several years, muds became much more sophisticated, and the connection to Dungeons and Dragons diminished.

For a time, people would say that MUD stood for "multiuser dimension" or "multiuser domain", but today we use the term "mud" as a word in its own right, so it really doesn't stand for anything.

Aside from muds, the Net also has a large number of graphics-based 3-D imaginary environments based on a system called VRML (Virtual Reality Modeling Language). These environments are called VRML WORLDS. (In this sense, VIRTUAL refers to objects and experiences that exist only on the Net.) When you talk about VRML, you can pronounce the name in two ways: either as four separate letters, "V-R-M-L", or as the single word "vermal".

Within a VRML world, you can move in three dimensions. As you do, you travel through imaginary landscapes, structures and settings, all created for 3-D exploration. If you enjoy being creative, you can learn how to build your own virtual domains for other people to visit.

Many VRML worlds are multiuser, and when you are not exploring or building, you can spend time talking to other people. VRML worlds are good places to make friends, and once you do, you can collaborate with your friends to add new features to that particular world.

To access a VRML world, you use a special program called a plug-in (see Chapter 10) that works with your regular browser to offer VRML capabilities. There are a variety of such programs available for free on the Net.

hint

Reality is just a crutch for people who cannot cope with fantasy.

Telnet

TELNET is a service that allows you to connect to a remote computer and run programs. Telnet was the first service developed for the original Arpanet (the network that grew into the Internet). In those days—the late 1960s—the only way to use a computer interactively was via a device called a TERMINAL. A terminal had a keyboard, a monitor, and not much more, and had to be connected directly to the computer, which was called the HOST. To use the computer, you would turn on the terminal and LOG IN by typing a user name and a password. You could then use your terminal to type commands which would be carried out by the host.

Telnet was developed to allow people to log in and use a remote computer over a network. Without telnet (or something like it), you could not interact with a computer unless you had a terminal that was physically connected to the host.

To use telnet, you run a TELNET CLIENT program on your computer. The telnet client connects to the remote host and then begins to act like a terminal. (In computer talk, we say that the telnet program EMULATES a terminal.) You can now log in by typing your user name and password.

In general, you can't use telnet unless you have an account (a user name and password) on a remote host. In years past, there were computers on the Net that would allow public telnet access for certain specific services, such as library catalogs or BBSs (bulletin board systems). Nowadays, though, most such services have moved to the Web, where you can access them by using your browser.

WHAT'S IN A NAME?

telnet

The ancestor of the Internet was called the Arpanet (named for the Advanced Research Projects Agency, a part of the U.S. Department of Defense). The first goal of the Arpanet researchers was to create a way for people to access remote computers. Here is an excerpt from one of their early memos [named RFC-5], written on June 2, 1969:

"The initial ARPA network working group met at SRI [Stanford Research Institute] on October 25-26, 1968. It was generally agreed beforehand that the running of interactive programs across the network was the first problem that would be faced."

Telnet was formally proposed in a technical note [RFC-15] written by C. Carr and dated September 25, 1969, and, as I mentioned, telnet became the first service offered over the new network.

The origin of the name "telnet" is unknown. My best guess is that Carr chose it to incorporate the words "teletype" (an early device that was used as a terminal) and "network".

The word "telnet" is often used as a verb; for example, "In the olden days, people would telnet to a computer in order to use it remotely."

Making Sense of It All

There is a lot to do on the Internet, and there is a lot to learn. To make sense out of it all, just remember these three basic ideas:

- The most important services on the Net are mail, the Web and Usenet.
- The Internet is based on a client/server system. You run client programs on your computer. Your clients connect to various servers on the Net in order to carry out your requests.
- The most important program you need to learn how to use is your Web client, called a browser. The most popular browsers, Internet Explorer and Netscape, are integrated with mail and Usenet clients, so you can use one main program for almost everything.

For reference, Figure 2-1 contains a summary of the clients and servers we have discussed. The fact that you understand this summary means that you now know more about the Internet than almost everyone else in the world.

Figure 2-1: Important clients and servers used on the Internet

Internet Service	Client	Server
Mail	Mail program	Mail server
The Web	Browser	Web server
Usenet	Newsreader	News server
FTP	FTP program	FTP server
IRC	IRC client	IRC server
VRML world	VRML browser	Web server
Mud	Mud client	Mud
Telnet	Telnet client	Host

3

Everything You Need to Connect to the Net

To use the Net, you need a computer, software and an Internet connection. In this chapter, I will discuss what type of computer to buy, where to get your software, and the best way for you to get connected.

Even if you are already using the Net, I would still like you to read this chapter for two reasons. First, I am going to explain a lot of basic computing terms that I want you to know; second, you may learn about something that will help improve your current setup.

The Summary in Advance

What computer, software and Internet access do you need?

Here is the wisdom from this chapter, condensed into a short summary. Don't worry if you don't understand all the words and abbreviations; I will explain them all as we go through the chapter. I just wanted to get everything into a few paragraphs to give you a preview of what we're going to talk about. Once you have finished the chapter, you can copy this page, and take it with you when you go computer shopping.

Harley Hahn's Quick Guide to What You Need to Use the Internet

Buy a PC running Windows 98, with at least 64 MB of RAM. The computer should have a fast processor, a V.90 56K modem, speakers and a microphone. Get a built-in Ethernet port if one is available. Don't buy a Macintosh unless you are a professional graphics designer.

For software, if you want a word processor, get Microsoft Word. For everything else, wait until you see what software comes with the computer and what you can find for free on the Net. You don't need to buy an antivirus program right away.

Get the fastest Internet connection you can afford. DSL and cable are better than ISDN, and ISDN is better than a regular dialup connection. Choose an ISP that gives you a flat rate with reasonable customer service. Don't use AOL unless you know for sure that you want the extra content.

Processors

If you were to open a PC (personal computer), you would see some circuit boards, some metal boxes and various wires. On the circuit boards, you would see a large number of small, flat electrical chips.

The main circuit board is called the MOTHERBOARD. The whole PC is built around this board. One of the chips on the motherboard is the PROCESSOR, the most important component of the whole computer. To the extent that a computer can be said to have a "brain", the processor is the brain. In Chapter 1, I explained that programs were actually long lists of instructions. Well, when you run a program, the processor is the part of the computer that executes the instructions. Thus, the speed and power of your computer depend on the speed and power of the processor.

Processor speed is measured in MEGAHERTZ, abbreviated MHz. For example, a 333-MHz processor is faster than a 266 MHz processor. (I chose these numbers because they are actual processor speeds.)

The power of the processor varies, depending on what family it is in. Most PC processors are created by the Intel Corporation, and Intel makes several families of processors. The most modern families are the Pentium, Pentium Pro and Pentium II. When you buy a new PC, get a fast Pentium II processor.

hint

Get the fastest computer you can afford. You will not regret it.

Memory

Within a computer, data is organized into units called BYTES, each byte storing a single character. For example, it takes 11 bytes to store the name "Harley Hahn". (The space counts as one character.)

When we talk about quantities of memory, we use names based on the metric system: A KILOBYTE (abbreviated KB) is a thousand bytes, a MEGABYTE (MB) is a million bytes, a GIGABYTE (GB) is a billion bytes, and a TERABYTE (TB) is a trillion bytes. So, for example, 1 MB = 1,000 KB. (There is actually a little more to it than I explain here. See the following technical hint.)

Computers have two types of memory: working memory and long-term storage. The working memory is called RAM. The name stands for "random-access memory" and is used for historical reasons, so don't try to make sense out of it.

You will remember that I explained that the processor is the "brain" of the computer. Well, RAM is working memory, used by the processor. When you turn off your computer, all the data stored in RAM is lost. This is why, each time you turn on a computer, you have to wait for everything to reload. This is also why, when you start a new program, it sometimes takes a few moments. You are waiting for the program to be copied from the long-term storage to RAM. (The long-term storage is the hard disk, which I will discuss as follows.)

Inside your computer, RAM is provided by electronic chips that plug into the motherboard. RAM is measured in MB (megabytes). The more RAM you have, the better. With most computers, you can upgrade the memory by buying more RAM chips and plugging them into the motherboard.

hint

When you buy a new PC, make sure it has at least 64 MB (megabytes) of RAM. More is better.

The cheapest way to make a computer faster is to buy more memory.

When we talk informally, we often refer to megabytes as "megs", and gigabytes as "gigs". Thus, if you were visiting the White House, you might hear the President tell his intern, "On your way back from McDonald's, pick me up a new computer—something real fast, with at least 64 megs of RAM and a 10-gig hard drive—and maybe a few donuts, those chocolate ones with the sprinkles."

technical hint

In the metric system, kilo means a thousand (1,000), mega means a million (1,000,000), giga means a billion (1,000,000,000), and tera means a trillion (1,000,000,000,000). However, when we talk about computer memory or storage, we use slightly different values for these prefixes.

Computer scientists and programmers work with computer memory by using a mathematical system called the BINARY SYSTEM. The binary system is based on powers of 2 (such as 1, 2, 4, 8, 16, 32, and so on), and within this system, it is more convenient to have "kilo" stand for 1,024, not 1,000. This is because 1,024 is 2^{10} (2 to the power of 10), and in the binary system, 2^{10} is a round number. Similarly, "mega" stands for 2^{20}, "giga" stands for 2^{30}, and "tera" stands for 2^{40}.

The following table shows these prefixes and their values when used to measure computer memory:

Kilo	2^{10}	1,024
Mega	2^{20}	1,048,576
Giga	2^{30}	1,073,741,824
Tera	2^{40}	1,099,511,627,776

I won't go into the details except to say that, unless you are a computer scientist or a programmer, none of this really matters. For normal people, 1 KB of memory is about a thousand bytes, and 1 MB of memory is about a million bytes, and that's all that counts. When you compare memory sizes, 2 MB is twice as much as 1 MB no matter how you measure it.

Disks

Inside a computer, long-term storage is furnished by a number of different devices called disks. All PCs come with a HARD DISK, a small box inside the computer. The name comes from the fact that, inside this box, data is stored on several hard disc-shaped plates. Unlike RAM, data on a hard disk does not disappear when you turn off the computer. The data is stored permanently, until you (or one of your programs) erase it. In fact, when you turn on the computer, the system will spend a minute or two copying data from your hard disk (long-term storage) to RAM (working memory).

The capacity of a hard disk is measured in GB (gigabytes). Typically, a new PC will have a hard disk with a capacity between 5 to 10 GB or even more, but you don't have to worry about the exact size. Modern PCs come with enough long-term storage.

A second long-term storage device is a FLOPPY DISK DRIVE. This is a small box inside your PC with an opening into which you can insert a FLOPPY DISK (often called a FLOPPY). Each floppy disk can hold up to 1.44 MB (megabytes) of data.

WHAT'S IN A NAME?

floppy disk

The outside of a floppy disk is hard plastic. However, in the olden days, floppy disks were larger and thinner, and really were floppy. Even today, if you open one up, you will find a flexible, wafer-thin disc. So inside, floppies are still floppy.

hint

Get yourself an extra floppy disk and open it up for fun. (Just pull it apart.) The disk will become unusable, but floppies are cheap and it's interesting to see what is inside.

For extra fun: If you are going to perform this demonstration in front of other people, stick a label that says "Master Tax Files" on the disk before you pull it apart.

Aside from hard disks and floppy disks, PCs also have CD-ROM DRIVES, which can read CDs (compact discs). The term "ROM" stands for "read-only memory", and indicates that the drive can read the CD, but not change what is on it. CDs are commonly used to distribute software, as they can hold several hundred megabytes of data. Moreover, most CD-ROM drives can also read regular music CDs. Thus, your computer can double as a stereo, and you can listen to music as you work. Some PCs have writable CD drives, which allow you not only to read standard CDs, but write on your own CDs or special cartridges.

WHAT'S IN A NAME?

disk
disc

When we talk about CDs, we use the word "disc" (as in compact disc), but when we refer to hard disks and floppies, we use the word "disk". This dates back to the original IBM PC (1981), in which floppy disks were called "diskettes".

Operating Systems (Windows)

An OPERATING SYSTEM is a master control program that runs a computer. Almost all PCs use an operating system called WINDOWS. Windows is made by Microsoft, and, every now and then, they come out with a new version. The latest version is Windows 98. Before that was Windows 95.

The first Windows was version 1.0. This was followed by 2.0, 3.0, 3.1 and 3.11. It wasn't until version 3.0 that Windows became widely used. Even today, there are many computers that still run Windows 3.0, 3.1 or 3.11. For convenience, these versions are referred to collectively as 3.x.

In 1995, Microsoft came out with a new version of Windows that was totally different from the old ones, so, for marketing reasons, they made a big change in the name. Instead of calling the new operating system version 4.0, they called it Windows 95. (For Microsoft, this is considered a big change.) Since then, Windows 95 has undergone a variety of updates as well as two new major releases, but Microsoft did not change the name until Windows 98 (again, for marketing reasons).

When you buy a PC, it should come with the newest version of Windows already installed. So, if you buy a new PC, make sure it has Windows 98.

hint

Should you upgrade to a new operating system?

If your PC is running Windows 3.x right now, don't worry about upgrading. Your computer is so old that Windows 98 wouldn't run well (and may not even run at all). Don't waste your money adding more memory or a new processor in an attempt to make your old computer more powerful. Stay with what you have and save your money until you can get a brand-new computer.

If you are currently using Windows 95, you could probably upgrade if you want. If you are somewhat adventurous, read about the new features of Windows 98 and see whether they appeal to you. Otherwise, if your computer is working fine, stick with Windows 95 and get the new operating system when you buy your next computer.

Software

When you buy a new PC, it will come with a lot of free software. Not only will you get the current version of Windows, you will get a lot of programs that Microsoft includes with Windows. In addition, most PCs come with a variety of other software. When something is given away free as part of the overall purchase price, we say that it is BUNDLED with the main product. In this case, we can say that Windows, as well as other software, is bundled with the PC.

Having so many programs included with a new computer is convenient, as the software will already be installed and working. This is particularly important with respect to Windows, because installing an operating system is a time-consuming process with many potential pitfalls. Microsoft saves everyone (including themselves) a lot of trouble by having Windows already working on the computer when you buy it.

When you buy a new computer, the question may arise as to whether or not you should buy extra software at the same time. (If the question doesn't arise by itself, the salesman will probably offer some "suggestions".) Actually, you don't really need to buy any other software right away. A new PC comes with everything you need to use the computer and to connect to the Internet. You may want some extra programs to use various Internet facilities, but you can download these from the Net for free. In fact, there is so much software for free on the Net—in any category you could want—that I would suggest not buying anything extra until you have learned how to download software and explored the many free software archives. (We'll talk about how to download software from the Net in Chapter 11.)

So, with one exception, I would suggest not buying anything right away. The exception is, if you know you will be doing a lot of word processing, buy the newest version of Microsoft Word. This product is pretty much the standard in its category, and can be bought as part of a group of programs called Microsoft Office.

Such collections are called software SUITES. Other companies besides Microsoft offer suites, and they provide good value. Some computers come bundled with a suite of programs, so you may get what you want for free anyway.

One last question: It is common for salesmen to suggest that you buy an antivirus program to protect your computer. Should you do so? I won't talk about computer viruses now (we'll do that in Chapter 8). However, I will say that the dangers posed by viruses, even on the Internet, are highly exaggerated by the companies that sell antivirus software, and by people who like to scare other people.

It is not necessary to pay extra for an antivirus program when you buy a new computer. Once you get connected to the Net, you will find a variety of free and inexpensive antivirus software to choose from. In addition, many new PCs already have such software installed on the machine.

hint

If you are worried about computer viruses, the following three precautions will provide the protection you need until you get an antivirus program:

- Never use a floppy disk to transfer a program from someone else's computer.
- Never allow your children to bring home floppy disks from school.
- Never run a program that someone has sent to you by email.

I will discuss these issues in more detail in Chapter 8.

As far as Internet software goes, I explained in Chapter 2 that you access the Internet by using client programs. The most important client program is a browser, which you use for the Web and other services.

All the Internet clients you need are available for free on the Net. To get started, you need only (1) the software that makes the actual connection to the Net (this software is included free as part of Windows) and (2) a browser. Once you are on the Net, you can use your browser to get whatever you need.

When you buy a new PC, chances are it already has a browser, probably Microsoft's Internet Explorer. If not, you should be able to get one for free from the company that provides your Internet connection. Don't worry about getting the newest version of the browser. Any browser will do to start. Once you get on the Net, you can download the newest versions of Internet Explorer or Netscape for free. (These are the two major browsers.) We will talk about browsers in more detail in Chapter 7.

hint

Both Microsoft and Netscape offer free suites of Internet software. Aside from a browser, each suite contains a variety of other Internet client programs, all of which are integrated to work well with one another. The Microsoft suite is called Internet Explorer (named after the browser), while the Netscape suite is called Netscape Communicator.

Figure 3-1 shows each of these suites along with the four most important components. I have included this information to make it easy for you to figure out which programs do what.

Figure 3-1: Microsoft's and Netscape's suites of Internet software

Type of Program	Microsoft Internet Explorer	Netscape Communicator
Web client (browser)	Internet Explorer	Navigator
Mail client	Outlook Express	Messenger
Usenet client (newsreader)	Outlook Express	Collabra
Web channels	Internet Explorer	Netcaster

What Type of Computer Should You Buy?

What type of computer should you buy to use the Internet? You have two basic choices: a regular computer or a special-purpose Internet computer. Most people use regular computers, so let's talk about those first. In this section, I'll summarize the points we have discussed so far and tell you what to buy.

When it comes to computers, you can get a PC or a Macintosh. Get a PC. Virtually all software and all new development, especially on the Internet, is for PCs running Windows. If you get a Macintosh, you will be left out of the mainstream.

Your PC should come with Windows 98 already installed. As I explained earlier, the computer should have at least 64 MB of RAM (memory)—more if possible. In addition, make sure the PC has a CD-ROM drive and speakers. I suggest that you also get a microphone (often included). This will allow you to talk to other people over the Net, and to record voice messages, which you can send by email.

Make sure the computer's processor is fast. Processor speeds are measured in MHz (megahertz) and, within the same family of processors, all you need to do is compare the numbers. For example, a Pentium II processor running at 450 MHz is faster (and better) than a Pentium II running at 266 MHz. When it comes to processing power, you get what you pay for, so if you can afford it, pay more for a faster processor. Whatever you do, don't buy a PC with the older Pentium processor. It will be too slow.

Other companies besides Intel make processors, and Intel spends a lot of money trying to convince people they should only buy PCs with Intel processors. Forget the advertisements. Although most PCs do have an Intel processor, it's okay to buy a PC with another brand. Just make sure it compares favorably to a fast Pentium II. (You may have to do some research.)

Finally, make sure that any computer you buy has the facilities you need to connect to the Net. For fast connections such as DSL and cable (discussed later in the chapter), you will need an Ethernet port. For slow connections, you will need a modem (also discussed later).

ETHERNET is a technology used to connect computers into a local network. For example, if you have more than one computer in your home, you can connect them into an Ethernet and share resources, such as files and printers. Many businesses and schools have Ethernets.

An ETHERNET PORT is a socket, which you can use to connect your PC to a network. When you use DSL or cable for Internet access, you actually connect to a network, so you need Ethernet capability. If your computer does not have a built-in Ethernet port, you will have to install a special Ethernet adapter in the machine. (You will sometimes see this adapter called an Ethernet NIC—network interface card.)

With respect to modems (discussed later in the chapter), make sure the computer has a 56K V.90 modem.

What about the other parts of the computer? For example, do you need to worry about the size of the hard disk? If you follow the advice I have given in this section, you don't have to worry about anything else. The size of the hard disk is important (as are other considerations), but if you get the type of computer I recommend, it will include everything you need.

How Much Should You Pay for a Computer?

How much you should pay for a computer is an important question. The best answer is that it's cheaper in the long run to make sure you don't pay too little. Here is why.

Computer technology changes quickly, and every few months, new, more powerful computers come on the market. Moreover, computer software changes just as fast, and the new programs will not work well on the old hardware. For example, the current version of Windows (98) will not run on the machines that were suitable for the old versions of Windows (3.0 and 3.1). As a general rule, new programs don't run well on old machines, because the programmers who design the programs depend on the power, speed, and increased memory of the newer computers. However, software is being improved all the time, and you certainly don't want to be stuck with old programs.

This is why computers become obsolete so quickly: It's because software becomes obsolete, and you need a new computer to run the new software.

This consideration is important when you buy a new PC, especially when you plan to use it to access the Internet. No matter what machine you buy, I guarantee that two years from now it will look old, and three years from now it will be screaming to be replaced.

Thus, instead of buying the most inexpensive computer, I want you to spend a little more now and buy one with a faster processor and more memory. My goal is for your machine to last three years, rather than two.

Of course, nobody will make you buy a new computer in two to three years. If you want, you can use one for five years or more. There are no Internet police who will arrest you for trying to run new programs on old machines. However, the programs won't run well, and maybe they won't run at all.

For this reason, I suggest that—in the U.S.—you spend at least $1,500 for a new computer (including the monitor). The number, of course, is a guideline, but if you follow my advice I know you will be pleased with your PC, and it will serve you well for as long as possible. In today's marketplace, computers are commodities, which means that brand names aren't all that important. What's important is to recognize that the more you pay, the more you get; and the more you get, the longer it will last without becoming obsolete.

hint

The only way anyone can give you a very low price on a new PC is by selling you last year's technology (and last year's technology is well on its way to being obsolete).

I want you to remember that a computer is a tool for your mind, and you deserve the best such tool you can afford. A friend called me recently and said, "I went computer shopping, and I can't decide whether I should buy my son a $900 computer or a $1,500 computer. What do you think?"

"That depends," I told him. "Does your son have a $900 mind or a $1,500 mind?"

Alternatives to Regular PCs (Such as WebTV)

A regular PC running Windows is a general-purpose tool. You can use it for a lot of things besides accessing the Internet. If all you want is the Internet, there is an alternative you may want to consider.

There are special-purpose computers used primarily for accessing the Internet. As such, they are simpler to use than regular PCs and a lot less expensive. Of course, they do not run regular programs. On the other hand, you don't have to deal with learning how to use Windows 98 and manage a PC (which can take a while).

There really isn't a standard name for such computers, but sometimes they are referred to as INTERNET APPLIANCES. One of the more well-known Internet appliances is called WebTV. WebTV, like other such devices, is designed specifically for the consumer Internet market and costs much less than a PC. One reason is that, instead of requiring a special computer monitor, the Internet appliance connects to your television set.

A special-purpose Internet computer is suitable for you if (1) you know for sure that you want only Internet access, and (2) you don't want to spend much money. Be aware, though, that hardware is only part of the cost. You will still have to pay for the Internet service. For example, with WebTV, you must pay the WebTV company a monthly fee. However, this fee usually compares favorably to what you have to pay to access the Internet with a PC. Personally, I'd rather have a full-fledged computer, but people who use devices like WebTV generally like them, so you may want to consider it as an alternative.

hint

Before you buy a special-purpose Internet computer, find out how it connects to the Net. Many such computers use a dialup connection, which pretty much guarantees that your experience is going to be a terribly slow one. (Read the next few sections in this chapter, and you will see what I mean.)

Types of Internet Connections

Once you have a computer and software, you need to arrange two things in order to use the Internet.

You need to buy Internet access from an INTERNET SERVICE PROVIDER or ISP. (We will discuss how to choose an ISP later in the chapter.) For this service, you will pay a monthly fee. Some ISPs also charge a one-time setup fee.

You will also need to arrange a way to connect your computer to the ISP. For a home computer, there are four choices:

● Dialup connection
● ISDN
● DSL
● Cable

The first three use a telephone line, while the fourth one uses the same cable that brings your TV service. There are various details you need to know, so I will discuss each of these choices later in the chapter.

The table in Figure 3-2 shows the various ways to connect to an ISP. Dialup connections are available everywhere. For the other three, you will have to check with your local telephone and cable companies. If you have a choice, go with the fastest one you can get.

Figure 3-2: Various ways to connect to an ISP

Name	Speed	Connect Via
Dialup	Slow	Regular telephone line
ISDN	Medium	ISDN telephone line
DSL	Fast	Regular telephone line
Cable	Fast	TV cable

The Speed of an Internet Connection

When you connect to the Net, the most important consideration is the speed of your connection. Faster is better, and a lot faster is a lot better. In fact, you can't get a connection that is too fast.

Why? Your mind works quickly, and no matter how fast you connect to the Net, the information will never appear fast enough for your brain. Waiting is irritating and interferes with your thought processes.

The main communication links inside the Internet are very fast. However, what you see on your computer is considerably slower. This is because, no matter how fast data travels within the Net, it must pass through one last link—the one to your computer— and that link is always the slowest. For this reason, when you arrange for your Internet connection, you should get one that is as fast as possible.

To measure speed on the Internet, we describe how much data is transmitted per second. However, before I can explain the terminology, we need to talk about how data is organized within a computer. Earlier in the chapter, I explained that data is measured in bytes, where each byte holds one character. Inside a computer, a byte is actually stored as a series of smaller entities called BITS. There are 8 bits in each byte, so that it takes 8 bits to store a single character.

Consider the name "Harley Hahn", for example. This name consists of 11 characters (counting the space) and, hence, within a computer, would be stored as 11 bytes, which is the same as 88 bits.

WHAT'S IN A NAME?

bit
byte

Within a computer, data is stored as bits (8 to a byte). Mathematically, it is possible to work with bits by representing them as numbers using the binary system. Within the binary system, each bit is represented by a single digit, either a 0 or a 1. The word "bit" stands for "binary digit".

The word "byte" doesn't stand for anything in particular. It's just a cute word that was chosen to represent something that was bigger than a bit. Since it could be confusing to have both bits and bites, we spell it with a "y" (byte).

By the way, just for fun, here is the word "Harley" encoded as bits:

```
    H         a         r         l         e         y
01001000  01100001  01110010  01101100  01100101  01111001
```

On the Internet, we measure speed in BITS PER SECOND, usually abbreviated as BPS. For example, if I tell you that a particular connection to the Internet has a maximum operating speed of 56,000 bps, it would be the same as saying you can transmit up to 7,000 bytes per second through that connection. In practice, we mostly use such numbers to compare relative speeds. For instance, I might say that 56,000 bps is significantly faster than 33,600 bps, but not nearly as fast as 128,000 bps.

To make the numbers easier to manage, we use the abbreviation K to mean 1,000. For example, instead of saying 56,000 bps, we would write 56K bps. Similarly, we would say 33.6K bps or 128K bps. We also use M to mean 1,000,000. For example, you might read about a 1.5M bps connection.

A related term, BANDWIDTH, means the capacity to transmit data. For example, a 128K bps (128,000 bits per second) connection has about four times the bandwidth of a 33.6K bps connection; a 1.5M bps connection has a great deal more bandwidth.

On the Net, we sometimes use this word more generally. For instance, you may see people complain that spam (unsolicited advertising) wastes a lot of bandwidth.

hint

When it is clear that we are talking about the speed of an Internet connection, we often leave out the "bps".

For instance, you might hear someone say, "I used to have a 56K dialup connection, but I recently changed to a 128K ISDN service, which is a lot better. However, I can't wait until cable or DSL is available in my neighborhood, so I can get a 1.5M connection like my Uncle Gil."

Analog and Digital

Before we continue, I want to digress for a moment to discuss an important topic, the difference between analog and digital. (If you live in the U.K., you can pretend we are talking about analogue and digital.)

We use the word ANALOG to describe quantities that can vary continuously from one value to another. We use the word DIGITAL to describe quantities that can take on only specific, discrete values.

The most common way to appreciate these differences is to think about analog and digital clocks. An analog clock is an old-style one, with hour and minute hands. A digital clock shows you exact numbers. If you look at an analog clock, you might say the time is "a quarter to six" or "a bit past eleven". With a digital clock, you would see an exact time, 5:45 or 11:02.

Here is another example. In a car, an analog speedometer has a needle that moves back and forth. You might look at such a speedometer and say, "We are traveling somewhere between 50 and 55 miles per hour." If your car has a digital speedometer, you would see an exact number, say, 52 miles per hour.

Within a computer, all data is stored in a digital format as exact values (the bytes and bits we talked about earlier). This makes the data easy to manipulate (for a computer). Moreover, as this short example will illustrate, digital data is less susceptible to error than analog data.

Singing is an analog experience, so imagine yourself singing a tune that you just made up. You sing the tune to a person, who then sings it to another person, who then repeats it to another person, and so on. After several such transmissions, the tune probably wouldn't sound much like the original.

Now try a digital experience. You write down a list of ten numbers on a piece of paper. You then give the list to another person who copies the numbers onto another piece of paper and passes it to a third person. This person copies the numbers once again and passes them to a fourth person. As long as you can all read and write, you can transfer the digital data (in this case, numbers) as many times as you want without introducing mistakes.

And this is how it works on the Internet. All the computers and communication links (with one important exception) are digital, and data is passed from one computer to another with a minimum of errors. This is not to say that there are never mistakes in a digital system—after all, it is perfectly possible to write down a set of numbers so that one or two of them are illegible—but the Internet has ways to find such errors and correct them. (This is done by TCP, which I discussed in Chapter 1.)

Modems

Everything on the Net is digital, with one important exception: the link between you and the Net. The signal that goes over the telephone line or cable is actually analog, so you need a way to convert outgoing digital data (inside your computer) to analog data (for the phone line or cable). Similarly, incoming data (from the phone line or cable) has to be converted to digital data (for your computer). All of this is done automatically by a device called a MODEM.

Each type of connection requires its own type of modem. For a dialup connection, you can use the regular modem that came with your computer. For an ISDN, DSL or cable connection, you will need a special ISDN, DSL or cable modem. Telephone and cable companies usually make it easy for you to buy or rent the type of modem you need when you use one of these services.

WHAT'S IN A NAME?

modem

In technical terms, the process used to convert digital data to analog data is called MODULATION. The process used to convert analog data to digital data is called DEMODULATION. Thus, the device that performs this job is called a modem: a modulator/demodulator.

hint

I said earlier that most of the connections on the Net are digital with one exception: the connection between your PC and your ISP. Actually, this is true only if you use a dialup connection, DSL or cable. ISDN actually uses a digital signal.

Thus, there is an exception to our exception, which serves to illustrate something important about life (and if I were a philosopher, I could tell you what it was).

So, strictly speaking, the device that acts as an ISDN interface—the so-called ISDN modem—is not really a modem. For this reason, I want you to be prepared for the following situation.

You are at a party, talking about high-speed Internet access, when an electrical engineer named Norman comes over and says:

"You know, of course, that ISDN modems are not really modems, because they do not modulate and demodulate."

When this happens, the correct response is:

"How nice for you, Norman. Would you please pass the onion dip?"

Dialup Connections

A DIALUP CONNECTION uses a modem and a regular telephone line. To access the Net, you run a program that causes the modem to dial the phone number of your ISP (Internet service provider). At the other end, another modem answers the phone and connects to your modem. Your program then sends your user name and password to log you in. You are now on the Net.

Before there were faster alternatives, virtually all Internet access from home computers was via a dialup connection. Even today, many people still connect to the Net in this manner.

There are three main advantages of a dialup connection: It is available everywhere, it is convenient if you travel with a computer, and it is cheap. Moreover, virtually all new PCs come with a modem, and a dialup account with an ISP is economical. (In the U.S., it costs only about $20/month.)

There are two disadvantages. Most importantly, dialup connections are slow. Even the fastest such connection can be irritatingly slow compared to ISDN, DSL or cable.

The second disadvantage is that a dialup connection ties up the telephone line, so you can't use the Net and talk at the same time. For this reason, many people install an extra line just for Internet access. This is convenient, but it will pretty much double your monthly cost.

hint

When you buy a new computer, make sure you get a 56K modem, not one of the older 33.6K modems.

Also, you should know that there used to be two incompatible types of 56K modems: K56Flex and X2. These two systems have been reconciled into one universal standard called V.90 (pronounced "vee-dot-90"). Make sure you get a real V.90 56K device, not an older K56Flex or X2.

Modern modems are advertised as running at 56K bps, while the older modems are said to run at 33.6K. However, these numbers are misleading in two ways.

First, the numbers are theoretical maximums. Analog phone lines are susceptible to electrical noise, and this noise decreases the speed at which your modem can make a connection. A 56K modem with a good telephone line will usually connect at somewhere between 30K and 45K. A 33.6K modem will connect at 20K to 28K. The importance of these numbers is shown in Figure 3-3.

Figure 3-3: Relative speeds of dialup connections

Type of Connection	Speed
Dialup using a 56K modem	Slow
Dialup using a 33.6K modem	Very slow

Second, 56K modems are 56K only with incoming data (downloading). With outgoing data (uploading), 56K modems behave like 33.6K modems. The reason is that, for outgoing data, the change from digital (your computer) to analog (the phone line) causes problems that restrict the modem's speed. This discrepancy isn't as bad as it sounds, though, because most of the time you are downloading data to your computer, not uploading data to the Net.

Once you have some experience, you will notice that modem advertisements (and computer salesmen) never volunteer the knowledge that your modem will not give you the advertised speed. You might ask, don't the modem manufacturers and the salesmen know about this? The answer is, of course they do. However, before you judge them too harshly, consider the following real-life observation:

hint

Everyone who sells connectivity hardware *always* misrepresents the speed.

Traditionally, modems have been advertised with speeds that are theoretical maximums, never to be seen in real life. Today, this tradition is honorably continued with the newer forms of connectivity. For example, the people who sell cable access (which we will discuss later in the chapter) exaggerate horribly about the speed you will get. (In fact, if this wasn't a family book, I would say that the cable modem people lie through their teeth.)

ISDN

ISDN (Integrated Services Digital Network) is a service offered by the phone company that allows you to connect to an ISP using all-digital technology. Because there are no analog links in the connection, ISDN is much faster than a dialup connection using a modem and a regular (analog) phone line.

An ISDN line consists of three separate parts called CHANNELS, each of which furnishes a specific amount of bandwidth. There are two B-CHANNELS and one D-CHANNEL. The B-channels carry your data, and each one provides 64K of bandwidth. Thus, a single ISDN line can offer a 128K connection to the Internet. The

D-channel has 16K, but it is used to carry the internal control information that makes everything work, and is not available for data.

Because the whole system is digital, ISDN lines are not affected by electrical noise the way modems are. Thus, unlike modems, ISDN really does provide close to the full amount of advertised bandwidth. Moreover, ISDN lines can also be used for telephones, and it is possible to use a single line for both voice and an Internet connection at the same time.

WHAT'S IN A NAME?

B-channel
D-channel

In ISDN terminology, "B-channel" stands for "bearer channel". The name was chosen because B-channels bear (transport) the computer or voice data.

"D-channel" stands for "data channel". However, "data" refers to the internal control information, not computer data.

To use ISDN you need three things. First, you need an Internet service provider (ISP) that offers ISDN connections.

Second, you need an ISDN phone line to connect to your ISP. ISDN service varies from place to place, but is widely available. Check the prices carefully. Some companies charge a per minute rate as well as a monthly fee, and this can get expensive. If possible, get a flat rate, so you can stay connected to the Net for long periods of time.

The final thing you need is an ISDN modem to provide an interface between the ISDN line and your computer. When you shop for an ISDN modem, look for one that promises to be easy to configure, because ISDN can be difficult to set up. You may find that your phone company offers an ISDN modem as part of an all-inclusive package.

hint

Many people have an ISDN line for the computer, and a regular phone line for voice. However, an ISDN line can support both data and voice at the same time. If you want to take advantage of this capability, choose an ISDN modem that allows you to plug in a regular (analog) telephone. Otherwise, you will have to buy a special digital phone.

Upstream and Downstream

In Chapter 2, I explained that receiving data from the Net is called downloading, and sending data to the Net is called uploading. We use similar terminology to describe the direction of data transmission: DOWNSTREAM and UPSTREAM.

When you use the Internet, you tend to receive a lot more data than you send. For example, with the Web, you click your mouse and type a little, and, in return, you receive huge amounts of data: text, pictures, sounds, animation, even video. For this reason, the technologies used for high-speed consumer Internet connections are designed to devote more of the available bandwidth for downstream transmission than upstream transmission. When the bandwidth is distributed unevenly, we say that it is ASYMMETRIC.

The reason I mention this is that both DSL and cable are asymmetric services. For example, you might see an advertisement for a DSL service that offers 256K downstream, but only 64K upstream.

DSL

DSL (Digital Subscriber Line) is a technology that allows high-speed Internet connections over telephone lines. DSL is fast, and if it is available in your area for a reasonable price, it should be one of your top choices for an Internet connection.

DSL uses a regular phone line without interfering with the voice service. Thus, a single line can support both voice and a high-speed Internet connection at the same time. DSL is much faster than a dialup connection or ISDN. I can't tell you an exact speed, because phone companies offer various services, but, at a minimum, you should be able to get several hundred bps (bits per second), and, perhaps, much faster.

A DSL connection is always turned on. With a dialup connection, you are not on the Net until your modem dials the phone and makes the connection. However, with DSL, you are connected permanently, until you either stop the service or die (whichever comes first).

There are different types of DSL. The type used for home Internet connections is asymmetric, with more downstream than upstream bandwidth. For that reason, this type of DSL is called ADSL.

WHAT'S IN A NAME?

DSL
ADSL

DSL (Digital Subscriber Line) is actually a family of loosely related technologies, the most well-known of which is ADSL. The following table shows the names of the various DSL technologies and what they mean.

ADSL   Asymmetric Digital Subscriber Line
HDSL   High-bit-rate Digital Subscriber Line
RADSL   Rate Adaptive Asymmetric Digital Subscriber Line
SDSL   Symmetric Digital Subscriber Line
VDSL   Very high-bit-rate Digital Subscriber Line

ADSL is the system that telephone companies use to connect home computers to the Internet, and, as such, it is the most common member of the family—the other DSLs are relatively rare. For this reason, the word "DSL" is usually used as a synonym for "ADSL". For example, when you read about DSL Internet services, it really means ADSL Internet services. When we want to avoid any possible ambiguity, we use the term xDSL to refer to the family as a whole.

To use DSL, you need three things: DSL service from your phone company, an account with a DSL Internet service provider (ISP), and a DSL modem. The DSL modem connects to your PC via an Ethernet port, so if your PC does not have such a port, you will have to install an Ethernet adapter.

hint

When you analyze the monthly cost for DSL, remember that you can use a single phone line for both DSL and voice. Unlike a dialup connection, there is no need to pay for a second line if you want to use the Net and talk on the phone at the same time.

Cable

Cable Internet connections are provided by cable TV companies. Such connections use the same wire—called a COAXIAL CABLE—that is used for television. However, the Internet signal is separate from the television signals, so you can use the Internet and watch TV at the same time (although I don't recommend it, as you run the risk of having your brain explode).

Like DSL, cable connections are fast and are always turned on. Also like DSL, cable connections are asymmetric, with more downstream than upstream bandwidth.

Cable connections are usually easy to arrange. Your cable company will supply you with everything you need, including a cable modem and an Ethernet adapter for your computer (if your PC does not have an Ethernet port). In addition, the cable company will probably be your ISP, providing Internet access as well as the connection.

When you check out prices, you will have to factor this all in. There will be a significant startup fee, which will include installation and the Ethernet adapter. But the monthly fee will cover the use of the cable modem as well as Internet access. Remember, also, you do not need to pay for an extra phone line.

Compared to dialup connections, cable Internet connections are great, but there are some caveats. First, you should realize that you are sharing the cable with everyone in your neighborhood. As more people use the cable, there will be less bandwidth for you, and the speed of your connection will decrease, especially during times of heavy use. This is not the case with ISDN or DSL.

Second, the speed you get will be fast, but not as fast as the cable company's advertisements will lead you to believe. One common number you will see is 10M bps. This is because cable modems connect to your computer via an Ethernet port, and the theoretical maximum for Ethernet is 10M bps. Don't believe it. The speed they provide won't be anywhere near this number (and even if it were, the hardware in your PC would have trouble handling even 3M bps).

Let me tell you about a real-life example. I have a friend who shall remain nameless (Josh) who uses a cable Internet connection. As an experiment, Josh and I decided to test the speed of his connection. According to the cable company, Josh's connection can support 10M bps (which we know isn't true), and he should get at least about 4M bps downstream. Upstream, Josh should get 768K bps.

To run the test, Josh downloaded a large file from one of Microsoft's Web sites. (The file was the current version of Internet Explorer, and was 10.631 MB.) As a control, I downloaded the same file to my computer. I have a very fast, dependable connection called a T1, running under HDSL. A T1 connection (which is very expensive) has a maximum speed of 1.544M bps. We ran the test on a Sunday afternoon, a typical time for a home user to be accessing the Internet.

The results were as follows. Josh's cable connection downloaded the file in 8 minutes and 2 seconds, an average speed of 176K bps. My T1 line downloaded the file in 1 minute 22 seconds, which works out to 966K bps.

Compared to the large bandwidth the cable company promised, 176K looks small, and some people might be disappointed. However, 176K—a real 176K—is not all that bad. Realistically, 176K is more than five times the actual speed you get with a 56K modem, and cable is a lot more convenient. There's no need for an extra phone line, and you don't have to wait for a modem to dial a number and connect each time you start a new work session.

Josh loves his cable connection and is completely satisfied, especially when he compares it to his old dialup connection. For me, 966K is like greased lightning (to coin a phrase), and I wouldn't want to live without it. However, my T1 costs a *lot* of money, and Josh pays only $40/month.

What Type of Internet Services Are Available?

In order to use the Internet, you will need to pay money to someone. This is not a usage fee, as the Internet itself is open to everyone. Rather, you are paying for a connection to the Net. There are a variety of Internet services you can purchase, so it's a good idea to understand what is available. I'll explain each one in turn, but let's start with the full list just to get an overview:

- Basic access
- Mail
- Usenet news
- Web site hosting
- DNS service (custom address)

The basic service you need is access to the Net. To get Internet access, you arrange an account with an Internet service provider (ISP). You pay a monthly fee, and, in return, they arrange for you to connect to the Internet through their system.

Just having a connection provides you with access to a lot of the Net, including all of the Web. However, you do need at least two other services: the use of a mail server and an email address (so you can send and receive email), and access to a Usenet news server (so you can participate in Usenet discussion groups). ISPs generally provide email and Usenet news at no extra cost when you pay for basic Internet access.

In addition, there are two other services you may want: Web site hosting (so you can have your own Web site) and DNS service (which allows you to have a personalized address, like `harley.com`). We'll talk about these topics later in the book.

Although your ISP will probably offer all these services, you do have choices. It is possible to buy your basic access from one ISP, and get mail, Usenet, Web site hosting and DNS from other providers. In fact, mail service and Web site hosting are widely available for free. The catch is, you will have to look at advertisements when you read your mail, and your users will have to look at advertisements when they look at your Web page. We will discuss all of these issues later in the book.

The important point is that basic Internet access can be unbundled from anything else. Just because you use one ISP for basic access doesn't mean you have to depend on the ISP for everything.

Why You Might Want Two Internet Accounts

Most people have only one Internet account, but in some circumstances you may want an extra one.

Let's say that your home Internet connection is a fast one (DSL, cable or ISDN), but when you travel, you like to carry a notebook computer so you can check your mail no matter where you are. Unfortunately, your portable computer will not be able to access your home connection. The only way to use the Net when you travel is via a modem and a dialup connection.

For this reason, you may want to maintain two accounts: one for fast access at home, another for dialup access whenever you travel. The two accounts do not need to be with the same ISP.

Finding Internet Service Providers (ISPs)

One of the two most common questions people ask me is, "How do I find an Internet service provider?" (The other question is, "How many copies of your books should I buy?") In this section, I will discuss how to find and select an ISP, so you can understand the choices and make a wise decision. (The answer to the second question, by the way, is, "One copy for everyone you know.")

Do not begin to look for an ISP until you have chosen the type of Internet connection you want. Start by checking to see whether DSL, ISDN or cable is available where you live. If DSL or cable is available, it should be your first choice. Otherwise, ISDN should be your second choice. If none of these services is available in your area, you will have to use a dialup connection.

Once you have decided how to connect to the Net, you can choose your Internet service provider. This is the company that will provide you with Internet access. If you use a cable connection, you probably won't have a choice—the cable company will be your ISP (or will arrange for an ISP). With other types of connections, you do have a choice. The widest choice will be with dialup connections.

hint

When you buy a new computer, there will be a lot of software already installed, including Windows 98 from Microsoft. It is common to find that your PC is set up to make it easy to connect to one or more ISPs. This is because Microsoft or the computer company has made marketing deals with the ISPs.

Ignore what is already on your computer. Follow the advice I give in this chapter and find the ISP that is best for you. If it happens to be one of the ISPs whose software is on your computer, so much the better, but don't choose blindly.

When it comes to ISPs, you have two broad choices. You can choose a local/regional provider, or you can choose a large national company. If you plan on moving, a national provider is convenient as you will not have to change your email address. Aside from that, the main considerations should be the ones I mention as follows.

How do you find ISPs that serve your area? First, if your local telephone company is selling DSL or ISDN connections, they may know which ISPs in your area offer Internet access using those services. If the customer service person at the phone company has no clue (not uncommon), try their Web site.

Second, talk to people who already have Internet access. This is a good way to find out the names of some ISPs, and at the same time get an opinion as to the quality of the service.

Third, use the Web. There are a number of Web sites that maintain directories of ISPs organized by area code. In my experience, it is a good idea to check more than one directory, because none of them are complete. (If you don't have Web access, ask a friend who is already on the Net to find the information for you. Alternatively, many public libraries have computers with an Internet connection that can be used for free.)

Choosing an ISP

How do you evaluate an ISP? There are two ways. First, ask people in your area what ISP they use and what they think of the service. Asking around in this way is important, as it will allow you to avoid those ISPs that are not providing good service. Second, do a bit of research. Call each ISP and inquire about their services. If you have Web access (say, at work or at school), check their Web sites. As you do your research, consider the following:

Price: Make sure you get a flat monthly rate, not an hourly rate. (You will use the Net more than you think.) In the U.S., monthly rates vary from about $20/month (for dialup) to $60/month for ISDN, DSL, or cable. If you have a dialup connection, you will probably want a second telephone line, so you can talk on the phone while you are using the Net. Be sure to consider the price of this line when you figure your overall costs. However, when you compare prices, don't worry about small differences in the monthly fee. Go for the fastest connection you can afford.

Mail: Are you going to share your Internet connection (say, with your family, your spouse, or a roommate)? Some ISPs will give you several different mail addresses with a single Internet account. Mail works better when each person has his or her own email address. This is especially true for husbands and wives. Even if you are the only person using an account, it can be handy to have more than one address. For example, if you run your own business, you can use one email address for business and another address for personal correspondence.

Usenet news: Does the ISP offer Usenet news service? If so, make sure they use filters to reduce the spam (junk advertising). This will make your Usenet experience a lot more pleasant.

Technical support: The profit margins in the ISP industry are small, and it is unrealistic to expect a lot of technical support. For example, no ISP can afford to spend time teaching you how to design your own Web page, or even how to use the Web. What you can expect is enough help to get started. If you can't figure out how to make your connection work, an ISP should help you until it works. Moreover, if you need special software to get connected, an ISP should provide it. At the very least, there should be a telephone number you can call for assistance. (Be prepared, however, to wait a long time.) When you investigate an ISP, see whether they provide support on their Web site. Once you are connected, such support can be a great help.

The points we have covered so far are important no matter how you connect to the Net. However, if you are going to use a dialup connection, there are a few extra considerations:

Local phone number: Each time you use the Net, your modem is going to have to dial the phone number of the ISP and connect to a modem at the other end of the line. To keep your costs down, make sure that you choose an ISP you can access with a local phone call.

The larger ISPs have local numbers for various parts of the country. Each of these access points is called a POP (Point of Presence). So in nerd language, we can say that you should look for an ISP that has a POP in your area.

Adequate phone lines: All ISPs have a large number of phone lines. To use the service, you dial a central number. If there is an empty line, you are connected to it—otherwise, you get a busy signal. One of the biggest complaints about ISPs is that many of them do not have enough phone lines. When you use such an ISP, you will spend a lot of time being frustrated because you can't get through. This is especially true during times of peak usage (evenings and weekends).

Fortunately, checking whether an ISP has an adequate number of lines is easy. Find out the local access number, the one your modem would call to connect you to the Net. (This number will be different from the customer service number.) Then use the phone yourself to call the number and see what happens. Call the local access number at various times on different days. If you get through each time, that is a good sign. If you get a busy signal a lot of the time, you have found an ISP to avoid.

56K modems: Earlier in the chapter, I explained that you should use only a 56K bps modem. (The older 33.6K modems are just too slow.) Make sure that the ISP you are considering supports 56K. Moreover, make sure they support the type of 56K modem you are using. The standard 56K modem uses a system called V.90. The older 56K modems used either K56Flex and X2 (which are not compatible).

*I*NTERNET RESOURCE Lists of Internet Service Providers (ISPs)

```
http://thelist.internet.com/
http://www.boardwatch.com/isp/
http://www.cnet.com/content/reviews/compare/ISP/
```

Does It Matter Whether Your Dialup ISP Has Lots of POPs?

If you travel with a notebook computer, you will want to be able to use the Net wherever you are. For example, it's handy to be able to check your mail. At home, you dial a local number to connect to your ISP, so there is no long distance charge. When you are traveling, however, you would have to pay extra for a phone call to your ISP at home.

All the large, national ISPs have local access numbers (POPs) all over the country, so if you use such an ISP, there will probably be a local number for you to dial when you travel. "Wow," you say, "I can check my mail wherever I go and not have to pay for a long distance call."

But wait—does it really cost that much to call long distance for a few minutes? Compared to your other travel costs, calling long distance to check your mail isn't expensive at all. For some reason, it seems cool to dial a local number when you travel, but realistically, it's just as easy, and not that expensive, to dial anywhere in the country. Here is a real-life example that illustrates what I mean.

Jack and Jill both work for the same large company. Occasionally, the company sends them on a business trip, and when they travel, they each take a notebook computer to check their email so they can stay in touch. Recently, Jack and Jill both went to New York. During the trip, their expenses were pretty much the same. Both Jack and Jill flew on the same airline, ate at the same restaurants, and stayed at the same hotel (in separate rooms, of course; this *is* a family book).

However, there was one difference. Jack has a dialup account with a national ISP, so while he was in New York, he was able to access the Net via a local phone number. Jill uses a local ISP, so every time she wanted to check her mail, she had to pay for a long distance telephone call.

At the end of the trip, both Jack and Jill added up all their expenses. Jack's trip cost $940. Jill had to pay the long distance bill, so her trip cost more: $955 (but that also included $3 for a chocolate bar she bought at the New York airport on her way home).

The moral of the story? When you travel, if all you do on the Net is check your mail, choose the ISP you want, because saving a few bucks on long distance charges won't make much of a difference. (However, you may want to bring your own snacks. Chocolate can be expensive at the New York airport.)

What About AOL?

AOL is, by far, the largest ISP in the world. In America, the name AOL stands for America Online. In Europe, in deference to local sensitivities, AOL is just plain AOL.

AOL has something that the other ISPs do not have: a lot of extra services. The most popular services are the many chat rooms, where people gather to talk 24 hours a day. In addition, AOL offers information that is available only to their customers as well as regular presentations. For example, there are events where famous people answer questions and talk to a live audience (by typing, of course, not voice). Overall, AOL tries to maintain the feeling of a large community, a feeling that many of their users share.

However, to access the Internet, you can use any ISP you want, and there are a number of good reasons why you should avoid AOL. First, they have a huge number of customers, and they have real trouble keeping up with the demand. AOL users often have trouble connecting over phone lines at peak periods (evenings and weekends).

Second, in general, the Internet is free and uncensored. People can do whatever they want. AOL is a private environment. Although there is a lot of freedom, there is definitely Someone-in-Charge. This may or may not bother you.

Third, AOL is slow. Accessing the Web through a regular ISP is almost always a faster, more enjoyable experience.

Finally, AOL is not primarily an Internet service provider. *AOL is a marketing company that sells Internet access in order to attract customers.* The distinction is an important one.

AOL makes the bulk of their money from advertising revenues, by selling merchandise to their customers, and by making sales deals with other companies. If you use AOL, you are going to look at a lot of ads.

My recommendation is that you forget AOL. Get yourself a regular ISP, and enjoy the Net. However, I do recognize that many people want the special AOL features, so if you think you would enjoy being an AOL customer, I have a suggestion.

You do not have to use them as an ISP in order to be a customer. For a smaller monthly fee, AOL allows you to connect to their services through any ISP. Of course, you still have to pay that ISP, so overall, it costs you a little more, but you will be getting the best of both worlds: faster and better Internet service, and full access to everything at AOL.

The Summary Once Again

At the very beginning of this chapter, I showed you a summary of what you were going to learn. We have covered a lot of ground since then, and I want you to appreciate how much you've learned, so take a moment and read the summary one more time. By now, you should understand it all.

Harley Hahn's Quick Guide to What You Need to Use the Internet

Buy a PC running Windows 98, with at least 64 MB of RAM. The computer should have a fast processor, a V.90 56K modem, speakers and a microphone. Get a built-in Ethernet port if one is available. Don't buy a Macintosh unless you are a professional graphics designer.

For software, if you want a word processor, get Microsoft Word. For everything else, wait until you see what software comes with the computer and what you can find for free on the Net. You don't need to buy an antivirus program right away.

Get the fastest Internet connection you can afford. DSL and cable are better than ISDN, and ISDN is better than a regular dialup connection. Choose an ISP that gives you a flat rate with reasonable customer service. Don't use AOL unless you know for sure that you want the extra content.

4

Internet Addresses

On the Internet, every computer, every person and every resource has its own address. One of the basic skills I want to teach you is how to understand and use these addresses. For example, here is the address of a particular Web page:

`http://www.harley.com/25-things/index.html`

By the time you finish this chapter, you will understand each part of this address, as well as the most important ideas related to Internet addresses.

Hostnames and Top-Level Domains

Every computer on the Internet has its own, unique name. Because Internet computers are sometimes referred to as HOSTS, these unique names are called HOSTNAMES. Here are some typical examples:

`www.harley.com`
`ftp.microsoft.com`
`architecture.mit.edu`
`ucsd.edu`
`www.senate.gov`
`eff.org`
`mail.pacbell.net`
`www.dofa.gov.au`
`www.austemb.org.cn`
`www.culture.fr`
`www.royal.gov.uk`
`www.rcmp-grc.gc.ca`
`www.cs.ait.ac.th`

Notice that each hostname has two or more parts separated by periods. When you say such a name out loud, you pronounce the period as "dot". For example, `www.harley.com` is pronounced "w-w-w dot Harley dot com".

Hostnames are part of a system called DNS, the domain name system (which we will discuss in detail later in the chapter). DNS is the system that allows us to give a unique name to every computer on the Internet.

The rightmost part of the name is called the top-level domain (for a reason I will explain later) and tells us general information about the host. For instance, within the name `architecture.mit.edu`, the top-level domain (`edu`) tells us that this computer is managed by an educational institution (in this case, MIT).

hint

When you type on a computer keyboard, small letters are called LOWERCASE and capital letters are called UPPERCASE.

With hostnames, you can use either lower- or uppercase letters or a mixture. For example, the following hostnames are all equivalent:

```
www.harley.com
WWW.HARLEY.COM
Www.Harley.Com
```

On the Internet, the custom is to use lowercase, and that is what you will see almost all the time. Although you can use uppercase when you type a hostname, I personally think lowercase looks nicer, because it is more uniform, and, as always, I encourage you to think like me.

There are two types of top-level domains: ORGANIZATIONAL DOMAINS and GEOGRAPHICAL DOMAINS. Organizational domains describe a category, while geographical domains indicate a particular country. For example, the organizational domain **edu** is for educational institutions, while the geographical domain **au** indicates the country of Australia.

Figure 4-1 shows the organizational domains. Figure 4-2 shows some of the geographical domains. There are actually a great many such top-level domains—one for every country on the Net—and for reference I have put the complete list in Appendix A.

As a general rule, organizational domains are used inside the U.S., while the geographical domains are used in other countries. You will, however, see exceptions.

Figure 4-1: Organizational top-level domains

Domain	Description
com	Commercial
edu	U.S. universities (educational)
gov	U.S. federal government
int	International
mil	U.S. military
net	Network providers
org	Miscellaneous organizations

Figure 4-2: Examples of geographical top-level domains

Domain	Description
at	Austria
au	Australia
be	Belgium
ca	Canada
ch	Switzerland (Confoederatio Helvetica)
cn	China
de	Germany (Deutschland)
dk	Denmark
es	Spain (España)
fr	France
gr	Greece
ie	Republic of Ireland
it	Italy
jp	Japan
nz	New Zealand
th	Thailand
uk	United Kingdom
us	United States

hint

When you see a hostname, look at the top-level domain (the rightmost part of the name). If the name has three or more letters, it is an organizational domain, and you can look up the meaning in Figure 4-1.

If the name has two letters, it is a geographical domain, probably representing a country. If you don't recognize the abbreviation, look it up in Figure 4-2 or in the master list in Appendix A.

Why Are There Two Types of Top-Level Domains?

In its formative years, the Internet was confined to the United States, and there were only a handful of top-level domains: **edu**, **com**, **gov**, **mil**, **org**, **net** and **int**. When the Internet expanded to other countries, the geographical domains were added so that each country could have its own top-level domain.

The original intention was that, eventually, all Internet hostnames would use geographical domains, and, indeed, the United States does have a **us** domain. However, by the time this domain was introduced, the organizational domains had been used for so long that few people in the U.S. were willing to change.

For this reason, you will see two main types of top-level domains: the organizational domains, used mostly in the U.S., and the geographical domains, used everywhere else. (This should not surprise you. After all, the United States is the only country in the world that does not use the metric system.)

hint

The U.S. geographical domain (**us**) is used by many schools and local governments. For example, the address of the Web site for Austin Community College in Texas is **www.austin.cc.tx.us**, and the address of the Web site for the city of San Francisco, California, is **www.ci.sf.ca.us**.

However, many people prefer to avoid the **us** top-level domain because the names are too complicated.

Exceptions to the Rules

How nice (but how boring) life would be if everyone always cooperated. Although the guidelines for using top-level domains are clear, not everybody follows the rules.

To be sure, most of the top-level domains are used consistently. Within the United States, for instance, **gov** is used only by the federal government, **mil** is used only by the military, and **edu** (educational) is used only by universities. Similarly, outside the U.S., the two-letter geographical top-level domains (**au**, **ca**, **jp**, **uk**, and so on) are almost always used appropriately.

However, **com**, **net** and **org** are a different story. The **com** designation is supposed to be for commercial organizations, **net** is supposed to be for network providers, and **org** is supposed to be for organizations that do not fit into any other category, such as nonprofit organizations. Nevertheless, there are many hostnames that use **com**, **net** or **org** that do not meet the criteria. The reasons are threefold.

First, in the mid-1990s, the Internet expanded so fast as to surprise almost everyone. Many people and organizations in the U.S. wanted their own unique hostnames, but there were not enough good names to go around. At the same time, the organization that administered the **com**, **net** and **org** top-level domains did not enforce the guidelines, so people pretty much did as they pleased.

So what do you think happened when the network administrator at the Acme Company tried to register the name **acme.com**, and he found that the name was already taken? He simply registered **acme.net** or **acme.org** instead. (I explain how to register a name in Chapter 16.)

Moreover, as the organizational top-level domain names became popular, many people wanted their own personalized hostnames, so they registered names like **alan.com**, **wendy.com** and **harley.com**. Other people who found these names already taken registered variations like **alan.net**, **alan.org**, **wendy.net**, **wendy.org**, and so on.

Finally, to make matters even more confusing, people and organizations outside the U.S. started to use these same top-level domains as well (even though they should have used their own geographical top-level domains).

Through it all, the registrations for **com**, **net** and **org** were accepted without anyone checking whether or not they were being used according to the guidelines. As a result, there are many hostnames that end in **com** that are not used by commercial entities, and there are hostnames that end in **net** or **org** that are not used by network providers or organizations.

Is this bad? Maybe yes and maybe no. How you feel about the situation depends on how much you like things to be orderly and well organized. One thing, however, that everyone can agree on is that the Internet needs more names, especially in the United States. As I explained earlier, there is a **us** top-level domain, but few people want to use it because the hostnames are so complicated.

Understanding Hostnames

The secret to understanding hostnames is to look at each part of the name, reading from right to left. In general, the rightmost two parts of the name will tell you which organization manages that particular computer. If a name has more than two parts, the extra parts may provide even more information.

Consider the name **ucsd.edu**. Reading from right to left, we see that this name represents a computer at a university (**edu**), which is the University of California at San Diego (**ucsd**).

Now look at the name **architecture.mit.edu**. The **edu** tells us this is also a computer at a university; the **mit** designation tells us that the university is MIT; and the third part, **architecture**, shows us that the computer is managed by the architecture department.

Let's take a look at one last example, **www.royal.gov.uk**. The rightmost part of the name (**uk**) tells us that this computer is in the United Kingdom. The next part of the name (**gov**) shows us that the computer is a government computer. The third part (**royal**) indicates that this computer has something to do with the British royal family.

But what about the leftmost part of the name, the **www**?

When the Web was first developed, it was called the World Wide Web. As the World Wide Web evolved, the name was shortened, but the old name left a legacy: It has become customary to use the designation **www** to indicate a computer that acts as a Web server. Thus, **www.royal.gov.uk** is the name of the Web site of the British royal family.

As you use the Net, you will see many other hostnames that begin with **www**. All of these are names of Web sites. For example, **www.ibm.com** is IBM's Web site, **www.microsoft.com** is Microsoft's Web site, and **www.harley.com** is my Web site.

You will also see similar patterns with other types of resources. For instance, there are many Anonymous FTP servers whose hostnames begin with **ftp**. (Anonymous FTP is a system that allows people to download programs and other files for free.) In addition, there are also many mail servers (that provide email services) that have names beginning with **mail**.

Here are two examples: The computer named **ftp.microsoft.com** is Microsoft's Anonymous FTP server, while the computer **mail.pacbell.net** is the mail server for an Internet service provider named Pacific Bell Internet.

There are no rules forcing people to use special hostnames, and there are some Web sites whose names do not begin with **www**. However, when you do see **www** (or **ftp** or **mail**) at the beginning of a hostname, you will know what it means.

Before we leave this section, let's look at one last hostname, **www.cs.ait.ac.th**. Reading from right to left, we start with the top-level domain **th**. This is the geographical top-level domain for Thailand.

The next part of the name is **ac**, a designation commonly used to indicate a university (**ac** stands for "academic community"). We then see **ait**, an abbreviation for the Asian Institute of Technology; **cs**, an abbreviation for "computer science"; and **www**, which indicates the computer is a Web site.

Thus, the hostname **www.cs.ait.ac.th** represents the Web site of the computer science department at the Asian Institute of Technology in Thailand.

Now, do I expect you to be able to figure out such names instantly? No, of course not. Unless you are already familiar with a country, you probably won't recognize its top-level domain or the names of its national organizations. However, I do want you to appreciate that many hostnames are constructed to make sense, at least to the people who make up the names.

hint

The organizational top-level domains—particularly **edu**, **com** and **gov**—are used widely within the U.S. In other countries, you will see a number of variations. In particular, you will see **ac** (academic community), **co** (commercial) and **gov** (government), followed by a two-letter geographical top-level domain.

For example, in Thailand, the Asian Institute of Technology uses **ait.ac.th**, while in England, Oxford University uses **ox.ac.uk**. Similarly, the *Times* newspaper in England uses **the‑times.co.uk**, while the Bank of Tokyo-Mitsubishi in Japan uses **www.btm.co.jp**, and in Australia, the Department of the Treasury uses the name **treasury.gov.au**.

In general, there are no absolute rules. Each country can use whatever hostnames it wants. However, as you gain experience on the Net, you will learn to recognize a number of common patterns that are followed around the world.

Domains

So far, we have talked about hostnames—the names used for computers on the Internet. I now want to discuss the more subtle concept of domains and how all the hostnames on the Internet are organized.

A DOMAIN is a set of hostnames that have the rightmost part of their names in common. For instance, all the hostnames that end in **edu** belong to the **edu** domain. Some examples are:

```
architecture.mit.edu
www.ucsd.edu
www.med.harvard.edu
```

Similarly, all the hostnames that end in **uk** belong to the **uk** domain. For example:

```
www.royal.gov.uk
ox.ac.uk
the-times.co.uk
```

(Notice, by the way, that a hyphen is a legitimate character within a hostname.)

The most general domains, such as **edu** and **uk**, are called TOP-LEVEL DOMAINS, because if you draw a diagram of hostnames, showing the most general names above all the others, these domains would be at the top.

As I explained earlier, there are two types of top-level domains: organizational domains and geographical domains (see Figures 4-1 and 4-2).

When hostnames have the two rightmost parts of their names in common, we say that they belong to the same SECOND-LEVEL DOMAIN. For instance, the following four hostnames all belong to the second-level domain **pacbell.net**:

```
pacbell.net
news.pacbell.net
mail.pacbell.net
www.pacbell.net
```

Similarly, these hostnames all belong to the second-level domain **gov.au**:

```
treasury.gov.au
hcourt.gov.au
health.gov.au
```

In such cases, we say that the more specific domain is a SUB-DOMAIN of the more general domain. Thus, **pacbell.net** is a sub-domain of **net**, and **gov.au** is a sub-domain of **au**.

Similarly, the hostname **www.royal.gov.uk** belongs to the **royal.gov.uk** domain, which is a sub-domain of **gov.uk**, which is itself a sub-domain of **uk**.

Thus, all the hostnames in the Internet are organized into one large hierarchical system based on domain names. This system is called DNS, the DOMAIN NAME SYSTEM.

IP Addresses

In a minute, we'll talk about DNS in more detail, but first I want to introduce you to the idea of IP addresses.

As you know, hostnames are the unique names we use to identify computers on the Internet. Hostnames are convenient because they are simple to use, and (once you get used to them) they are easy for human beings to remember.

However, the real work on the Internet is done by computer programs, not by human beings, and it is easier for programs to deal with numbers, not names. For this reason, every computer on the Internet is given a unique number, and, internally, the Net uses these numbers, not hostnames, to identify specific computers. (These numbers are similar, in spirit anyway, to the personal identification numbers—such as the U.S. Social Security number—that most countries issue to their citizens.)

In Chapter 1, I explained that the glue that holds the Internet together is a family of protocols (technical specifications) called TCP/IP. The most important protocol is IP (Internet Protocol). For this reason, the numbers used to identify Internet computers are called IP ADDRESSES or IP NUMBERS.

As we discussed in Chapter 1, we make use of the Internet by using client programs to request information from servers. For instance, to access the Web, we use a Web client, called a browser, to contact various Web servers on our behalf. What you need to understand is that, the way the Internet is set up, your browser must have an IP address in order to contact a server.

Of course, when we tell a client program the name of a computer, we use a hostname. This means that, before the client can carry out our request, it must translate that hostname into the corresponding IP address.

Let's say, for example, you want to visit my Web site. The address is **www.harley.com**. In order to contact my Web server, your browser must find out the IP address that corresponds to this address. To do so, the browser calls upon DNS to translate the hostname into an IP address. In this case, the IP address happens to be **207.155.37.136**, and once the browser has this information, it is a simple matter to connect to computer number **207.155.37.136** and request data from the Web site.

hint

When we talk about the "address" of a computer, we can mean two different things.

To a person, the address of a computer is its hostname. To a program, the address of a computer is its IP address.

All IP addresses have the same structure: four numbers separated by periods. The numbers can range from 0 to 255, but the actual details need not concern us, because, after all, IP addresses are for programs and computers, not for people.

For fun, however, here are some of the hostnames I mentioned earlier in the chapter, along with their IP addresses:

Hostname	IP Number
www.harley.com	207.155.37.136
ftp.microsoft.com	198.105.232.1
architecture.mit.edu	18.80.2.226
ucsd.edu	132.239.1.1
www.senate.gov	199.95.76.23
eff.org	204.253.162.2
mail.pacbell.net	206.13.28.55
www.dofa.gov.au	147.211.50.70
www.austemb.org.cn	202.94.1.136
www.culture.fr	143.126.211.220
www.royal.gov.uk	193.32.28.6
www.cs.ait.ac.th	192.41.170.15

DNS

The main job of DNS—the domain name system—is to translate hostnames into IP addresses. Everything is done behind the scenes, but I do want to take a moment to explain a bit about how it works, because it is so cool I know you will appreciate it.

Suppose someone gave you the task of keeping track of all the hostnames in the world and their corresponding IP addresses. How would you do it? One way would be to maintain a master table of all the hostnames and IP addresses. Whenever you had a specific inquiry, you could look up the hostname in the table and read off the appropriate IP address.

This is more or less the scheme that was used in the early days of the Internet, but as the years passed and the Net grew large, the hostname table grew as well, and, eventually, became much too big. Moreover, new hostnames were being added continually, and it became very difficult to keep the table up to date. The solution was to distribute the responsibility around the Net.

As I explained in Chapter 1, the Internet is constructed such that every organization manages its own part of the Net. For this reason, it makes sense for each organization to manage its own hostnames as well. In particular, specific domains are used by organizations, who are then responsible for maintaining all the hostnames and IP addresses within those domains. For example, IBM has **ibm.com**, Harvard University has **harvard.edu**, the Australian government has **gov.au**, and so on. Each organization must arrange for at least two computers, called NAME SERVERS, to provide addressing information for all the hostnames in its domain. (Two servers are used in case one of them goes down temporarily.)

Because DNS distributes the management of the various domains, there is no need for anyone to maintain a gigantic master list of every computer on the Net. Whenever a program needs to translate a hostname into an IP address, all the program has to do is find the name server that handles that particular domain.

But out of all the name servers on the Net, how can a program find the one it needs? The solution is to start with the top-level domain and work its way down.

At various places around the Net, there are a number of special computers called ROOT NAME SERVERS. Each root name server maintains a list of the name servers that handle top-level domains (**com**, **edu**, **au**, **uk**, and so on). Each of these name servers maintains a list of other name servers that handle the second-level domains, and so on.

When a program needs the IP address for a hostname, the program starts at a root name server and works its way from one server to the next until it finds the one that has the required IP address.

Here is an example. Say that a program needs to find the IP address of the hostname **www.ibm.com**. The program starts by contacting a root name server to get the IP address of the **com** name server. The program then contacts the **com** name server to get the IP address of the **ibm.com** name server. Finally, the program contacts the **ibm.com** name server to get the IP address of **www.ibm.com**.

In this way, using DNS, it is simple for any program to find out the IP address of any computer on the Net, even though no one maintains a master list. DNS works well because, as the Internet grows, DNS grows as well. For example, when the IBM network administrators create new hostnames (using new IP addresses), all they need to do is update the information in the **ibm.com** name servers.

Is DNS cool, or what?

How DNS Works for You

Your access to DNS is provided by your ISP (Internet service provider). All ISPs maintain DNS SERVERS for the use of their customers. When one of your client programs needs to find the IP address of a particular computer, the program sends a request to your ISP's DNS server. The DNS server does whatever is necessary to find the IP address, which it then sends back to your program.

Let's take an example.

You decide to visit my Web site, so you tell your Web browser to go to **www.harley.com** (the hostname for my site). In order to get the appropriate IP address, your browser sends the hostname to your ISP's DNS server.

The DNS server contacts the root name server and gets the IP address of the **com** name server. The DNS server then contacts the **com** name server and gets the IP address of the **harley.com** name server. Finally, the DNS server contacts the **harley.com** name server and gets the IP address of **www.harley.com**. In this case, the IP address happens to be **207.155.37.136**. This information is then sent to your browser, which can now use the IP address to contact the Web server directly.

DNS is a good system, but it does involve a certain amount of overhead. To save time, each server at every level keeps a list of the most recently requested names and addresses. If a subsequent request comes in for the same information, the server is able to respond right away.

For example, once your DNS server has gone to the trouble of finding the IP address for **www.harley.com**, the information is kept for a certain period of time in case another program requests the same address.

hint

As you use the Web, you will sometimes notice a delay after you type the address of a Web site. There are several reasons for this delay.

First, your browser must send the hostname to the DNS server and wait for a reply. Once the IP address is sent back, your browser then uses that address to contact the Web server. You then have to wait for data to be sent from the Web server to your computer.

During these delays, you will see informative messages, showing the progress. With the Internet Explorer browser, you will see a series of messages like:

```
Finding site www.harley.com
Connecting to site 207.155.37.136
Web site found. Waiting for reply.
```

With the Netscape browser, you will see messages like:

```
Looking up host www.harley.com
Host www.harley.com contacted. Waiting for reply.
```

Now when you see these messages, you will know what they mean.

Mail Addresses

The most important service on the Internet is electronic mail. To send someone mail, you need to know his MAIL ADDRESS. Similarly, if someone knows your mail address, he can send you mail.

Once you understand hostnames, mail addresses are easy. They all follow the same pattern: a name, followed by an **@** character (the "at" sign), followed by a hostname:

name@hostname

Here are some examples:

billg@microsoft.com
charles@royal.gov.uk
stevecase@aol.com
president@whitehouse.gov
abuse@netcom.com

When you say a mail address out loud, the **@** character is pronounced "at". For example, the address **billg@microsoft.com** is pronounced "Bill G at Microsoft dot com". The address **charles@royal.gov.uk** is pronounced "Charles at royal dot gov dot U.K.".

Mail addresses are not case sensitive. Thus, the following three addresses are equivalent. However, we generally use all lowercase letters (as in the first address) because it looks nicer:

president@whitehouse.gov
President@Whitehouse.Gov
PRESIDENT@WHITEHOUSE.GOV

Today, electronic mail is used widely, and mail addresses are ubiquitous. (For instance, some phone companies list email addresses in their telephone books.) For this reason, it is common to hear people use the word ADDRESS to refer to an email address.

hint

If you are talking to someone on the Net, and he uses the word "address", you can assume he means an email address. If the person wants to refer to a regular street address, he will usually make it clear by context. This idea is illustrated in the following real-life example:

(A conversation that might take place in a Web chat room.)

Unknown Person: Excuse me, do you use Windows on your PC?

You: Yes, I do. Why do you ask?

Unknown Person: Well, I am Bill Gates, and I am interested in what you think of Windows and other fine Microsoft products. If I give you my personal address, would you mind sending me email with your comments?

You: Not at all, Bill, I would be glad to help.

Unknown Person: Thank you, that would be great. To show my appreciation, if you give me your postal address, I would be pleased to send you a box of money.

You: Sorry, Bill, but I make it a point to never give out personal information on the Net. I hope you understand.

Unknown Person: Of course I do, and I admire your good judgment. Well, bye for now.

Where does your personal email address come from? In most cases, you get your address from the company that supplies you with mail service. If you use an ISP for mail service, they will assign you a name to use. For example, if your name is Benjamin Dover and your ISP is the Undependable Internet Company, your email address might be **bendover@undependable.com**.

Sometimes you can get your ISP to assign you a special name if it is not being used by someone else. So if everyone calls you Benjy, you might ask for the address **benjy@undependable.com**. The main rule everyone has to follow is that no two people can have the exact same address.

Most addresses are used by a person. However, there are some addresses that are used for special services. Companies often use names like **sales**, **support** or **feedback** to provide mailboxes for the general public. You might, for example, see the Undependable Internet Company set up the address **support@undependable.com** for customers who need a place to send a message when they have a problem.

Almost all mail systems have a standard address called **postmaster** to which you can send messages pertaining to the mail service. If you are having trouble sending mail to someone at, say, IBM, you can send a message to **postmaster@ibm.com**.

hint

Many ISPs (Internet service providers) set up a mailbox with the name **abuse** to field complaints about problems caused by the ISP's customers. For instance, AOL uses the address **abuse@aol.com** and Netcom uses **abuse@netcom.com**.

If someone sends you threatening messages or bothers you with unsolicited advertising (spam), send a note to the **abuse** mailbox at that person's ISP. If the ISP does not have an **abuse** mailbox (and your mail comes back with an error message), send the complaint to **postmaster**.

All ISPs take such complaints seriously.

URLs

At the beginning of this chapter, I said that every computer, every person and every resource on the Internet has its own address. We have already talked about two types of addresses: hostnames (for computers) and mail addresses (for people). We will now talk about the addresses we use to identify the vast number of resources available on the Net.

The most popular resources on the Net are the many millions of Web pages stored on Web servers all over the world. Anyone with an Internet connection and a browser (Web client program) can access these pages. Of course, in order to fetch a Web page for you, your browser needs to know where to find the page. To describe the location of Web pages, we use a special type of address called a URL or UNIFORM RESOURCE LOCATOR. The name URL is pronounced as three separate letters, "U-R-L".

When we use a URL to specify the address of a particular resource, we say that the URL POINTS to that resource. For example, here is the URL that points to the main page of my Web site (don't worry about the details just yet):

http://www.harley.com/

Web sites can consist of many separate Web pages, and, strictly speaking, a URL points only to a single page. However, when a URL points to the main page of a Web site, we often say, informally, that the URL points to the site as a whole. Thus, I might say that the URL above points to the Harley Hahn Web site.

URLs can be used to point to all types of resources, and not just Web pages. For this reason, URLs were designed to be as general as possible. As you use the Net, you will see two slightly different formats:

*scheme***://***hostname***/***description*
*scheme***:***description*

Here are some examples:

```
http://www.harley.com/
http://www.harley.com/25-things/index.html
http://www.ibm.com/
mailto:billg@microsoft.com
news:rec.pets.cats.anecdotes
ftp://ftp.microsoft.com/Products/msmq/demos.zip
```

The SCHEME (short for "addressing scheme") identifies the type of resource. Figure 4-3 shows the most commonly used schemes. As you use the Web, most of the URLs you will encounter will point to Web pages and, hence, will use the **http** scheme. (The name stands for Hypertext Transfer Protocol, the protocol used to transfer Web page data.) However, you will also see mail addresses (**mailto**), Usenet newsgroups (**news**), and Anonymous FTP files (**ftp**).

Figure 4-3: The most common schemes used within URLs

Scheme	Meaning
http	Web page (hypertext)
mailto	Mail address
news	Usenet newsgroup
ftp	File accessed via Anonymous FTP
file	File on your computer

Although there are many other schemes, the ones I talked about are the most common. The only other scheme you are likely to see is **file**, and you will see it only if you use your browser to display a file that is stored on your own computer.

After the scheme, the next part of a URL is the hostname. This is the name of the computer on which the resource resides. For instance, the following URL points to a Web page on the computer named **www.harley.com**:

```
http://www.harley.com/25-things/index.html
```

Here is another example. This URL points to a file that is available via Anonymous FTP from the computer named **ftp.microsoft.com**:

```
ftp://ftp.microsoft.com/Products/msmq/demos.zip
```

If you look at our previous list of examples, you will notice that some types of URLs do not need hostnames. These URLs point to resources that, by their nature, do not reside on a specific computer.

An example of this format is **mailto**, the type of URL that specifies a mail address. If you see a Web page with a **mailto** URL, and you click on it, your browser will start your mail program and send it the specified address. This makes it easy for you to send a message to that particular address. For example, the following URL will set up a message to be sent to the person whose email address is **billg@microsoft.com**:

mailto:billg@microsoft.com

Aside from **mailto**, there is another common type of URL that does not require a hostname. This type of URL specifies the name of a Usenet newsgroup (discussion group). For instance:

news:rec.pets.cats.anecdotes

(By the way, this newsgroup is the one to which people send stories about cats.)

To read the articles in a newsgroup, you use a client program called a newsreader to access a news server. There are many news servers on the Net.

Before you can access Usenet, you need to tell your newsreader the hostname of the news server you will be using. Then, whenever you encounter a URL with a newsgroup name, your newsreader knows which computer to contact. Most people use a news server maintained by their ISP (Internet service provider) as a service to their customers.

For this reason, a URL that points to a newsgroup cannot contain a specific hostname. The URL contains the name of the group, but it is up to your browser to know the location of your news server.

So let's summarize what we have discussed so far.

URLs are designed to describe a variety of resources. There are two common variations of URLs:

*scheme***://**hostname**/**description*
*scheme***:**description*

The *scheme* identifies the type of resource described by the URL. The *hostname*, if it is included, specifies the location of the computer that contains the resource. The last part of the URL, the *description*, contains whatever other information is needed to find the exact resource.

With a **mail** URL, the *description* is a mail address; with a **news** URL, the *description* is the name of a Usenet newsgroup. However, with an **http** or **ftp** URL, the *description* must show exactly where a particular file resides. Such descriptions can be complicated, so we will discuss them in more detail, one step at a time.

File Names and Extensions

A computer FILE is a collection of data stored under a specific name. Files can hold any type of data that can be stored in a computer: text, numbers, pictures, sounds, video, and so on. In particular, the Web pages we view with our browsers are all stored in files on some computer or another. Thus, when we use a URL to point to a Web page, we need to specify not only the hostname of the computer, but the name of the exact file we want to look at.

Different computer systems have different rules for how files can be named. I won't go into all the variations, but I do want to mention one common characteristic: File names usually have two parts. The first part is chosen to describe the contents of the file in some way, the second part indicates the type of data stored in the file, and the two parts are separated by a period. Here are two examples:

```
invoice.doc
sales-order.doc
```

By looking at the first part of these file names, we can guess that the first file holds an invoice and the second file holds a sales order. The second part of a file name is called an EXTENSION. In this case, both files have the same extension, **doc**, which indicates that the files are documents. (It is common for word processor programs, such as Microsoft Word, to save files with an extension of **doc**.)

On the Internet, there are a number of extensions that you will see a lot. The most common is **html**. This indicates a file that contains hypertext—that is, a Web page. Now take a look at the following URL:

```
http://www.harley.com/25-things/index.html
```

Notice it ends with the name of a file, **index.html**. This tells you that the URL points to a Web page (although I still haven't explained all the details).

There are many different file extensions, and Figure 4-4 shows the ones you are most likely to see on the Internet. For now, don't worry about each type of file and what it means. We will discuss the various types of files as we encounter them throughout the book. I just want you to see a list of the most common extensions all in one place.

Figure 4-4: The most common file extensions used on the Internet

Extension	Pronunciation	Meaning
html	"h-t-m-l"	Web page
htm	"h-t-m"	Web page
asp	"a-s-p"	Web page generated in a special way
gif	"giff" or "jiff"	Picture stored in GIF format
jpg	"jay-peg"	Picture stored in JPEG format
wav	"wave"	Sound/music file
txt	"t-x-t" or "text"	Plain text
zip	"zip"	Compressed collection of files
exe	"e-x-e"	Executable program

When we talk about a file name, we pronounce the period as "dot." The pronunciations of the extensions vary and are shown in Figure 4-4. As an example, the name **index.html** is pronounced "index dot h-t-m-l", while the name **cat.jpg** is pronounced "cat dot jay-peg".

WHAT'S IN A NAME?

html
htm
asp

Web pages are written using a set of specifications called Hypertext Markup Language or HTML (which we will discuss in Chapter 15). For this reason, Web pages are commonly stored in files with the extension of **html**.

Some computer systems do not allow more than three characters in a file extension, and, on such systems, Web pages are given the extension **htm**.

Files with an **asp** extension contain hypertext, just like **html** files, but are generated by a special system called Active Server Pages. (Hence the extension **asp**.) However, when you use your browser to look at an **asp** page, it works the same as a regular **html** page.

Directories and Subdirectories

Computers have so many files that we need a way to organize them. We do so by grouping files into DIRECTORIES. Each directory is given a name and can hold any number of files. For example, you might use a directory called **documents** to hold your word processing documents. It is easy to create and delete directories, so, on your own computer, you can modify the storage arrangement as you see fit.

Directories can contain not only files, but other directories. When a directory contains another directory, we call the first one a PARENT DIRECTORY and the second one a SUBDIRECTORY. A directory can have as many subdirectories as you need. The power of this system is that it allows you to create a hierarchy of directories to reflect a particular way of organizing files. Moreover, as your needs change, it is a simple matter to modify the directory structure and to move files from one directory to another.

Here is an example. You create a directory named **documents** to hold your word processing documents. This works fine for a few weeks, but then you notice that you have too many files in one directory, so you decide to reorganize. Within the **documents** directory, you create three subdirectories, **letters**, **writing** and **miscellaneous**. You then move each file in the **documents** directory to one of the three new subdirectories.

hint

With Windows 98 and Windows 95, the program you use to work with files and directories is called WINDOWS EXPLORER. With Windows 3.x, the program is called FILE MANAGER.

On some computer systems, it is customary to refer to directories as FOLDERS. This idea arose in the early days of PCs, when it was thought that personal computers were too intimidating for many people and everything should be "user friendly". The idea was that, by referring to directories as "folders", people would see the analogy between directories that contain computer files and folders in a filing cabinet.

Personally, I think the whole idea was pretty lame, and, to this day, computer companies (especially Microsoft and Apple) still continue to underestimate the intelligence of the average consumer. Thus, you will see both terms being used. When you do, just remember that a folder is the same thing as a directory, and a subfolder is the same as a subdirectory.

In general, people who like and understand computers use the word "directory", not the word "folder".

hint

If you are a "directory" person, do not marry a "folder" person.

Pathnames

Now that we have discussed file names and directories, we can fill in the last part of the URL puzzle. You will remember that one type of URL uses the following general format:

*scheme***://***hostname***/***description*

The *description* is nothing more than a list of directories and a file name. Take a look at one of our previous examples:

http://www.harley.com/25-things/index.html

In this case, **25-things** is the name of a directory. Thus, the *description* refers to a file named **index.html** within a directory named **25-things**.

Here is another example:

ftp://ftp.microsoft.com/Products/msmq/demos.zip

In this URL, there are two directory names, **Products** and **msmq**. Thus, the *description* refers to a directory named **Products**. Within this directory lies a subdirectory named **msmq**, and within this subdirectory is a file named **demos.zip**. Or, to say it another way, the **demos.zip** file is in a directory named **msmq** that itself is in a directory named **Products**.

As you use the Web, you will see a lot of URLs that have a series of directories ending with the name of a file. Such specifications are called PATHNAMES or, more simply, PATHS. Within a pathname, we use a slash (/) character to separate the various directory and file names.

Once you understand pathnames, it's easy to make sense out of most URLs if you remember the format:

*scheme***://***hostname***/***description*

The *scheme* shows you the type of resource, the *hostname* tells you the name of the computer, and the *description* contains a pathname.

technical hint

When you write URLs, you use slash (/) characters to separate the directory names. For example:

`http://www.harley.com/25-things/index.html`

When you are working within Windows, however, you use backslash (\) characters in pathnames. For instance, here is a typical Windows pathname that points to a file named **quikview.exe**:

`C:\Windows\System\Viewers\quikview.exe`

In this example, the file resides in the **Viewers** directory, which is a subdirectory of the **System** directory, which is a subdirectory of the **Windows** directory on the **C:** disk.

Don't ever be confused. Within Windows, we use backslashes in a pathname, but in a URL we always use slashes.

URL Abbreviations

Since URLs often contain a pathname, they can be quite long, and it's nice to be able to abbreviate whenever possible. To meet this need, there are conventions followed by Web servers that allow us to shorten URLs under certain conditions.

First, most Web servers follow a rule that says if the URL specifies a directory but no file name, the server will automatically look for a file with a specific name. Some servers look for a file named **index.html**, while others look for a file named **default.html** or **default.asp**. That means that, if you see a URL that ends in **index.html**, **default.html** or **default.asp,** you can usually leave off the file name and the URL will still work. Consider this URL from my own Web site:

`http://www.harley.com/25-things/index.html`

When you see a URL like this, you can guess that it might be okay to leave out the **index.html**, and most of the time (but not always) you will be right. With our example, it will work just fine if you use:

`http://www.harley.com/25-things/`

Similarly, either of the following URLs will point to the main Web page at my Web site:

`http://www.harley.com/`
`http://www.harley.com/index.html`

Another convention that lets us abbreviate has to do with the browser. If you ever type a URL that does not have a scheme at the beginning, your browser will assume the URL points to a Web page and insert **http://** for you.

In addition, if you leave out a final slash (/) character, the browser will usually insert the slash for you. For example, if you want to visit my Web site, either of these URLs will work:

www.harley.com
http://www.harley.com/

hint

How does a Web server know whether a pathname ends with a directory or a file name?

The Web server assumes that if the pathname ends with a slash (/), it indicates a directory. Thus, if you type a URL that does not have a file name at the end, you should be sure to include the slash. For example, use:

http://www.harley.com/
http://www.kingfeatures.com/comics/

not:

http://www.harley.com
http://www.kingfeatures.com/comics

A lot of the time, such URLs will work, even without the slash, but it is proper to include it, and, as one of my readers, I know you take pride in being proper at all times.

One More URL Abbreviation

Aside from the abbreviations we just discussed, there is one more I want you to know about. As you use the Web, you will encounter a great many URLs of the form:

http://www.*something***.com/**

Some browsers will allow you to specify such URLs simply by typing the *something*. The browser will change the URL for you by inserting **http://www.** at the beginning and **.com/** at the end. For example, try giving your browser the URL of:

harley

Of course, this is not a valid URL, and your browser will not be able to connect to it. However, after a moment, the browser will give up and change the URL to:

http://www.harley.com/

The browser will then try the new URL, which will work.

Test whether your browser will do this. If so, try it with your own name and see what you get.

Case Sensitive Pathnames

There are just a few more ideas I want to explain before we finish our discussion of pathnames. However, in order to do so, I need to talk about operating systems for a moment.

An operating system is the master control program that runs a computer. Most PCs use a version of the Windows operating system: either Windows 98, the older Windows 95, or the very old Windows 3.x. For more powerful computers—especially those providing database and networking services—there are special versions: Windows 2000, as well as the older Windows NT. (At one time, the name stood for "new technology".)

Aside from Windows, there is a completely different family of operating systems called Unix. There are many types of Unix—with different names—that run on all types of computers, not just PCs.

The reason I mention this is that most of the Web servers on the Net run either Windows 2000/NT or Unix, and the two systems use slightly different rules for pathnames.

First, with Windows, you can write pathnames using either lower- or uppercase letters. For example, within a URL, the following pathnames are all equivalent (as long as the server is running some type of Windows):

```
products/msmq/demos.zip
Products/msmq/demos.zip
Products/Msmq/Demos.Zip
PRODUCTS/MSMQ/DEMOS.ZIP
```

Unix *always* distinguishes between lower- and uppercase. For instance, in Unix, the name **demos.zip** is considered completely different from the name **Demos.zip**. We describe such names as being CASE SENSITIVE.

Recall our example:

```
ftp://ftp.microsoft.com/Products/msmq/demos.zip
```

If the computer to which this URL points is a Windows computer, you could use a lowercase **p** and the URL would still work. However, if the server is a Unix machine, the URL would not work.

In this case, the server does run Windows (which you might guess from looking at the hostname), so the following URL will work just fine:

`ftp://ftp.microsoft.com/products/msmq/demos.zip`

On the other hand, consider this URL:

`http://www.cnn.com/STYLE/`

This Web page resides on a server where pathnames are case sensitive, and the last part of the pathname, **STYLE**, must be in all uppercase letters. If you change these letters to lowercase, the URL will not work.

hint

If you type a URL that doesn't work, check to see whether you might have accidentally typed some uppercase letters in lowercase.

What a ~ (Tilde) Means in a Pathname

You will sometimes see a ~ character within a pathname. For instance:

`http://www.psych.ucsb.edu/~kopeikin/`

This character is called a TILDE (pronounced "til-duh"). In the United States, the standard PC keyboard has the tilde in the top left corner, above the **Tab** key. To type a tilde, you need to hold down the **Shift** key. (By the way, the character you get if you don't hold down the **Shift** key is called a backquote [`` ` ``]. The backquote is rarely used.) In other countries, the location of the tilde will vary. In the U.K., for example, the tilde is just to the left of the **Enter** key.

The tilde character is used primarily in Unix systems. Unix is designed to support many users at the same time, and each user is given a HOME DIRECTORY in which to store his files. A Unix user can create whatever files and subdirectories he wants in his home directory.

Within Unix, a tilde combined with a name refers to the home directory of a particular person. For example, if you had an account on a Unix computer under the name **harley**, your home directory would be known as **~harley**.

Thus, when you see a URL that has a directory name beginning with a tilde, it means the Web site resides on a Unix system, and the directory is someone's home directory. In the preceding example, the URL points to the Web site of Hal Kopeikin, a member of the Department of Psychology at the University of California at Santa Barbara.

Putting It All Together

At the beginning of the chapter, I promised that by the time you finished this chapter, you would be able to understand addresses like this one:

`http://www.harley.com/25-things/index.html`

Notice how easy it is to understand such addresses once you understand the pattern. Just look for the general format:

*scheme***://***hostname***/***description*

Then identify the various parts. In this case:

- The scheme, **http**, tells you the URL points to a Web page.
- The hostname, **www.harley.com**, is the address of the Web server.
- The description, **25-things/index.html**, is the pathname of the Web page.

In other words, this URL is the address of a Web page named **index.html** in the **25-things** directory on the **www.harley.com** Web server.

If only all of life were so easy.

5

Mail

When I was a kid, I had to walk three miles in the freezing snow every time I wanted to check my electronic mail. Then, after checking my mail, I had to walk three miles back (and it was uphill both ways) just to get a peanut butter sandwich.

Today, life is a lot easier. Once you have Internet access, you can send and receive all the mail you want from the privacy (and warmth) of your own home.

In this chapter, I'll explain the basics: what you need to get you going and keep you going. In Chapter 6, I will give you some extra help and teach you how to use email well. After all, you are one of my readers, and it is my job to ensure that your usage of the Internet is elegant and skillful enough to carry you head and shoulders above the pressing crush of humanity.

So read on. By the time you finish these two chapters, mothers will hold up their children as you walk by and say, "Look at that person. Now, there's someone who *really* knows how to use email."

The Basic Ideas

In Chapter 2, we talked a bit about how mail works. Let's take a moment to have a quick review and add a few more details.

On the Internet, we commonly use the word MAIL to refer to EMAIL (electronic mail). Anyone who has your mail ADDRESS can send you mail. Similarly, you can send mail to anyone whose address you have. Mail addresses are in the form:

name **@** *hostname*

For instance:

`billg@microsoft.com`

Like all Internet services, mail uses a client/server system. You run a client, called a MAIL PROGRAM, on your computer. Whenever necessary, your mail program contacts a MAIL SERVER to request services on your behalf. Most people use the mail server provided by their ISP (Internet service provider). However, there are other options, which we will discuss later in the chapter.

To send mail, you use your mail program to compose a message. When you are finished, you tell your program to send the message. Your program contacts the server, and sends it the message. The server then delivers the message to the recipient's mail server.

Similarly, when someone sends a message to your mail address, it is received and stored by your mail server. From time to time, your mail program contacts the server to see whether there are any messages waiting for you. If so, your program receives the messages and shows them to you.

Whenever you start your mail program, it will check for messages. After that, it will check at regular intervals (say, every 10 minutes). So although it is possible to tell your program to check for new mail, you usually won't need to. Incoming messages will arrive automatically.

SMTP Servers and POP Servers

In Chapter 1, I explained that clients and servers communicate with one another by using various protocols. There are three different protocols you will encounter within the Internet mail system. Although you don't need to concern yourself with the details, it is important to at least know the names of these protocols and what they do.

The three protocols are SMTP (Simple Mail Transfer Protocol), POP (Post Office Protocol) and IMAP (Internet Message Access Protocol). SMTP is used to send messages to a mail server, while POP and IMAP are used to receive messages from a mail server. To explain how this all works, let's take a look at when these protocols are used when you send a message.

Using your mail program , you compose a message and address it to a friend. Once the message is ready for delivery, your program uses the SMTP protocol and transfers the message to your ISP's mail server. The mail server then uses SMTP to transfer the message to the mail server used by your friend. When the message arrives at the destination mail server, it is stored until your friend picks it up.

Now, consider what happens when you receive a message. When it is time to check for messages, your mail program uses the POP protocol to connect to your ISP's mail server (where all your incoming mail is stored). If there are messages waiting for you, your program uses POP to download them to your computer. Your program then shows you a summary of the incoming messages, which you can read whenever you want.

Thus, SMTP is used to send messages to a mail server, while POP is used to receive messages from a mail server. (We'll talk about IMAP in a moment.)

Thus, it follows that, before your mail program can send and receive mail, it must know the hostname (computer name) of your SMTP server and the hostname of your POP server. In principle, the SMTP server and the POP server can be completely different computers. However, in practice, both servers usually run on the same computer.

Here is an example. A fellow named Benjamin Dover signs up for Internet service with the Undependable Internet Company, and is assigned an address of **bendover@undependable.com**. At the time he signs up, Benjamin is told that his SMTP and POP servers both have the same hostname: **mail.undependable.com**. So, before he uses his mail program for the first time, Benjamin must configure the program by specifying this information. If Benjamin ever changes ISPs, he must reconfigure his program by specifying a new address for himself, his SMTP server, and his POP server.

By the way, notice that the hostname of the mail server begins with **mail**. This is a common convention used by many ISPs.

hint

> Some ISPs give you a special installation program to run to set up your service. (For example, they may send you a CD to use to get started.) When you run this program, it will install a lot of software, such as a browser and a mail program. You may also find that the program configures your mail program for you. In such cases, you will not have to type in the host-names of your SMTP and POP servers by hand. However, it is interesting to look and see what they are.

IMAP Servers

The system I have described so far uses SMTP to send messages and POP to receive messages. IMAP (Internet Message Access Protocol) is sometimes used as an alternative to POP.

When you use POP, all your messages are downloaded to your computer and deleted from the mail server. This is fine when you always check your mail from the same computer. However, if you routinely use POP to check mail from different computers, you may have a problem, because your messages can end up in different places.

For example, let's say you work for a company that provides you with a computer in your office as well as a notebook computer to use when you travel. In addition, you sometimes do office work at home using your own computer. All your work-related mail is sent to only one mail server—the one at the office—but you need to be able to check for mail from all three computers.

If you use POP, your messages will be deleted from the mail server as they are downloaded and will end up being distributed on three different computers: at the office, on your notebook, and at home. With IMAP, your mail client can manipulate messages on the server without having to download them. Thus, your messages stay on the server and are accessible from any computer you may use. (Of course, you can delete your messages from the server whenever you want.)

Most ISPs would not want their customers to use IMAP, because the tendency would be for people to leave all their messages on the ISP's server. Eventually, the IMAP server would fill up, and there is no graceful way for an ISP to delete their customers' messages. However, within a well-managed private environment, IMAP can work well, as it allows people to check their mail from any computer they want and still keep all their messages in one place.

To use this system, you need both a mail server and a mail client that support IMAP.

Web-Based Mail Services

The systems I have described so far involve mail client programs using SMTP and POP (or IMAP) to communicate with mail servers. This is the way most people send and receive email. However, there is an alternative system you should know about.

A number of companies offer Web-based mail services that allow you to send and receive mail using only your Web browser. With such systems, your browser acts as a simple mail client, while a special Web server at the other end acts as a mail server. Since browsers are not designed to handle mail, virtually all of the work is done by the server. All your browser does is show information and let you make choices.

There are advantages and disadvantages to Web-based mail services. The first big advantage is that, in most cases, they are free: The companies make their money by selling advertising. Free services are nice, but while you are composing, reading, or sending mail, you will have to look at advertisements. Personally, this bugs me a lot, although you may not mind it as much as I do. In addition, some services also put a short advertisement at the end of each message you send out. Moreover, you may find yourself the recipient of unsolicited advertising messages. Again, this is all something you may be glad to put up with in return for free mail.

Another advantage to Web-based email is that you can use it from any computer in the world that has an Internet connection. This means that, when you are traveling, you can check your mail from anywhere you can find access to a browser. With the regular mail system, you need to be at your own computer, running your own mail program. (Even with IMAP, you still need a mail client configured for your account.)

Web-based mail makes it possible for people without computers to use mail. For example, many libraries have public Internet access. If you don't have your own computer, you can use a browser at the library to establish and maintain a Web-based mail account. Obviously, this would not be your first choice, but it's remarkable that such a choice even exists.

Finally, Web-based services provide a large measure of anonymity. When you register for such a service, you can specify any name and password you want. This is handy, for instance, when your only Internet access is at the office, and you don't want to use your work address for personal correspondence. You can get yourself a Web-based mail account, give out that address to your friends, and then use your browser at work to check your personal mail. (Although, if anyone asks, you didn't hear this idea from me.)

As you might imagine, the convenience and anonymity of such systems has not escaped the notice of the troublemakers of the world, and there are a lot of dishonest and shady characters hiding behind free, Web-based mail addresses.

A more immediate concern, if you have children, is that any kid with Internet access can register for a free mail address and then use a browser to access the mail when no one is looking. This is something you should be aware of, especially if you are a teacher whose students seem too well-behaved when they are using the computer lab.

Perhaps the biggest disadvantage to Web-based mail services is that they are slow to use. With regular mail service, your mail client runs on your own computer, and all your messages reside locally on your own hard disk (with POP) or on a special server (with IMAP). With a Web-based service, everything is stored at the Web site, and working with individual messages one at a time over the Web can be a frustrating experience.

So do you need a Web-based mail account? For your day-to-day mail, you are better off using the regular mail account with your ISP. But if you have a special need (such as checking your messages when you travel or hiding your mail from prying eyes), you might want to try a Web-based service.

hint

The distinctions between regular and Web-based mail services occasionally blur. Some Web-based services offer a POP server, so you can use a regular mail client instead of a browser to check your mail (although you may have to pay for this service).

Conversely, some ISPs offer Web access to their mail server, so you can check your mail away from your own computer.

*I*NTERNET RESOURCE Web-Based Mail Services

```
http://www.iname.com/
http://mail.yahoo.com/
http://www.hotmail.com/
http://www.eudoramail.com/
http://www.rocketmail.com/
http://www.netaddress.com/
http://altavista.iname.com/
```

Which Mail Program Should You Use?

The two most popular browsers, Microsoft Internet Explorer and Netscape Navigator, are bundled with a free mail program. Why is this? Both Microsoft and Netscape are trying to control the browser market, and one way to do so is to provide lots of other software that is tightly integrated with the browser. In that sense, the strategy works, because most people use the mail program that comes with their browser. Internet Explorer comes with a mail program called OUTLOOK EXPRESS, and Navigator comes with a program called MESSENGER.

Since the mail protocols (SMTP, POP and IMAP) are standardized, you can use any mail program you want. Both Outlook Express and Messenger will work fine (although, in my opinion, Outlook Express is better and less frustrating). However, you can use a completely different program, one that has nothing to do with your browser. My favorite such program is Eudora Light, and, indeed, that is the program I use personally.

Regardless of which mail program you use, you will find it has more features than you need and more options than you will ever understand. Do not get frustrated. In this chapter and in Chapter 6, I will explain the basic features of all mail programs. I suggest that, after you read these chapters, you take a good amount of time—at least a few hours—and experiment with your particular program. Investigate all the menu items, and take a look at all the options. (They may be called "preferences".) Eventually, you will figure out what features you need and what you can ignore.

If you use the Internet at work, you may be forced to use the same mail program as everyone else. In my experience, people who work for large companies often do not like the standard corporate mail program. If you do work in such a company, take advantage of your freedom at home, and choose a program that suits you.

If you are new to the Net, don't worry about making a choice right away. Use whichever mail program is installed on your computer and, once you get some experience, you can download other programs and experiment. If you find a mail program you like better than the one you are using, there is no problem making a switch whenever you want.

hint

Some software companies offer both free and commercial versions of the same program, and you can tell them apart by looking at the names.

With Microsoft, programs whose names end in "Express" are free. Thus, Outlook Express is free, while the commercial version, Outlook 98, costs money. Similarly, programs whose names end in "Light" are often free. Thus, Eudora Light is free, while another version, Eudora Pro, is not.

In such cases, the programs that cost money have extra features. However, in my experience, the free programs are usually adequate, and there is no need to pay for a commercial product unless you really want the extra features.

In this book, I have chosen free resources whenever possible.

_I_NTERNET RESOURCE Mail Programs

```
http://www.microsoft.com/ie/
http://eudora.qualcomm.com/eudoralight/
http://www.netscape.com/comprod/products/communicator/
```

Note: At the Microsoft Web site, look for Outlook Express. At the Netscape Web site, you need to download Communicator to get Netscape Messenger.

The Parts of a Message

Conceptually, mail is simple: You type a message and then send it to someone else. Through the years, however, electronic mail has evolved, and the nature of a message has become complex to the point where it can have up to five separate parts. These parts are the header, the body, attachments, a signature and a vCard. In this section, I will give you a quick overview. We will then discuss each part in more detail.

At the beginning of every message is a HEADER consisting of a number of specific HEADER LINES. These header lines contain technical information needed by the mail system: the name and address of the sender, the time and date the message was sent, the subject of the message, the name and address of the recipient, and so on.

After the header comes the BODY, the main content of the message. Most of the time, the body will be simple text that you have typed, but, if you want, you can also include other elements, such as pictures or links to Web pages.

Along with the body of a message, you can also send a file. When you do, we say that you ATTACH the file to the message, and the file itself is referred to as an ATTACHMENT. For example, you might send a message to a friend to which you have attached a sound file containing a song. When your friend receives the message, he can save the file to his hard disk and then listen to the song.

A SIGNATURE is a small amount of information (which you create) that your mail program puts at the end of every message you send. Having a signature is optional, though many people use one. A typical signature might contain your name, mail address, and a link to your Web site (if you have one).

A VCARD (pronounced "vee-card") is a sort of electronic business card. You can create a personal vCard with information about yourself and attach it to your outgoing messages in the same way as you might fasten a business card to a regular letter. Modern mail programs have a built-in facility that makes it easy to use vCards to exchange information automatically.

vCard

The idea of a vCard was developed by the Versit Consortium, a group formed by IBM, Siemens and Lucent. In December 1996, Versit transferred the rights to vCard to a noncommercial organization called the Internet Mail Consortium. Today, the vCard standard has been adopted by many different software companies and can be used with a variety of mail programs.

The odd spelling of vCard originally came from the name Versit. However, if you want, you can think of the "v" as meaning "virtual".

The Most Important Header Lines

Each time you send a message, your mail program automatically generates a header with technical information and places it at the beginning of the message. Similarly, when you receive a message, it will have a header which you can look at if you want.

All headers more or less have the same format, but what you see on your system depends greatly on which mail program you use. Some programs attempt to dumb down everything that looks the least bit technical and hide most of the header from you. Other programs show you all or some of the header. Regardless, there is always a way to look at the full header if you really want to, although how to do so may not be obvious. You may have to use the help facility that comes with your program, or just experiment and figure it out by trial and error.

hint

When you first start to use a mail program, take a moment and find out how to look at the full header of a message.

Microsoft Outlook Express: Using your mouse, right-click on the message and then select "Properties". Now click on the "Details" tab.

Netscape Messenger: You must be viewing a message. Use your mouse to pull down the "View" menu. Select "Headers", then "All".

Eudora Light: You must be viewing a message. Use your mouse to click on the icon that says "Blah Blah Blah".

A few of the header lines are crucial, and you must be able to understand them. Others are less important and can be safely ignored. Let's start with a typical message, shown in Figure 5-1. This message shows the most important parts of the header: the **From**,

To, **Subject**, **Cc** and **Date** lines. All mail programs show these lines, or at least the information they contain.

Figure 5-1: A typical mail message

```
From: Arthur Irwin Choke <artichoke@whitehouse.gov>
To: Harley Hahn <hhahn@little-nipper.com>
Date: Wed, 8 Apr 1998 18:23:01 -0400
Subject: VP wants to meet with you
Cc: Charles Wagon <chuckwagon@whitehouse.gov>

To Harley Hahn:

The Vice President of the United States has
asked me to see if you are free to meet with
him next week.  He hopes you will be able to
help him install Windows 98 on his PC.

Arthur Irwin Choke
Special Assistant, Computer Stuff,
Office of the Vice President
```

From: This line tells you the address and name of the person who sent the mail. In most cases, you can simply take the information at face value. However, if the mail seems strange in any way, you should be suspicious. It is simple for someone to configure their mail program so as to specify any name and address they want. Moreover, if you know what you are doing, you can forge mail so that it looks like it comes from another computer. This is a common trick of spammers (people who send unsolicited advertising by email.) So when in doubt, be careful. If you get a message with an invitation to meet the Vice President of the United States, you might want to check carefully before you make your plane reservation.

To: This line shows the mail address to which the message was sent. In most cases, you will see your own address. However, this is not always the case. For instance, a message can be sent to more than one person simply by putting more than one address in the **To** line. So if you see other addresses besides yours, it means that all the other people received a copy of the message. If you belong to a mailing list (see Chapter 13), the messages from the list are addressed to a special list address, not to you personally. Thus, if you see a mailing list address in the **To** line, it means the message went to everyone on the list.

Subject: The information on the **Subject** line is specified by the person who sent the message. The purpose of this line, as you can guess from its name, is to provide a short summary of the contents of the message. When incoming mail arrives, your mail program shows you the subject line of each message. You won't actually see the contents of the message (the body) until you open it. Thus, whenever you look at the list of incoming mail, you are really looking at the **Subject** lines created by the senders of those messages.

hint

When you compose a message, take a moment to create a good **Subject** line. The description you write should be short, no more than a few words, but as meaningful as possible. Remember, your subject line is the only description the recipient is going to see to identify your message among the many others in his mailbox.

This is especially important when you send mail to a Very Busy Person. Some people receive so much mail that they literally do not have time to read it all. A VBP is more likely to read a message with the subject **Need a free ticket to the game?** than one with the subject **Question for you.**

Cc: When you compose a message, it is possible to send it to more than one person by putting more than one address in the **To** line. Alternatively, you can send a copy to someone by putting his address in the **Cc** line. (I will show you how this works later in the chapter.) The important thing I want you to remember is that, when you receive a message, look at both the **To** line and the **Cc** line. Everyone whose address is in one of these lines has received a copy of the message.

Date: This line shows the date and time that the message was sent. The date portion is straightforward, but when you read the time you must be careful. The Internet is used around the world, and local time is not meaningful unless you know the time zone. For this reason, the time zone is always specified in some way. In our example, the time is shown as:

`18:23:01 -0400`

The first part of the time tells you the message was sent at 6:23 PM local time. (The Internet uses a 24-hour clock, so 18:23 means 6:23 PM.) However, how do you know what time zone this refers to? The **-0400** shows you. It indicates the number of hours difference between the local time where the message originated, and GMT (Greenwich Mean Time). In this case, the local time zone is 4 hours behind GMT. (This happens to be Eastern Daylight Time.)

For more information, see Appendix B, where I discuss these topics in more detail. Such calculations can be a bit confusing. Moreover, you may see other time zone formats than the preceding one I have shown.

A Few More Header Lines

Aside from the **Date**, **From**, **To** and **Subject** lines, there are a number of other header lines. In this section, I will describe those lines that are important enough for you to care about. As an example, Figure 5-2 shows a typical message containing these extra lines.

Figure 5-2: A typical mail message showing the full header

```
From: Harley Hahn <hhahn@little-nipper.com>
Received: from mail.little-nipper.com ([198.68.156.50])
  by mail.whitehouse.gov
Message-Id: <199804061852.WRM012367@little-nipper.com>
Reply-To: Harley Hahn <hhahn@little-nipper.com>
Date: Wed, 8 Apr 1998 20:50:17 -0700
Organization: The Little Nipper Foundation
To: Arthur Irwin Choke <artichoke@whitehouse.gov>
Subject: re: VP wants to meet with you
X-Mailer: Microsoft Outlook Express 4.72.2106.4
Cc: Charles Wagon <chuckwagon@whitehouse.gov>

> To Harley Hahn:
>
> The Vice President of the United States has
> asked me to see if you are free to meet with
> him next week.  He hopes you will be able to
> help him install Windows 98 on his PC.
>
> Arthur Irwin Choke
> Special Assistant, Computer Stuff
> Office of the Vice President

Art:

I am sorry, but I will not be able to accept
your invitation to meet with the Vice President
next week.  Please tell him I will be too busy
surfing the Information Superhighway.
I'm sure he will understand.

— Harley Hahn


================================================
Harley Hahn              http://www.harley.com/
(202) 456-1414           hhahn@little-nipper.com
================================================
```

Received: Each time a message passes through a computer, the mail program on that computer inserts a **Received** line into the header. Thus, the header always contains at least one such line. You can look at these lines to trace the path followed by the message to your mail server. In the example in Figure 5-2, we see one **Received** line. (Although it is so long as to be physically broken into two parts, it still counts as one line.)

```
Received: from mail.little-nipper.com ([198.68.156.50])
  by mail.whitehouse.gov
```

From this line, we can see that the message was sent from a computer named **mail.little-nipper.com** with an IP address of **198.68.156.50**, and was received by a computer named **mail.whitehouse.gov**. Both of these computers, of course, are mail servers. When you look at **Received** lines, you will often see other types of information. Such information is usually highly technical and can almost always be ignored.

Message-Id: Every time a message is mailed on the Internet, the originating mail server assigns the message a unique identification code. In our example, we see:

```
Message-Id: <199804061852.WRM012367@little-nipper.com>
```

This information in itself is not all that useful to a human being. However, what *is* useful is that part of the code is always the domain name of the mail server that sent the message. Thus, if someone mails you a message with a forged address, the best way to track down the person is to look at the **Message-Id** line. It is very difficult to forge this line unless you have control over the mail server. Some spammers are sophisticated enough to do so, but most troublemakers—such as mischievous college students—are not.

hint

If someone sends you a bothersome or harassing message from a forged address, look at the full header and find the **Message-Id** line. This will show you the name of the mail server from which the message was sent. You can then send a message to **postmaster** at that address and ask for help. When you do, be sure to include the entire original message, including the full header. This will help the postmaster track down the miscreant.

Here is an example. You receive a threatening letter with the following header line:

Message-ID: <3529D136.5B6B6CCC@shsu.edu>

Send the message, along with the full header, to **postmaster@shsu.edu** and ask for help.

Reply-To: When you reply to a message, your mail program will usually send the reply to the address in the **From** line. For example, if Eloise Q. Abernathy sends you a message, you want the reply to go to Eloise Q. Abernathy. However, there are times when this is not appropriate. In such cases, you will see a **Reply-To** line along with an address. When this line is present, your mail program will send the reply to this address, rather than to the address in the **From** line. You will often see this with mailing lists (see Chapter 13) in which each message is sent to everyone on the list. Every time a message is sent to the list, the mailing list program will insert a **Reply-To** line to ensure that all replies go back to the list, and not to the person whose address is in the **From** line.

Organization: You will sometimes see this header line. The intention is to tell you the name of the organization to which the sender of the message belongs. Such information can be useful, but is easy to falsify, so do not depend on it.

X-Mailer: When the original technical specification for Internet mail headers was developed, a certain number of standard header lines were described. However, it was recognized that there would be a need for other, nonstandard lines, so the rules say that anyone can put extra lines in a header as long as they begin with the characters **X-**. When you look at the full header for a message, you will often see several **X-** lines, usually inserted by the sender's mail program. One common line is **X-Mailer**, used to show the name of the mail program used to compose the message. Such information may or may not be significant in your life, but if you need it, it is there. I find the **X-Mailer** line useful when I am helping someone who is having trouble with mail, and I want to know what program he is using.

The Body of a Message

The body is the main part of the message, and is usually plain text, so when you compose a message, you just type whatever you want.

Some mail programs, however, allow you to include more than plain text by using RICH TEXT. Rich text can contain different typefaces, as well as italic and boldface. It can also contain pictures, links to Web sites, and various other elements that might appear on a Web page. To create rich text in a message, your mail program uses HTML (hypertext markup language), the same system that is used to specify the appearance of Web pages.

HTML is complex, but you don't have to understand it to use it in a mail message. You just compose the message the way you want, and your mail program automatically builds the required HTML specifications for you. Not all mail programs support rich text, but the most popular ones do, and they make it easy to insert special features into your messages.

Rich text might seem like a good idea, and when used judiciously it can be cool. Mostly, though, people who use rich text tend to go overboard at first and use it to excess. In addition, many mail programs do not support rich text, and when you send such a message, there is a chance the person receiving it will not be able to read it properly. I will talk more about these problems in Chapter 6.

Attachments

Along with the body of a message (either plain text or rich text), you can send one or more files. These files are called attachments and can hold anything you want: a picture, a word processing document, a program, and so on.

I have a friend named Terry who talks to people in Greece using a chat facility. Before they start the conversation, Terry and her friends use attachments to send one another sound files containing Greek music. Then, as they are talking, they use their computers to listen to the music at the same time.

hint

Whenever you send an attachment, make it easy for the recipient to understand what the message is supposed to contain.

Although it is possible to send a message that contains an attachment and nothing else, it is always a good idea to include a short note describing the file you are sending, along with a relevant `Subject` line in the header.

Signatures

If you find yourself typing certain routine information in all your letters, think about putting that information into a signature: a small amount of personalized information that your mail program automatically inserts at the end of each outgoing message. All you need to do is create a SIGNATURE FILE to hold whatever information you want, and then tell your mail program the name of the file. (Your mail program allows you to turn this feature on and off as necessary.)

Traditionally, signatures are used for information such as a phone number, Web page address, and street address. An example of this is the signature from the message in Figure 5-2:

```
=================================================
Harley Hahn              http://www.harley.com/
(202) 456-1414           hhahn@little-nipper.com
=================================================
```

Some people like to include a witty or pithy saying within their signature. This is fine: After all, we all like wit, and the person does not live who can't use a bit more pith in his life. Just make sure that your signature does not get too long.

To use a signature, all you have to do is create a small file with some text. Then tell your mail program where the file is, and the contents of the file will be appended automatically to the end of all your outgoing messages. Here is how to set up your signature file:

Within Outlook Express (Internet Explorer), pull down the Tools menu and select "Stationery". Click on the Mail tab and then on the Signature button.

Within Messenger (Netscape), pull down the Edit menu and select "Preferences". In the Category box, click on "Identity" under Mail & Groups and then specify the name of the signature file in the appropriate box. (If there is nothing showing under Mail & Groups, click on the + [plus sign] character to show the various choices.)

hint

Over the years, experienced Internet users have determined, by trial and error, that signatures should be no more than four lines. Anything longer is irritating to other people.

Remember, your signature is going to be read by everyone to whom you send mail, every time they receive a message from you. For example, in the course of a month, if you send your girlfriend 100 messages, she is going to have to read your signature 100 times.

(The same advice, of course, goes for messages to a boyfriend. However, in my experience, it is almost always the men who are chronic large-signature-offenders.)

vCards

A vCard is a facsimile of an electronic business card attached to a message. The specifications for vCards have been standardized and adopted by various software companies. In particular, vCards created with the Netscape mail program (Messenger) will work with the various Microsoft mail programs (such as Outlook Express), and vice versa. However, many other programs do not understand vCards and wouldn't know what to do with one if it were handed to them on a plate of watercress.

To some people, vCards are très cool (which is French for "hot stuff"). Other people see them as a silly solution in search of a problem. My suggestion is to try them with your friends and see what you think.

You create a vCard by using your mail program. (The details vary from one program to another.) Once you have a vCard, you can then tell your program to attach it to your outgoing mail. When someone receives a message with a vCard, his mail program will recognize it (you hope). When the recipient looks at the message, he will see the card and have the option of displaying all the information it contains.

Mail programs that support vCards make it easy to copy the information from a card directly to your personal address book. (We will talk about address books later in the chapter.)

How Mail Is Stored (Folders)

As the days pass, you are going to accumulate a lot of messages. To help you store them conveniently in an organized fashion, your mail program creates a set of FOLDERS, each of which can hold as many messages as necessary. If you want, you can create more folders and move messages between them, but you will probably find that the standard folders will work just fine.

The names of the folders will vary from one program to another, but their use should be obvious. In the following table, I have put the names of the folders used by two popular mail programs.

Outlook Express (Microsoft)	Messenger (Netscape)
Inbox	Inbox
Outbox	Unsent Messages
Drafts	Drafts
Sent Items	Sent
Deleted Items	Trash

The Inbox holds all your incoming mail. The Outbox (or as Netscape calls it in their own cunning way, the "Unsent Messages folder") holds messages you have composed that are ready for delivery, but have not yet been sent. Once messages are sent, they are moved to the Sent folder.

The Drafts folder is a temporary storage area for messages that are partially typed, but not yet ready to send. For instance, if you are typing a message and you have to quit the program before the message is finished, you can save it in the Drafts folder. Some mail programs will automatically save unfinished messages to this folder when you quit the program. Other programs will not do so automatically; you must save the message yourself before you quit. (I suggest you take a minute right now and run a test to see exactly how your program works.)

As you read your incoming messages, you will want to delete them. Similarly, you will want to delete messages from your Sent folder. When you delete messages, they are not really deleted, they are simply moved to your Trash (Deleted Items) folder. This gives you a chance to look at your old messages should the need arise. Eventually, though, you should delete the messages in your Trash folder. Once you do, the messages are gone forever.

For reference, Figure 5-3 shows the life cycle of a mail message.

Figure 5-3: The life cycle of a mail message

Outbox (Unsent Messages)
↓
Sent Items folder
↓
your mail server
↓
recipient's mail server
↓
Inbox
↓
Deleted Items (Trash)
↓
oblivion

hint

It is a bad idea to let the mail in your Sent and Deleted (Trash) folders build up indefinitely, so you should clean them out from time to time. My suggestion is to get rid of all but the last three months' mail. That way, you can always go back in time a bit if necessary.

Realize, however, that most people are not so well organized. If you foolishly sent an embarrassing message to a friend several years ago, it is probably still in his Trash folder, waiting for you to became famous enough to make it worthwhile for your friend to sell the message to the *National Enquirer*.

Address Lines Within the Header (To, Cc, Bcc)

When you compose a message, there are three lines in the header on which you can specify addresses: the **To** line, the **Cc** (copy) line, and the **Bcc** (blind copy) line. Each of these lines can hold one or more addresses, and every address you specify will be sent a copy of the message.

The **To** line and the **Cc** line are similar. The main difference is one of interpretation by the people who receive the message. When you put someone's address in the **To** line, it shows you consider the message to be of direct importance to that person. When you put someone's address in the **Cc** line, it shows you want the person to see the message, but only for his own information; you don't expect him to act upon it.

For example, say you live in the U.S., and you think your taxes should be lower. You decide to mail a message explaining your situation to the Commissioner of the Internal Revenue Service. You also decide to send copies to the President of the United States, the Vice President of the United States, the Chief Justice of the Supreme Court, and your mother. The proper etiquette is to put the address of the Internal Revenue Commissioner on the **To** line and all the other addresses on the **Cc** line:

```
To: commissioner@irs.ustreas.gov
Subject: Please lower my taxes
Cc: president@whitehouse.gov, vice-president@whitehouse.gov,
    chief@supreme-court.gov, mom@happy-family.com
```

Aside from the **To** and **Cc** lines, you can also put addresses on the **Bcc** line. The addresses on this line will receive an identical copy of the message, however, no one else will know about it. Thus, you can use the **Bcc** line to send secret copies of a message. When you do, the copies are called BLIND COPIES.

In our example, you might decide it would intimidate the IRS commissioner too much if he found out that other powerful people were sent a copy of your message. So you decide to send a blind copy to the most intimidating people, and a regular copy to the other, less powerful people:

```
To: commissioner@irs.ustreas.gov
Subject: Please lower my taxes
Cc: president@whitehouse.gov, vice-president@whitehouse.gov,
    chief@supreme-court.gov
Bcc: mom@happy-family.com
```

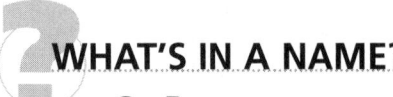

WHAT'S IN A NAME?

Cc, Bcc

In the olden days, before computers and copiers, people used typewriters to write letters, and, once a letter was written, there was no easy way to make a copy.

The solution was to use carbon paper. You would put a piece of carbon paper between two pieces of regular paper and insert all three pieces into the typewriter. As you typed, the keys striking the top paper would press on the carbon paper underneath and cause a copy to be made on the bottom paper. When you were finished, the bottom paper would be a duplicate of the top paper. This duplicate was called a CARBON COPY and would normally be filed in your records. (If you are not sure what carbon paper is, ask an old person.)

If you needed to send an extra copy of a letter to someone, you would have to use a second piece of carbon paper with an extra piece of regular paper, and make two copies instead of one. This extra copy could then be sent to a second recipient. To indicate that a copy was sent, you would type "Cc:" followed by that person's name at the bottom of the letter.

For example, say you were typing a business letter to Rick Shaw, with a copy to Mary Q. Contrary. At the bottom of the letter, you would type:

`Cc: Mary Q. Contrary`

When Rick saw this line, he would know that Mary was sent a carbon copy of the letter.

That is why, to this day, we use a `Cc` header line within an email message to indicate who is to receive a copy of that message. The `Bcc` (blind copy) designation is simply a variation of `Cc`.

Using an Address Book

If you send many messages, it is convenient to have a permanent list of names and addresses. All mail programs let you do this by maintaining a personalized ADDRESS BOOK. The address book contains a number of entries, each of which has room for a name, a mail address and miscellaneous notes. The actual details depend on your program. Some store only this basic information; others allow you to put in other types of information, such as a company name, a postal address, phone numbers (work, home, fax), and so on.

To use an address book, you create one entry for each person to whom you send mail. Then, whenever you want to send a message, you can select a name from the address book and the program will fill in the details (such as the address). Some programs will automatically look in your address book whenever you start to type a name in the **To** line of a new message. If the program can guess which name you are starting to type, it will do its best to fill in the rest of the name for you.

Most mail programs make it easy to create an address book. In particular, as you read a message, there will be a way to tell your program to extract the name and address of the person who sent the message and automatically create a new entry in your address book. Thus, it is easy to build a personal address book one entry at a time as you receive messages from various people.

If you use vCards, it is even easier. Whenever you receive a message with a vCard, you can tell your program to take the information from the vCard and create a new entry in your address book.

hint

Take a moment now and find out how to create an entry in your address book by using your mail program. In particular, find out how to save the name and address from a message directly to your address book.

Microsoft Outlook Express: From the Inbox, double-click on a message to display it within its own window. Then, on the **From** line (in the header), right-click on the name of the person who sent the message and select "Add to Address Book".

Netscape Messenger: While you are reading a message, pull down the Message menu, and select "Add to Address Book".

Eudora Light: While you are reading a message, pull down the Special menu, and select "Make Address Book Entry". (Alternatively, as a shortcut, you can press **Ctrl-K**.)

Replying

After you have read a message, you can REPLY to the person who sent it to you. The details vary depending on which mail program you use, but they should be simple.

If the message was sent to more than one person, your mail program will give you two choices: You can reply only to the person who sent the message, or you can reply to everyone who received a copy (that is, to everyone whose address appears on the **To** and **Cc** lines). Before you choose, take a moment and ask yourself: Do I really want everyone to see my reply?

When you reply to a message, your program creates a new message, all ready to send. The old message will be included as part of the new message, so you can use all or part of it within the reply, and will be marked in some way to make it stand out. The most common convention is to preface each line of the old message with a > (greater-than) character.

When you include part of the original message within a reply, we say that you QUOTE the original message. For an example of what this looks like, take a look at the message in Figure 5-2.

It is important to make your replies as readable as possible. Do not always quote the entire original message. Instead, quote only what you need and delete the parts that are irrelevant. Sometimes a message will go back and forth several times, with new text added each time, and, if you don't edit and prune the message as it develops, it will grow excessively long and become difficult to understand.

Here is an example to illustrate how to write a good reply. A person named Rick sends the following message to a person named Ilsa:

```
Ilsa:

Would you like to meet me this evening after the club
closes?

We could talk over old times and have a drink.  We haven't
seen each other in years, and I would love to spend some
time with you again.

If you come, please wear a pink carnation so I will be
sure to recognize you.

-- Rick
```

When Ilsa replies to Rick, she quotes only the parts of the original message that are relevant to her reply. She also makes sure to put Rick's name at the top of the message and her name at the bottom.

```
Rick:

> Would you like to meet me this evening after the club
> closes?

Yes, that would be great.

> If you come, please wear a pink carnation so I will be
> sure to recognize you.

I don't know if I can get a carnation on such short
notice.  Would a ranunculus be okay?

-- Ilsa
```

Rick now replies to Ilsa's reply. Notice that parts of the very first message are now marked by >> (two greater-than characters). This is because a single > character is inserted into the old text each time you reply. Notice as well that Rick, like Ilsa, has deleted all but the relevant parts of the message to which he is replying.

```
Ilsa:

>> If you come, please wear a pink carnation so I will be
>> sure to recognize you.

> I don't know if I can get a carnation on such short
> notice. Would a ranunculus be okay?

That would be fine. See you tonight.

-- Rick
```

When you reply to a message, your mail program will change the **Subject** line slightly by inserting the characters **Re:** at the beginning of the subject. This lets the recipient knows he is looking at a reply. For example, say you send a message to your friend Vladimir with the following **Subject** line:

Subject: Do you need a banana?

When Vladimir replies, the **Subject** line will look like this:

Subject: Re: Do you need a banana?

If you would like to see another example of how this works, take a look at the messages in Figures 5-1 and 5-2 earlier in the chapter. The message in 5-2 is a reply to the message in 5-1.

People often use mail to have a discussion of some topic in which each message is a reply to the previous one. In such cases, we refer to the sequence of messages as a THREAD. Within a thread, the **Subject** lines of the messages will all be the same.

When looking back over old messages, it can be convenient to view them arranged in threads. To do so, just tell your mail program to sort the messages by subject. (All programs have a way to do this.)

hint

When you reply to a reply, your mail program will *not* insert a second **Re:** at the beginning of the **Subject** line.

Thus, when you see **Re:** at the beginning of the subject, you won't be able to tell whether you are looking at the first reply or a subsequent reply until you open the message.

Forwarding

From time to time, someone will mail you a message that you want to send to a third person. When you do, we say that you FORWARD the message. Like replying, forwarding is easy (though the details vary from one mail program to another).

When you forward a message, some (but not all) mail programs insert a few characters at the beginning of the **Subject** line to let the recipient know he is looking at a forwarded message. Microsoft Outlook Express uses **Fw:**, while Netscape Messenger uses **Fwd:**. For example, say you receive a message with the following **Subject** line:

Subject: I am having a party on Friday

You use Outlook Express to forward the message to your friend Wendy. When Wendy receives the message, it will have the **Subject** line:

Subject: Fw: I am having a party on Friday

Forwarding mail is so easy that people do it a lot, and it is common to receive a message that contains information that has been forwarded many times, from one person to another. Sometimes this is okay, such as when a collection of jokes is being sent around the Net.

Other times, forwarding is not so benign. For example, it is all too common for people to receive a message with false, but alarming, information, and to immediately forward a copy to thirty of their closest friends. An enormous amount of misinformation is circulated throughout the Net in just this manner.

Whenever you receive a forwarded message, never believe what it says unless you can independently verify the facts. Be especially suspicious of messages that purport to alert you to something bad or outrageous. Such messages are almost always wrong.

hint

If you receive a forwarded message telling you about a dangerous new computer virus, do not worry. Such messages are *always* wrong, and are forwarded around the Net by misinformed people who think they are doing their friends a favor.

One common such message warns you about "mail viruses". Supposedly, certain mail messages contain a virus that can cause damage if you read the message. This is not true: Such viruses do not exist. The real damage—scaring people needlessly—is caused by the foolish people who forward such messages.

hint

When someone forwards you a message alerting you to something bad or outrageous, do not forward the message unless you are sure it is true.

Misinformation not withstanding, the worst forwarding problems come from people who pass on messages that were meant to be confidential. Some people are incorrigible forwarders, and they love to send messages all over the place. The only way you can stop such people is to not send them confidential mail in the first place.

Once you mail a message, there is no way to get it back, and there is no way to keep someone from forwarding it. Moreover, there are probably copies of the message stored on various computers, so nothing you send is ever completely private. If it seems like a lot of trouble to be careful about sending mail, take a few moments and imagine what fun a jealous co-worker or a disgruntled girlfriend/boyfriend might have with your old messages.

hint

Never, ever send a message that would cause you problems or embarrassment if it were to be made public. When you have something delicate to say, do so over the phone, where you will not leave a permanent record that can be saved and forwarded to the world at large.

Although this guideline may seem awkward, it can save you more trouble than you would ever believe (until it happens to you).

Understanding Mail Error Messages

Occasionally, you will mail a message that cannot be delivered. In such cases, the message will be returned to you. We describe this by saying that the message BOUNCED. For example, a friend might tell you, "I got a message from Tom Cruise last week. He didn't know your email address, and he wanted to know if you would like to spend the weekend at his ranch. I sent you mail, but it bounced, so I had to go instead."

There are various reasons why a message might bounce. Usually, either your mail server could not send the message, or the recipient's mail server could not accept the message. In either case, one or both of the servers insert a comment into the header of the message before sending it back. Thus, when you receive bounced mail, the first thing to do is look at the full header. Some of the header lines will be highly technical and hard to understand, but if you look carefully, there will be some clue as to what went wrong.

When you look at the header of a bounced message, you will probably see a notation of a "permanent fatal error". Don't panic, no one died. This is just nerd talk for "the mail server gave up because it encountered a problem that didn't go away".

To help you figure out why a message bounced, here are some of the more common terms you may encounter:

User unknown or Invalid recipient: The recipient's mail server did not recognize the name at the beginning of the address. Check the address. You may have used an incorrect name, or you may have spelled it wrong.

Host unknown or Host not found: Your mail server could not find the computer to which you tried to send the message. Check the address. The hostname may be incorrect, or you may have spelled it wrong.

Time out: Your mail server gave up waiting for the recipient's mail server to respond. Try again later. The recipient's mail server may be down temporarily. If mail keeps bouncing, make sure you are using the correct address.

Mailbox full: The system to which you are sending a message has limits on the amount of storage space for each individual user. The person to whom you are sending a message has so much unread mail that his mail server will not accept any more messages on his behalf. Try again later.

Connection refused: For some reason, the recipient's mail server would not accept a connection from your mail server. Try again. If the message keeps bouncing, check the address.

No route to host: Your mail server could not find a way to contact the recipient's mail server. Try again. If the message keeps bouncing, check the address.

6

Using Mail Well

Mail is important, and I want you to be able to use it well. Every time you send a message, it does more than convey words from one place to another. The messages you send also represent you to another person.

With what you learned in Chapter 5, and with a little practice, you will be able to send and receive mail quickly and easily. However, you must make sure you are not misunderstood and that you do not accidentally offend someone. You also have to safeguard your privacy, follow the accepted conventions, and learn how to control the mail system to your advantage.

In this chapter, I will teach you the nuances and give you an understanding of a few advanced tools. You already know how to use mail. By the time you finish this chapter, you will know how to use it well.

Email Conventions

When you talk in person or on the telephone, there is more to the conversation than your words. Your voice has certain tones and rhythms that help you communicate. In person, your gestures and body language also have meaning. Even more important, as you talk with someone, you can interact with him or her in such a way as to avoid serious misconceptions.

Sending mail on the Internet is a lot different. Moreover, unlike postal mail, email is easy to send, and you don't have to worry about envelopes, postage, delivery time, and so on. You can send a message whenever you want and read your incoming messages at your convenience. What you can't do, however, is be with the other person when he or she reads your mail.

Electronic mail has been used for years, and in that time people have found it all too easy to send a message that is misunderstood. To avoid such problems, a number of conventions and practices have been worked out over the years. At first, you may decide that some of these conventions don't make sense and don't apply to you. Remember, though, what I am telling you in this chapter is based on the experience of many people. If you don't understand why something is necessary, all I can say is you will. If you follow the guidelines in this chapter, you will be doing the right thing.

hint

When you start to use a system that millions of people are already using, it is not a good idea to try to redefine the rules.

Make Sure Your Messages Look Nice

Whenever you send mail, take an extra moment and make the body of the message neat, orderly and easy to read. Just like a regular letter, each email message should start with the name of the recipient and end with your name. If you choose, you can have a signature appended to the end of the message (see Chapter 5). Take care to divide your message into paragraphs, fix spelling mistakes, and edit out any problem areas. In other words, take the same care with an email message as you would with a regular letter.

As an example, compare the message in Figure 6-1 with the one in Figure 6-2. You might think that Figure 6-2 is an exaggeration, but it is not. I get mail like this all the time.

Figure 6-1: An example of a good mail message

```
Harley:

Your books have changed my life. I didn't realize how much
the Internet had to offer, and how much I could do on the
Net until I read your Yellow Pages book.

I like the name Harley because I think motorcycles are cool.
I used to have one of my own, but I had to sell it when I
went to college.

My father and mother are just starting to use the Net and I
gave them your book.  I told them your Web site is cool and
they should be sure to check it out.

Ever since my mom got a computer, she has been sending me
email notes about life.

Thanks again for writing such cool books.

-- Fester Bestertester
```

Figure 6-2 has a lot of obvious mistakes (including spelling), but there is one particular problem that is not so obvious: The person has written the message as one long paragraph. Remember, people will be reading your messages on a computer screen, which is not as easy as reading a letter on paper. Thus, it behooves you to use short, well-constructed paragraphs.

Figure 6-2: An example of a bad mail message

```
Your bOoks have changed my life. I DIDn't

realize how much the Internet
had to offer, and how much i could the Net until i
read your Yellow Pages bOOK. i like the name
Harley because I think motorcycles are cool""!!
I used to have one of my own but I had to sell it when I
went to colege.My fathr and mothr are    just
starting to use the Net and i
gave them your bookI told them your Web site is cool
and
they should be sure to check it out. eVER SINCE MY MOM GOT
A COMPUTER, SHe has
been sending me email notes about life. Thanks again for
writing such cool books. Fester BEstertester
```

Here is a real life example. I have a friend who is a highly educated professional and a master at writing business letters. However, he has little experience with email and the Internet, and when he composes a message, he tends to write one huge paragraph that is very difficult to read. Like a lot of people, he doesn't treat email as if it were as important as "real mail". This is a mistake.

hint

Before you send a message, re-read it in its entirety. As you re-read, check your spelling and take a moment to fix any writing mistakes.

As a general rule, your message will be easier to read if you use small, well-structured paragraphs. Remember, the person who receives your message will be looking at a computer screen, and he will be reading a lot faster than you did when you typed the message.

Thank-You Notes

Whenever someone gives you a present, no matter how small, you are obligated to send that person a thank-you note. This is not optional. No matter what other people may do in such situations and no matter what your friends may think, thank-you notes are required, and you must send them. (If you don't believe me, ask your grandmother.)

The reason I mention this topic is because I have noticed a distressing tendency for people to use mail on the Internet to fulfill certain social obligations in a highly inappropriate manner. Electronic mail is great for just about anything: planning a meeting, talking to a friend, asking a question, passing around information, debating an issue, or discussing the meaning of existence. However, there are a few important times in life when you must not use email, no matter how convenient it may be. In such situations, you must either send a letter on paper or talk in person.

So, for future reference, I now declare that you may not use electronic mail to:

● Send a thank-you note
● Ask someone to marry you
● Break off a relationship
● Inform a loved one of a death
● Fire someone

Smileys and Other Communication Conventions

Reading a textual message on the Internet does not convey the same nuances and subtleties as a face-to-face conversation or even a telephone conversation. For this reason, people on the Internet have developed a number of important conventions that are used to ensure good relations. These conventions are used not only in mail, but anywhere people on the Net communicate via the written word: in Usenet discussion groups, on IRC (Internet Relay Chat), in chat rooms, and on Web pages.

Perhaps the most important convention is the SMILEY, a series of characters that looks like a sideways face. There are several variations of a smiley, but the basic one looks like this:

`:-)`

You will also see:

`:)`

(To see the smiling faces, tilt your head sideways to the left.)

The role of the smiley is to tell the reader that what you are saying should be taken as inoffensive. In spoken conversation, you can use a certain tone of voice, a facial expression or a wink. In a mail message, you use a smiley. For example, say you are replying to a message in which a friend has asked you to have lunch with him. You might write:

```
I'll be glad to have lunch with you on Friday.
I can use a free meal :-)
```

In this case, the smiley says, "I am making a joke, so don't be offended." Smileys are also useful when you are demonstrating a devastating wit that a lesser mind might erroneously interpret as sarcasm:

```
Of course, I think your new dress is lovely. I used to
have one just like it when I was a kid. :-)
```

Sometimes you will see the word `<grin>` or, more simply, `<g>` used instead of a smiley. When you do, it means the same thing:

```
Of course, I think your new dress is lovely. I used to
have one just like it when I was a kid. <grin>
```

```
Of course, I think your new dress is lovely. I used to
have one just like it when I was a kid. <g>
```

Another convention to understand is that writing in all uppercase letters means (figuratively) that you are shouting. For example, compare the following two sentences:

```
I NEED YOU TO SEND ME THAT REPORT BY TOMORROW.
```

```
I need you to send me that report by tomorrow.
```

We sometimes refer to words that are entirely in uppercase as being in ALL CAPS (all capital letters). On the Net, typing in all caps is considered to be highly emphatic and rarely appropriate, so don't do it unless you really mean to.

On a more personal level, there is a convention regarding how you refer to yourself. The Internet is an informal place, where people are judged mainly by the quality of their ideas. Thus, it is customary for people to refer to themselves by their name only, omitting titles such as Doctor, Professor, Mrs., Mr., Ph.D., and so on.

For example, say your name is Laura Schlessinger, and you have a Ph.D. in physiology. In your personal life, you might puff yourself up by swanking around, demanding that people call you Dr. Schlessinger or even Dr. Laura. However, on the Net, you are better off signing your messages as "Laura" or "Laura Schlessinger". Using the title "Dr." would give people the impression that you are insecure and pretentious.

hint

When you configure your mail program, you will need to specify your full name. This is the name that is used in your return address.

On the Net, it is customary to use your name only. Do not use an honorific, such as Dr. or Prof., or a designation, such as M.D. or Ph.D. It will only make you look pretentious.

The final convention I want to mention has to do with abbreviations and acronyms. Because all mail messages must be typed, many people use abbreviations to save time. Figure 6-3 shows some of the more common abbreviations used in mail messages.

Figure 6-3: Common abbreviations used in mail messages

Abbreviation	Meaning
BTW	by the way
CUL	see you later
CUL8R	see you later
F2F	face to face ("in person")
FAQ	frequently asked question list
FWIW	for what it's worth
FYI	for your information
IMHO	in my humble opinion
IMNSHO	in my not so humble opinion
IMO	in my opinion
IOW	in other words
LOL	laughing out loud
OTOH	on the other hand
POV	point of view
ROFL	rolling on the floor laughing
ROTFL	rolling on the floor laughing
TTFN	ta-ta for now ("good-bye")
TTYL	talk to you later
TYVM	thank you very much

Such abbreviations are used wherever people type messages, not only in mail, but in Usenet discussion groups, IRC (Internet Relay Chat), chat rooms, and so on. For reference, I have put a more comprehensive list of common abbreviations in Appendix C. Take a moment now and give the list a quick glance.

Be Careful What You Write

Once a message is sent, you can't get it back. For this reason, I want you to get into the habit of using your very best judgment when it comes to sending mail. For example, it is common for someone to receive a message that makes him angry, and, without thinking, to fire off an angry reply. A few hours later, the person is less angry, but it is too late—the message has been sent. Even if you change your mind ten seconds after a message has been sent, it is too late to stop it from being delivered.

Moreover, electronic mail can be stored indefinitely. The message you send today will exist as long as the person who receives it decides to keep it, and a year from now, it is just as easy to forward a message to someone else as it is today. Furthermore, it doesn't take much effort to put the text of a mail message on a Web page, where it is accessible to the general public.

I have a friend who sent a private message to someone and later was astonished to find that a third person had seen the message. My friend was astonished because that person doesn't even have email access. How could this be? Simple. The person who received the message printed it out and delivered a copy to the third person.

The following hint may seem over-cautious, but I promise you, it is one of the most valuable pieces of advice you will ever read. If you follow this advice, you will thank me over and over.

hint

Whenever you receive a mail message that makes you angry, *always* force yourself to wait 24 hours before answering the message.

No exceptions.

Aside from anger, you also need to be careful when it comes to romance. Although you may be tempted to use email to send romantic missives to the adorable object of your affections, you must remember that messages are easy to save and easy to forward. It doesn't take much imagination to see how an ex-boyfriend or ex-girlfriend, armed with a collection of your email love letters, could wreak havoc with your life. This is especially true if your messages were even the least bit suggestive. My advice is, if you want to get romantic or sexy, forget email and confine yourself to the more traditional methods of sending special notes back and forth (like using your employer's FedEx account).

To be completely safe, you should never write anything in a mail message you would not want to be made public. I know this sounds extreme and unrealistic: Rules that guarantee complete safety are always extreme and unrealistic. However, I do want you to remember that mail on the Internet is *not* always private, and a wise person uses judgment and discretion.

This guideline is important when you use the mail system at work. From day to day, you may feel you have complete freedom to send whatever mail you want, but that is an illusion. You and I need to be very clear here: If you send and receive mail at work, your employer has every right to look at it and, if it serves his interest to do so, he *will* look at it.

I know someone who once used the mail system at work to send a message to a friend in which she described a co-worker as a "psycho bitch from hell". No doubt there was some truth in this assessment, but I can only imagine that such a revealing description would be difficult for that person to explain during her next performance evaluation.

My suggestion is to never, ever use your employer's mail system for personal messages. Save your social correspondence for your leisure hours at home. If you really do find it necessary to send personal mail at work, get yourself an anonymous Web-based mail account (see Chapter 5) and use your browser. And, for goodness sakes, don't get caught.

hint

Mail is not private.

Every message you send is only a few keystrokes away from being forwarded to anyone on the Net.

Is It Okay to Use Rich Text?

Most messages are composed of plain text (letters, numbers, punctuation, and so on). However, in Chapter 5, we talked about a variation called rich text. With rich text, your message is still mostly characters, but these characters can be in a variety of different typefaces, as well as italic and boldface. Underneath, rich text is actually HTML, the same stuff out of which Web pages are made. This means you can create messages that contain the same types of elements you might see on a Web page: pictures, graphics, links to Web sites, and so on. Some mail programs (like Outlook Express) allow you to go even further, by making it easy to use backgrounds that give your messages the look of real stationery.

Rich text is wonderful when you really need to dress up a message. The thing is, how often do you really need to dress up a message? What I notice is that people get carried away with different typefaces, backgrounds, pictures, and so on, and, most of the time, it is all unnecessary.

Having said that, I don't want to discourage you from using rich text at all, but try to think of it as perfume. When used judiciously, rich text can add excitement and charm to an otherwise pedestrian experience. However, a little goes a long way.

The ultimate effect of rich text depends a great deal on what mail program the recipient uses to read your messages. If you send a message full of rich text to someone who is using the same mail program as you, what he sees will be pretty much what you want him to see. However, if he is using a different program, the results may not be what you intended. For example, I have received many messages that were next to unreadable, because they were composed with a type of rich text my mail program couldn't handle well.

There is also another potential problem with rich text. It is common for people to reply to a message, and, when they do, the text of the original message is usually quoted within the reply (see Chapter 5). If you use rich text and send a message to someone with a different mail program, there is a good chance the quoted part of the reply will be screwed up. (I have seen this happen a lot.)

Thus, my advice is to use rich text only when you know for sure that your recipient is using a mail program that can handle the type of rich text your program produces. If you both use the same program, rich text is a safe bet. Otherwise, the two of you should send a few test messages back and forth to see whether rich text will work with your programs.

Still, even if you can get rich text to work perfectly for you, use it sparingly. It is often better to spend a few extra moments looking for better words rather than to use rich text to enhance a mediocre message. Although there will be times when you think you need boldface or italic, what you might really need is a better verb.

hint

Configure your mail program so that plain text, *not* rich text, is the default. Only use rich text when you know the recipient will be able to view it properly. Some programs allow you to specify (in your address book) that particular recipients should always (or never) receive rich text. Specifying such preferences is a good idea.

Putting URLs in Messages

There will be many times when you will want to send someone the address of a particular Web site. To do so, all you need to do is include the URL (Web address) in a message. When the recipient reads your message, his mail program will recognize the address as a URL and turn it into a live link. This makes it easy to go to that Web site. All the person has to do is click on the URL. When he does, his mail program will send the URL to his browser.

Almost all mail programs will recognize URLs within a message, but may not be able to do so unless you specify the entire URL. In Chapter 4, I explained that you can abbreviate URLs when you type them into your browser. In particular, you can omit the `http://` at the beginning of the address.

For example, a browser considers the following URLs to be equivalent:

`http://www.harley.com/`
`www.harley.com`

A mail program, however, may not. Most mail programs will recognize the first URL, but some will not recognize the second one without the `http://`. Since you don't know which mail program your recipient is using, you should always be sure to specify the entire URL, including the `http://`.

hint

Whenever you put a URL into a mail message, be sure to use the entire URL, including the **http://** at the beginning. The best, most reliable way to do so is as follows:

1. Use your browser and navigate to the Web page you want.
2. Click on the URL within the address bar. This will select the entire URL.
3. Copy the URL to the clipboard.
4. Change to your mail program.
5. Paste the URL right into your message.

My advice is to always copy and paste URLs. Never re-type them: It is too easy to make a mistake.

Using the Windows Clipboard

In the previous section, I talked about using the clipboard to copy and paste a URL. Being able to use the clipboard in this way is one of the fundamental skills you need as a Windows user, so, in case you are not sure how it all works, here is a quick summary.

The CLIPBOARD is an invisible storage area maintained by Windows to allow you to copy or move data from one place to another, even between windows. You start by putting some data in the clipboard. (I'll explain how in a moment.) You then move to the place where you want the data and insert the contents of the clipboard.

You can put data into the clipboard in one of two ways, by copying or by cutting. COPY puts the data into the clipboard, but does not change the original. CUT deletes the original data as it is moved to the clipboard.

Once data is in the clipboard, you can copy it into a different location. We say that you PASTE the data.

To copy or cut, start by selecting (highlighting) the data you want to go into the clipboard. You can select data by using either the mouse or the keyboard:

- While holding down the left mouse button, move the mouse pointer over the data you want to select.
- While holding down the **Shift** key, use another key (**Left**, **Right**, **Up**, **Down**, **PageUp**, **PageDown**) to move the cursor over the data you want to select.

Once the data is selected, you can either copy or cut it. To copy, pull down the Edit menu and choose "Copy". To cut, pull down the Edit menu and choose "Cut." The data is now in your clipboard.

Next, move to where the data should go. This can be anywhere you want, even within a different window. Click your mouse at the exact position where you want to insert the data, then pull down the Edit menu and choose "Paste".

If you like shortcuts, there are two different sets you can use instead of the Edit menu. First, when you are ready to copy or cut, you can right-click on the selected data (press the right mouse button). This will display a menu from which you can choose "Copy" or "Cut". After you move to the place where you want to paste, you can right-click again. This will display a menu from which you can choose "Paste".

The second set of shortcuts is to use the keyboard as follows:

Operation	Shortcut Key
Copy	**Ctrl-C**
Cut	**Ctrl-X**
Paste	**Ctrl-V**

Personally, I prefer the shortcut keys as they are a lot faster than using the mouse.

Once you copy or cut something, it stays in the clipboard until you replace it with new data (or until you turn off the computer). This means you can paste the same data over and over. However, you must be careful. The clipboard is meant to be a *temporary* storage area. As soon as you put anything into the clipboard—even a single character— all the previous data is lost forever. For this reason, it is safer to copy, not cut.

Cutting is faster when you want to *move* data, and you know you do not need to preserve the original. However, if you are working with large amounts of data, especially in different windows, it is better to copy. Then, after you have verified that the data is safely pasted, you can return to the original location and delete what you don't need.

Remember, you can't see the clipboard, and even a simple mistake will wipe out the entire contents.

hint

Once data becomes invisible, it is easy to lose.

Sending Mail to a Group of People

You can send a message to more than one person simply by putting more than one address in the **To**, **Cc** or **Bcc** lines in the header (see Chapter 5). People commonly do this when they want to share information. For example, someone mails you a collection of grapefruit jokes, and you decide to forward a copy to all your friends.

In such cases, do *not* send a message with a whole bunch of addresses in the **To** line. Put the addresses in the **Bcc** line. Here is why:

Each person who receives the message will see all the addresses on the **To** line and the **Cc** line. Some of your friends, however, may want their email addresses kept private. Moreover, out of all the people who receive the message, some are going to forward it to friends of their own, and (unless they have read this book) they will not bother to edit out the header of the original message. If the information in the message is interesting, it will be forwarded again and again, and in a short amount of time, the names and addresses in the original message will be spread around the Net.

In such cases, the best thing to do is to address the message to yourself, and send blind copies to all your friends. (A blind copy is one in which the recipient's address does not appear. See Chapter 5 for the details.) In other words, put your address in the **To** line and put your friends' addresses in the **Bcc** line.

Here is an example. Let's say I wanted to send a message to several friends. The right way to do it would be as follows:

```
From: Harley Hahn
To: Harley Hahn
Subject: Grapefruit jokes
Bcc: Charles Wagon, Arthur Irwin Choke, Ben Dover,
 Al Abaster, Ellie Fant, Mel Norman Collie, mom
```

The wrong way would be to put all these names in the **To** line:

```
From: Harley Hahn
To: Charles Wagon, Arthur Irwin Choke, Ben Dover,
 Al Abaster, Ellie Fant, Mel Norman Collie, mom
Subject: Grapefruit jokes
```

If you have a group of people to whom you send mail regularly, you can put an entry in your address book to represent a group of addresses. For example, if I were to create an entry in my address book called **friends** that contained this list of addresses, I could simply mail a message to **friends** and a copy would be sent to everyone on the list:

```
From: Harley Hahn
To: Harley Hahn
Subject: Grapefruit jokes
Bcc: friends
```

(For a general discussion of address books, see Chapter 5.)

When you use an entry in an address book in this way, to represent more than one address, the name of the entry is called an ALIAS. In this case, the name **friends** is an alias for a list of seven different addresses.

hint

When you send a message or reply to a message, be careful of any addresses that do not look familiar. If you are suspicious, send a test message.

I have a friend who once sent highly sensitive mail to an address that, unknown to him, was an alias for a large, public mailing list.

Finding Someone's Mail Address

There are millions of people on the Internet, but as we discussed in Chapter 1, the Net itself is not run by any particular organization. For this reason, there is no central directory in which you can look up someone's address. Nor is there an easy way to see whether a particular person is even on the Internet.

So what do you do when you want to send mail to someone, but you don't know his address? There are several things to try.

First, although this may sound simple, the very best way to find out someone's address is to ask him. Although it is possible to search for an address on the Net (as I will explain in a minute), nothing is faster than calling a person on the telephone and asking him, "What is your email address?" If you have trouble reaching the person you want, a good bet is to ask someone who knows that person.

For example, say you want the email address of someone who works at a company, but you can't reach him by phone. Call the company and ask the receptionist for that person's email address. Similarly, if you want to get in touch with an old friend you haven't seen in years and you don't have his phone number, you can often get better results by calling his mother than by searching the Net.

hint

Occasionally, you may find yourself talking to someone who wants to give you his mail address, but who doesn't know what it is. This is especially common with people who are brand new to the Net and don't understand how things work.

In such a case, give the person your address, and tell him to send you a message. When the message arrives, you can look at the header and see the person's address in the `From` line. Even easier, you can tell your mail program to look at the message, extract the return address, and put it in your address book automatically. (See Chapter 5.)

If you do need to search for an address, there are mail address directories on the Net you can use. These directories use a standard protocol called LDAP (Lightweight Directory Access Protocol). Using LDAP, your mail program can query such a directory on your behalf and display the results. All you need to do is specify a name, and, if that person is listed, you will be given their address. When you find an address you want, it is easy to add it to your address book.

Mail programs that support LDAP usually come with a built-in list of directories that are available for searching. You can add to the list whenever you want, if you find an LDAP directory.

It addition, the public LDAP directories all have their own Web sites, which you can access directly by using your browser.

INTERNET RESOURCE Mail Address Directories

```
http://www.four11.com/
http://www.bigfoot.com/
http://www.whowhere.com/
http://www.infospace.com/
http://www.switchboard.com/
```

hint

To search for an address from within a mail program:

With Microsoft Outlook Express (the mail program that comes with Internet Explorer), go to your address book and click on the Find button.

With Netscape Messenger (the mail program that comes with the Netscape browser), pull down the Edit menu, and select "Search Directory".

When you perform such a search, there will be a number of directories to choose from. Each directory is different, so do not give up until you have searched them all.

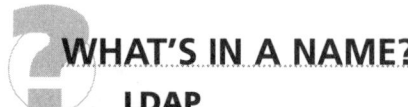

WHAT'S IN A NAME?

LDAP

Most of the mail address directories on the Net support a protocol called LDAP: Lightweight Directory Access Protocol. By using this protocol, a client, such as your mail program, can query such a directory (LDAP server) on your behalf and display the results.

LDAP was developed as an alternative to other, more complex protocols. The word "Lightweight" was chosen to indicate that LDAP is simpler and easier to use than these other protocols. (It's a nerd joke.)

The LDAP directories contain a great many names, so there is some chance you will find the person you want. However, there are many millions of people on the Net, and most of them are not in such a directory, so you may have to search further.

When all else fails, the final way to find an address is to search the Net for some trace of the person. For example, if you can find a person's Web site, you will usually find his mail address on one of the Web pages. Or, if you can find an article the person has posted to a Usenet discussion group, there will be a mail address in the header of the article.

To search the Web, you use one of the Web search engines, which we will discuss in Chapter 9. To search Usenet, you use a Usenet search engine, also discussed in Chapter 12.

Spam and Privacy

There are various reasons why you might want to keep your mail address private. The most important reason is spam (which I discuss in Chapter 2).

SPAM is advertising that is sent to your mail address without your permission. A person or company that sends spam is called a SPAMMER. Receiving spam is similar to receiving junk mail from the regular post office system. However, there is a major difference. With postal mail, it costs significant money to send a letter. There are printing costs, handling costs and postage. For this reason, junk mailers do not want to send mail to people who have no interest in their products. Although this may seem hard to believe (especially if you get a lot of irrelevant junk mail), it is true. If you call a junk mailer and ask to be taken off their list, they will do so, because spending good money to reach the wrong people only raises their overhead.

Spam is different, because it costs nothing to send an email message. If a spammer sends 90 percent of his mail to people who are not interested in the product, what does he care? Thus, unlike the postal junk mailers, email spammers have no economic motivation to make an effort to send their mail only to those people who might be interested. More important, they have no economic motivation to take you off their lists once they have your address.

If you don't mind spam (and some people don't), that's fine. However, if you are like me and you dislike unsolicited messages in your mailbox, you need to learn how to keep your address private.

The first thing to realize is that many spammers are basically dishonest people. Here is why:

Every ISP (Internet Service Provider) has a strong policy against spamming. When an ISP sees a customer using their system to spam people, they cut off that customer immediately. In addition, there are many technically adept people on the Net who hate to receive spam, and if they find the email address of a spammer, they will retaliate in some way (say, by spamming *his* system).

For these reasons, virtually all spammers structure their mail messages to have a fake return address and to hide the origin of the spam. Otherwise, they would lose their ISP and incur the wrath of tens of thousands of people. In other words, just to be in business requires that a spammer be dishonest.

hint

From time to time, you may receive a spam message that apologizes for sending you mail you may not be interested in. The message will say, if you want to be taken off the mailing list all you need to do is send a reply, say, with the word "REMOVE" in the body of the message.

They are lying. Do not reply.

They will not take your address off the list. By replying, you confirm that your mail address is a real one. All that will happen is that the address will be sold and resold to other spammers. You may not see the exact same advertisement again, but I guarantee you will see a lot more.

There is only one sure way to keep yourself out of the spam lists: Do not allow your address to get on a list in the first place. So, to understand how to keep your mail address private, you need to understand how spammers get such addresses in the first place.

First, they sell and trade them in *huge* lists. In fact, you may get advertisements inviting you to pay money to send a message to millions of people.

Second, spammers use automated programs to scan vast numbers of Web pages looking for email addresses. This is called TROLLING.

Third, spammers use programs to scan all the articles from all the Usenet newsgroups looking for return addresses in the headers. (We will talk about Usenet articles in Chapter 12, but basically, they have headers similar to mail headers.)

In other words, spammers will do everything they can to get as many addresses as they can. Once they do, they will sell the addresses repeatedly. (After all, it doesn't cost anything to copy a file of data.)

The following hints will help you protect the privacy of your address. Some hints are more extreme than others, so you will need to decide for yourself how much you really want to be private.

Harley Hahn's List of Seven Ways to Keep Your Email Address Private

1. **Be selective about giving out your address**: Give your address only to the people you want to have it, and ask those people not to give it out without your permission.

2. **Lie about your address**: There are many Web sites that demand that you "register" before you can access the site. As part of this registration, you are asked for your address. Why do you think they want it? Even if you are dealing with a legitimate company that promises not to sell your address, they still want to send you their own spam. The best solution is to specify something that looks like an address, but is fake, for example **z@z.gov**.

   You might ask yourself, is this a moral thing to do? The answer is yes. No one on the Net has a right to demand your mail address for any reason.

   In some cases, you may have to give a real address to access the site. (For example, they may want to send you a personal password by mail.) In such situations, think carefully and decide whether giving out your address is worth access to that site.

3. **Get a throwaway address for nonprivate mail**: An alternative to using a fake address is to get a free address from a Web-based mail service (see Chapter 5). You

can treat such addresses as temporary, throwing them away whenever you want. This allows you to register all you want at Web sites, while keeping your personal address completely private.

4. **Don't register your software**: Many software programs ask you to "register" (there is that word again). Of course, as part of the registration they want your address. Don't register. Your software will still work.

5. **Use a disguised address when you post to Usenet**: Unfortunately, Usenet has suffered greatly from spammers in two ways. First, they send a great many advertisements to the Usenet newsgroups, and, second, they steal legitimate addresses from the headers of messages for their mailing lists. To protect yourself, use a disguised return address when you post Usenet articles. To do this, modify your address in a way that a person would recognize the change, but an automated spam program would not. For example, say your real address is:

bendover@undependable.com

When you post a Usenet article, you might use a return address of:

bendover@undependableREMOVE.com

If someone wants to reply to your article, he will know to delete the characters **REMOVE** from the address. However, an automated program trolling for addresses will be fooled.

6. **Don't put your address on your Web page**: Either omit your email address entirely from your Web page, or use a disguised address as I discussed previously.

7. **Don't put your address in your Web browser**: When you configure your browser, there is a place to specify your mail address. For complete privacy, do not do so. As you navigate the Web, it is possible for a Web site you happen to be visiting to run a program on your computer that, without your permission, sends back your address as well as all the other personal information your browser knows about. Omitting this information from your browser's configuration data protects your privacy. However, there is a price. If you don't specify an email address, you won't be able to use your browser for mail, so you will have to use another mail program. (For example, if you use Internet Explorer for browsing, and you don't tell it your address, it will be inconvenient to use Outlook Express for mail.)

Filters

Some mail programs have a facility called FILTERS that allow you to process incoming mail automatically in various ways. For example, you can arrange that all mail from a particular address should be deleted before you even see it. (This is an easy way to eliminate some types of unwanted mail.) Or you might want all messages that have a specific **Subject** line to be moved to a special folder.

You can create as many filters as you need, each one having its own name and its own characteristics. To create a filter, you specify one or more criteria and choose what you want to happen whenever an incoming message meets those criteria. As incoming messages arrive, your mail program will check each message and perform the appropriate actions automatically.

As you gain experience with mail, you will probably come up with useful ways to use filters to preprocess your messages and to help you organize your incoming mail. One nice thing is that you can create as many filters as you want, and turn them on or off to suit your needs.

The details of creating a filter differ from one mail program to another, so it is best to spend some time experimenting with your particular program.

hint

To use filters:

With Microsoft Outlook Express, go to your Mail window, pull down the Tools menu and select "Inbox Assistant". To create a new filter, click on the Add button.

With Netscape Messenger, go to the Message Center window, pull down the Edit menu, and select "Mail Filters." To create a new filter, click on the New button.

Encryption and Security

In certain circumstances, you may need to be absolutely sure that the messages you send and receive are completely private. For example, you may want to use the mail system to send someone a confidential document. You need to ensure that, even if someone else gets a copy of the message, he will not be able to read it. You do this by encoding (scrambling) the message in such a way that only the intended recipient can read it. When you do, we say that you ENCRYPT the message.

An encrypted message looks like meaningless gibberish. The message won't make any sense until it is DECRYPTED, so it doesn't matter if anyone else sees it. What makes the system secure is that it is possible to encrypt a message so that it can be decrypted by only one person in the world—your recipient.

On the Internet, there are a number of systems used for encrypting and decrypting mail. The most common such system uses a protocol called S/MIME (Secure Multipurpose Internet Mail Extensions). The details of S/MIME are complex and involve a lot of mathematics. We can skip the math, however, because your mail program will do the work automatically.

Each person who wants to use S/MIME needs two special items, a PUBLIC KEY and a PRIVATE KEY. (In this context, a KEY is a unique pattern of bits—a data pattern—that is stored in a file.) The idea is that you send your public key to anyone with whom you want to exchange secure messages. Likewise, these people send you their public keys. Your private key, however, you keep only for yourself.

When you want to send a secure message to someone, your mail program will use that person's public key to encrypt a message. Once this is done, the only way to decrypt the message is to use that person's private key. Since only that person has his private key, he is the only one in the world who can decrypt the message.

Similarly, when someone uses your public key to encrypt a message, the only way to decrypt it is by using your private key. As an extra safeguard, when you decrypt a message, you are asked to type in a password (which you have chosen previously). This keeps your mail absolutely private, even in the unlikely event that someone is able to steal your private key.

The system is designed so all the encryption and decryption is done automatically by your mail program. For convenience, your program stores your private key, as well as other people's public keys. This means that, once you set things up, you can send and receive secure messages relatively easily. Moreover, when you attach a file to a message that is to be encrypted, the file is encrypted along with the text of the message. This affords you a completely secure way to send and receive any type of data across the Internet.

So how do you get started? The first thing you need is a set of private/public keys. The pair of keys is actually stored together in a single file. Microsoft and Netscape, in deference to their longstanding tradition of mutual noncooperation, use different terminology for this file. Microsoft calls it a DIGITAL ID, while Netscape calls it a CERTIFICATE. (However, in spite of the different names, the systems are compatible because they both use S/MIME.)

To get a digital ID (or certificate), you must visit the Web site of an organization called a SIGNING AUTHORITY. There are a number of signing authorities around the world. However, there are separate Web sites for Microsoft users (who need digital IDs) and Netscape users (who need certificates).

Digital IDs and certificates are not free: You do have to pay for them (although not very much). The money goes toward maintaining the system. However, most signing authorities will give you a free digital ID or certificate that will last for a limited time, typically 60 days.

hint

To get a digital ID or certificate:

With Microsoft Outlook Express, pull down the Tools menu and select "Options". Click on the Security tab, and then click on "Get Digital ID".

With Netscape Messenger, go to the Message Center. Then pull down the Communicator menu and select "Security Info". Click on "Yours" (under "Certificates") and then click on "Get a Certificate".

Once you get your digital ID or certificate, you will need to learn how to use it with your mail program. The details vary from one program to another, and take some time to understand, so I will make only a few general comments.

I remarked earlier that once you set things up, you can send and receive secure messages *relatively* easily. The catch here is the word "relatively". Both Microsoft and Netscape have made their systems difficult to figure out and to set up. If you can muddle through and get everything to work, the system is usable and will run smoothly. Between here and there, however, you may have a lot of frustration.

Between us, complete security sounds nice, but you probably don't need it. The chances are remote that anyone will ever intercept your mail messages in transit. Although it is possible to imagine a situation in which bulletproof mail security is absolutely necessary, the plain fact is that the regular mail system is safe enough for almost everybody.

hint

If you have a need for encryption, it's probably a psychological one.

The Web

As you read the next few chapters and as you explore the Web on your own, you will find many new things to investigate and many new technical terms. At times, you may feel that the Web is overwhelming and the features of your browser are incoherent. If so, I want you to remember a secret that will make your life a lot easier:

You don't need to understand everything.

In recent years, the Web has become extremely popular, and the programs we use to access the Web (the browsers) have become the focus of an intense, sustained marketing war between Microsoft and Netscape. One consequence is that new browsers are planned, implemented, and rushed to market without long-term testing. For example, whenever I evaluate a new version of a browser, I can see that many of the features were put there for marketing reasons and not because of careful, deliberate study based on the legitimate needs of the users (you and me).

To compound the problem, both Microsoft and Netscape perceive that the road to success lies in making their browsers the center of a grand array of programs and features. "Use *our* browser," the vendors seem to say to us, "and we will lead you through the portal of the Web and show you the magnificent treasures of the Internet."

In marketing terms, the goal of these companies is to "own the desktop." To further their efforts, they have created a complex suite of interdependent programs—mail programs, Usenet newsreaders, Web page editors, and much, much more—all based on their respective browsers. Unfortunately, there has been little effort toward mutual planning and even less care regarding standardizing the terminology.

The result is that Microsoft and Netscape have unwittingly created two large impenetrable hodgepodges of self-serving commercialism. Moreover, the Microsoft programs and the Netscape programs are designed *not* to work well together. This means that, before you start to learn about the Web, you pretty much have to decide whether you want to commit yourself to the Microsoft hodgepodge or the Netscape hodgepodge.

In general, learning how to use the Web leads to an interesting paradox. At the beginning, it only takes a few minutes to learn how to look at a Web page and click on the links, and, much of the time, that's all you really need to know. However, to use the Web *well*, you need to understand some of the details as well as the idiosyncrasies of your browser, and that takes a lot more time than it should.

As you use the Web, there will be occasions when things happen that you don't understand. At such times, remember that everything you see was created by a person, not a mysterious force of nature, and there is nothing on the Web you can't understand (at least in general terms) if you are willing to take the time to learn about it.

On the other hand, it is not necessary to know everything. Believe me, you could walk into any conference of Internet experts, close your eyes and throw a brick, and not have to worry about hitting anyone who completely understands the Web (or even his browser).

The Web is the medium for much of the innovation in the Internet, and as a result, you will find a huge number of resources. However, many of these resources and many of the new ideas are experimental and have not yet stood the test of time. Starting with this chapter, I will help you understand the most important, most useful and most enduring parts of the Web. However, the Web contains far more than any one person needs to understand, so let us recall the following observation:

hint

You don't need to understand everything.

The Basic Ideas

In Chapter 2, I discussed the basic ideas related to using the Web. Before we move on, let's take a moment to go over those ideas.

The WEB is an information delivery system. You can use the Web to look at many different types of information and to access a variety of services. Like all Internet resources, the Web is based on a client/server system. You use a client program, called a BROWSER, to access the information on WEB SERVERS (of which there are millions around the world). The two most widely used browsers are INTERNET EXPLORER (from Microsoft) and NETSCAPE.

Information on the Web is organized into WEB PAGES (although they are not real pages like in a book). A WEB SITE is a collection of related Web pages. Many organizations and people have their own Web sites. For example, IBM has a Web site, the U.S. Senate has a Web site, and I have a Harley Hahn Web site. If you are so inclined, you can create your own Web site and make it available to everyone on the Net. (We will talk about how to do this in Chapter 15.) Note: You will sometimes see "Web site" spelled as a single word "website".

Web pages can contain all types of information including TEXT (characters), GRAPHICS (pictures and photographs) and MULTIMEDIA (animation, video, and sounds). The defining characteristic of Web pages is that they can contain links to other pages or resources. This type of information is called HYPERTEXT (for a reason I will explain in a minute).

As you read a Web page, you will see the LINKS. If you click on a link (using your mouse), your browser will fetch and display the Web page to which that link points. When this happens, we say you are FOLLOWING the link. From your point of view, it looks as if you are jumping from one Web page to another, just by clicking on a link.

If you are a science fiction fan, you will be familiar with the idea of rocketships that jump from one part of space to another via "hyperspace". On the Web, information that contains links allows you to jump from one Web page to another. Thus, the name hypertext.

Now that you know about hypertext, you can understand two of the common technical terms you will see on the Web: HTML and HTTP.

HTML (HYPERTEXT MARKUP LANGUAGE) is the system of specifications used to define the appearance and structure of Web pages. That is why the files that contain Web pages have names that end with **html** or **htm**, for example, **index.html**. (The **html** part of the name is called an extension.) We will talk more about HTML in Chapter 15.

HTTP (HYPERTEXT TRANSFER PROTOCOL) is the protocol used to transfer data between Web servers and Web clients (browsers). In Chapter 4, we talked about URLs (uniform resource locators), the types of addresses that point to Web resources. Now you see why so many URLs start with the letters **http**. For example, the URL for my Web site is:

http://www.harley.com/

The **http** designation tells your browser that the resource in question contains hypertext and must be accessed via the **http** protocol.

The best way to learn how to use your browser is to take some time to explore its features and to experiment. In the following sections, I will explain how to use your browser to perform the most important tasks. There will be slight differences depending on whether you are using Internet Explorer or Netscape. Where the differences are important, I will point them out along the way.

I do want to tell you that I find using a mouse slow and awkward, and I would rather use the keyboard. So, whenever I can, I will show you keyboard shortcuts that can make using your browser faster and easier.

If you would like to experiment with different browsers to see which you like best, I encourage you do to so. After all, when you choose a browser you are (in most cases) also choosing a mail program and a Usenet newsreader. The following Internet Resource shows the URLs where you can find the latest versions of Internet Explorer and Netscape.

In addition, I have also included the URL for another browser called OPERA. Opera is fast, well-designed and easy to use, especially if you are a smart person. I like it because you can do everything you want with the keyboard; you don't have to use a mouse (although you can).

Unlike Internet Explorer and Netscape, Opera costs money. You can try it for free, but if you like it and you want to use it, you must pay for it (although not much). As a general rule, I include only free resources in this book, but I have made an exception in this case because Opera is a good product, and it provides an important alternative to Internet Explorer and Netscape.

hint

Even if you already have a browser, check to make sure you have the latest version. The browser companies release new versions every now and then, and it is a good idea to keep your software current.

If some of the instructions in this chapter don't match exactly what you see in your browser, it may be because you are using an old version.

INTERNET RESOURCE Browsers

```
http://www.operasoftware.com/
http://home.netscape.com/download/
http://www.microsoft.com/ie/download/
```

Before we move on, take a look at Figures 7-1 and 7-2. They show what Internet Explorer and Netscape look like while viewing a typical Web page. From time to time, I will refer to the particular parts of the browser window, and, if necessary, you can refer to these figures. By the way, don't worry if your browser looks a bit different. The appearance sometimes changes from one version to another, but the changes are usually minor.

Options and Preferences

Browsers are complex programs and, as such, have a variety of settings you can change. These settings give you some measure of control over the operation of your browser (although, if you are like me, not as much control as you would like). Microsoft calls the settings OPTIONS, while Netscape calls them PREFERENCES.

There are many such settings, but generally, there are two types:

- Configuration information that you set once (for example, your name, email address, mail server, Usenet news server, and so on)
- Settings that control the operation of your browser (for example, control over how links should be displayed)

Figure 7-1: A typical Web page within Internet Explorer

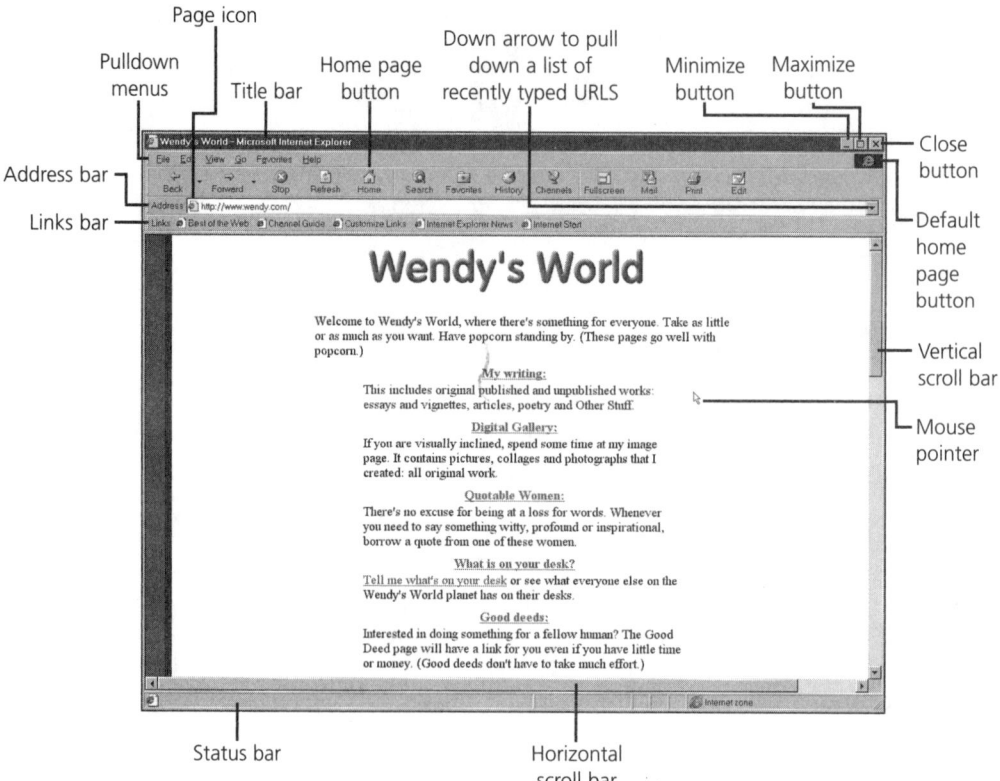

It is important for you to know where these settings are and how to change them when you want, so here is how to find them:

Within Internet Explorer, pull down the View menu and select "Internet Options". Alternatively, you can get at the same setting via the Control Panel. Click on the Start button (on the Windows taskbar), select " Settings", click on "Control Panel", and then double-click on "Internet" or "Internet Options".

Within Netscape, pull down the Edit menu and select "Preferences".

Once you find the settings for your browser, you may want to experiment, and I encourage you to do so. The only warning I would give you, however, is to not change settings that look crucial unless you are sure you understand what they do. As a precaution, you might want to write down the current settings before you make any changes, so you can restore the original values if you want.

Figure 7-2: A typical Web page within Netscape

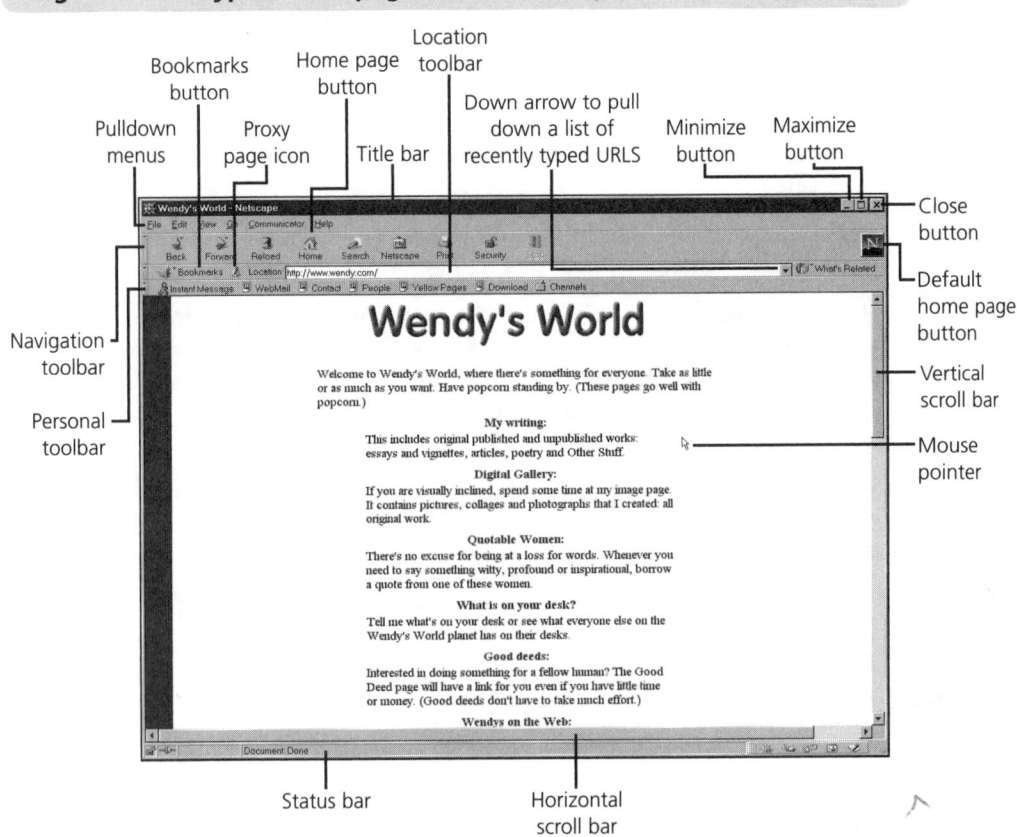

Aside from changing the settings, you can change the appearance of your browser. Pull down the View menu and test the various choices. By doing so, you can add, remove, and even change the size of the various buttons and bars.

Blocking Advertisements

If you hate to look at advertisements, there are two ways to avoid most of them. The first technique is based on the fact that most advertisements are graphics (pictures), not text, and, within your Options (or Preferences), there is a setting that tells your browser not to load graphics automatically.

The setting was intended for people with slow Internet connections, because it takes a lot longer to load graphics than text. People with slow connections can turn off the graphics to decrease the time spent waiting for Web pages to load.

However, regardless of your type of Internet connection, turning off graphics effectively cuts out the ads. Instead of seeing irritating pictures, you will see only outlines of boxes, showing where the pictures would go if you had loaded them. Here is how to tell your browser not to load graphics automatically:

Within Internet Explorer, pull down the View menu and select "Internet Options". Click on the Advanced tab. Go down to the Multimedia section, and uncheck the box next to "Show pictures".

Within Netscape, pull down the Edit menu and select "Preferences". In the Category box, click on "Advanced", then uncheck the box next to "Automatically load images."

From time to time, you may see a page in which you want to see one of the pictures. In such cases, there is an easy way to override the default setting and tell your browser to load a picture on the current page. All you need to do is use your mouse to point to the picture, click the right button, and select "Show Picture" (Internet Explorer) or "Show Image" (Netscape).

With Netscape, there is also a way to show all the graphics on the page at once. Just click on the "Images" button. (It appears in the row of buttons near the top of the browser window whenever you have the "Automatically load images" setting turned off.)

So, if you hate the ads, you don't have to look at them. You can block all the graphics (and virtually all the ads) as a default, and look at only those pictures *you* want to see. This method isn't foolproof, because you have to block all the graphics, and some of them are not ads. However, at least you have some measure of control over your own computer.

hint

If your kids use the Web, think about turning off the graphics on their browser. This will keep the kids from having to look at a zillion ads (as well as other, possibly offensive pictures).

The second way to avoid advertisements is to use software that is designed to block the ads. Such software acts as a barrier between your browser and the outside world, by filtering out the ads before they even get to your browser. Some of these programs cost money, but they work well, and if you hate ads, the money is well spent.

INTERNET RESOURCE Ad-Blocking Software

```
http://www.atguard.com/
http://www.intermute.com/
http://www.junkbusters.com/ht/en/ijb.html
```

Where to Get Help

A moment ago, I told you not to change a crucial setting unless you understand it. But where do you go for assistance if you have trouble understanding something? There are two important sources of help.

First, every program has a built-in help facility. There are two ways to access it: You can either pull down the Help menu or you can press the **F1** key.

hint

Press the **F1** key whenever you need help.

This is worth remembering because, as a general rule, **F1** is the standard help key in almost all programs, not just browsers.

The second way to get assistance is to ask other people for help. This is important because the built-in help facility will often not answer your questions, or will answer them in a way that you can't understand. (Don't feel bad. It's not your fault. Most help systems just aren't all that good.)

When all else fails, the best place to get help is from someone who knows more than you. For this reason, I strongly suggest you cultivate the friendship of one or two computer nerds.

hint

During times of total confusion, the phone number of a nerd is worth more than all the built-in help facilities in the world.

Entering a URL

The basic function of a browser is to let you look at Web pages, so the first thing you need to learn is how to tell your browser to go to a particular URL.

There are several ways to do this. First, near the top of your browser window is an area called the ADDRESS BAR. In Internet Explorer, the address bar is just to the right of the word "Address". In Netscape, the address bar is to the right of the word "Location".

To enter a URL, use your mouse and click anywhere in the address bar. Then type a URL and press the **Enter** key.

If you want to try an example, use the following URL:

`http://www.wendy.com/`

(This is the Web site of Wendy Murdock, my chief researcher.)

Once you press **Enter**, your browser will contact the appropriate Web server, download the information from that site, and display it for you in the large window.

hint

Within Netscape, you will normally see the word "Location" to the left of the address bar. However, as soon as you start to type within the bar, the word changes to "Go to". Once the browser contacts a Web server, the word changes back to "Location".

Note: If your browser connects to a site that is running a Netscape Web server, you will see the word "Netsite" instead of "Location".

Although it is easy to type a URL into the address bar, there are two alternatives that you may prefer. First, use your mouse to pull down the File menu and select "Open". Your browser will display a small window in which you can type a URL. Type the URL and press **Enter**.

An easier way to do this is to press **Ctrl-O**. This is a shortcut that will display the small window immediately. This is the way I enter a URL, as I find it a lot faster than using the mouse.

hint

The fast way to enter a URL is to:

Press **Ctrl-O**, then type the URL and press **Enter**.

hint

From time to time, a program you are using may need you to enter a bit of information or make a choice of some type. The program will display a window with a place for you to type something, some buttons to press, or both. This window is called a DIALOG BOX.

When you are using a browser and you press **Ctrl-O**, you get a dialog box into which you can enter a URL.

Shortcuts When Typing URLs

Most browsers have several ways to make typing long URLs easier. First, as I discussed in Chapter 4, there are several ways to abbreviate a URL and your browser will insert the missing letters for you. For example, the following two addresses will both work:

```
http://www.wendy.com/
www.wendy.com
```

(In Chapter 4, I also describe other useful abbreviations.)

Another facility offered by Internet Explorer is called AUTOCOMPLETE. As you are entering a URL, your browser tries to guess what you are typing, based on the addresses of the Web pages you have already visited. As soon as you have typed enough letters for AutoComplete to make a guess, it will fill in the rest of the letters for you.

You now have three choices:

- You can ignore the suggestion and keep typing.
- If you like the suggestion, you can stop typing and press **Enter**.
- You can press the **Down** key (the one with the down arrow) and go through a list of other URLs that fit the same pattern.

If you want to reuse a URL you have typed recently, there is an easy way to do so. Use your mouse and click on the small down arrow at the right end of the address bar. This will pull down a list of the URLs you have typed. All you have to do is select the one you want.

Finally, Internet Explorer has one more feature you will find useful. As you know, there are many URLs of the form:

`http://www.`*something*`.com/`

Within Internet Explorer, all you need to do is type the *something* and then press **Ctrl-Enter**. (That is, hold down the **Ctrl** key and press **Enter**.) The browser will immediately fill in the rest of the URL for you. For example, to go to my Web page, just type **harley** and press **Ctrl-Enter**.

hint

If you use Internet Explorer, click on the address bar, type your first name, and press **Ctrl-Enter** (just to see what happens).

Navigating

As you use the Web, a lot of your time will be spent changing from one Web page to another. We call this activity NAVIGATING. The metaphor is a convenient one, and I will use it myself, because it is handy to talk as if we are actually moving from one place to another. However, as you use the Web (and as you read this book), don't lose track of the fact you are not really moving through some mysterious universe. What is really happening is that your browser is presenting one page after another for your perusal.

In other words, there is no "cyberspace". (See Chapter 1.)

Most Web pages contain links to other pages, and the simplest way to move from one page to another is to follow a link. To do so, move your mouse pointer to the link and click on it. Your browser will then do whatever is necessary to get you the information to which the link points. Typically, your browser will contact the appropriate Web server, request the new Web page, wait for it to arrive, and then display it on your screen. How long you have to wait depends on several factors, the most important of which is the speed of your Internet connection.

After a while, using the Web takes on a peculiar rhythm to which your mind will begin to synchronize:

Click... *wait*... read... Click... *wait*... read... Click... *wait*... read...

When you are reading a Web page, how do you know where the links are? There are several ways. First, most links are attached to words, and these words will be displayed in a special way. For example, they may be a different color than the rest of the text, or they may be underlined, or both. Most browsers have settings that give you some control over how links are displayed. Experiment with your browser and see what you prefer.

There are two other ways to tell whether something is a link. When you point to a link with your mouse, the mouse pointer will change to a picture of a hand, and the browser will display the address (URL) of that link in a special box at the bottom of the browser window. (This area is called the STATUS BAR.)

Aside from words, links can also be attached to pictures. Usually, the pictures are small ones, referred to as icons. (Within Windows, an ICON is a small picture that represents a resource.) If you point to such a picture, you will see the address of its link in the status bar. To follow the link, just click on the picture.

One special type of picture is an IMAGE MAP. With an image map, various parts of the picture correspond to different links. Here is a typical example. You are visiting a Web site that has travel information about the United States. The main Web page has a picture of the U.S. showing all the states. To see information about a specific state, you simply click on that state. In this case, you are looking at an image map in which each state points to a different Web page.

As you jump from one Web page to another, you will often want to go back to a previous page, and once you do, you may want to move forward again. This is easy: Your browser has Back and Forward buttons. Just click on the one you want.

For a more elaborate way to move forward into the past, you can use the HISTORY LIST, a record that your browser maintains of your recent Web page visits. With Internet Explorer, click on the History button. With Netscape, pull down the Go menu and you will see the various items on the history list. Just select the one you want.

hint

Although it is possible to move back and forth within your recently visited Web pages by clicking on the Back and Forward buttons, that is for weenies.

The fast, cool way to move around is by using the keyboard and pressing **Alt-Left** or **Alt-Right**. (That is, hold down the **Alt** key and press the key with the left arrow, or hold down the **Alt** key and press the key with the right arrow.)

Alt-Left moves back, and **Alt-Right** moves forward. Most people don't know about these shortcuts, but they are so cool I want you to memorize them right now.

Reading a Web Page

Reading a Web page is mostly straightforward: You read it. However, I do have a few hints to help you have more control over your Internet experience. Some of these hints, by the way, are general Windows techniques that apply to any program you may be using, not just to browsers.

Many Web pages are so long that the complete page will not fit within the browser window. In order to read the parts of the page that are not visible, you need to move the page up and down (or left and right) within the window. This action is called SCROLLING, and you can do it with either your mouse or with the keyboard. Let's start with the mouse.

When a Web page does not fit into the browser window, your browser will show you as much as will fit and will place SCROLL BARS alongside the border of the window. (You can see scroll bars in Figures 7-1 and 7-2.) There are two ways to use a scroll bar. You can either click on one of the arrows at the end of a bar, or you use your mouse to drag the slider within the bar.

(To DRAG an object, move the mouse pointer over it, press the left mouse button, and move the mouse while holding down the button.)

The scroll bar on the right is called a VERTICAL SCROLL BAR because it moves the Web page up and down. The scroll bar on the bottom is called a HORIZONTAL SCROLL BAR because it moves the Web page left and right.

hint

Your browser will show scroll bars only when necessary. If the entire page fits in your browser window, you won't see any scroll bars at all.

If the Web page is narrow enough to fit horizontally, but too long to fit vertically, you will see only a vertical scrollbar (because that is all that is necessary).

Aside from using the mouse to scroll, you can also use the keyboard. The **Up** and **Down** keys move the Web page up and down by a small amount. The **PageUp** and **PageDown** keys move the Web page up and down in larger jumps. (If you experiment, you will see what I mean.) In addition, if the page is too wide to fit in the window, you can use the **Left** and **Right** keys to move it horizontally. Finally, for large movements, you can use **Ctrl-Home** to jump to the very top of the Web page and **Ctrl-End** to jump all the way to the bottom.

hint

Within Windows, you can control only one window at a time. The window that is currently under your control is said to have the FOCUS. To move the focus to a particular window, all you need to do is use your mouse and click anywhere in that window.

The reason I am telling you this is because, on occasion, you will press a key (say, the **PageUp** or **PageDown** key) and nothing will happen. Usually this means that the window you want to control—the one containing the Web page—does not have the focus.

In such cases, just click on the Web page. Once the window has the focus, you will be able to control the Web page by using your keyboard.

Most Web pages are displayed using the entire window. Some Web pages, however, are divided into sections, each of which lies within a small window of its own. These sections are called FRAMES.

Frames are used when the Web page creator wants to have more than one independent window within a single page. This is useful when the sections of a page may need to be manipulated individually. For example, one frame might contain a table of contents that is always available, while a second frame contains information that changes. When you click on a link in the first frame, the results are shown in the second frame.

Figure 7-3 shows a Web page that has three frames. The first frame, near the top, contains a navigation banner. The second frame, on the left, contains links. The third frame, on the right, contains text.

FIGURE 7-3
A Web page with
frames

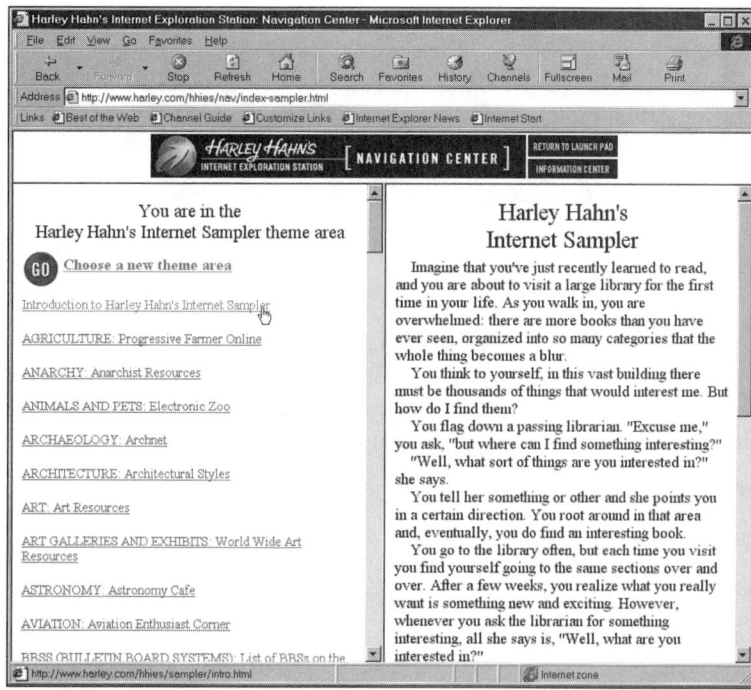

When you read such a page with frames, you can control the scrolling of each frame independently, either with the mouse or with the keyboard. With the mouse, each frame will have its own scroll bars as necessary. With a keyboard, you can use the same keys within the frame as you do for a full-sized window (**Up**, **Down**, **PageUp**, **PageDown**, **Ctrl-Home** and **Ctrl-End**). However, before you can control a specific frame, you will have to click inside the frame in order to give it the focus.

Right-Clicking

When it comes to using your mouse, you usually press the left button. Indeed, throughout this book, when I say to CLICK on something, I mean to point to it with your mouse and press the left button. When I say DOUBLE-CLICK, I mean to press the left button twice in a row. However, you will sometimes need to press the right button, and when you do, we say that you RIGHT-CLICK.

Although you use the left mouse button most of the time, the right button is important. As a general rule within Windows, right-clicking on an object displays a CONTEXT MENU containing selections relevant to that object. For example, if you right-click on an icon, you will see a context menu with selections relating to icons.

hint

Although most people don't know it, there is a way to use the keyboard to simulate a right-click on your mouse: Just press **Shift-F10**.

Right-clicking is important because, typically, the context menus allow you to manipulate an object and look at its properties. Thus, if you become familiar with the various context menus, you will be able to use your programs (and Windows) more efficiently.

The reason I mention all this is because I want you to right-click on the various parts of your browser window just to see what happens. In particular, load a Web page and right-click on the page, away from a link. Now right-click on a link. Notice that you get different context menus depending on where you right-click.

hint

Whenever you feel like a quick break, take a moment and right-click on something, just to see the context menu.

You can't do any harm by right-clicking.

If you are left-handed, you can reverse the function of the left and right mouse buttons by changing a setting via the Control Panel.

Click on the Start button (on the Windows taskbar), select "Settings", click on "Control Panel", and then double-click on "Mouse". You will see the mouse settings panel.

Using the Buttons page, you can now change your mouse setting from right-handed to left-handed.

What to Do When a URL Doesn't Work

From time to time, you will have a problem with a URL that doesn't work properly. For instance, you may try to connect to a Web page and, instead, you get an error message.

There are two types of error messages. First, you may see a message like "File not found". This means that your browser was able to connect to the Web server, but the server could not find the file you wanted. (Remember, each Web page is stored in a file.) Sometimes, you will see a "File not found" message with error code 404. This is the standard error code sent by a Web server when a file cannot be found. (There is nothing cosmic about the number 404.)

A second type of error occurs when your browser cannot even connect to the Web server. In such cases, you will see a message like "Cannot open the Internet site" or "There was no response".

There are several things that might be wrong. First, if you typed the URL yourself, you may have made a spelling mistake. Check the spelling carefully. Many URLs are complex and it is easy to make a mistake.

If you click on a link and get an error message, it may still indicate a spelling problem, because the person who created the Web page may have made a spelling mistake when he typed the address. Such mistakes are more common than you might think.

If you think the address is correct, the next thing to do is make sure your Internet connection is working. An easy way to do so is to try an address that should always work, such as:

```
www.microsoft.com
www.netscape.com
www.ibm.com
```

If URLs like these do not connect, you are probably having a problem with your Internet connection.

If your Internet connection is working, and you are sure the URL is spelled correctly, the address itself may be bad. This can happen when a Web site is reorganized and some of the addresses that used to work stop working.

In such cases, I have a trick for you: Chop off the rightmost part of the URL and try again. For example, let's say you try to connect to the following URL, but it doesn't work:

```
www.harley.com/freestuff/valuables/money/news.html
```

In this case, the rightmost part of the URL is **news.html**. Chop it off and try again:

```
www.harley.com/freestuff/valuables/money/
```

If that doesn't work, repeat the process:

```
www.harley.com/freestuff/valuables/
www.harley.com/freestuff/
www.harley.com
```

Eventually, either something will connect, or you will have proven that the Web site itself is not working.

Managing Your Browser Window

In this section, I am going to show you a number of ways in which you can control your browser window. I am mentioning these procedures here because they are useful while you are using the Web. However, most of what I am about to show you are general techniques that will work for any program running under Microsoft Windows. In particular, I am going to show you how to move, resize, minimize, maximize and close your browser window.

Now, I have to mention that whenever I run up against stuff like this, I'm never quite sure how much detail to explain. After all, there are lots of new users who don't know much about Windows, and if I simply assumed they know all the basics, the conversation might go like this:

Me: "If you have trouble reading a Web page, you can always resize the browser window."
New User: "What's a resize?"
Me: "Or you can maximize the window to get more room."
New User: "What's a maximize?"
Me: "And if you want to put away the window temporarily, you can always minimize it to the taskbar."
New User: "What's a ...?"

Well, you get the idea.

On the other hand, if you are an experienced user, you may already know how to manipulate windows, and I certainly don't want to bore you while I attend to the newcomers. "Old hat," I hear you say (or, if you are French, *"Vieux chapeau."*). So, if you already know how to use Windows, it's okay if you let your attention wander for a few minutes. After all, there are plenty of other things you might be doing: feeding the cat, putting away those old magazines in the garage, or maybe just catching up on your stamp collection.

All set now? Okay, let's push on.

The Web browser and everything it displays is contained within a window. You can control that window in various ways. First, you can change its size by making it as large as possible. To do this, use your mouse and click on the MAXIMIZE BUTTON in the top-right corner of the window. The maximize button is the one with the picture of a small square (see Figures 7-1 and 7-2).

When you click on this button, your window will expand to fit the entire screen. (We say that you have MAXIMIZED the window.) When a window is maximized, the single square on the button is replaced with a small picture of two overlapping rectangles. If you now click on the button again, the window will shrink back to its original size.

An alternative way to maximize a window is to use your mouse to double-click on the TITLE BAR (the bar at the very top of the window). Once the window is maximized, you can restore its original size by double-clicking on the title bar once again. In other words, double-clicking on the title bar alternates the window from maximized to nonmaximized.

Another way to change the size of a window is to use your mouse to drag a corner or an edge. When you drag any of the corners, you make the entire window larger or smaller. When you drag an edge, you make the window larger or smaller in one direction only. For example, to make a window wider, you would drag either the left or right edge outward.

When you change the size of a window in this way, we say that you RESIZE or SIZE it. Whenever you resize a browser window, the browser automatically redisplays the contents to fit the new size, creating or removing scroll bars as necessary.

When you are finished with a browser window, you can close it by clicking on the CLOSE BUTTON. This is the button with an "X" on it, in the top-right corner of the window, just to the right of the maximize button. (See Figures 7-2 and 7-3.) Alternatively, you can use the keyboard to close a window by pressing **Alt-F4**.

hint

Think carefully before you close a window. Once you close it, the contents are gone for good.

If you want to close a window temporarily, without losing the contents, you can click on the MINIMIZE BUTTON. This is the button with a single small line, just to the left of the maximize button. When you click on the minimize button, the window will disappear and we say that you have MINIMIZED it.

A minimized window is not closed. You can restore it to its original size whenever you want, by clicking on the appropriate button on the taskbar. (The TASKBAR is the long bar that contains the Start button, as well as buttons for the various programs that are running.)

An alternative way to restore a minimized window is to press **Alt-Tab** repeatedly and select the program you want. (A lot of this will make sense when you try it.)

hint

When you minimize a window, the program inside it does not stop running.

Thus, if you are waiting for a program to finish a long operation, you can minimize its window and move on to something else. This is convenient when you are downloading a large file, and you want to do something else while you are waiting.

The last basic operation you need to know is how to move a window. Just drag the title bar, and the entire window will move. In other words, move the mouse pointer to the title bar, hold down the left mouse button, and then move the mouse while holding down the button.

Opening a New Browser Window

There will be times when you will want to look at more than one Web page at a time. You can do so by opening a new browser window. In fact, you can open as many browser windows as you want. You can then switch from window to window, using each one as you see fit.

If you accumulate extra windows you don't need, you can get rid of them by closing them. When you close the last browser window, it stops the browser program itself.

Opening a new window is easy.

Within Internet Explorer, pull down the File menu and select "New", then "Window".

Within Netscape, pull down the File menu and select "New", then "Navigator Window".

In either program, it is even easier to use the keyboard: Simply press **Ctrl-N**.

hint

I get bored easily, so I tend to open a new browser window whenever I have to wait for anything.

For example, let's say I am reading the daily comics. I connect to a Web site to read *Doonesbury*, but it takes too long to load. I immediately press **Ctrl-N** to create a new window, and use that window to start loading *Cathy*. Then I switch back to the original window and read *Doonesbury* (which has loaded by now).

After reading *Doonesbury*, I press **Alt-F4** to close the window and switch back to the other window to read *Cathy*.

(Although this scenario sounds complicated, it's actually fast and easy. Try it.)

*I*NTERNET RESOURCE Daily Comics

```
http://www.comiczone.com/
http://www.kingfeatures.com/comics/
http://www.washingtonpost.com/comics
http://www.creators.com/comics/comics.asp
```

So far, I have described how you can create a new browser window intentionally. It is possible, however, for a new window to be created automatically.

Sometimes this is useful. For instance, a Web page might be designed to serve as a table of contents for various resources. When you click on a link, the resource you choose can be automatically displayed in a second window so as to keep the original window available (so you can choose one resource after another).

Most of the time, however, automatic window creation is used for a more aggravating reason: to make an advertisement pop up in your face. Unfortunately, there's not much you can do about this except to avoid the Web sites that do this. In my experience, some of the worst offenders are the sites that offer free Web site hosting services. They seem to be "free", but only because they make the people who visit the pages look at lots of ads.

(Actually, I have seen worse. I have come across Web pages designed to create a whole cluster of new browser windows, each of which contains an ad, and each of which must be closed separately.)

hint

When a Web site creates an unwanted browser window on your screen, remember the two ways to close a window:

You can either click on the close button in the top-right corner or press Alt-F4.

Reloading a Web Page (the Cache)

It can take a long time to download all the information for a Web page, and while it is downloading, you have to wait. For this reason, your browser uses a temporary storage area, called the CACHE, to save the information from recently viewed Web pages. Whenever you want to load a page, your browser looks in the cache to see whether the page is already there. If so, there is no need to reload the page from the Internet. Thus, the second time you look at a Web page, it should load much faster (because it is in the cache).

Using a cache is great, because it can really speed things up. However, there is a problem. The content of Web pages changes from time to time, and if you always load a particular page from the cache, you will never know whether the page has changed.

To obviate this problem, your browser will keep information in the cache for only a predetermined amount of time. After that, if you request the same Web page, your browser will go to the Net and reload it over again, just to make sure you get an up-to-date copy.

There are two important ways you can control the operation of the cache. First, if you feel the need, you can force your browser to ignore the cache and reload the current Web page from the Internet.

Within Internet Explorer, click on the Refresh button. Within Netscape, click on the Reload button. In both browsers, you can also press **Ctrl-R**.

The second way to control the cache is by changing certain settings that specify when your browser should automatically discard information.

hint

To see the cache settings within Internet Explorer, pull down the View menu and select "Internet Options". Click on the General tab, and then, under Temporary Internet Files, click on the Settings button.

To see the cache settings within Netscape, pull down the Edit menu and select "Preferences". In the Category box, look under Advanced and click on "Cache". (If there is nothing showing under Advanced, click on the + [plus sign] character to show the various choices.)

Creating a Shortcut to a Web Page

In your adventures on the Internet, you will find lots of Web pages you want to visit again. For example, you may have a news source you like to check each day for the latest scoops, or you may find an interesting site you want to take a closer look at when you have some free time.

There are two ways you can save such URLs: You can either create a shortcut to the Web page, or you can save the address on a special list. In this section, we will talk about shortcuts. In the next section, I will show you how to create a list of URLs for your favorite Web pages.

A SHORTCUT is an icon that represents a resource (such as a URL). Normally, a shortcut resides on your desktop, the area represented by the background of your display area. (The DESKTOP is what you see when you have no open windows.) Once a shortcut is on your desktop, it is a simple matter to access the Web page. All you have to do is double-click on the icon. This action sends the URL right to your browser. (If your browser is not already running, it will be started automatically.)

hint

If your browser is already open, there is an easier way to use a shortcut. Just use your mouse to drag the icon and drop it on the browser window.

A typical way to use a shortcut is to point to your favorite news site. Then, whenever you want to check the news, all you have to do is double-click on the icon or drag it over to your browser window.

So how do you create an icon? There are several ways. As you are reading a Web page, use your mouse and right-click anywhere on the page. When the context menu pops up, select "Create Shortcut". A shortcut to the current page will be created and placed on your desktop.

hint

You can use the keyboard to simulate a right-click on your mouse by pressing **Shift-F10** (as long as the focus is on the window).

Thus, while you are reading a Web page, the fast way to create a shortcut to that page is to press **Shift-F10** and select "Create Shortcut".

Another, more interesting way to create a shortcut is to use the small icon just to the left of the address bar. This icon represents the URL of the current page. In Internet Explorer, the icon is called a PAGE ICON, while in Netscape, it is called a PAGE PROXY ICON.

(Do you ever wonder if there are people who stay awake at night thinking of these names?)

Take a moment and look at Figures 7-1 and 7-2. I have labeled these special icons so you can see exactly where they are.

Once you know where the page icon is, creating a shortcut to the current page is easy. All you need to do is use your mouse to drag the page icon to the desktop. A shortcut will appear automagically. Try it.

So far, we have talked about creating a shortcut to the current Web page (the one you are reading). As a convenience, it is possible to create a shortcut to a specific link on the current page without having to click on the link and wait for the page to download. Just use your mouse and drag the link to the desktop. This creates a shortcut to the link, rather than to the current page.

For example, say you are looking at a Web page that has weather information. The page contains links to information about particular cities, and you want to create a shortcut to the Web page for your city. Just drag the appropriate link over to the desktop.

hint

Once you create a shortcut, there are several ways to customize it:

To rename an icon, click on it and press the **F2** key. Type the new name and press **Enter**. (Alternatively, you can right-click on the icon and select "Rename".)

To move an icon, use your mouse and drag the icon to a new location.

To delete an icon, click on it and press the **Delete** key. (Alternatively, you can right-click on the icon and select "Delete".)

Saving URLs in a List (Favorites and Bookmarks)

In the previous section, I mentioned there are two ways to save URLs. The first way is to create a shortcut stored as an icon on your desktop. Shortcuts work fine for a small number of URLs, but as you use the Web over a period of weeks and months, you are bound to encounter more than a few Web pages whose URLs you want save, and the best way to do so is by making a list.

All browsers allow you to create and maintain such a list, however, the name of the list and the details of how it works differ from one browser to another. With Internet Explorer, the list is called the FAVORITES LIST. With Netscape, it is called the BOOKMARKS LIST.

A Favorites/Bookmarks list consists of a number of ITEMS. Each item has a name and represents a specific Web page. (Within the item is the URL for that page.) The various items are stored in FOLDERS, which you can organize as you see fit. Thus, you can customize your list to be exactly the way you want it.

When you first use your browser, the Favorites/Bookmarks list will already have some folders and items. These are set up for you by the browser company, but you do not have to keep them. You can delete anything you want and create your own, brand-new list.

The items in the preset list did not get there by accident. They were put there by the browser company to help promote their products and their marketing programs. Netscape, in particular, starts you off with a bunch of Bookmark items pointing to Web sites from companies that have paid Netscape to put them on the list. The Microsoft items are somewhat less commercial, but awfully proprietary.

So don't feel bad about deleting the entire list if you feel like it and building your own from scratch. As one of my readers, you are a thoughtful, imaginative individual with important human needs—not a mindless pawn to be manipulated by big companies and their advertisers.

It is worth your while to spend some time learning how to use and organize your Favorites/Bookmarks list, and to get you started, I am going to explain the most important things you need to know: how to use the list, how to create a new item, how to edit your list, and how to make a backup copy to guard against accidental loss. Although the basic ideas are the same for both browsers, the details are a bit different, so I am going to talk about each browser separately (so just read the section that applies to you).

Before we start, though, I want to give you a hint:

hint

In my experience, if you don't save a URL the first time you see a Web page, you will probably never see that page again. Although you may think you will remember how to find it, you won't. So, if you are looking at a Web page and you feel like you may want to return, don't hesitate to save the URL to your Favorites or Bookmarks list.

Don't worry about saving too many URLs. From time to time, you can edit your list and get rid of the junk.

Internet Explorer: Using the Favorites List

To see the Favorites list, just use your mouse to pull down the Favorites menu. You will see that the list has a number of folders. You can navigate in and out of the folders just by moving your mouse. (Try it.) When you see an item that looks interesting, click on it. The URL for that item will be sent to your browser, which will fetch the appropriate Web page and display it for you.

As an example of what an open Favorites list looks like, take a look at Figure 7-4. It shows a typical Favorites list with a number of folders open. Notice that I have used my mouse to navigate to a particular item (the one that contains the URL for Wendy Murdock's Web page). If I were to click on that item, my browser would fetch that Web page for me.

In this example, I created the folder named "Harley's Picks" as well as everything it contains. All the other folders were created by Internet Explorer automatically when I installed the browser. Here is what they contain:

● **Channels:** This is a collection of various channels to which you may want to subscribe. (A channel is a facility that allows a remote server to send information to your computer automatically. For more information, see the description in Chapter 2, as well as the discussion later in this chapter.)

FIGURE 7-4
A typical Favorites list
within Internet Explorer

- **Imported bookmarks:** When you install Internet Explorer, it checks to see whether Netscape is already installed. If so, Internet Explorer creates a copy of your Bookmarks list and puts it in a folder named "Imported bookmarks". This allows you to switch from Netscape to Internet Explorer without losing the items in your Bookmarks list.

- **Links:** This folder contains the same items that are on the Links bar (see Figure 7-1). In our example, the items are the ones that came with the browser—"Best of the Web", "Channel Guide", and so on—although you can change them if you want.

- **Software updates:** Here you will find items to help you keep your Internet Explorer software up to date.

hint

> When you start to organize your own Favorites list, feel free to remove any of the preset items and folders. Nothing bad will happen.

Creating a new item is easy. Whenever you find a Web page worth remembering, use your mouse to pull down the Favorites menu and click on "Add to Favorites". You will then be shown a dialog box.

If you click on "OK", the item will be saved to the bottom of the Favorites list.

If you want to put the item in a particular folder, click on the "Create In" button, and you will be shown a diagram of all the folders in your Favorites list. To indicate where you want to place the new item, just click the folder of your choice. (If you see a folder with a plus sign [+] next to it, it means there are subfolders. To look at the subfolders, click on the plus sign.)

hint

Whenever you see a Web page you might like to save on your Favorites list, just add it to the bottom of the list.

Later, when you get a spare moment, you can edit the list and process all the new items that have accumulated, deleting them or putting them into folders as you see fit.

To edit your Favorites list, open the Favorites menu and select "Organize Favorites". Your browser will create a new window containing the entire list.

Once you see the new window, you can make any changes you want. The details are straightforward, so I won't go into them here. Just experiment for a while, and it won't be long before you will be able to do whatever you want.

hint

Whatever items you place in the Links folder will automatically appear as buttons on the LINKS BAR (see Figure 7-1). Thus, by organizing this folder the way you want, you can create your own convenient, custom buttons.

The last thing I want to teach you about your Favorites list is how to make an extra copy of it, just in case something goes wrong and you lose the original. (Such a copy is called a BACKUP.)

Internet Explorer stores your Favorites list as a folder in the Windows directory on your hard disk. The best way to make a backup is to use Windows Explorer (the Windows file management program) to make a copy of the entire Favorites folder. My suggestion is to save the backup folder in a completely different location, away from the Windows folder.

If you do not know how to use Windows Explorer to copy folders, ask someone to help you. Don't muck around with your Favorites folder unless you are sure you know what you are doing.

Netscape: Using the Bookmarks List

To start work with your Bookmarks list, you need to display it, and there are two ways to do so. You can either click on the Bookmarks button, or you can pull down the Communicator menu and select "Bookmarks". Try both methods and see which one you like better.

Once you display the Bookmarks list, you will see a number of folders. You can navigate in and out of the folders just by moving your mouse. (Try it.) When you see an item that looks interesting, click on it. The URL for that item will be sent to your browser, which will fetch the appropriate Web page and display it for you.

As an example of what an open Bookmarks list looks like, take a look at Figure 7-5. It shows a typical Bookmarks list with a number of folders open. Notice that I have used my mouse to navigate to a particular item (the one that contains the URL for Wendy Murdock's Web page). If I were to click on that item, my browser would fetch that Web page for me.

FIGURE 7-5

A typical Bookmarks list within Netscape

In this example, I created the folder named "Harley's Picks" as well as everything it contains. All the other folders were created by Netscape when I installed the browser. In particular, the six folders below "Harley's Picks" contain a variety of links that are mostly advertising. The bottom folder, "Personal Bookmarks", is empty. It was thoughtfully provided by Netscape as a place for my personal items. (As you can see, I created my own folder instead: "Harley's Picks".)

hint

When you start to organize your own Bookmarks list, feel free to remove any of the preset items and folders. Nothing bad will happen.

Creating a new item is easy. Whenever you find a Web page worth remembering, open your Bookmarks list and select "File Bookmark". You will then be shown a display of the various folders in your list. All you have to do is choose a folder and click on it. Your browser will create a new item that points to the current Web page, and place that item in that folder.

hint

In this context, the word "File" is used as a verb. When you select "File Bookmark", you are telling your browser: "I would like you to create an item that points to the current Web page, and then file that item in my Bookmarks list."

A faster way to create a new item is to open the Bookmarks menu and click on "Add Bookmark". This saves the URL of the current Web page to the bottom of the list. As a convenience, you can do the whole thing from the keyboard just by pressing **Ctrl-D**. (Think of **D** as "dumping" an item into the list.)

hint

Whenever you see a Web page you might like to save on your Bookmarks list, just press **Ctrl-D**. This will save the URL of the current page at the bottom of the list.

Later, when you get a spare moment, you can edit the list and process all the new items that have accumulated, deleting them or putting them into folders as you see fit.

To edit your Bookmarks list, open the Bookmarks menu and select "Edit Bookmarks". Your browser will create a new window containing the entire list. (As a shortcut, you can make this window appear by pressing **Ctrl-B**.)

Once you see the new window, you can make any changes you want. If you pull down the File menu (within this window), you will see a list of choices of various operations you can perform. The details are straightforward: You can use your mouse to drag an item or a folder to a new location. Just experiment for a while, and it won't be long before you will be able to do whatever you want.

hint

It is possible to create your own convenient, custom buttons on the PERSONAL TOOLBAR (see Figure 7-2). Edit your Bookmarks list, and create a folder containing the items you use most frequently. Now click on the folder, pull down the View menu, and select "Set as toolbar folder".

The items in the selected folder will now appear as separate buttons on the personal toolbar.

The last thing I want to teach you about your Bookmarks list is how to make an extra copy of it, just in case something goes wrong and you lose the original. (Such a copy is called a BACKUP.)

A Netscape Bookmarks list is an ordinary text file containing HTML (just like a regular Web page). To make a backup, all you have to do is save this file to a different location.

To do so, open the Bookmarks menu and select "Edit Bookmarks". A new window will appear containing your Bookmarks list. Once the new window appears, pull down the File menu (in the new window) and select "Save As". Then specify where you want to save the backup file. My suggestion is to save it in a completely different folder, away from the Netscape folders.

Sending a URL or a Web Page to Someone

There will be lots of times when you see a cool Web page that you want to share with a friend (and one of the best things about the Internet is that sharing is easy). At such times, you have two choices: You can send the URL or you can send a copy of the actual page.

My preference is to send the URL. This is because a URL is only a single line of text—much smaller than an actual Web page—and it is more efficient to send the address of a page than the page itself. When someone receives a message that contains a URL, his mail program will recognize the URL as a Web address and will display it as a link. All the person has to do is click on the link and the URL will be sent to his browser automatically. Moreover, if he wants to share the Web page with another person, he can forward the message.

There are several ways to send a URL to someone. The basic idea is simple: Get the URL into a message and mail it. One way is to copy the URL to the clipboard and paste it into a message. (I discuss how to do this in Chapter 6.) My advice is to always copy and paste URLs. Never retype them, because it is too easy to make mistakes.

Internet Explorer (but not Netscape) makes it easy to create a mail message containing the URL of the current Web page. Use your mouse to click on the Mail button and then select "Send a Link". Alternatively, you can pull down the File menu, then select "Send" and "Link By Email".

The second way to share a Web page is to send a copy of the actual page. Doing so is the same as sending a message with rich text. In Chapter 6, I discuss the problems involved when you send rich text. The biggest problem is that you can't count on your recipient being able to view the rich text properly unless he uses the same mail program as you. Thus, I discourage you from sending Web pages rather than URLs.

Having said this, I will now tell you how to do it.

Within Internet Explorer, click on the Mail button and then select "Send Page"; or pull down the File menu, then select "Send" and "Page By Email".

Within Netscape, pull down the File menu and select "Send Page". Alternatively, you can right-click anywhere on the page and select "Send Page".

Setting Your Home Page

Each time you start your browser, it automatically loads a specific Web page. We call this your HOME PAGE. The first time you use a browser, it will have the address of a default home page. However, you can change it to whatever you want. All you have to do is change the home page setting. Here is how to find it:

Within Internet Explorer, pull down the View menu and select "Internet Options". Then click on the General tab (if it is not already showing).

Within Netscape, pull down the Edit menu and select "Preferences". In the Category box, click on "Navigator".

Once you know how to find the home page setting, you can change it as you see fit, so experiment and see what you like best. If you find a home page you really like, there is an easy way to jump to it whenever you want: Just click on the Home button near the top of your browser window.

hint

On the Internet, you *can* go home again (whenever you want).

WHAT'S IN A NAME?

home page

The term "home page" is used in two different ways.

First, your home page is the Web page your browser displays automatically whenever it starts. In this sense, "home" refers to the place from which you begin your Internet explorations.

Second, we use the term to refer to the main page of a Web site: the place from which you start to explore that site. It is common for Web sites, especially the larger ones, to have one main page act as a starting place. Typically, this page—the home page—contains an introduction to the site, navigation aids, news about the site, and so on.

With respect to your default home page, I am going to tell you something interesting that many people don't realize. The location of this page is an extremely valuable commodity. Most people don't bother to change their home page, so each time they start their browser, they see the default home page. Overall, this creates a vast amount of traffic to this page, making for a huge captive audience.

For this reason, both Microsoft and Netscape have created elaborate home pages, which they set as the default for their respective browsers. These home pages provide a variety of links to useful information, as well as a great deal of self-promotion and advertising.

Just how valuable is it to control the default home page for a browser? Netscape uses their default home page (which they call the Netcenter) to sell a lot of advertising and to engage in a great deal of commercial promotion. According to the company's financial reports, the money they made from this site in 1997 accounted for 17.8 percent of their total revenue!

So you can see why the browser companies use their default home pages to create a huge captive audience to whom they can show massive amounts of advertising. My feeling is you should change your home page just on general principles.

Aside from Microsoft and Netscape, other companies have created Web sites to act as generalized starting points for using the Internet. Such Web sites are called PORTALS. Each portal offers a variety of services, the idea being to tempt you into using that particular Web site as your home page.

Changing your home page doesn't mean you lose access to the default pages. Look near the top-right corner of the browser window. Notice the button with the logo of your browser (see Figures 7-1 and 7-2). If you click on this button, you will be taken to the default home page automatically.

Alternatively, if you really like the default home page, you can add it to your Preferences or Bookmarks list. In fact, why not look at *both* pages and see whether you like either one? Each browser is capable of accessing the other company's page.

*I*NTERNET RESOURCE Default Home Pages

```
http://home.microsoft.com/
http://home.netscape.com/
```

If you are not sure what to use as your home page, you may want to use my Web site:

```
http://www.harley.com/
```

This is the easiest way I know to show your friends and family that you are a person of great distinction and excellent taste.

hint

Regardless of what you choose for your home page, my advice is: *Take control.*

Channels

When you enter the URL of a Web page, your browser contacts a Web server and requests the data for that particular page. Thus, data is not sent to your computer until your browser sends a request to the server.

However, there are certain types of servers that can send data to your computer automatically, according to a predetermined schedule. These facilities are called CHANNELS. Channels are particularly useful when you have a need for information that, by its nature, needs to be updated. For example, if you want to look at up-to-the-minute news, or if you enjoy reading a magazine whose content changes regularly. Although many channels are sophisticated, they display the same type of information you might see on a Web page, so don't be confused. Channels are basically the same as fancy Web pages; they are *not* like television channels.

The system that supports channels is called PUSH, and it works as follows. You run a PUSH CLIENT program on your computer. To access a channel, you must put it on a list that is maintained by your push client. To do so, you tell your client that you want to SUBSCRIBE to that channel. (Subscribing to channels is almost always free.) At any time, you can tell your push client to take a channel off the list by UNSUBSCRIBING.

Your push client takes care of all the details automatically. Each channel has a schedule specifying when the information for that channel should be updated. Your client monitors the schedule, and, at the predetermined times, contacts the appropriate servers to download any new information. This means that whenever you decide to look at a channel, the latest information will already be on your computer.

What happens if you turn your computer off and miss an update? The next time your push client starts, it will check the channel schedules and update the channels appropriately.

Although we refer to this system as "push", it is really your client that initiates the channel updates. In other words, the channel servers don't really push—your client pulls. However, since everything is done behind the scenes, it gives the illusion that servers are sending information to your computer automatically.

When you subscribe to a channel, there will be a suggested update schedule. For example, a news channel might be updated every half hour, while a magazine channel might be updated only once a week (when a new issue comes out). However, regardless of what schedule is suggested for a particular channel, you have control, and you can change it whenever you want.

hint

Whenever you want, you can tell your push client to update a channel immediately. This will cause all the latest information from that channel to be downloaded and stored on your computer.

Once a channel is updated, you can access it without having to be connected to the Internet. Thus, if you travel with a portable computer, you can update your channels just before you leave, so you can look at them during your trip. (Just the thing for a long plane ride.)

There are various types of push systems. Each one has its own client and its own types of servers. Unfortunately, they are not compatible with one another.

Within Internet Explorer, channels are referred to as ACTIVE CHANNELS. (Microsoft likes the word "active".) Internet Explorer comes with a built-in push client, so if you have the browser, you are ready to start using channels. To do so, all you have to do is press the Channels button.

Netscape also has a push client, but it is a separate program called NETCASTER. You can download Netcaster for free as part of the Communicator suite of software. Once Netcaster is installed, you can access channels just by starting the program. (From the browser, pull down the Communicator menu and select "Netcaster".)

Other companies have their own push systems. Three that I will mention here are Backweb, Downtown (the company is called inCommon) and Pointcast. To use one of these systems, you need to download and install the appropriate push client. (See Chapter 11 for a discussion of how to download software.)

The following collections of Internet resources will help you get started with channels. First, get yourself a push client if you don't already have one. Then start the client, and look at the list of channels to which you can subscribe. For more variety, visit one of the following channel guides, where you will find a large selection of available channels.

*I*NTERNET RESOURCE Push Clients for Using Channels

```
http://www.backweb.com/
http://www.incommon.com/
http://www.netscape.com/
http://www.pointcast.com/
http://www.microsoft.com/ie/download/
```

*I*NTERNET RESOURCE Channel Guides

```
http://www.phlip.net/
http://www.pushcentral.com/
http://www.iechannelguide.com/
http://home.netscape.com/netcenter/cf/index1.html
```

The Active Desktop

The ACTIVE DESKTOP is a facility created by Microsoft to enhance Windows. (As I mentioned earlier, Microsoft likes the word "active.") The Active Desktop allows you to place active elements—that is, things that change—on your desktop. In particular, you can put channels on your desktop. This allows you to have information from the Web displayed on your desktop and updated regularly.

In addition, the Active Desktop allows you to configure Windows so that Windows Explorer (the file manager program) looks and works a lot like Internet Explorer. The idea is to make things look as if your computer has blended with the Web to form one large, seamless system.

All of this may or may not appeal to you, but you should give it a try to see whether you like it. My experience is that, if you are not used to the Active Desktop, you won't like it at first, especially the changes in Windows Explorer. However, give it a chance—many people like it once they get used to it.

To use the Active Desktop, you must have Internet Explorer installed on your system. If you have Internet Explorer, here is how to see if the Active Desktop is installed. Right-click on an empty part of the desktop, and you will see a list of menu choices. If one of the choices is "Active Desktop", it is installed on your computer.

If you have Internet Explorer, but you don't have the Active Desktop, here is how to get it:

1. Click on the Start button. Select "Settings" and then "Control Panel".

2. Double-click on "Add/Remove Programs". This will start the Windows Add/Remove facility.

3. Scroll down the list of installed programs and click on "Microsoft Internet Explorer". Then click on the Add/Remove button.

4. You will now see a dialog box with several choices. Click on "Add the Windows Desktop Update". Then click on the OK button.

5. This will take you to a Web page where you can download various Internet Explorer components. Select the one for the Windows desktop and follow the instructions.

Once the Active Desktop is installed, you can turn it off and on as follows. Right-click on the desktop. When a menu pops up, place your mouse pointer over the words "Active Desktop" and you will see several choices. In particular, you will see "View As Web Page". This selection acts a switch. You can click on it to turn the Active Desktop off and on. (If you see a checkmark, the Active Desktop is turned on.)

Once the Active Desktop is activated, there are various ways you can customize it. To do so, right-click on the desktop and select "Active Desktop", then "Customize my Desktop".

Safety, Security and Privacy

There are millions of people on the Net—and millions of computers to which you might connect—and you and I have no control over any of them. Using the Internet connects your personal computer to the outside world, and that brings up several important concerns: safety, security and privacy. In this chapter, I will talk about all of these issues, and show you how to make your time on the Net pleasant and comfortable. (In addition, you may also want to take a look at Chapter 6, where I discuss privacy as it relates to email.)

Before we start, let me assure you that safety, security and privacy on the Internet are not big problems. As long as you follow a few common sense guidelines—which we will talk about—there isn't all that much for you to worry about.

Is It Safe to Send Personal Information Over the Web?

SECURITY on the Internet refers to protecting yourself against problems that might arise as you interact with the outside world. In the broadest terms, there are two types of situations in which you might encounter a security problem:

- When data is going out of your computer
- When data is coming into your computer

In this chapter, I will discuss the various possibilities, along with potential problems and how you should think about them. Let's start with a real-life example of what happens when information leaves your computer.

Imagine you are using the Web, and you happen upon the Web site of the Acme Internet Shopping Company. As you peruse the site, you see a stuffed Bill Gates doll on sale for only $29.95. You immediately recognize this as an ideal Mother's Day present and decide to order one right away. To do so, you need to fill out a form on the Web site, so you enter your name, address and credit card number. Let's pretend that you have just finished filling out the form, and are about to click on the "Send" button. What is going to happen when you click that button?

So far, everything you have typed is still on your computer. However, once you click the "Send" button, the information on the form is going to be sent to a remote Web server run by the Acme Internet Shopping Company. At that point, the data will be processed by a program which, presumably, will do whatever is necessary to initiate your order for the stuffed Bill Gates doll.

As long as everything works perfectly, it seems like a good system. After all, it might take you months to find a nearby store with stuffed Bill Gates dolls, and it is certainly more convenient to buy one over the Web. However, before you press that button, you need to ask yourself, "Is it safe to send my personal information over the Web to the Acme Internet Shopping Company?"

This question really has two parts. First, is your personal information secure as it travels from your computer to the remote Web site? Second, do you trust the Acme Internet Shopping Company to use the information responsibly?

The answer to the first question is easy: Your personal information is secure as long as no one intercepts it along the way. In theory, a gang of bad guys with sophisticated equipment, exceptional skills, a lot of time, and enormous motivation might find a way to intercept your data as it travels from your computer to the remote Web site. These guys could make a copy of all your data and then analyze it so as to extract your credit card number, which they would then use for nefarious purposes. However, the chances of all this happening are about the same as you being hit by a meteor right now as you read this. In other words, don't worry—the Internet is secure.

Consider the following analogy. Suppose the Acme Internet Shopping Company takes orders over the phone, and instead of using their Web site, you decide to call them to place an order. Is that really safe? After all, someone could be tapping your phone illegally, listening day and night on the off-chance that, eventually, he might overhear some valuable information. Since such a scenario is technically possible, shouldn't you be afraid to say your credit card number out loud over the telephone?

Of course not. Although it is possible for someone to tap your phone line, it's not likely to happen, so you don't worry about it. I can tell you it's a lot harder to intercept data on the Internet than to tap a phone line, and no one is going to do either one just to steal your credit card number. People who steal such numbers have ways to get them that are far easier and much less risky.

So, the answer to our first question—is your personal information secure as it travels from your computer to the remote Web site?—is yes, so don't worry about it.

But what about the second question: Do you trust the Acme Internet Shopping Company? After all, you *are* sending them your credit card number. This is the same question you need to answer before you place an order with any company you don't know, whether your order is over the phone, by regular mail, or on the Internet. You need to ask yourself whether you feel comfortable doing business with that company.

The nature of the Web is such that you can't judge a company by the quality of its Web site. On the Net, it is easy for a small, one-person business to look like a large, well-established firm. Questionable companies will often design a great-looking Web site that very carefully gives no information about how to reach a real person. So here is my advice.

Never do business with anyone over the Web unless their Web site gives their phone number and postal address. Before you send in your order, call the company on the phone and check them out. At the very least, ask whether the item you want is in stock, confirm the price, and have them explain their refund policy. If you can't get a real person on the phone, or if you get a funny feeling about the company, do not do business with them.

hint

When it comes to sending personal information on the Web, you can assume that the Net itself is safe.

However, you do need to confirm that the people who will be receiving the information are trustworthy.

Unnecessary Security Warnings

From time to time, you may see a warning, telling you that you are about to send data from your computer to the Internet. Typically, this will happen when you have filled out a form of some type and have just pressed a button to send the information. Figure 8-1 shows a typical warning you might see with Internet Explorer. Figure 8-2 shows a similar warning from Netscape. When you see such a warning, you must choose whether or not you want to continue with the data transmission.

FIGURE 8-1
Security warning when sending data with Internet Explorer

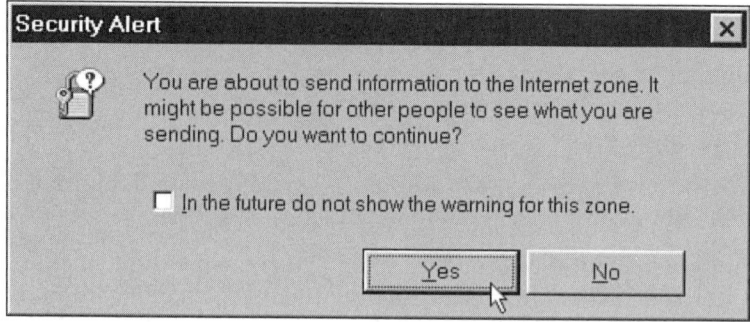

These warnings are useless, and you can always ignore them. In fact, you should select the option within the warning box to indicate that you never want to see these warnings again.

So why are these warnings used in the first place? After much thought, the only reason I can come up with is to limit the legal liability of the browser company. Once Microsoft or Netscape shows such a warning to you, you cannot sue the company and say their browser sent information to the Internet without your knowledge. This is why, if you don't want to see the warnings all the time, you must turn them off explicitly.

Surely no one at Microsoft or Netscape actually believes you need a reminder that information is being sent to the Internet: not after you have just used your browser to fill out a form and have clicked on a "Send" button.

Secure Connections

When electronic commerce started on the Internet in the mid-1990s, the Web was still new, and many people were reluctant to use it for sending personal information, such as credit card numbers. This, of course, was an obstacle to business on the Net, and a number of companies, feeling that a lot of money was at stake, decided to do something about it.

Their goal was to make people feel comfortable about online transactions. To do so, they popularized the idea that what was holding back commerce on the Net was the lack of a completely secure means of data transmission. So, having invented a nonexistent problem, they proceeded to create a solution: a way to encrypt (scramble) data as it is sent over the Web. At the other end, the remote Web site that receives the data automatically decrypts it. When data is transmitted in this way, we say that it is sent over a SECURE CONNECTION.

Once secure connections were available, the Internet industry announced that electronic commerce was now "safe". As long as data is encrypted, they declared, you have nothing to worry about, because even if some bad guys do intercept a data transmission, they will not be able to read it.

Actually, as I explained earlier in the chapter, there is nothing inherently insecure about sending information over the Net, and, in real life, secure connections are never necessary. What you need to worry about is *what* you send, and to *whom* you are sending it, not the safety of the actual transmission.

The reason I mention all this is because your browser has a lot of unnecessary security features. I won't go into them in detail, but I do want to mention them so you won't waste time worrying about silly ideas. Moreover, I do not want you to get a false sense of security.

> *hint*
>
> Technology, no matter how sophisticated, is not a substitute for common sense.

There are a number of systems and protocols used on the Web to provide secure connections. The two most common protocols are SSL and PCT. SSL (Secure Sockets Layer) was developed by Netscape. (A "sockets layer" is a facility used by programs to pass data back and forth.) PCT (Private Communications Technology) was developed by Microsoft.

On occasion, you may see Web pages whose URLs begin with **https** (as opposed to **http**). The extra letter, **s**, indicates that the page uses a secure connection to transmit data. However, if you would like to know when you are using a secure connection, there is an easier way to tell. Just look on the status bar (the bottom line of your browser window).

Within Internet Explorer, a secure connection is indicated by a small picture of a locked padlock on the right side of the bar. When the padlock is not there (most of the time), it indicates a normal connection.

Within Netscape, a secure connection is indicated by a picture of a locked padlock at the far left of the bar. With a normal connection, the padlock is unlocked.

Cookies

As you wander around the Web, have you ever asked yourself, "Can a remote Web server track what I am doing?" The answer is, yes, it can, to a limited extent. Such tracking is done by using what are called cookies.

A COOKIE is data sent by a remote Web server and stored in a file on your computer by your browser. At any time, a Web server (either the same one or a different one) can request a particular cookie, at which time the browser will look in the file, get the cookie, and send it to the server. In other words, cookies are a way for any Web server in the world to store information on *your* computer for later retrieval.

WHAT'S IN A NAME?

A cookie   *is very good expleained*

The term "cookie" dates back to systems that are much older than Windows. In technical terms, a cookie is a small token of data that is passed between two programs in order to relate the current transaction to a later one. Consider the following analogy.

In many parking lots, you get a ticket as you enter, and on the ticket are the time and date. Later, when you leave the lot, you give the ticket to an attendant, who uses the information to tell you how much you need to pay. The parking lot ticket is a cookie.

Nobody knows the exact origin of the word "cookie", but, clearly, it reflects a spirit of whimsy—neatly capturing the idea of a small object that is passed from one program to another. In the Unix operating system, cookies are often referred to as "magic cookies", and it is from Unix that the word "cookie" was appropriated for use on the Web.

In principle, cookies can be used to store just about any type of textual data. In practice, they are usually used to track your identity, your preferences and your actions as you navigate the Web.

Obviously, this is a gross invasion of your privacy. Why, you might ask, would the browser companies build a cookie facility into their products? The answer to this question lies in understanding who are Microsoft's and Netscape's real customers. You and I are not their customers. We got our browsers for free, and no one makes money giving away free software. The real customers are the companies that pay for the server software and the programming tools used to build commercial Web sites. These companies want a way to track what you do on the Web, and that's why Microsoft and Netscape put a cookie facility into their browsers.

This is not to say that cookies are always bad. They are often used to keep track of information in a way that makes your life a bit easier. For example, there is a movie information site called Movielink that I often use to find out the names and times of movies playing in my town. The first time I used Movielink, I entered my zip code, which the Movielink Web server stored as a cookie on my computer. Now, each time I use Movielink, it retrieves my zip code automatically, and shows me information about the movies in my area.

INTERNET RESOURCE Movie Information

`http://www.movielink.com/`

Here is another example. Say that you visit an online shopping site in which you move from one Web page to another, putting various items in your "shopping basket". When you are ready to "check out", the Web server sends you an order form containing a list of all the items you have chosen to buy. How does the server keep track of what you want? By storing cookies on your computer.

In such cases, cookies serve the legitimate needs of commerce. All too often, however, cookies are used to track your movements and your decisions as you use the Web. For example, it is possible for a Web server at a large company to store a cookie documenting what you did when you visited the site. Later, that cookie can be retrieved by any server at the same company. In this way, a company can keep track of you no matter which of their Web sites you use.

Similarly, a marketing company can put up attractive advertisements around the Web in order to induce you to click on them. Once you do, the server to which you connect might show you various types of information in order to gather data about your preferences and habits. This data can be stored on *your* computer, to be picked up later by the Web site of any company that subscribes to that particular marketing service.

So what can you do about cookies? You have three choices:

- You can look upon cookies as a necessary evil and forget about them.
- You can force your browser to ask your permission each time a remote Web site wants to store a cookie on your computer.
- You can tell your browser to never accept cookies on your behalf, and you can delete the cookies you already have.

If you want some control over how your browser handles cookies, there are various settings you can control. Try the different choices, and see what you prefer—you can't hurt anything by experimenting. If you want, you can look at your cookies, or even delete them. The details are different for each browser, so I will explain them separately. Just read the part you need.

Controlling Cookies with Internet Explorer

To change the cookie settings:

Pull down the View menu and select "Internet Options". Click on the Advanced tab. Scroll down to the Security section and look for the Cookie settings.

To look at your cookies:

Internet Explorer keeps two copies of each cookie. The first copy is in your cache (see Chapter 7). The cache consists of a collection of files stored in a directory named **Temporary Internet Files**. This directory lies in the **Windows** directory. That is:

```
C:\Windows\Temporary Internet Files
```

A duplicate of each cookie is kept in a directory called **Cookies**, also within the **Windows** directory:

C:\Windows\Cookies

To get rid of your cookies:

To delete the cookies, use Windows Explorer to delete the cookie files from *both* directories. It is not enough to delete the files in the **Cookies** directory.

hint

It is possible to tell Internet Explorer to clean out the cache for you. (Look on the General tab in the Internet Options.) However, doing so will delete only regular files, not cookies. You must delete the cookies yourself.

Controlling Cookies with Netscape

To change the cookie settings:

Pull down the Edit menu and select "Preferences". In the Category box, click on "Advanced". You will then see the Cookie settings.

To look at your cookies:

Netscape stores all the cookies in a single file named **cookies.txt**. To find this file, look in the directory in which Netscape is installed. You will see a subdirectory called **Users**. Within the **Users** director, lies another subdirectory called **default**. This is where you will find the cookie file. In other words, your cookies are stored in the file:

Netscape-directory\Users\default\cookies.txt

If you have set up more than one User Profile, each user will have his own cookie file within his own subdirectory under **Users**. (It will be obvious when you look.)

To get rid of your cookies:

The cookie file is an ordinary file. You can delete it in the regular manner using Windows Explorer.

hint

If you look inside the cookie file, you may see a warning not to delete the file. Don't worry, deleting the cookie file is completely safe. If the need arises, Netscape will create a new file automatically.

Java and ActiveX

Earlier in the chapter, I said there are two types of situations in which you might encounter a security problem:

- When data is going out of your computer
- When data is coming into your computer

We have already discussed what can happen when data leaves your computer. I would now like to talk about the possible risks of data from the outside world entering your computer and causing a problem.

The term "data" is a general one. It encompasses anything that can be stored on a computer. However, it is important to realize that the only type of data that can damage your computer is data that actively does something (such as a program). Data that just sits there (such as text or pictures) can't hurt you.

A program running amuck on your computer can cause a lot of damage. Such a program might freeze the entire system, modify important settings, or delete a lot of files. A cookie file, on the other hand, might contain information that invades your privacy, but the file itself won't damage your computer. Only a program that is running can damage your computer.

So, when we look at risks from the outside world that can harm your computer, we have to ask the question: Is it possible for a program to enter your computer, without your knowledge, and start running automatically? If so, such a program poses a possible security risk.

Before I can answer this question, I need to digress for a moment and talk about two ideas called Java and ActiveX.

The Web was originally developed as a system to display various types of information. Information is sent from a Web server to your browser. The browser receives the information, and does whatever is necessary to process it for you.

Some years ago, programmers realized that the power of the Web could be increased significantly if Web servers could send more than information to be displayed. If there were a way for a Web server to send a program that would be run on your computer automatically, such a facility could open the door to a lot of cool and useful stuff.

Of course, a system that downloads programs from the Net and starts them running on your computer also opens the door to a massive amount of potential problems. For example, imagine you are using the Web, and you see an advertisement for free money. You click on the ad, and it takes you to a Web site, where the server automatically sends a program to your computer that wipes out all the files on your hard disk.

Such catastrophes do not necessarily need to be the work of an evil mind. Even a legitimate program can have a bug that causes damage accidentally. The point is, if you are going to design a system in which programs can be run automatically on someone else's computer, you have to be very careful.

The programmers who wanted to develop such systems were well aware of these considerations. The first such system, JAVA, was developed by Sun Microsystems and, from the very beginning, was designed with safeguards. (By the way, the name Java doesn't mean anything in particular.)

Java was based on a system that Sun had originally designed for controlling consumer electronic devices such as microwave ovens and telephones. The basic idea is to create small programs, called APPLETS, that are embedded within a larger system. (On the Web, Java applets are embedded within Web pages.) To maintain security, applets can run only within a special operating environment. This environment—called the JAVA VIRTUAL MACHINE—is provided by your browser. The Java system is designed very carefully to ensure that no applet can ever cause a problem on your computer, either on purpose or by accident. Moreover, Java is portable, so that an applet created for one type of computer (say, a PC) can run on another type of computer (such as a Macintosh). In particular, Netscape has licensed Java and put it in their browser.

The design of Java draws a clear line between your computer and the outside world. There is a basic assumption that programs that arrive from the outside world cannot be trusted. Thus, they are allowed to run only in a restricted environment (the Java virtual machine) that sets limits on what the program may do.

At Microsoft, they have a different philosophy. Microsoft (and especially Bill Gates) feels that there should not be a well-defined line between your computer and the rest of the world. You should be able to look at data and programs anywhere, and use them without caring where they are. Within this vision, a program on a computer down the hall (or on the other side of the world) should be as accessible as a program on your own computer.

Thus, when Microsoft wanted their own Web-based facility to download and run programs automatically, they developed two completely different solutions.

First, they licensed Java from Sun Microsystems and created a Java system of their own. Thus, Internet Explorer (as well as Netscape) will run Java applets.

Second, they created a brand new system called ACTIVEX. ActiveX is based on Microsoft's family of programming tools, and is promoted as a richer, more powerful alternative to Java.

Unlike Java, ActiveX programs (which aren't really applets) are not constrained to run within a restricted environment. Thus, they have no limitations and, as such, are the cornerstone of Microsoft's vision that there is no real line between your computer and the outside world. Of course, having no limitations also means that it is possible for an ActiveX program to cause damage to your computer.

Obviously, there is a security problem here. If you can't guarantee that a program is safe, how can you feel comfortable running it on your computer? The answer is, you can't, so there is a clear tradeoff:

- Java keeps its programs safe, but, by doing so, limits their usefulness.
- ActiveX is not safe, but it allows more powerful and more useful programs.

So what did Microsoft do about this? After all, customers—especially corporate customers—are uneasy knowing that every time a person clicks on a link, he might be downloading and running a potentially damaging program.

To reconcile all these considerations, Microsoft created a system of security settings within Internet Explorer that gives you the *illusion* of safety without limiting the power of ActiveX. To me, this is a remarkable achievement—a triumph of marketing and double-talk over rational thought.

Are you intrigued? Read on.

Security Settings in Your Browser

One day, a total stranger walks over to where you are sitting, hands you a cup containing an unknown liquid, and says, "Drink this." He then walks away.

Would you drink the liquid or would you be too suspicious?

Now, suppose your mother offers you a similar-looking drink. Would you be more likely to try it? As far as Microsoft is concerned, the answer is yes, because you trust your mother more than you trust a total stranger.

This is the idea behind the Internet Explorer security settings.

As I explained in the previous section, Java applets are inherently safe, but limited in what they can do for you. ActiveX programs can be much more powerful, but pose a definite security risk. ActiveX, however, is Microsoft's first choice, so, to deal with the uncertainty, they have devised a complex scheme that is implemented within Internet Explorer by a system of security settings.

There is no way to guarantee that any particular ActiveX program is safe. However, you can ask yourself, "Who created the program, and do I trust that person or organization?" For example, if an ActiveX program comes from the Web site of an unknown college student, you might think twice before allowing the program to run on your computer. On the other hand, if a program comes from, say, Microsoft's Web site, you would feel more comfortable about letting the program run on your computer. At least, that's the theory.

To put this theory into practice, Internet Explorer requires you to classify all Web sites as being in one of four different categories, called ZONES. You can then assign a particular SECURITY LEVEL to each zone. Whenever you visit a Web site, Internet Explorer checks to see what zone it is in. Then, based on what security level you have assigned to that zone, the browser knows what to do if the Web site sends an ActiveX program to your computer.

The details, as you might imagine, are appalling, and the whole system is pretty much useless. However, as I said earlier, the system does give the *illusion* of safety, which is not to be sneezed at. In real life, very few programs on the Web actually cause trouble, and, realistically, there isn't all that much to worry about. As such, there is a lot to be said for making people feel more secure.

In case you want to investigate the Internet Explorer security system for yourself, I'll give you a quick summary, and then tell you where to find the actual settings.

The four different zones are as follows:

- **Local Intranet Zone**: This zone contains all the Web sites within your organization's internal network (which doesn't mean much unless you have an organization with an internal network).
- **Trusted Sites Zone**: This zone contains all the Web sites you believe will *not* cause damage to your computer.
- **Restricted Sites Zone**: All the Web sites you believe *might* cause damage to your computer.
- **Internet Zone**: All the Web sites that are not part of another zone.

Your job is to assign a specific security level to each zone. You have four choices:

- **High Security**: Never do anything that could potentially cause trouble.
- **Medium Security**: Warn the user and ask for permission before doing anything that could potentially cause trouble.
- **Low Security**: No warnings, no protection. (Just do it!)
- **Custom Security**: A customized security level, based on selections you make from a large list of confusing choices.

Of course, all of this begs the question, how do you know whether or not a Web site has the potential to cause a problem? Microsoft's solution is to recommend that Web sites use a SECURITY CERTIFICATE, an electronic confirmation that a particular Web site is "secure and genuine".

For example, let's say you are willing to put a particular IBM Web site into your trusted sites zone, as long as you are sure that the site really does belong to IBM. The way IBM convinces you the site is really theirs (and hence, can be trusted) is by obtaining a security certificate for that site. Whenever you go to the site, the IBM Web server sends your browser the security certificate, which your browser can verify automatically.

Are you confused? So is everyone else. My advice is to just ignore the whole thing and hope for the best. The chances of your ever running into a damaging ActiveX program are very low. In fact, I have never met anyone who has had trouble—it's mostly a psychological problem.

If you want to look at the Internet Explorer security settings, pull down the View menu and select "Internet Options". Then click on the Security tab.

If you use Netscape, they have their own, much simpler security settings. To see them, pull down the Edit menu and select "Preferences". In the Category box, click on "Advanced". The security options are above the Cookie settings.

When I was in medical school, I had a good friend named Tim Rutledge who once made a philosophical observation I will never forget. The reason I mention it here is that Tim's comment is the very best advice I can give you about browser security settings:

hint

"When you get serious about bullshit, you're getting into serious bullshit."

Computer Viruses

You have probably heard about computer viruses, but you may not understand exactly what they are. Is a computer virus like a real virus? Computers don't really get sick— or do they?

The answer is, a computer virus is not a real virus. The idea is a metaphor. A computer VIRUS is a small program that is designed to insert itself into a file containing another program. When the second program runs, the virus becomes active. Depending on how the virus is designed, it may or may not cause a problem. Thus, computer viruses are *not* biological organisms. They are small, carefully crafted programs deliberately designed by bad people.

The only way you can get a virus on your computer is to run a program that already contains a virus. Since the largest repository of software in the world is the Internet, it is natural to wonder whether the Internet is a source of dangerous virus-laden programs.

The answer is no. There are hardly any viruses circulating on the Internet, and the chances of your encountering one are small. Personally, I have downloaded more software than I can remember, and I have never even seen a virus. Moreover, I don't know anyone who has ever encountered a virus by downloading programs from the Internet.

There are two important reasons for this. First, as I mentioned, viruses are uncommon. Second, people who run software repositories would immediately remove any program that was found to contain a virus.

The biggest virus problems I know of occur when people use floppy disks that have been in a public computer, such as the ones in a library or in a school. Because so many people bring their own disks to use with public machines, it sometimes happens that such computers have a program containing a virus.

For example, it is common for children to use a floppy disk to bring home a program from a computer at school. They then copy the program to the hard disk on the family computer. This is one way a virus can spread.

What about email? Is it possible for a virus to get to your machine via a mail message? Only if someone sends you a message with an attachment that contains a program, and you run that program. Remember, the only way a virus can be activated on your computer is if you run the program that contains the virus. So, if you want to be completely safe, just don't run any programs you receive by mail. If a friend of yours gets a cool program from the Net, tell him to send you the URL, and you can download the program for yourself.

To help detect and protect against viruses, there are a variety of ANTIVIRUS PROGRAMS available. Such a program will scan all the files on your hard disk, looking for telltale signs of known viruses. Some programs also run in the background, continuously checking for viruses as you work.

Do you need an antivirus program for your home computer? Not if you confine yourself to commercial software and to programs you download from the Net. If so, the chances are slim that you will ever encounter a virus.

hint

If, after reading this section, you are still worried about viruses, the following three precautions (which I mentioned in Chapter 3) will protect you just fine:

- Never use a floppy disk to transfer a program from someone else's computer.
- Never allow your children to bring home floppy disks from school.
- Never run a program that someone has sent to you by email.

On the other hand, there are two situations in which it *is* prudent to install a good antivirus program. First, if you are responsible for computers that are used by many people, such as in a school or in a corporate network. In such cases, there is no way to keep people from using their own floppy disks or accepting programs from other people, so you need to protect the network.

Second, if you have a home PC and you can't get your kids to follow the three preceding rules, an antivirus program can be important. Personally, I lean toward keeping outside floppy disks away from my machine. However, that may not be possible in your home.

*I*NTERNET RESOURCE Antivirus Programs

```
http://cws.internet.com/32virus.html
http://www.davecentral.com/virus.html
http://tucows.tierranet.com/virus95.html
http://tucows.cableinet.net/virus95.html
```

Virus Hoaxes

Far more troublesome than actual viruses are virus hoaxes. Information spreads rapidly on the Internet, and rumors and myths spread fastest of all. A VIRUS HOAX is an erroneous belief that a particular virus (which may or may not exist) is a potential source of trouble. Virus hoaxes spread by mail and on Usenet discussion groups when well-meaning people warn other people about nonexistent problems.

If you have ever received a message warning you about a virus, I can tell you right now the message is wrong. Perhaps it is human nature, but many people are all too eager to believe that forces beyond their control (such as computer viruses) are lurking nearby, ready to swoop down and cause a catastrophe. Unfortunately, too many people are willing to accept such a warning, no matter how unfounded it may be, simply because they don't understand the details.

The most common virus hoaxes purport to describe EMAIL VIRUSES. Such a hoax comes in the form of a message that warns you not to read messages with specific words in the subject line. The warning declares that even the mere act of opening such a message may trigger a virus that will damage your computer. The virus hoax spreads because well-meaning people, who don't know any better, send copies of the warning to all their friends, thus perpetuating the hoax.

In real life, virus hoaxes are far more common (and far more disconcerting) than actual viruses. In fact, some people feel that the real viruses are the hoaxes themselves.

hint

The only way to activate a virus on your computer is by running a program in which the virus is embedded.

It is impossible to activate a virus by reading a mail message.

INTERNET RESOURCE Virus Hoaxes and Myths

```
http://www.kumite.com/myths/
http://www.afcert.kelly.af.mil/hoaxes.html
http://www.icsa.net/services/consortia/anti-virus/alerthoax.htm
```

Children and the Internet

There is an interesting paradox about how we think about children. On one hand, we know that children need supervision and guidance. No matter how grown up they may act, they are not adults. On the other hand, we sometimes treat children as if they are fragile, worrying about them more than we need to.

There is an irony here, because we were all children ourselves at one time. Think back, and I bet you can remember how silly the adults seemed when they worried so much about things that were perfectly harmless. However, as we grow up, our memories fade, and one day we find ourselves having the same types of worries as our parents. Of course, now it is different, because these are *our* children.

So how should you think about the Internet when it comes to your children? Different children have different needs, and you have to do what you think is appropriate. My intention is to give you a few guidelines to consider and then talk a bit about the nature of the Internet, so you can figure out what's best for you and your kids.

Harley Hahn's List of Five Guidelines for Happy Family Internet Usage

1. Learn about the Internet yourself. In particular, learn how to send and receive mail and how to use the Web.
2. Develop a *realistic* sense of what might hurt your children.
3. Spend some time with your children using the Internet together.
4. As your children get older and more responsible, give them time alone to enjoy the Internet by themselves.
5. Set a *few* basic rules to let your children know what you expect from them, and then enforce those rules.

In general, the Internet is a safe place. After all, when your kids use the Net, they are indoors, not wandering around the outside world. Because of the nature of the Net, you do need to show your children how to evaluate information and how to maintain their privacy. However, you do not need to worry about physical danger.

But what about those stories you read in the newspaper? Isn't it true that there was a kid who met an adult on the Internet, who then lured the kid to a real-life meeting in which something bad happened?

Perhaps somewhere in the world, at some time, something like this actually happened, but let me assure you, it's not going to happen to your kids. Millions of children around the world use the Internet every day in perfect safety. The scary stories you see in the newspaper are exaggerated and *extremely rare*.

Actually, what your kids already know about talking to strangers is most of what they need to know about the Internet. Tell them there are certain things they should not talk about (make up your own list) and certain types of people they should avoid.

Just as important, help your children understand that they must protect their privacy. Young children should know they cannot give out a mail address, phone number or street address without asking you first. Some parents do not let their kids fill out any form that requests information until they have shown it to a parent. For example, you may not want your children to fill out surveys that ask for marketing information about your family. Similarly, you might make a rule that your children are not allowed to download any files or programs without your permission.

Explain to your children that the Internet is a place where you really don't know whom you are talking to unless you already know the person in real life. For example, just because someone in a Web chat room says she is a 15-year-old girl, it doesn't mean she really is a 15-year-old girl. It is common, and perfectly acceptable, for your kids to use an alias (pretend name) when they talk to people on the Net.

What really helps is to find time to explore the Net together with your kids. As you use the Net, explain to them that they can't believe something just because they see it on the computer. Young children especially may not understand that anyone can create a Web site with whatever content they want.

Show your children that you expect them to make active judgments about the quality of the information they see. Teach them how to decide whether or not to believe what they read. At the same time, you may also want to talk to them about the massive amount of advertising they are going to encounter, and how they should think about it.

A great way to help your children is to steer them toward Web sites that are suitable for their age level. There are several ways to do so. First, you can spend some time searching for Web sites you like and build your kids a customized Favorites or Bookmarks list (see Chapter 7). You can also trade URLs (Web addresses) with other parents.

With young children, it is best to start with a Web site that has lots of activities for kids their age. If you let them play on their own, take a look from time to time to make sure they haven't accidentally wandered off track.

Similarly, you can introduce your little ones to electronic mail in a gradual fashion. Have them send mail to friends you know, and read the replies together. As your kids get older, you can give them more freedom. Eventually, you can let them send and receive mail on their own, but they should know that you control the computer, and you have the right to look at any mail whenever you want.

If you would like some ideas about Web sites for your kids, I have a few suggestions. First, take a look at my book *Harley Hahn's Internet & Web Yellow Pages* (published by Osborne McGraw-Hill), where you will find lots of Internet resources. In particular, there is a "Kids" section for younger children, and a "Young Adults" section for teenagers. There is also a "Families and Parenting" section just for parents.

Another book you may want to get is *The Internet Kids & Family Yellow Pages* (also published by Osborne McGraw-Hill). This book is written by a friend of mine, Jean Armour Polly (the same Jean Armour Polly who coined the expression "Surfing the Internet"—see Chapter 1.) Jean, also known as "Net-Mom", has filled the book with a large number of interesting Web sites, all of which are safe for children.

Aside from books, another good way to find Web sites for your kids is on the Internet itself. Here are some places to get you started:

*I*NTERNET RESOURCE Collections of Web Sites for Children

```
http://www.yahooligans.com/
http://db.cochran.com/li_toc:theoPage.db
http://www.netmom.com/ikyp/samples/hotlist.htm
http://www.ala.org/parentspage/greatsites/amazing.html
```

Filtering Software and Rating Systems

The very best guardian for a young child is the eye of a parent. However, you can't be everywhere all the time. For this reason, there are various programs you can buy to restrict your children's use of the Internet. These programs are called FILTERING SOFTWARE or CENSORWARE, depending on your point of view. (You will also see a lot of other euphemisms, such as parental control software, content filters, blocking software, and so on.)

There are two basic approaches to such programs. Some operate with a list of forbidden sites called a BLACKLIST. The program works with your browser to make sure your child cannot go to any of the Web sites on the blacklist. Other programs use a WHITELIST of approved sites. In this case, the program allows access to only those Web sites that are *on* the list.

Such programs usually have a number of options that can be changed, but only by someone who knows the password (which you set). Thus, you can turn the various features off and on as you see fit.

The big question, of course, is how does a particular Web site get on a blacklist or a whitelist? Usually, these lists are maintained by the companies that sell the filtering programs, and as you might imagine, there is a lot of controversy. Although filtering software seems like a noble idea, in practice, such programs are restrictive and highly arbitrary. In my experience, parents who understand the Net well do not use these programs.

What works best is to tell your children what is acceptable and what is not, and then enforce the rules. With young kids, it is a good idea to use the Net together. With older kids, you can talk about their Internet activities around the dinner table. In this way, you can keep a careful eye on what your kids are doing, while having the same type of sparkling conversation that you already enjoy about their school activities:

Parent: So, what did you learn on the Net today?
Child: Nothing.
Parent: And what did you do?
Child: Nothing.
Parent: Well, whom did you talk to?
Child: No one.

(You get the idea.)

Another approach to parental control is to use Web site ratings. The idea is to have many Web sites rated in some manner, and to use a browser that looks at the rating for each Web site before loading it. By changing various settings within the browser, you can control access to Web sites based on their ratings.

Toward this end, a set of standards called PICS has been developed for creating rating systems. (PICS stands for "Platform for Internet Content Selection".) Internet Explorer has a built-in facility, called the CONTENT ADVISOR, that lets you control access to Web sites, based on ratings from any PICS-compliant rating service. To access the content advisor, pull down the View menu and select "Internet Options". Then click on the Content tab. For more information about the Web site rating systems, you can check out the following resources:

INTERNET RESOURCE Web Site Rating Systems

```
http://www.rsac.org/
http://www.safesurf.com/
http://www.peacefire.org/
```

However, before you rush into any of this, I want to have a few more words.

The Internet is a public arena used by millions of people all over the world. Some of those people are bad, and some of the ideas on the Net are bad, and it is possible that your children could get hurt in some way by using the Net. However, the chances of anything bad happening are slight, and there is no reason why you can't feel comfortable letting your kids use the Internet.

Filtering software and rating systems may seem like worthwhile ideas, but my advice is to avoid them. Why? With any filtering system, you always have to ask, who is the censor? Who gets to decide for *your* kids what is okay and what is not okay? In my opinion, many (but not all) of the people involved in these schemes are utter fanatics who see the world as a scary place and are doing their very best to scare as many other people as they can.

Moreover, filtering software and rating systems are far from foolproof, and using them can give you a false sense of security. In spite of what the children may think, they do need our guidance—the child who doesn't need rules has yet to be born. However, it is also true that youngsters are far more resilient than we sometimes realize. (Just remember back to when you were a kid.)

Realistically, there is no such thing as a computer program or a ratings system that is going to protect your children. On the Internet, as in other aspects of life, the children who do best are the children who have the help of the people who love them more than anyone else in the world: their parents.

hint

As your children use the Internet, their safety and security are guaranteed by their behavior, your good judgment, and the innate goodness of the Net itself.

Finding Stuff on the Internet

The Internet is one of the best sources of information in the world. There are hundreds of millions of Web pages and tens of thousands of Usenet discussion groups: the products of people all over the world who contribute and share.

However, information is useful only if you can find it, and there is no central directory to the Net. Since no one is in charge, there is no one to organize everything. Nevertheless, once you understand what is out there and how to access it, there are ways to find what you want when you want it.

In this chapter, I am going to show you how it all works by answering one of the most common questions people ask me: How do I find stuff on the Net?

Starting a Search

Searching the Net requires more than skill and knowledge. It requires time to develop your skills. I was once at an Internet conference, when a young man came up to me and asked, "How do I find information about Carnegie Hall?" My answer was, "Practice, practice, practice."

I spend a lot of time finding stuff on the Net. For some years now, I have published a book called *Harley Hahn's Internet & Web Yellow Pages* (the original Internet Yellow Pages). Every year, I revise the book and spend many, many hours looking for information on the Internet, so I guess you could say I search the Net for a living.

I published the first edition of the book in 1992, and, since then, I have watched the Internet grow and change. Although the Internet is much larger than when I started, it is, in my opinion, easier to search than ever before. The main reason is that millions of people are compiling information and creating resources and putting it all on Web sites to share with everyone else.

For example, say you are looking for information about ancient Roman coins. Somewhere on the Net, other people with the same interest have created Web sites devoted to this topic. When you visit these sites, you will find more than information and picture; you will also find links to other Web sites about ancient Roman coins.

When I am searching for something, I often start by looking at the Web pages of people who are fanatics about that particular topic. Such people almost always collect links to related resources.

Search Engines

A SEARCH ENGINE is a program that can search a large database for specific information. On the Web, there are a number of search engines devoted to keeping track of everything on the Web, and you can use them for free. (The companies that maintain them make their money by selling advertising.) Each search engine is different, and you must learn to use it in its own way. As an example, let me talk about two of my favorite search engines, Yahoo and Altavista. Both of these search engines keep track of a great deal of the content on the Web, but they do so in completely different ways.

The YAHOO! search engine seeks to categorize everything on the Web. When you use Yahoo to search for something, the results are given as a list of categories related to that something. If you select a category, you will be shown links to Web pages in that category.

The ALTAVISTA search engine has a different emphasis. Altavista does its best to maintain a copy of all the information on the Web. You use Altavista to look for specific words, and it responds by showing you a list of links to Web pages that contain those words.

The following example should make it clear. If you search Yahoo for my name, **Harley Hahn**, the results look something like this:

Business and Economy: Companies: Books: Computers: Titles: By Author
⬤ **Hahn, Harley**

The first line shows a sequence of categories and subcategories. Following this line is a list of all the resources in the rightmost subcategory. (In this case, there is a link to my Web site.) In other words, Yahoo has classified my Web site as belonging to the category of computer book authors.

In our example, the results were a single item within a single subcategory (perhaps because there is only one Harley Hahn). More often, the results of a Yahoo search will be a list of subcategories, each of which contains multiple items.

Now let's compare this to an Altavista search. If you search Altavista for my name, the results will consist of a very long list of links to all the Web pages in the database that contain the words **Harley** or **Hahn**. Altavista will display this list one page at a time, organized in such a way so that what you want is often near the top of the list.

When I performed this search, the results page contained the following messages:

About 393176 documents match your query.

Word count: hahn: 207363; harley: 377433

The Altavista database is huge, and within that database, there are a lot of Web pages on the Net that contain either the word **Harley** or the word **Hahn** or both. However, the results are organized with the most relevant links first. In this case, the very first item was:

```
1. Harley Hahn's Web Site
    Welcome to the Web site of Harley Hahn, the best-selling
Internet author of all time and the creator of: Harley
Hahn's Internet & Web...
    http://www.harley.com/ - size 7K - 18-Mar-98
```

The first few lines of information (the title and some text) are taken from the beginning of the actual Web page. They are included to help you decide whether or not you want to look at that page. If so, you can click on the title, which is a link to the URL shown in the last line.

I chose these examples because they were simple. Yahoo, Altavista and all the other search engines have far more complex capabilities than what you see here. Every search engine has built-in help information, and you should take the time to read it. Knowing even the basic ideas will make a big difference in the type of results you get, and, ultimately, in your ability to find stuff on the Net.

For reference, here are the URLs for a few of the best search engines. If you have a copy of my Yellow Pages book, look in the section called "Finding Stuff on the Net", where you will find a more comprehensive collection of resources.

*I*NTERNET RESOURCE Search Engines

```
http://www.yahoo.com/
http://www.lycos.com/
http://www.hotbot.com/
http://www.altavista.com/
http://www.webcrawler.com/
```

Techniques for Using a Search Engine

The best way to learn how to use a search engine is to read the help information and practice. To get you started, I will show you a few techniques that should work with most search engines.

First, if you want to search for words that must be together, you can put them within quotation marks. In the previous section, I used Altavista to search for:

Harley Hahn

This caused Altavista to search for all Web pages that contain either the word **Harley**, the word **Hahn** or both, anywhere on the page. It would be more expedient to search for pages that contain the two words **Harley Hahn** together. To do so, put the words in quotation marks in the order you want to see them:

"Harley Hahn"

The better the search criteria, the more exact the results. However, you have to be careful. If you search for this pattern with Altavista, you will get good results. If you use the same pattern with Yahoo, it won't find anything, because Yahoo classifies author names first name last:

Hahn, Harley

Thus, if your first search doesn't find what you want, it is a good idea to try different combinations (especially with Yahoo).

Sometimes the best way to use a search engine is to specify a list of words that are related to what you want. For example, the other day, I wanted to cook pizza for someone who is a vegetarian. To find a suitable recipe, I said to myself, "What words are related to what I need?" I then used Altavista to search for:

recipe vegetarian pizza

The results contained over 400,000 items. Why? Because I asked for all the Web pages that contain any of these three words in any order. To narrow it down, I specified that the words **vegetarian** and **pizza** must be together:

recipe "vegetarian pizza"

This still yielded way too many items, because I was picking up all the Web pages with the word **recipe** regardless of the context.

When this happens, there are two easy ways to narrow the search.

- Use a plus sign (**+**) to indicate you want only Web pages that contain a specific word.
- Use a minus sign (**-**) to indicate you want only Web pages that do not contain a specific word.

So, to narrow down the pizza search, I searched for pages that contained both of my search terms:

`+recipe +"vegetarian pizza"`

Now the search was more successful: There were 256 items. However, as it happens, the person I was going to cook for does not like celery (this is a true story), so I needed to eliminate all the recipes with celery. To do so, I searched for:

`+"vegetarian pizza" +recipe -celery`

I was now down to 205 items. Then I remembered that my friend *does* like artichokes, so I changed the search to:

`+"vegetarian pizza" +recipe -celery +artichoke`

This yielded a nice, manageable set of results: 41 items. Within these items, I was able to find several suitable recipes for vegetarian pizza with artichoke but no celery. Thus, thanks to the Web (and a search engine), I was able to cook the pizza I wanted, and a good time was had by all.

Use the plus or minus signs when you suspect in advance that a particular set of words is going to yield a lot of spurious results. For example, say I was looking for information about the movie *Rocky* made by Sylvester Stallone. I could search for Web pages that contain either **stallone** or **rocky**:

`stallone rocky`

However, since I know I want to eliminate as many irrelevant pages as I could, I would start with a more specific search:

`+stallone +rocky -mountain -bullwinkle`

In this case, by specifying **-mountain -bullwinkle** I am able to eliminate a great many unwanted items.

Usenet Search Engines

In my experience, searching the Web allows you to find what you need almost all of the time. The Web is mature enough that virtually everything you might want is out there somewhere. Sometimes, however, you need more than information. There will be times when what you really need are people's opinions, particularly those having to deal with personal experience and preferences. At such times, you can often get better results by searching Usenet.

Usenet is a global system of thousands of different discussion groups. I described Usenet generally in Chapter 2, and will talk about it in detail in Chapter 12. For our discussion here, there are only a few important points you need to know.

To access Usenet, you use a program called a newsreader. (For historical reasons, Usenet discussion groups are often called "newsgroups", although they don't really contain news.) Anyone with an Internet connection can participate, and millions of people around the world have been doing so for years. There is a Usenet newsgroup for every topic you can imagine, including current events of all types. In fact, I would be inclined to say there is not much that happens in the world that isn't discussed somewhere on Usenet.

Within a specific newsgroup, people from all over the Net post (send in) articles that are seen by everyone who reads that group. Thus, one of the best ways to find help is to post a message to the appropriate Usenet newsgroup, especially if what you need is unusual or timely.

For example, I have a friend who wanted to buy a certain type of camera, but she wasn't sure exactly what to choose or where to buy it. She posted a message asking for help to one of the Usenet photography groups, and a half dozen people sent replies. Over the next few days, she was able to correspond with some of these people by email, and ask more questions as she narrowed down her search. The people who wrote her gave a lot of good advice, and, as a result, she was able to find exactly what she needed at a good price. Moreover, she made a few friends who know a lot about photography, people who would be glad to help her if she has a problem in the future.

hint

No matter what you need to know, there are people on the Net who already know it and would be glad to help you. You can use Usenet to help you find those people.

Earlier in the chapter, I described how I used a Web search engine to look for a recipe for a particular type of vegetarian pizza. Probably, at some time, someone on Usenet discussed a similar recipe. However, the conversation on Usenet is always changing, and the articles are kept for only a short time. Nevertheless, there is a way to search through old articles.

There are a number of Usenet repositories on the Net that are maintained as archives. To search an archive, you use a USENET SEARCH ENGINE. These search engines allow you to access the vast number of articles that have been posted to all the newsgroups around the world. Like the Web search engines, Usenet search engines are free to use. (They are run by companies who make money by selling advertising.)

As with the Web search engines, it can take a bit of time to learn how to use these tools well, so be sure to read the help information. Moreover, your searching will be a lot more rewarding if you understand what Usenet is and how it works, so do take some time to read Chapter 12, where I discuss these topics in detail.

*I*NTERNET RESOURCE Usenet Search Engines

```
http://www.dejanews.com/
http://www.reference.com/
```

Accessing Your Favorite Search Engines Quickly

You will notice that your browser has a Search button. When you press it, you see some type of search facility. (Try it.) At first, having a built-in Search button seems like a nice idea. After all, people do search the Net a lot, so having a single button devoted to searching should be convenient.

Well, it would be, except for one important flaw: The button is actually there as a marketing tool. The browser companies know if they put a Search button in their browser, a lot of people will click on the button. So they use the button to make marketing deals and sell ads based on this captive audience. Thus, when you press the Search button, what you see depends on the current marketing deals made by your browser company. You will not necessarily get the search engine you want.

Pressing the Search button is easy, but I can show you two better ways to make it easy for you to select the search engine you want, when you want it.

First, you can put the addresses of your preferred search engines in your Favorites (Internet Explorer) or Bookmarks (Netscape) list. (I explain how to do this in Chapter 7.) My suggestion is to create a folder named "Search Engines". If you are not sure which ones you like best, start with the ones I mention in this chapter. Put them all in one folder, and experiment over time. Eventually, you will develop your own favorites.

Accessing a search engine (or any Web site) from your Favorites/Bookmarks list is easy, but for sites you visit a lot, you can make things even faster by creating customized buttons. (Again, this is something I explain in Chapter 7.)

With Internet Explorer, you can create custom buttons on the links bar. Simply place items in the Links folder of your Favorites list. Internet Explorer will create a custom button for each of these items.

With Netscape, you can create custom buttons on the personal toolbar. Place the items in any folder you want. Then designate that folder as the "toolbar folder". Netscape will create a custom button for each of these items. (While editing your Bookmarks list, click on the folder you want, pull down the View menu, and select "Set as toolbar folder".)

Figure 9-1 shows custom buttons with Internet Explorer. Figure 9-2 shows the same for Netscape.

FIGURE 9-1
Custom buttons for accessing search engines with Internet Explorer

FIGURE 9-2
Custom buttons for accessing search engines with Netscape

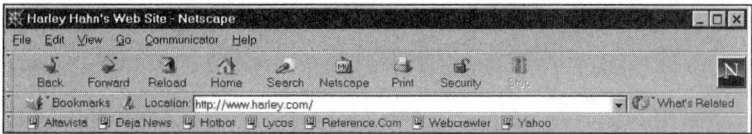

Cool Browser Tricks

Since searching the Web is such a common activity, your browser has a special feature to make the job easier. Wherever you can type a URL, you can also enter a ? (question mark) character followed by a list of search words. When you press **Enter**, your browser will automatically submit the words to a search engine and then display the results. For example, to search for information about cats, you can click on the address bar and type:

? cats

This is shown in Figure 9-3. (Note: With Internet Explorer, you must be sure to put a space after the question mark.)

FIGURE 9-3
Entering a search request into the address bar

If you'd like, you can search for multiple words. For example:

? travel cruise bahamas

However, you can't, as a general rule, use more complex searches like the ones we discussed earlier in the chapter. If you want to use special characters (such as **+** and **-**), you need to use a search engine directly.

When you enter a query directly to your browser, how do you know which search engine will be used? The choice of search engine depends on the current marketing agreements the browser company has with the various search engine companies. As you probably will have guessed, making deals to send your queries to this or that search engine is another opportunity for browser companies to make money. (Are you starting to get a feeling why both Microsoft and Netscape want to control the browser market?)

hint

When typing a search request, you can use either a **?** (question mark), the word **find**, or the word **go**. For example, the following search requests are equivalent:

? cats
find cats
go cats

If you are searching for more than one word at a time, you can even leave out the **?** character. For example:

travel cruise bahamas
? travel cruise bahamas
find travel cruise bahamas
go travel cruise bahamas

hint

As I mentioned in Chapter 7, you can press **Ctrl-O** to display a window into which you can type an address. Well, you can also type a search request into this same window.

Thus, a quick way to perform a simple search is to press **Ctrl-O**, type **?**, followed by one or more search words, and then press **Enter**. For example, try this:

1. Press **Ctrl-O**
2. Type **? cats**
3. Press **Enter**

If you are entering more than one word, you can leave out the **?** character. Try this:

1. Press **Ctrl-O**
2. Type **travel cruise bahamas**
3. Press **Enter**

You can see such a search being initiated in Figure 9-4.

FIGURE 9-4

Entering a search request into an address window

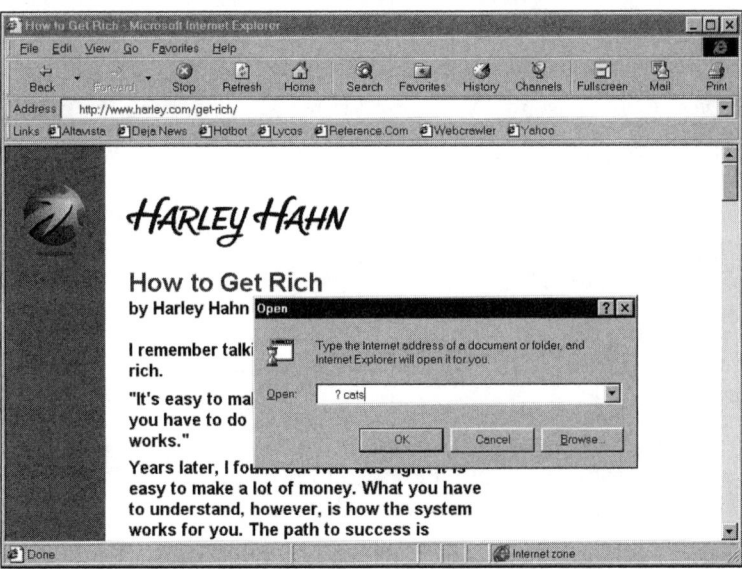

FAQs (Frequently Asked Question Lists)

It was a beautiful, sunny Southern California day. I was sitting on my beachfront patio, watching the intricate patterns of the waves as they lapped lazily on the sand. In the distance, a school of dolphins frolicked playfully, while the pelicans flew in tight formation, skimming down low, barely a foot above the tips of the whitecaps.

I had just finished an early morning surfing session and was relaxing in a comfortable chair, sipping a tall, cool fruit smoothie. I listened to the distant cry of the seagulls as they foraged for their breakfast. I closed my eyes and listened to the rhythmic sound of the waves and the gentle stirring of the wind as it rustled the leaves of the nearby palm trees.

It hadn't been more than five minutes when I felt a shadow cross my chair, and without even opening my eyes, I could tell who it was. Only a cop would walk with that heavy, thumping, flat-footed gait, even on the sand.

"Go away, Lieutenant," I said. "I told you never to bother me before noon. Why aren't you off catching criminals somewhere?"

"Aw... why do you have to be like that? You know we always cooperate with you. Why can't you help us out once in a while?"

"Because I don't like cops, especially dumb cops, and especially in the morning. What do you want? I assume you didn't come all the way to the beach just to get a suntan."

"They told me that someone named the Colonel has the whatcha-ma-hoosers."

"The what?"

He pulled a small beat-up notebook out of his pocket, and flipped through a couple of pages. "The FAQs," he said.

I sat bolt upright in my chair and took off my lime-green sunglasses. "The Colonel's got the FAQs? If that's true it means trouble for you. Lots of trouble. How did it happen?"

The Lieutenant produced a stained white handkerchief and wiped his brow. He was sweating profusely. "I don't know, but if Inspector Babin finds out, I'll be back pounding the street within a week. What are these FAQ things anyway?"

"How much do you know about finding information on the Internet?" I asked.

"The regular stuff, what they teach in the Academy. But I never heard of FAQs."

I lay back in my chair and closed my eyes. "A FAQ," I began, "is a Frequently Asked Question List. Years ago, people who used Usenet noticed that newcomers always seemed to ask the same questions. For example, whenever people join, say, the cat discussion group, they ask the same basic questions about cats.

"So, in many Usenet groups, someone would prepare a list of all the frequently asked questions along with the answers. This list, a FAQ, would be posted to the group regularly, as well as to one or two special groups used for periodic postings. Over time, a great many FAQs were written dealing with many, many topics.

"Today, there are hundreds of different FAQs, just from Usenet alone. As a matter of fact, when I am looking for information, I often search for a FAQ from a related Usenet group. For example, if you wanted some information about cats, you could check to see whether the cat discussion group had a FAQ. If so, there is a good chance that what you need would be in the FAQ."

The Lieutenant thought about it. It took him a few minutes. Thinking was not his strong point. "So how do you find a FAQ when you need one?"

I laughed. "Don't you learn any of this at the Academy? What do you do, ride horses all day long?"

He snorted like a bulldog choking on a bone.

"There are several ways to find a FAQ," I continued. "First, there are Web sites that act as FAQ repositories. You can check those, or you can use a search engine to look for a FAQ related to the topic you want. For example, to find a FAQ about cats, you could search for:

`+cats +FAQ`

"Alternatively, you can use your Usenet newsreader and look in the appropriate discussion group. As I told you, FAQs are posted regularly to the related groups. If you know the name of a discussion group, that's always a good place to look for a FAQ. For cats, that would be **rec.pets.cats**.

"Another group to check is **news.answers**. This is a special Usenet group to which people post copies of all the FAQS and other periodic Usenet postings. When you look in **news.answers**, you'll see all kinds of FAQs. Sometimes I look just for fun, to see what's there.

"And, of course, you can use one of the Usenet search engines. That's often the fastest way to find a FAQ and get the information you need."

The Lieutenant nodded. "I see. But what does that have to do with the Colonel?"

"The idea of a FAQ," I answered, "has proven to be very popular. People make up FAQs on all different topics, not just those associated with Usenet groups. For example, I have a FAQ on my Web site to answer the most common questions people ask me.

"Now, I happen to know that for the last six months, Inspector Babin has been working on a set of FAQs about police procedures and tracking down criminals on the Internet. These FAQs are highly confidential and were never supposed to leave your internal computer network. Just before he left for Guatemala, he encoded everything. Evidently, the Colonel has found a way to break into your system and decode the files."

"So, can I find the Colonel?" The Lieutenant was really beginning to sweat now. "Can you help me get back the FAQs before it's too late?"

"The Colonel is a very talented hacker in the pay of a foreign power. Fortunately for you, we are dealing with a highly secretive person who moves slowly and deliberately. Chances are, yes, if we find the Colonel quickly, we can get the FAQs back before it is too late."

"So what should we do?"

"Hold on." I went inside and used my high-speed connection to make a few fast searches on the Net. "You're in luck," I told the Lieutenant. "I think I know where we can find the Colonel. Let's take my car."

We jumped into the red BMW 328i, and in twenty minutes, we pulled up outside a nondescript gray building. Fifteen seconds later, we were knocking on the door of #127.

"Better call for a patrol car and then get your handcuffs out, " I said.

We heard the sound of gentle footsteps and, a moment later, the door was opened by a ravishing ash blond woman with a set of curves that could cause a traffic jam in the Gobi Desert. She was wearing a black and gray skin-tight outfit that accentuated just about every natural resource in her collection. Her eyes were a chilled blue, the color of the ocean on a winter afternoon, and her plump crimson-lined lips were twisted upward, in a shallow, half-smirking smile. If she was surprised, she didn't show it.

"Lieutenant," I said, "may I present Colonel Valerie Babushka." I walked into the room and picked up a disc from the table. "And here, if I am not mistaken, are the missing FAQs."

She tried to run, but the Lieutenant had his own ideas. It was the work of a moment for him to produce the handcuffs, clamp them over the Colonel's thin, feminine wrists (from which I caught just a hint of fragrance of *chypre*), and hustle her out the door.

I threw the disc to the Lieutenant. He looked at me gratefully. "The entire department," he said, "is in your debt."

The Colonel looked up at me, pouting. "You're a good guy," she said. "Can't you help me? Without your expert testimony, they haven't got a case. Couldn't we make a deal?"

"Sorry, sister, but you play too rough for me. You used Sammy to get the FAQs, but when he wanted more than you agreed on, you hired Starkwell to bump him off. And when Starkwell wouldn't play along, you took care of him yourself that night with the dwarf and the one-eyed harmonica player. You thought you could get away with it then, and you think you can play me for a sap now. Well, you can't. You were just about to skip town, to sell the disc to the Little Nipper and stiff your own people, weren't you?"

At the mention of the Little Nipper, her blue eyes grew wide with fear and her mouth quivered. "I don't know what you're talking about," she said.

I motioned to the Lieutenant and pointed at the police car which had just driven up. "Take her in," I said. "I'll catch up with you later. "

As the car started, she began to panic. "Look," she said, "it isn't too late. We can still make a deal. What do you need? I'll give you anything you want."

The color of her eyes changed to a deeper, more magnetic blue, and her pupils widened. Her mouth took on a wry, vulnerable smile as she raised her carefully manicured eyebrows like two question marks. As I watched the car pull slowly away from the curb, the nearby jacaranda trees cast a pattern of bar-like shadows over her face, and her expression changed to a silent and fearful plea for help.

She twisted her body toward me and leaned out the window. "Surely, there must be something I can give you. Isn't there anything you want? Anything at all?"

"Just the FAQs, ma'am," I said, as I pulled down my lime-green sunglasses, slipped into my red BMW 328i and drove off into the warm, California sun.

INTERNET RESOURCE FAQs (Frequently Asked Question Lists)

```
http://www.faqs.org/faqs/
http://familiar.sph.umich.edu/faq/
http://www.cs.ruu.nl/cgi-bin/faqwais/
http://www.lib.ox.ac.uk/search/search_faqs.html
http://www.cis.ohio-state.edu/hypertext/faq/usenet/➥FAQ-List.html
```

Web Rings

A WEB RING is a collection of Web sites organized into a loop. From any Web site in the ring, you can follow a link to move forward to the next site, or a different link to move backward to the previous site. If you keep moving in one direction, you will eventually traverse the entire ring and end up where you started.

The idea behind Web rings is to make it easy to visit a group of related Web sites. There are literally tens of thousands of Web rings devoted to a variety of subjects:

movies, computers, sports, health, hobbies, pets, and so on. A popular topic will have many different rings; a more esoteric topic will have only a single ring. A typical Web ring might have 10 or 20 Web sites, although many rings are larger, some with well over a hundred sites.

The Web ring system is organized by a group of people who manage a central Web site containing a catalog of the various rings. They also maintain the software that makes the whole thing operate. The content of the rings, however, consists of hundreds of thousands of regular Web sites created by individuals around the Net.

If you have a Web site, it is free to have it become part of an existing Web ring. Similarly, anyone is allowed to start a new ring, which is also free. Each Web ring is administered by a volunteer called a RINGMASTER, usually the person who started the ring. He or she will maintain a master list of the Web sites in the ring and ensure that the links stay intact as various sites join and drop out. The ringmaster will also build up the ring by inviting people to add new sites.

I like Web rings because they are useful for finding information. The best way to do so is to start at the main Web ring site (see the following), where you can search for rings devoted to a particular topic. Once you find such rings, you can check the individual Web sites for what you need.

One caveat: There are a great many Web rings and not all of them work properly. Remember, the rings are maintained by volunteers, so don't be disappointed if you encounter a link that doesn't work. Just try another site, or go back to the main Web site and look for another ring.

*I*NTERNET RESOURCE Web Rings

    `http://www.webring.com/`

An Approach to Searching the Net

In this chapter, I have discussed a variety of different tools and techniques you can use to find information on the Net. However, tools and techniques take you only so far. In my experience, the best Internet researchers develop a feeling for the Net and an innate sense of how to approach a problem. To help you develop a style of your own, I have a few final hints for you.

1. **If you have a copy of my book *Harley Hahn's Internet & Web Yellow Pages*, use it as a starting place.**

   Every year, as I revise the book, I look for the best items I can find in each category. I particularly look for resources that will lead you to other resources. I often use the book myself as a shortcut when I need to find something fast.

2. **Pick at least two different search engines and learn how to use them well.**

   Search engines are complex tools and help you in many ways if you know how to ask for that help. Each search engine is different and has its own strengths and weaknesses. The more you use them, the better they will work for you. Take time to read the help information and experiment with different types of searches.

3. **Become familiar with Usenet and how it works.** (See Chapter 12.)

   The strength of Usenet lies in the millions of people who participate in the discussion groups. There will be times when you will find the help of other people invaluable, so it is a good idea to learn about Usenet now. Once you are familiar with Usenet, spend a little time with the Usenet search engines. They are valuable tools that will often help you find what you need when all else fails.

4. **The more you know about your topic, the easier it is to find what you want.**

   If you are looking for information about which you are not particularly knowledgeable, it is often a good idea to start by looking up some of the basic facts and terminology. This helps you in two ways. First, you will be able to think of better search words. Second, when you do find information, you will more likely be able to make sense out of it. The Net covers a lot of topics, but in many areas, there is a significant paucity of introductory material.

   Preparing for a search is especially important if you are a student. The Internet is a great place for research, but it is not a substitute for the library. I can tell you that, although I search the Internet for a living, I have over 40 different reference books on my bookshelf, and, generally speaking, the information in my books is more reliable.

5. **Ask other people for help.**

   If you find a Web site that is close to what you want, you can send a polite note to the person who maintains the site asking for help. Most people who create Web sites are willing to help people with similar interests.

   However, don't be disappointed if you do not get an answer. Some popular Web sites take a lot of work to maintain, and there isn't always time to answer every message, especially when someone receives a lot of mail.

6. **Learn to search creatively.**

   The best researchers learn to be creative in how they look for something. If your first search doesn't return what you want, change the search words and try again. You will often find that you need to slowly close in on your target. However, with practice, you will become faster. Some of my researchers are so fast that just watching them is an awe-inspiring experience. You would not believe how quickly they can break an idea into parts, and try various combinations, one after the other, until they get what they want.

My goal is to teach you more than how to use search engines, FAQs and Web rings. What I want is for you to begin to think in a new way. There is no central Internet administration, but that does not mean there is no order. The information on the Net (and the Web in particular) tends to organize itself in certain ways that you can teach yourself to understand. The Internet has a rhythm, and once you tune into this rhythm, you will almost always be able to find whatever you want, whenever you want it.

hint

Give a man information about a fish, and he will be satisfied for a day. Teach a man how to find information about fish on the Internet, and he can satisfy his needs for a lifetime.

Plug-Ins and Controls

On its own, your browser can do a lot. However, there are ways to enhance your browser that can expand its power enormously.

In this chapter, we will talk about plug-ins and ActiveX controls, two types of tools that allow a plain, ordinary browser to do just about anything it is possible to do. We will also discuss the incredible amount of innovation such tools bring to the Net, along with examples you can try for yourself.

To lay the groundwork for understanding plug-ins and ActiveX controls, I am going to start by answering a basic question:

How does your browser recognize different types of data?

File Types and Extensions

When you click on a link that points to a Web page, your browser contacts the Web server for that page. The Web server then sends your browser a number of files containing the various parts of the page. The main file is the one that contains the text and description of the page, written in HTML (hypertext markup language). If the page has frames (see Chapter 7), each frame will also have its own HTML file. In addition, every picture, every graphic, and every separate element is sent in a file of its own. Your browser's job is to take all these files, put them together into a single Web page, and display that page on your screen.

Your browser does not wait for all the files before starting to display the page. The main HTML file is displayed as soon as it arrives, while the other files (pictures, usually) are displayed, one by one, as they become available. When a connection is fast and all the files arrive quickly, it may look as if the entire Web page was received at the same time. However, when a connection is slow, you will see the Web page being built before your eyes, one piece at a time. For instance, it is common for the text of the page to be visible, while you are still waiting for the pictures to arrive.

hint

As a Web page loads, look at the status line (at the bottom of the browser window), and you will see various messages as each file arrives in turn.

Web pages can contain different types of data: HTML, pictures, sounds, video, and so on. For this reason, it is important that, when a file arrives from a Web server, your browser be able to tell what type of data is contained within that file.

In Chapter 4, I explained that every file name has a suffix called an extension that indicates the type of data contained in that file. For example, if you see a file named **harley.html**, you know it contains HTML (that is, a Web page) because you see the

html extension. If you see the file **harley.jpg**, you know it contains a picture, because of the **jpg** extension.

The table in Figure 10-1 (copied from Chapter 4) shows a list of file extensions and what they mean. There are many more extensions in use than you see in this table, but these are the most common ones on the Web.

Figure 10-1: The most common file extensions used on the Web

Extension	Pronunciation	Meaning
html	"h-t-m-l"	Web page
htm	"h-t-m"	Web page
asp	"a-s-p"	Web page generated in a special way
gif	"giff" or "jiff"	Picture stored in GIF format
jpg	"jay-peg"	Picture stored in JPEG format
wav	"wave"	Sound/music file
txt	"t-x-t" or "text"	Plain text
zip	"zip"	Compressed collection of files
exe	"e-x-e" or "exy"	Executable program

hint

Within a file name, the **.** (period) character is pronounced "dot".

Thus, the name **harley.html** is pronounced "harley dot h-t-m-l". The name **harley.jpg** is pronounced "harley dot jay-peg".

File extensions are used by every program, not just by browsers. In fact, file extensions are so important that Windows keeps a master list. Each item in the list describes a particular type of data, its file extension, and the name of the program that handles that type of data.

To see the master list of file types, start the Windows Explorer program. Pull down the View menu, select "Options", and then click on the File Types tab. Within the box named "Registered file types" you will see a long list. Take a minute and scroll through the list just to see what's there.

This list is important because whenever you need to do something with a particular file, Windows must be able to know which program handles the type of data contained in that file.

For example, say you are using Windows Explorer and you double-click on a file named **harley.html**. (This tells Windows you want to "open" the file.) Windows looks at the extension and then checks the master list of file types to see which program processes **html** files. In this case, it would be your browser, so Windows launches the browser program (if it is not already running) and sends it the file **harley.html**.

Can you see how powerful this system is? Windows can figure out what to do with any type of data simply by looking up the file extension in the master table and launching the appropriate program.

As you use the Web, your browser has similar responsibilities. Every time a file arrives from a Web server, your browser must figure out how to process that file. First, your browser looks at the extension to see what type of data is in the file. Certain types of data can be handled internally by the browser itself, for example, **html**, **gif** and **jpg** files. Other types of data (and there are many other types) require the use of a separate program.

Thus, your browser needs its own master list of file types, in order to be able to look up an extension to find out which program should be used to process the data in a particular file.

For example, files with an extension of **mov** contain Quicktime movies (short movies that use the "Quicktime" format developed by Apple Corporation). On its own, a browser cannot display **mov** files, so whenever such a file is encountered, the browser must call upon another program to process the data.

Internet Explorer uses the same master list as Windows, which you can look at in the manner I described previously.

Netscape uses its own master list based on the Windows list. To look at the Netscape list, pull down the Edit menu and select "Preferences". In the Category box, look under "Navigator" and click on "Applications". If you do not see anything under "Navigator", click on the plus sign (**+**).

Plug-Ins

All browsers need auxiliary programs to process the various types of data the browser cannot handle by itself. Netscape and Internet Explorer use different approaches, but, regardless of which browser you use, I want you to understand both systems because they are both important.

Let's start with Netscape.

The Netscape browser is designed so that any programmer can extend its capabilities by creating a program called a PLUG-IN. The job of a plug-in is to process a particular type of data that the browser cannot handle on its own. For example, I mentioned earlier that browsers cannot process a file in Quicktime format. If you want to look at such files, you need a Quicktime plug-in. The idea of plug-ins is important, because it encourages people to create new Web-based products and services. Here is an example.

In 1995, the RealNetworks company (then called Progressive Networks) developed a new technology to send audio over the Web. At the time, listening to audio over the Web was a slow, frustrating experience. Audio is stored in sound files, and an entire file had to be downloaded before you could begin listening. In the days of slow Internet connections, this could take a long time.

RealNetworks developed a system, called RealAudio, in which you could start listening to the sound as soon as the beginning of the file reached your computer. While you were listening, the rest of the file would be transferred behind the scenes. Not only did this make listening to audio a lot more pleasant, it opened the door to continuous audio broadcasting, such as listening to a radio station. This whole idea is called STREAMING.

RealNetwork's main products were the RealAudio servers, which they hoped companies would buy in order to transmit audio over the Web. Of course, no one would buy a RealAudio server unless there was a way for people to listen to streaming audio. Since this capability was not built into the browser, the company created a RealAudio plug-in and gave it away free. As a result, RealAudio became a successful product.

The company later expanded their product line by creating new ways to broadcast sound and video, as well as new plug-ins. To this day, they still give away a free plug-in (now called RealPlayer, because it combines audio and video). They also sell an enhanced version of the plug-in for people who are willing to pay for more features.

The fact that the power of a browser can be augmented by plug-ins is responsible for a great deal of innovation on the Web. There are now more than a hundred plug-ins (almost all of which are free), providing many different services and features. Later in the chapter, I'll give you the URLs of some Web sites that act as plug-in repositories. I will also give you a list of some of the more interesting plug-ins in case you want to experiment.

WHAT'S IN A NAME?

plug-in
helper application

In the world of Netscape, most programs that augment the capabilities of the browser are called plug-ins. However, you will sometimes see some of these programs referred to as HELPER APPLICATIONS.

A plug-in is an adjunct to the browser that usually (but not always) does its work within the original browser window.

A helper application is a completely separate program that usually (but not always) does its work in a separate window.

In practice, the distinction between plug-ins and helper applications is not so important. I mention it only because when you see the term "helper application" (or "helper") I want you to know what it means.

ActiveX Controls

In the world of programming, a CONTROL is a self-contained program that can be used as a component within another program. Each control performs a specific function. This allows a programmer to use various controls as building blocks.

For example, let's say you are designing a program that, under certain conditions, must display a dialog box to ask the user a question. Instead of programming this yourself, you can simply use a standard dialog-box control. Conceptually, you just plug the control into the program wherever you need it.

In Chapter 8, I discussed ActiveX, a programming system based on Microsoft's family of programming tools. ActiveX is a rich system that can be used to create all types of programs. In particular, programmers use ActiveX to create controls to enhance the built-in capabilities of Internet Explorer. In other words, Internet Explorer uses ActiveX controls the way Netscape uses plug-ins (although the technical details are a lot different).

hint

The idea of plug-ins was developed by the Netscape company. However, Microsoft has designed Internet Explorer so as to be able to use Netscape plug-ins (a fact that most people do not know).

This means that, if you are an Internet Explorer user, you can use all the same plug-ins as the Netscape users. However, they cannot use ActiveX controls, because Netscape does not support ActiveX.

technical hint

On the Web, ActiveX controls are used to provide the same functionality as Netscape plug-ins and Java applets. However, because of their unrestrained power, it is possible for an ActiveX control to cause damage.

A Java class is interpreted byte code that runs within a "sandbox of functionality" provided by the Java virtual machine. The sandbox limits what a Java class can do, which (in principle) prevents it from causing damage.

Installing Plug-Ins and ActiveX Controls

Installing plug-ins is easy, and installing ActiveX controls is even easier. Let's start with plug-ins.

The best idea is to not worry about installing a plug-in until you need to. Use the Web as you always do, and, one day, you will encounter a new file type that your browser cannot handle. When that happens, you will see a message telling you that you need a plug-in. (Figure 10-2 shows a typical message.) Click on the "Get the Plug-in" button. You will be taken to a Web page from which you can download the plug-in.

FIGURE 10-2
A typical message telling you to get a plug-in

Sometimes, you will visit a Web site that has a notice telling you that you should have a particular plug-in to use some of the features on that site. In such cases, there will usually be a link for you to follow to get the plug-in.

You will usually download the plug-in from the Web site of the company that makes the plug-in. Such Web sites are sometimes designed poorly, and you may have to root around to find the download page. Don't be discouraged if you jump to a Web site to fetch a plug-in, and you can't find the place to start the download. Keep looking, it's there somewhere.

hint

Some companies force you to fill out a form with your name and mail address before they allow you to download a plug-in. You should *always* use a fake name and mail address to protect your privacy. (See the discussion in Chapter 7 regarding how to keep your mail address private.)

The program that processes the form checks to see whether your mail address looks real. Thus, in order to fool the program, you will probably have to type a fake mail address with the same format as a real address (such as **a@a.com**).

Eventually, you will click on a link that will start the download process. We will talk about downloading and installing programs in Chapter 11, so I won't go into the details here. Basically, you copy an installation program to your computer, and then you run the program. Plug-ins are particularly easy to install because the installation program figures out where to put the plug-in, so you usually don't need to make any decisions.

With Netscape, plug-ins are installed in a directory called **Plugins** within the browser's **Program** directory. If Netscape was installed in the standard location, the plug-ins will be found in:

C:\Program Files\Netscape\Communicator\Program\Plugins

With Internet Explorer, plug-ins are installed in a **Plugins** directory within the main browser directory. If Internet Explorer was installed in the standard location, the plug-ins will be found in:

C:\Program Files\Internet Explorer\Plugins

As I mentioned earlier, Internet Explorer will use Netscape plug-ins. Moreover, Internet Explorer is smart about finding them. If you have both browsers installed on your computer, Internet Explorer will automatically look for plug-ins in the Netscape directory as well as in its own directory.

Installing ActiveX controls is even easier. Whenever Internet Explorer encounters a resource which requires a control you don't already have, you will see a message like the one in Figure 10-3. All you need to do is click on the "Yes" button, and the control will be downloaded and installed on your computer automatically.

If you would like to see all your Web-related ActiveX controls, look in the following directory:

C:\Windows\Downloaded Program Files

FIGURE 10-3
Dialog box asking to download an ActiveX control

hint

Within Netscape, you can display a list of all your plug-ins by pulling down the Help menu and selecting "About Plug-ins".

Alternatively, you can type **about:plugins** into the address bar, the place where you normally would type a URL. (Most people don't know this.)

hint

Here is an easy way to make some money. Take a laptop computer into a bar and look for a group of people who are talking about browsers. Stand next to them and, at an opportune moment, announce that you will bet them that they cannot make Netscape display a list of all the installed plug-ins.

There will always be one wisenheimer who will smirk and take the bet. Turn on your computer and start Netscape. The wisenheimer will pull down the Help menu and select "About Plug-ins".

Do your best to look disappointed, and offer another bet that he cannot do the same thing without using the mouse. Tell him you deserve a chance to win back your money.

The wisenheimer will take the bet. He will then press **Alt-H** to pull down the Help menu, and use the **Down** key to select "About Plug-ins".

Pay the money, but be sure you look very disappointed. Then, in a voice of desperation, offer to bet them that they cannot display the plug-in list without using the mouse or the **Alt** key. When no one offers to take the bet, call them weenies, and say you are willing to bet double or nothing that *you* can do it.

Once they take the bet, press **Ctrl-O** (to bring up an address window), type `about:plugins`, and press **Enter**.

Cool Things to Do with Plug-Ins

A tremendous amount of innovation on the Web is based on plug-ins. However, you can't really appreciate all the creativity until you see (and hear) it for yourself.

Here are some plug-in resources I would like you to try. Each of these extends the power of your browser in important ways, and by the time you finish experimenting, you will appreciate how much more there is to the Web than simply clicking on links and reading.

hint

You don't have to install all the plug-ins—one from each category is enough. Most browsers come with a few plug-ins, so you may already have a few of these installed.

Streaming Audio/Video: These plug-ins use streaming (discussed earlier in the chapter) to allow you to access all kinds of audio and video, including radio stations, continuous music, prerecorded presentations and live events. The Internet does not have regular broadcasting (like cable TV), because the technology is a lot different.

However, there is a lot out there. Once you start to look around, you will find a variety that does not exist in the world of commercial radio and television.

INTERNET RESOURCE Streaming Audio/Video Plug-Ins

```
http://www.microsoft.com/ntserver/netshow/download.htm
http://www.real.com/products/player/downloadrealplayer.html
```

VRML: Virtual Reality Modeling Language (VRML) is a system that allows people to create imaginary 3-D environments. (In this sense, the word VIRTUAL refers to objects and experiences that exist only on the Net.) Such an imaginary environment is called a VRML WORLD.

Within a VRML world, you move in three dimensions through imaginary landscapes, structures and settings. If you enjoy being creative, you can learn how to build your own virtual domains for other people to visit. Many VRML worlds are multiuser, and when you are not exploring or building, you can spend time talking to other people. VRML worlds are good places to make friends, and once you do, you can collaborate with your friends to add new features to that particular world.

hint

The word VRML is pronounced in two different ways: either as four separate letters, "V-R-M-L", or as the single word "vermal".

INTERNET RESOURCE VRML Plug-Ins

```
http://www.microsoft.com/vrml/
http://cosmosoftware.com/download/player.html
http://www.intervista.com/cgi-bin/download.pl
```

Multimedia: There is a lot you can do with sound, images and animation, and there are a lot of people doing it on the Web. With these plug-ins, you will be able to look at video clips and animation, as well as many types of special effects.

*I*NTERNET RESOURCE Multimedia Plug-Ins

```
http://www.apple.com/quicktime/download/
http://www.macromedia.com/shockwave/download/
http://www.microsoft.com/ntserver/netshow/download.htm
http://www.clubvdo.net/store/products/vdonet/vdolive_player.asp
```

Music: There is a great deal of music waiting for you on the Web. These plug-ins provide a high-quality facility for listening to music on your computer. (Of course, your computer must have a sound card and speakers.) The Web has a wide variety of prerecorded music, including many original compositions, and these plug-ins help make it all available to you. In particular, there is a great deal of music available using the MIDI format.

*I*NTERNET RESOURCE Music Plug-Ins

```
http://www.liveupdate.com/dl.html
http://www.headspace.com/beatnik/plug-in/
```

360-Degree Photos: Imagine you are on a mountaintop, surrounded by a breathtaking view. As you slowly turn in a circle, enjoying the full 360-degree experience, you realize that there are so many things you just can't appreciate within the small field of view of a regular-size photo. "Why," you ask yourself, "can't someone invent a way to make 360-degree photos?"

Well, someone has, and they are on the Web now.

*I*NTERNET RESOURCE 360-Degree Photo Plug-Ins

```
http://www.ipix.com/viewers/plugin.html
http://www.livepicture.com/download/clients/lpviewer.html
```

Where to Look for More Plug-Ins: There are well over a hundred different plug-ins available. When you have a spare moment and you feel like experimenting, take a look at the following list, which contains Web sites that serve as plug-in directories. These sites are fun to explore when you are looking for something new. They are also handy when you need a particular type of plug-in, and you are not sure where to find it.

*J*NTERNET RESOURCE Places to Look for Plug-Ins

```
http://www.gol.com/users/oyamada/
http://cws.internet.com/32plugin.html
http://www.winfiles.com/apps/98/plugins.html
http://browserwatch.internet.com/plug-in.html
http://home.netscape.com/comprod/products/navigator/
    version_2.0/plugins/
```

Downloading and Installing Software

DOWNLOADING means copying a file from a remote computer to your computer. The Internet is the largest library of software in the world, and there are a vast number of programs available for you to download for free. Once you know how to find and download software, you will have access to virtually all the programs you will ever need: programs to use for fun, to help you with your work, and to increase the utility of your computer.

In this chapter, I will show you how to locate, download, and install programs from the Internet. The skills are important as the Internet is always changing, and you will always have a need for new software. My goal is to show you how to open doors that will change the way you think about your computer and about the Net itself.

Overview of the Download Process

Almost all programs consist of multiple files, and to use a program, you need all of its files. Let's say you wanted to download a program that required, say, 15 separate files. It would be a lot of bother to download the files one by one. You would have to initiate 15 separate download operations, and make sure that all 15 files ended up in the right place.

To solve this problem, the multiple files needed for a particular program are gathered together into a single large file called an ARCHIVE. It is the archive that is stored on the Internet and made available for downloading. Thus, no matter how many files a program may require, you need download only a single file, the archive.

Within an archive, files are compressed so as to take up less room. Thus, the size of an archive is less than the size of all the files together, which means that it is faster to download the archive than it would be to download all the separate files. Once you have downloaded an archive, you need to uncompress and restore the original files. We call this UNPACKING the archive. (We will talk about the details later in the chapter.)

Within the collection of unpacked files will be an INSTALLATION PROGRAM. The job of the installation program is to do everything necessary to make the software ready to run on your computer.

Thus, to download and install a program from the Internet, you follow these steps:

1. Find the program you want.
2. Download the archive for that program.
3. Unpack the archive.
4. Install the program.

Once you get used to it, this four-step procedure is simple, and you will be able to do it quickly.

There are a number of large Web sites that act as software repositories, and these are the best places to get free software. Most of the programs will be either FREEWARE (completely free) or SHAREWARE (try it for free and pay money only if you decide to keep using it). I use these Web sites a lot, either when I am looking for a particular program, or when I have a few spare moments and I would like to try something new just for fun.

What about safety? When you get software from one of these sites, is there a danger of downloading a program with a virus? The answer is no, so don't worry about it. (See Chapter 8 for the details.)

hint

When you visit a software repository, you will sometimes see programs described as either 32-BIT or 16-BIT. Be sure to choose the programs that are suitable for your system.

32-bit programs are for Windows 95, Windows 98, or Windows NT.

16-bit programs are for the older Windows 3.x systems.

INTERNET RESOURCE Software Repositories: Windows 95/98

```
http://www.nonags.com/
http://www.tucows.com/
http://www.winsite.com/
http://www.download.com/
http://www.hotfiles.com/
http://cws.internet.com/
http://www.winfiles.com/
http://www.thefreesite.com/software.htm
```

INTERNET RESOURCE Software Repositories: Windows CE

```
http://www.cemonster.com/software.htm
http://www.wincecity.com/software.html
http://hpc.net/scripts/windowsce/softpage.asp
```

Downloading a Program

Once you find a program to download, you will reach a point where you click on a link and the downloading will start. The first step in the process varies slightly depending on your browser. Some browsers (such as Internet Explorer) show a dialog box similar to the one in Figure 11-1. You are offered a choice to either run the program or save it to disk. For now, make sure "Save this program" is selected, and then click on the OK button. (We will discuss the other option later.)

FIGURE 11-1
Beginning a download with Internet Explorer

Ultimately, you will end up with a dialog box similar to the one in Figure 11-2. You are being asked to specify where to save the downloaded file. Just specify the directory (folder) where you want to save the file, click on the Save button, and your browser will start the downloading process. Once it finishes, you are ready to install the program.

Before we continue, let's talk for a moment about where you should save the file. I have a friend who has often had a problem installing new software. She would download the archive and then not be able to find it. (This is easier to do than you might think.) You can avoid this problem by putting all your downloaded files where they are easy to find. My suggestion is to use Windows Explorer to create a directory called **Download**, and to use this directory for all your downloaded files. (If you are not sure what a directory is, take a moment to review the discussion in Chapter 4.) In Figure 11-2, you can see I am about to save a file called **tpe32324.exe** into my **Download** directory.

FIGURE 11-2
Specifying where to
save a downloaded file

I want you to think of this directory as providing temporary storage only. Once you have finished installing a program, you can delete all the files in the download directory. There is no point keeping an old archive. If, for some reason, you ever want to reinstall the program, you can download the archive again. In fact, you will sometimes find a newer version of the program.

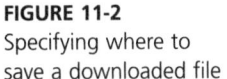

In Windows, the names you choose for directories and files are not case sensitive: You can mix upper- and lowercase letters. My suggestion is to use the following conventions:

- Directory names: Use a single uppercase letter followed by lowercase letters (**Download**).

- File names: Use all lowercase letters (**tpe32324.exe**).

Anonymous FTP

When you download a file from the Net, there are two different systems that might be used: HTTP (the same as is used to download Web pages) or Anonymous FTP (see Chapter 2). Either way, it doesn't matter much to you, because your browser knows what to do. In fact, the only clue that you are using Anonymous FTP might be the letters **ftp** in the name of the computer from which you are downloading (say, **ftp.microsoft.com**).

FTP (File Transfer Protocol) is used throughout the Internet to copy files from one computer to another, both uploading and downloading. When you use FTP, the remote server requires you to identify yourself by specifying a user name and password.

Anonymous FTP is a variation of this system that provides public access, for example, to download programs.

With ANONYMOUS FTP, the user name is always **anonymous**, and the password can be anything. Traditionally, people would use their mail address as a password, to allow whoever was maintaining the FTP server to know who is using the service. For privacy, however, your browser does not give out your mail address in this way.

With Netscape, it is possible to force the browser to use your mail address as the Anonymous FTP password (say, if you are using a private network and you do want to identify yourself). To do so, pull down the Edit menu and select "Preferences". In the Category box, click on "Advanced", and then check the box next to "Send email address as anonymous FTP password". Normally, you would leave this box unchecked.

Installing a Program

Once you have downloaded an archive, you are ready to install the program. However, before you do, you should take a minute and look at the Web site where you got the archive to see whether there are any installation instructions. If so, you should read the instructions *before* you install the program.

A moment spent reading the instructions can sometimes save you a lot of bother. For example, I have a friend who went through the entire process of downloading and installing a particular plug-in program (see Chapter 10). It was only after the program was installed that she read the instructions and found that the program would not work with the browser she was using.

Most programs come with a README FILE, usually named **readme.txt**. This file contains information that you should read before you use the program. You will often find that most of the information in the readme file is highly technical and not relevant to you. Still, you should spend a moment skimming this file. If, during the installation process, you are asked whether you want to look at the readme file, always say yes. With some programs, the readme file is available on the Web site where you got the program. If so, read the file before you start the download. With other programs, the readme file will not be available until after the program is installed.

Generally speaking, there are two types of archives. The first type is, in itself, an executable program. You can tell because the file name has an extension of **exe**, as with the file named **tpe32324.exe** in our previous example. With such archives, it is easy to start the installation process. Just use Windows Explorer to navigate to your download directory, and double-click on the archive file. Windows will start the program for you.

In most cases, once the program starts, everything is automatic. It will unpack itself and run the installation program. All you have to do is follow the instructions. When it is finished, you can clean up by deleting the archive.

hint

Many programs will put an icon on your desktop as part of the installation process. This is only for your convenience. If you don't want the icon, you can delete it so as to reduce the clutter.

There are two ways to delete an icon on your desktop:

- Click on it and press the **Delete** key
- Right-click on it and select "Delete"

The second type of archive is a ZIP FILE, so called because the file name ends in **zip**, for example, **harley.zip**. Zip files are not executable: You must unpack them yourself. This process is called UNZIPPING the file.

Unzipping an archive will create a collection of files. Within these files will be an installation program (usually called **setup.exe** or **install.exe**). Run this program to carry out the installation procedure. After the installation program is finished, you can delete it, along with the rest of the unpacked files and the archive.

To unzip an archive, you need a ZIP FILE PROGRAM. (Sometimes such programs are called COMPRESSION UTILITIES, because the zip format is used to compress files.) There are many zip file programs available, some freeware, some shareware. One of the most widely used shareware programs, my personal favorite, is called Winzip. I suggest you take some time now to select and install a zip file program. Once you start downloading software from the Net, I guarantee you will run into zip files, and it is best to have your zip file program ready.

When you install a zip file program, it registers itself with the Windows master list of file types (see Chapter 10) as being the program to handle all files with the **zip** extension. From then on, whenever you tell Windows to open a zip file, it will automatically start your zip file program.

Thus, to install a program that comes in the form of a zip file, follow these steps:

1. Download the zip file.
2. Use Windows Explorer to navigate to your download directory.
3. Double-click on the zip file to start your zip file program.
4. Use the zip file program to unzip the file into the download directory. (Your program may refer to this process by another name, such as "extract".)
5. Once the file is unzipped, look for and read the readme file.
6. Run the installation program. (If you don't see an installation program, look for instructions in the readme file.)
7. After the installation is complete, delete the files in the download directory, including the zip file.

hint

Some zip file programs come with special features to automate the installation process. For example, Winzip will look inside a zip file for files named **setup.exe** or **install.exe**. If Winzip finds such a file, it will display an Install button. Just click on this button, and Winzip will do everything for you automatically.

INTERNET RESOURCE Zip File Programs

```
http://www.winzip.com/
http://nng.simplenet.com/zip32.html
http://tucows.tierranet.com/comp95.html
```

Installing a Program Automatically

I mentioned earlier that some browsers offer you a choice when you download a file. Take a look at Figure 11-1. Notice that you can either run the program or save it to disk. If you select "run", your browser will download the program to a temporary location on your hard disk, start the program, and wait for it to finish. Once the program is finished, it will be deleted automatically.

Using this option can make the installation process a lot simpler. If the archive is in the form of an executable program (an **exe** file), you will not have to worry about saving it, running it, and deleting it. Everything will be automatic.

If the program is in the form of a zip file, the "run" option will still save you some bother, because when your browser "runs" the file, it will cause Windows to start your zip file program, which you can then use in the regular manner.

Some people prefer to save a program or zip file to their download directory, and then run the program themselves. This gives them more control over the installation process. Try it both ways and see which option you prefer.

hint

With large programs that take a long time to download, it is better to save the file before you run it. That way, if something goes wrong, and you need to rerun the program, you won't have to wait for it to download all over again.

Uninstalling a Program

If you have a program you don't want to use any longer, you can get rid of it by UNINSTALLING it. To do so, you must follow a specific procedure—do not simply delete the directory in which the program resides. Most installation programs make changes to your system that are hidden from you. These changes must be reversed when you uninstall the program.

The first step is to look in the directory where the program is installed and see whether there is a readme file. If so, look in the file for uninstall directions. (To read the file, double-click on it.)

If there are no uninstall directions, look for a special uninstall program. If you find one, run it.

Finally, if there are no uninstall instructions and you don't see an uninstall program, use the Windows Add/Remove facility. The steps are as follows:

1. Click on the Start button. Select "Settings" and then "Control Panel".
2. Double-click on "Add/Remove Programs". This will start the Windows Add/Remove facility.
3. Scroll down the list of installed programs and find the name of the program you want to uninstall. Click on the name and then click on the Add/Remove button. This will start the uninstall process.
4. When the uninstall is complete, close the Control Panel window.

Usenet

We hear people talk a lot about the Web, but the Web is only *part* of the Internet. There are other parts of the Net I want you to learn how to use, the most important of which is Usenet, the worldwide system of discussion groups.

Usenet is not only a lot older than the Web, it is far more important as a vehicle for communicating with other people. Usenet is where millions of people from many different countries and cultures come together to talk, argue, pose questions, share information and help one another.

The Basic Ideas

In Chapter 2, I discussed the basic ideas related to Usenet. Before we talk about Usenet in detail, let's take a moment to go over those ideas.

USENET is a system of discussion groups. There are thousands of different groups and millions of participants all over the world. Usenet was started in 1979. Originally, it was conceived as a way to send news and announcements between two universities in North Carolina (University of North Carolina and Duke University). Within a short time, Usenet spread to other schools and soon developed into a system of discussion groups. However, to this day, because of its origin, Usenet is still referred to as the NEWS (or sometimes, NETNEWS), even though it is not a news service. Similarly, the discussion groups are referred to as NEWSGROUPS.

Like other Internet services, Usenet uses a client/server system. To access the newsgroups, you need a Usenet client program called a NEWSREADER. (Thus, a newsreader enables you to access Usenet, in the same way that a browser allows you to access the Web.)

Usenet works as follows. People send messages, called ARTICLES or POSTINGS, to the various newsgroups. (When you send an article, we say that you POST it.) Most articles consist of text, but some also have pictures. The articles are propagated around the world (I'll explain how later) and stored on special servers called NEWS SERVERS. To look at the articles within a particular newsgroup, you use your newsreader to contact a news server. Your newsreader downloads the articles for that newsgroup and shows you a summary. You choose whichever articles you want to read, and your newsreader displays them for you.

How Does Usenet Work?

Usenet has no central authority, so there is no one to manage the system and no one to make any rules (and even if there were rules, there would be no way to enforce them). Usenet functions well because it is put together in a clever way, and because there is a lot of cooperation between the people who manage the news servers.

How are Usenet articles distributed? There is no central system to broadcast each new article to all the news servers in the world. Instead, each news server connects to other news servers at regular intervals. When the servers connect, they pass articles back and forth.

For example, let's say you compose an article for a particular newsgroup. When the article is finished, your newsreader will send it to your news server. Some time later, your news server will connect to another news server. At that time, your server will send a copy of your article to the other server. At the same time, the other server will pass on articles to your server. Eventually, the other server will connect to a third server and send it a copy of your article. Most news servers connect to only one or two other computers. But some news servers act as switching points by connecting to many other servers. When your article hits one of these major servers, it will fan out quickly to many different locations.

In this way, new articles are passed from one server to another, until they are propagated around the world. (Each article has a unique identification number so a server doesn't get more than one copy of the same article.) The system is designed so well that—although there is no central server and no one in charge—a new article will be distributed throughout most of the Internet within a day or two (and often much faster).

As you can see, Usenet does not require central management. Instead, each news server is managed by its own organization. In this way, the administration of Usenet is distributed in the same way as the administration of the Internet itself. So, although there is somebody in charge of each particular news server, there is no one in charge of the system as a whole.

The Usenet Tradition of Freedom

Since there is no central authority and no rules, people who use Usenet have wide latitude as to what they write in their articles, what pictures they choose to send, and, generally, how they behave. Usenet has a long tradition of being completely without censorship. This is important, as Usenet is the largest global forum for uncontrolled freedom of expression, with tens of thousands of discussion groups covering just about every topic a human being might care about.

The reason that the whole system does not degenerate into mindless anarchy is that, over the years, various conventions and traditions have been adopted by the people who participate in Usenet. For the most part, these traditions are followed voluntarily.

If you have never participated in a completely open discussion, it may take you a while to get used to the freedom in Usenet. Since there is total freedom, you are bound to encounter articles—and people—that you find offensive in some way. It may be because a particular article is truly tasteless, or it may be because you are not used to someone from another culture or someone who holds opinions that are extremely different from yours.

Whatever the case, I promise you, there will be times when you will be offended. When this happens, you have only two choices: You can either argue with the offensive person, or you can ignore him. (It doesn't do much good to complain because there is no one to complain to.)

I won't go on and on about what you are supposed to do and what you are not supposed to do. As you gain experience, you will learn from other people and from your own observations (and, as one of my readers, I know you are intelligent, sensitive and considerate). So, to help you get started, I will condense the entire body of Usenet etiquette into two simple rules.

Harley Hahn's Rules for Using Usenet Successfully

1. Be a nice person.
2. Ignore people who do not follow rule #1.

What Newsreader Should You Use?

To use Usenet, you need a newsreader to act as your client, and you need a news server to use as a source of articles. Let's talk about the newsreader first.

Both Internet Explorer and Netscape come with free newsreader programs. The Internet Explorer newsreader is OUTLOOK EXPRESS, the same program that acts as a mail client (see Chapter 5). The Netscape program is COLLABRA, part of the Netscape Communicator suite. Either one of these programs is okay, but if you get serious about Usenet, you should get yourself a better newsreader. There are a variety of such programs you can download for free. (For a discussion on how to download and install programs, see Chapter 11.)

As you will see in this chapter, Usenet involves a lot of details. Moreover, newsreaders have a large variety of options and features. As a result, newsreader programs are complex, and take more time to master than browsers and mail programs. My goal in this chapter is to teach you the basic ideas you need to understand Usenet. Then I want you to find a newsreader you like and learn how to use it well.

If you are not sure which newsreader to use, start with the one that comes with your browser. To begin, read through the built-in help information, then start practicing. Once you have some experience using Usenet, move on to another newsreader. Each newsreader has its own quirks, so you may have to experiment to find the one you like best.

There is an alternative to using a newsreader that you may want to try. A number of Web sites offer a free service (supported by advertising) that allows you to read the News with your browser. That is, the various newsgroups and their articles are made available as ordinary Web pages. These Web-based Usenet services are handy and easy to use. However, in the long run, you will be better off using a newsreader of your own to connect to a real news server.

Once you learn how to use a newsreader, you will have a lot more flexibility and power than a Web site can give you. Moreover, you will find that accessing Usenet with your own client program is faster than reading articles over the Web, and you won't have to look at advertising. Finally, some (but not all) of the Web-based Usenet services will show you only text, not pictures. This is a major disadvantage if you like to look at pictures. (See the discussion later in the chapter.)

*I*NTERNET RESOURCE Newsreaders

```
http://www.ksedb.no/ntnews/
http://www.microplanet.com/download.asp
http://www.winfiles.com/apps/98/news.html
http://www.forteinc.com/getfa/download.htm
```

*I*NTERNET RESOURCE Web-Based Usenet Access

```
http://www.talkway.com/
http://wren.supernews.com/
http://www.dejanews.com/info/toplevel.shtml
```

News Servers

In order to use Usenet, you must arrange to have access to a news server for two basic reasons. First, a news server acts as a repository for Usenet articles. When you want to read the articles in a particular newsgroup, your newsreader contacts your news server to get the articles. Second, when you post an article, your newsreader sends it to your news server, which distributes it to other servers.

Almost all ISPs (Internet service providers) maintain a news server for the benefit of their users. When you register with an ISP (see Chapter 3), they will tell you the name of the computer that acts as their news server. Typically, it will start with the word **news**. For instance, the news server for the Undependable Internet Company might be **news.undependable.com**.

The protocol (see Chapter 1) used to distribute news articles is called NNTP (Network News Transfer Protocol). For this reason, news servers are sometimes called NNTP SERVERS. You will also see the term NEWSFEED used to describe the service offered by a news server. For example, a friend who is looking for a better news server might ask you, "Where do you get your newsfeed?"

Although most people use the news server supplied by their ISP, there are a number of companies that offer newsfeeds to anybody on the Net. This service costs money, but some people choose to pay a bit extra for several reasons.

First, commercial newsfeeds provide a high-quality service that may be better than the one offered by your ISP. For example, the commercial services carry a very large variety of newsgroups. In addition, they use fast, powerful computers that minimize the time you spend waiting.

Another point has to do with how long articles are kept on a news server. There are so many articles sent over Usenet that it takes a large amount of disk space on a server just to keep the new articles that arrive each day. For this reason, news servers keep each article for a limited time, after which it is deleted automatically. When this happens, we say that the article EXPIRES. Thus, the longer a news server keeps its articles, the more there is for you to read.

A commercial news server will devote more disk space to their newsfeed than will most ISPs. Thus, a commercial server might keep articles for several weeks before letting them expire, while an ISP might keep articles for only a few days.

Another important point is that, as a general rule, commercial news servers connect to many other news servers and, thus, have better Usenet connections than most ISPs. For this reason, if you use a commercial server, you will have a larger variety of newsgroups to choose from and, within those groups, more articles to read. Moreover, when you post articles of your own, they will propagate throughout the Internet faster than if they were sent via your ISP.

The final issue has to do with spam. As we discussed in Chapter 2, SPAM consists of advertisements and other irrelevant articles that are posted to newsgroups. (Most of the ads, by the way, are for schemes to make money or for pornography.) Spam is a huge problem on Usenet, to the point where it has overwhelmed many existing groups.

There do exist special programs to ferret out and cancel spam before it can propagate too far. There is also software to allow a news server to identify and delete spam automatically as it arrives. Most commercial services and some ISPs use these programs to offer spam-free newsfeeds. If the newsfeed you get from your ISP is full of unwanted advertisements, you may want to subscribe to a commercial newsfeed, just to get rid of the spam.

*I*NTERNET RESOURCE Commercial Newsfeeds (Cost Money)

```
http://www.altopia.com/
http://www.newsfeeds.com/
http://www.supernews.com/
http://www.triton.net/news.htm
http://www.newscene.com/index.html
```

Newsgroups and Hierarchies

How many different Usenet newsgroups are there? There are two different answers to this question.

- There are between 30,000 and 60,000 different Usenet newsgroups, depending on who is doing the counting and how they are counting.
- There are only about 7,000 newsgroups you need to care about.

How can this be? I'll explain in a minute, but first we need to talk about hierarchies and newsgroup names.

Usenet was started in 1979 and, for several years, growth (by today's standards) was slow. For example, by the end of 1986, Usenet was carrying an average of 500 articles a day. Today, there are about 500 new articles posted *every minute*.

Within the first few years, the newsgroups were loosely organized into a few general categories, but it soon became evident that a better system was needed. Such a system was devised and implemented between the summer of 1986 and March of 1987. This system established seven categories called HIERARCHIES (shown in Figure 12-1), and each newsgroup was placed in a specific hierarchy. Six of the hierarchies had specific descriptions, while a seventh (**misc**) was used for all the groups that did not fit anywhere else.

Figure 12-1: The seven original Usenet hierarchies

Hierarchy	Contents
comp	Computers
misc	Miscellaneous
news	Usenet itself
rec	Recreation, hobbies, arts
sci	Science and technology
soc	Social and cultural issues
talk	Debate, controversial topics

As part of the reorganization of Usenet, a system was adopted for naming newsgroups. This system worked out so well that we still use it today. Each newsgroup name consists of two or more parts, separated by a **.** (period) character. The first part of the name shows the hierarchy in which the group resides. The following parts describe the topic of the group. For example, within the **rec** hierarchy, there is a group named **rec.humor** that is devoted to jokes and humor.

hint

Within a newsgroup name, the **.** (period) character is pronounced "dot". Thus, the name **rec.humor** is pronounced "rec dot humor".

(Of course, in the U.K. and Canada, it is pronounced "rec dot humour".)

Within the seven hierarchies, a new group could be established only by certain procedures: a discussion followed by a referendum in which anyone who was interested could cast a vote. In 1986, a new hierarchy named **alt** was established to offer more freedom. Within the **alt** hierarchy, anyone could create a new group without a formal vote, and it wasn't long before a variety of new, and often strange, newsgroups sprang up. At the same time, other hierarchies were established to serve various regions, schools and organizations. For example, there was a **can** hierarchy for Canadian newsgroups.

Now, as I mentioned earlier in the chapter, Usenet is controlled at a local level, by the people and organizations that administer the computers that provide the services. Each administrator chooses which newsgroups his or her computer will carry. Thus, the mere act of creating a new group in itself does not guarantee that the group will be propagated around the world. In order to become established, a new group must be accepted by a large number of Usenet administrators.

Most Usenet administrators accept all new groups that are established according to the traditional discussion/voting procedure. However, other groups are not accepted as widely, especially where resources (such as disk space) are limited. Thus, a group in the **rec** hierarchy, for example, will be carried by many more computer systems around the world than will a group in the **alt** hierarchy.

For this reason, the original hierarchies (including another that was added later, **humanities**) are called MAINSTREAM HIERARCHIES. All new groups in the mainstream hierarchies are created using a well-established, traditional procedure and, thus, receive the widest distribution. The eight mainstream hierarchies are shown in Figure 12-2.

Throughout the years, hundreds of other hierarchies have been established, most of which have few restrictions on creating new groups. However, only five of these hierarchies (including **alt**) are widely distributed. These are the ALTERNATIVE HIERARCHIES and are shown in Figure 12-2 along with the mainstream hierarchies.

Figure 12-2: Mainstream and alternative Usenet hierarchies

Mainstream	Alternative
comp	alt
humanities	bionet
misc	bit
news	biz
rec	k12
sci	
soc	
talk	

Together, the mainstream and alternative hierarchies comprise the most important part of Usenet, and contain virtually all the newsgroups most people care about. Figure 12-3 shows these hierarchies along with short descriptions. (Note: The **bit** hierarchy carries articles from a system of mailing lists called Bitnet, which we will talk about in Chapter 13.)

Figure 12-3: The most important Usenet hierarchies

Hierarchy	Contents
alt	Wide variety of miscellaneous topics
bionet	Biology
bit	Miscellaneous (from Bitnet mailing lists)
biz	Business, marketing, advertising
comp	Computers
humanities	Literature, fine arts
k12	Kindergarten through high school
misc	Miscellaneous
news	Usenet itself
rec	Recreation, hobbies, arts
sci	Science and technology
soc	Social and cultural issues
talk	Debate, controversial topics

As I mentioned, Usenet has several hundred hierarchies. Most of these, however, were established to serve a particular region of the world (such as a city or country) or a particular organization (such as a university or company). We call these REGIONAL and ORGANIZATIONAL HIERARCHIES, and you can see some examples in Figure 12-4. (For a full list, take a look at the Internet Resource.)

As you might imagine, the regional and organizational hierarchies are less important than the mainstream and alternative hierarchies and are not carried as widely. For the most part, you can ignore them unless you have an interest in a specific region or organization.

Figure 12-4: Examples of regional and organizational hierarchies

Hierarchy	Description
ba	San Francisco Bay area
ca	California
can	Canada
fr	France, French language
hepnet	High Energy Physics Network
japan	Japan, Japanese language
microsoft	Microsoft
netscape	Netscape
nyc	New York City
ox	Oxford University
ut	University of Toronto

*I*NTERNET RESOURCE Lists of Organizational and Regional Hierarchies

```
http://www.magma.ca/~leisen/master_list.html
http://www.faqs.org/faqs/usenet/hierarchies-config/
```

Now that you understand the idea of Usenet hierarchies, the system of naming newsgroups should make sense to you. Figure 12-5 shows some examples of typical newsgroup names. (I have chosen one from each of the mainstream and alternative hierarchies.) Notice that each newsgroup name starts with the name of its hierarchy.

Figure 12-5: Sample Usenet newsgroups

Newsgroup	Description
`alt.celebrities`	Celebrities
`bionet.biology.deepsea`	Deep-sea marine biology (moderated)
`bit.listserv.travel-1`	Travel
`biz.marketplace.international`	International business, import and export
`comp.lang.java.help`	Java programming, questions and answers
`humanities.classics`	Culture of ancient Greece and Rome
`k12.news`	News for teachers
`misc.creativity`	Creativity in all human endeavors
`news.newusers.questions`	Questions and answers for new Usenet users
`rec.parks.theme`	Theme parks
`sci.chem`	Chemistry
`soc.feminism`	Feminism and women's issues
`talk.environment`	Debate about the environment

There are literally tens of thousands of newsgroups, with more being created all the time. However, for various reasons, a large number of the newsgroups are not functional. We call these BOGUS groups.

The largest number of bogus newsgroups lie within the **alt** hierarchy, where, over the years, many new groups have been created but not widely propagated. For example, a good number of the **alt** groups were started as jokes, often with foolish names. Other bogus newsgroups used to be legitimate, but have outgrown their usefulness, and have since been abandoned or replaced. Still other groups have been deserted because of too much spam that choked out the legitimate discussions. (As I mentioned, spam has hurt Usenet significantly.)

So now let us return to the question I posed at the beginning of this section. How many Usenet newsgroups are there?

If you were to collect a list of every possible newsgroup name, from every hierarchy that ever existed, you would find between 30,000 and 60,000 names (depending on how selective you chose to be). Many of these newsgroups would be bogus, and many more would belong to regional and organizational hierarchies that have only a limited distribution.

Suppose, however, that you started with this huge list, selected only the newsgroups that belonged to the 13 mainstream and alternative hierarchies, and then eliminated the large number of bogus groups. How many groups would you have left?

The answer is, you would be left with about 7,000 legitimate groups that enjoy a global circulation. I know this because I maintain just such a master list. (I will talk about it later in the chapter.)

In other words, although there may be 30,000 different Usenet newsgroups, realistically, there are only about 7,000 groups you need to care about. However, don't feel deprived. These 7,000 newsgroups encompass a *huge* variety of topics. I can assure you that no matter what you are interested in, people are talking about it on Usenet.

Configuring Your Newsreader

Before you can use your newsreader for the first time, you must configure it by giving it certain information. In particular, you need to specify the name of your news server. (This is the computer from which your newsreader will download articles.) For help in choosing a news server, see the discussion earlier in the chapter.

Your newsreader may also want you to specify your name and email address. This information is put at the beginning of every article you post to Usenet. Such information is important, because when people read your articles, they will want to know who wrote them. Moreover, it is handy to have a mail address, in case people want to send private replies.

Against these needs, however, you must balance two considerations. First, you may want to maintain your privacy by being able to post articles without having people know who you are. You should understand that there are companies that archive every article posted to every newsgroup and store the information in publicly accessible databases. (See the discussion on Usenet search engines in Chapter 9.) Using one of these services, a person could read your article long after it has expired. It is also easy for someone to search for all the articles you have ever posted under your name.

The second consideration also relates to privacy: You may want to avoid getting on the lists of mail addresses used by spammers. (I talk about this problem in detail in Chapter 6.) Spammers use automated programs to scan every Usenet article in every newsgroup looking for new email addresses to add to their lists. This is done continually, and, if you ever post an article to Usenet with your real email address—even once—there is a good chance you will end up on spam lists. Before long, you will start to receive unsolicited advertising in your mailbox, and there will be nothing you can do about it.

So, when you configure your newsreader, you have several choices. You can specify your real name and your real address, and just not worry about the lack of privacy and the spam. Alternatively, you can specify a fake name and address, to protect your privacy. However, this will also make it impossible for the people who read your articles to send you private replies, unless you include your address in the body of the message or in a signature.

A good compromise is to use your real name, but to disguise your mail address. Change it in such a way that a person will know how to use it, but an automated spam program will not. For example, let's say your name is Ben Dover and your mail address is:

bendover@undependable.com

You can configure your newsreader to use an address similar to:

bendover@undependableREMOVE-ME.com

When a person replies to one of your articles, he will know to delete the letters **REMOVE-ME** from the address. The automated spam programs, however, will be fooled into adding the bogus address to their lists.

Reading Usenet Articles

As I mentioned earlier in the chapter, newsreader programs are complex, and the details vary widely from one program to another. In this section, I am going to help you get started reading the News. I will explain the basic ideas you need to understand and show you how they work with Outlook Express and Collabra. If you use a different newsreader, it won't be hard to figure out what to do.

To begin, start your newsreader. With Internet Explorer, pull down the Go menu and click on "News". (This will start Outlook Express.) With Netscape, pull down the Communicator menu and click on "Collabra Discussion Groups". (This will start Collabra.)

If you have not yet configured your newsreader, you must do so before you can use it. You may be prompted to enter the configuration information automatically. If not, you can do it yourself.

Within Outlook Express, pull down the Tools menu and click on "Accounts". Click on the News tab and then on the Add button. At this point, you will be led through the configuration procedure.

Within Collabra, pull down the Edit menu and select "Preferences". In the category box, look under Mail & Groups. (If there is nothing showing under Mail & Groups, click on the **+** [plus sign] character to show the various choices.) Now click on "Groups Server", to specify your news server, and "Identity", to specify your name and mail address.

Once your newsreader is configured, you need to tell it which newsgroups you want to look at. Your newsreader will download a list of all the available newsgroups from your news server, so you can see what is available.

Since there are so many newsgroups, the master list is huge, and it would be too much trouble to select your favorite ones each time you want to look at them. Instead, you designate certain groups as being the ones you normally want to read, and your newsreader keeps track of them for you.

When you choose a group in this way, we say you SUBSCRIBE to it. If you get tired of reading a particular group, you can UNSUBSCRIBE. (Actually, the term "subscribe" is a misnomer. All you are really doing is telling your newsreader to remember that you want to read a particular newsgroup.)

Subscribing to a newsgroup is easy. With Outlook Express, start by clicking on the Newsgroups button. (With Collabra, click on the Subscribe button.) Then choose a group and click on the Subscribe button. You can do this as often as you want and build up your subscription list to be as long as you want. (To practice, start with some of the newsgroups I listed in Figure 12-8.)

Once you have subscribed to some newsgroups, you are ready to read them. The details are as follows. (Warning: The details may look complicated at first, but once you figure out how it all works, it's easy.)

Click the OK button and close the subscription window. Within the main window, you will see the name of your news server. To the left of the name will be a **+** [plus sign] character. Click on the **+** character and you will see the list of all your subscribed newsgroups.

To read a group, click on it (double-click with Collabra). Your newsreader will now contact the news server and download a summary of the available articles. To read an article, just click on it in the summary list. Your newsreader will download the article and display it for you.

hint

Within your browser, it is possible to specify a Usenet newsgroup as a URL. Simply type **news:** followed by the name of the newsgroup. For example:

news:alt.celebrities
news:rec.parks.theme

Whenever your browser encounters such a URL, it passes the name of the newsgroup to your newsreader, which then displays the group. (This is also what happens when you click on a **news:** URL on a Web page.)

Thus, if you are using your browser, the quickest way to display a newsgroup is to enter **news:** followed by the name of the group.

Figures 12-6 and 12-7 show what it looks like to read an article with Collabra and Outlook Express, respectively. If you want, you can customize the appearance by changing the size and location of the various windows.

FIGURE 12-6

Reading a Usenet article with Collabra (Netscape)

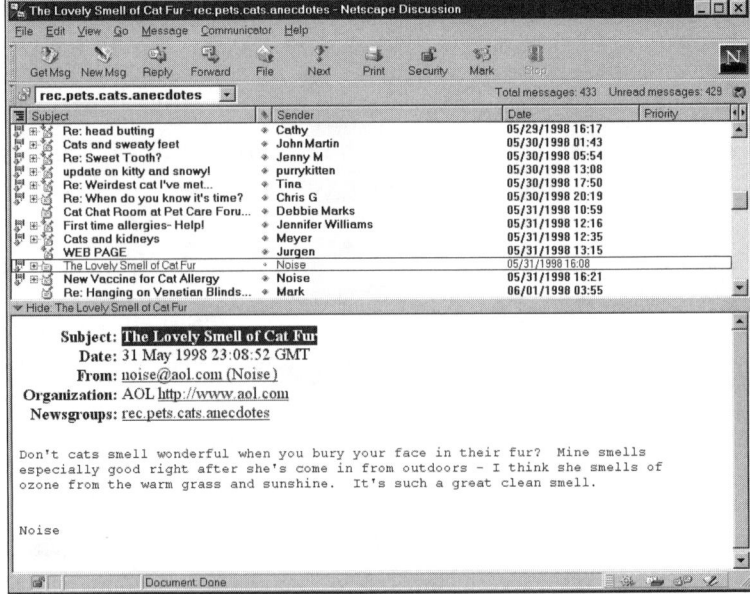

The Format of a Usenet Article

A Usenet article has three parts: a header, a body and an (optional) signature. If this sounds familiar, it is because it is the same format as a mail message. In fact, the description of a Usenet article is pretty much the same as for a mail message. The main difference is that Usenet articles have slightly different headers.

At the beginning of every article is a HEADER consisting of a number of specific HEADER LINES. These header lines contain technical information used by news servers and newsreaders. The most important header lines are as follows. For more information, please see the discussion about header lines in Chapter 5.

FIGURE 12-7

Reading a Usenet article with Outlook Express (Internet Explorer)

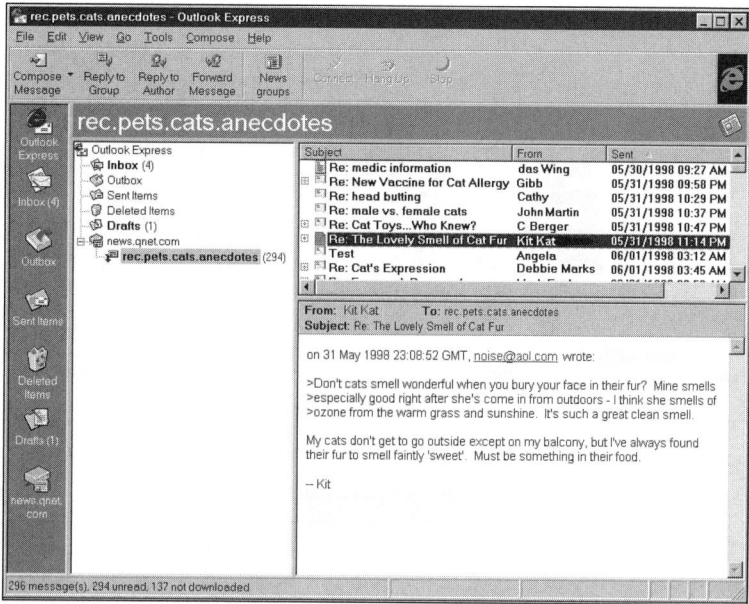

Header Line	Description
`From:`	Name and mail address of person who posted the article
`Newsgroups:`	Groups to which the message was posted
`Subject:`	The subject of the article
`Date:`	The time and date the message was posted
`Organization:`	The organization from which the article was sent
`Lines:`	Number of lines in the message (not counting the header)

hint

All newsreaders will show you the most important header lines by default. If you want to see the other header lines, you must tell your newsreader to show you more.

With Outlook Express, display the article. Then right click on the `Subject:` line within the Subject box. Choose "Properties" and then click on the Details tab.

With Collabra, display the article. Then pull down the View menu, point to "Headers" and select "All".

After the header comes the BODY of the article, the main content. Most of the time, the body will be simple text. However, it is possible to use rich text (HTML) in an article. (For a discussion of rich text, see Chapter 6.) Articles can also include pictures, similar to the attachments that can be sent along with a mail message. If the body of an article contains a URL, most newsreaders will recognize it as such, and turn it into a link you can click on.

A SIGNATURE is a small amount of personalized information included at the end of an article. Having a signature is optional, though many people use one. A typical signature might contain your name, mail address, and a link to your Web site (if you have one). Here is an example:

```
===============================================

Harley Hahn               http://www.harley.com/

(202) 456-1414            hhahn@little-nipper.com

===============================================
```

To use a signature, you create a small file, called a SIGNATURE FILE, and put whatever you want in it. Then you tell your newsreader that you want to use a signature and give it the location of the file. From then on, every time you post an article, your newsreader will automatically append the contents of your signature file to the end of the article.

Here is how to specify the location of a signature file:

Within Outlook Express (Internet Explorer), pull down the Tools menu and select "Stationery". Click on the News tab and then on the Signature button.

Within Collabra (Netscape), pull down the Edit menu and select "Preferences". In the Category box, click on "Identity" under Mail & Groups and then specify the name of the signature file in the appropriate box. (If there is nothing showing under Mail & Groups, click on the **+** [plus sign] character to show the various choices.)

Moderated Newsgroups

Usenet has been around for a long time, and throughout the years, people have developed a large number of customs and traditions. Some of these customs have to do with how Usenet is organized and maintained. Other customs involve how people talk, behave, and use certain words. The overall effect is to keep Usenet running smoothly, and to allow people to communicate well without face-to-face contact. In the next few sections, I am going to explain a number of important ideas and traditions you will encounter as you start to use Usenet.

In general, Usenet groups are available for everyone to read. However, some newsgroups are MODERATED, which means that posting articles to the group is controlled by a person called the MODERATOR. All articles that are posted with the name of a moderated newsgroup are first sent to the moderator. He or she looks at each article and decides whether or not to send it to the group.

Moderators do not censor. Rather, they discard articles that do not properly belong in the newsgroup. For these reasons, many people prefer moderated groups because the discussion is more focused, and there is no spam.

In most cases, you can't tell whether a newsgroup is moderated just by looking at the name. You will have to look at the articles within the group. If you use my master Usenet newsgroup list (discussed later in the chapter), it will tell you whether a group is moderated.

FAQs (Frequently Asked Question Lists)

An important Usenet tradition is the FAQ, or frequently asked question list. Over the years, it has been noticed that most newcomers to a newsgroup seem to ask the same questions. In the computer newsgroups, beginners always ask the same computer questions; in the cat-related newsgroups, beginners ask the same cat-related questions; and so on. In general, people on Usenet like to help one another and answer questions, but answering the same questions over and over (for years) gets tiresome.

As a solution, many of the newsgroups have a volunteer who produces a FAQ containing the frequently asked questions along with their answers. Usenet has hundreds of FAQs on a large variety of topics. Most FAQs are posted regularly (usually once a month) to the appropriate newsgroup. In addition, there are special newsgroups to which a copy of the FAQs are posted. These groups are shown in Figure 12-8.

Figure 12-8: Newsgroups to which FAQs are posted

Newsgroup	Description
news.answers	All the FAQs from every newsgroup
alt.answers	FAQs from the **alt** newsgroups
comp.answers	FAQs from the **comp** newsgroups
humanities.answers	FAQs from the **humanities** newsgroups
misc.answers	FAQs from the **misc** newsgroups
rec.answers	FAQs from the **rec** newsgroups
sci.answers	FAQs from the **sci** newsgroups
soc.answers	FAQs from the **soc** newsgroups
talk.answers	FAQs from the **talk** newsgroups

Whenever you start reading a newsgroup for the first time, it is a good idea to begin by checking out the FAQ. It will contain wisdom and knowledge that has been distilled from the newsgroup over a long period of time. Personally, I find the various FAQs fascinating, and I like to browse through them every now and then. For more information, including the addresses of Web sites that act as FAQ repositories, see the section on FAQs in Chapter 9.

hint

On Usenet, it is considered good manners to look in the appropriate FAQ before you ask questions.

Thus, when you start to read a newsgroup that has a FAQ, you must read the FAQ *before* you post your first article to that group.

Usenet Slang

People have been talking on Usenet for a long time, and over the years, certain words and expressions have evolved. Once you spend enough time reading newsgroups, you will begin to pick up the nuances. However, to help you get a head start, let's talk about a few of the words now.

To begin, people on Usenet use a great many abbreviations and acronyms. Such expressions are handy, and I want you to know what they mean. Figure 12-9 shows some of them, but when you get a moment, take a look at Appendix C, where I have included a much larger and more comprehensive list.

Figure 12-9: Some of the abbreviations commonly used on Usenet

Abbreviation	Meaning
:-)	smiley
:)	smiley
;-)	winking smiley
BTW	by the way
F2F	face to face (that is, in person)
FAQ	frequently asked question list
FWIW	for what it's worth
FYI	for your information
<G>	grin (same as a smiley)
IMHO	in my humble opinion
MOTAS	member of the appropriate sex
MOTOS	member of the opposite sex
MOTSS	member of the same sex
Ob-	(as a prefix) obligatory
Objoke	obligatory joke
ROFL	rolling on the floor laughing
SO	significant other

The meaning of most of these abbreviations is obvious, once you know what they mean, but I do want to discuss a few of them. Let's start with the smileys.

There are many different types of people on Usenet, and it is not hard to make a remark that might be misinterpreted. Usenet is used around the world, and your articles will be read by people from another countries, many of whom speak English as a second language and come from an entirely different culture.

For this reason, whenever you suspect that what you are saying might be wrongly interpreted as being insulting, it is customary to use a SMILEY: a short sequence of characters that, when looked at sideways, looks like a small smiley face.

The purpose of a smiley is to show a sense of irony, as if you mean to say, "Just kidding". For example, say you are taking part in a discussion about the best way to make pizza. You might write:

```
I can't understand why you don't like to put macaroni and
tuna fish on your pizza.  But then not everyone has good
taste like me :-)
```

(To see the smiling face, tilt your head sideways to the left.)

Smileys are important, and I want you to learn how to use them properly, so, when you get a moment, take a look at the section in Chapter 6 where I talk about them at length.

The next abbreviation I want to explain is the prefix **Ob-**. In some newsgroups, the participants make an effort to ensure that all the articles are relevant. For example, the group **rec.humor** is devoted to jokes and humor, and people do not like it when someone posts an article that does not have a joke. Of course, from time to time, someone does want to make a non-humorous comment, so, when they do, they always put at least one joke within the article. The tradition is to refer to this as an **Objoke** (obligatory joke). In other groups, you will sometimes see the **Ob-** prefix used in a similar way.

Sometimes the discussion of particular items does not belong in the same group as the items themselves. In such cases, there may be a separate newsgroup just for discussion. This group is often designated by a name ending with the characters **.d** (discussion). For example, the **rec.humor** newsgroup is supposed to be for jokes only. The group **rec.humor.d** is for related articles, such as the discussion of particular jokes or requests for jokes.

Here is another example. The newsgroup **alt.sex.stories**—an extremely popular group, by the way—is for people to post erotic stories (and only stories). Discussion about such stories must go to the group **alt.sex.stories.d**.

When you look at newsgroup names, another important suffix you will see is **.misc**. This indicates that there are several related groups, each devoted to a specific topic. The group whose name ends in **.misc** is for all the articles that don't belong in one of the other groups.

As an example, Figure 12-10 contains the names of newsgroups in which people discuss bicycles. Notice that most of the groups are for specific bicycle-related topics, while the **.misc** group is for everything else. In such cases, it is important to use the **.misc** group when appropriate. If you post miscellaneous articles to another, more specific group, it will dilute the focus of that group (and people will get mad at you).

Figure 12-10: Related Usenet newsgroups, including a `.misc` group

Newsgroup	Description
`rec.bicycles.marketplace`	Bicycles: buying and selling
`rec.bicycles.misc`	Bicycles: miscellaneous topics
`rec.bicycles.off-road`	Bicycles: mountain bikes
`rec.bicycles.racing`	Bicycles: racing
`rec.bicycles.rides`	Bicycles: tours and routes
`rec.bicycles.soc`	Bicycles: societal issues
`rec.bicycles.tech`	Bicycles: technical aspects

Returning to our discussion of Usenet slang, there are a few more words I want to mention. First, it is common for people on Usenet to disagree and to argue, and sometimes the discussion turns nasty. When this happens, someone will post a real stinker in which he criticizes another person or complains vociferously. We call such an article a FLAME. If an argument gets out of hand, with a lot of arguing back and forth, we call it a FLAME WAR. We also use the word as a verb, for example, "Sam got flamed by a lot of people because he didn't bother to read the FAQ before he started asking questions."

Another important word you will see is SPOILER. This refers to a description of a book, movie or play in which the ending is given away.

For example, let's say you are thinking about going to a particular movie. To make up your mind, you look in the newsgroup devoted to movie reviews (**`rec.arts.movies.reviews`**) to see whether anyone has posted a review of that movie. If, while you are looking, you see an article that says it contains a spoiler, you would know not to read that review as it gives away the ending of the movie.

The last few words I want to discuss have to do with posting articles. It is common for someone to read an article and post a reply. This is called a FOLLOW-UP article. When people start to post replies to the reply, the sequence of related articles is called a THREAD. You can tell your newsreader to arrange articles into threads, to make it easy to follow the various separate discussions within a newsgroup.

Finally, when you post an article, you specify the newsgroups to which the article should be sent. If you send an article to more than one group, we say that you CROSS-POST it.

Pictures (Binaries)

There are a huge number of pictures posted to Usenet groups, so if you like to look at pictures, you are in the right place. However, I do need to tell you that, by far, most of the pictures on Usenet are erotic (or pornographic, depending on your point of view). Even a cursory inspection of the pictures people post to Usenet is enough to show you that, regardless of what anyone might say in public, looking at erotic pictures in private is an extremely popular pastime for human beings.

Still, I don't want to mislead you. You will find more than naked men and women on Usenet. There are all kinds of pictures, such as flowers, landscapes, cartoons, and some absolutely wonderful images of paintings. You just need to know where to look.

Most of the pictures are posted to special newsgroups that are designated as being just for pictures. These groups are in the **alt** hierarchy and have the word **binaries** as part of their name. (I'll explain why in a moment.) Figure 12-11 shows a list of some of these newsgroups.

Looking at pictures is easy. Just read the articles in these newsgroups. If an article contains a picture, your newsreader will show it to you when you display the article.

If you decide you really like looking at pictures, there are a number of programs you can use to search through Usenet groups and automatically download all the pictures. (See the Internet Resource.)

Figure 12-11: Examples of Usenet newsgroups that contain pictures

Newsgroup	Contents
alt.binaries.clip-art	Clip art
alt.binaries.erotica	Erotic pictures
alt.binaries.erotica.pictures.redheads	Erotic pictures of redheads
alt.binaries.nude.celebrities	Nude celebrities
alt.binaries.pictures.autos	Automobiles
alt.binaries.pictures.cartoons	Cartoons
alt.binaries.pictures.celebrities	Celebrities
alt.binaries.pictures.fine-art	Fine art
alt.binaries.pictures.gardens	Gardens
alt.binaries.pictures.grotesque	Grotesque images
alt.binaries.pictures.horses	Horses
alt.binaries.pictures.motorcycles	Motorcycles
alt.binaries.pictures.movie-posters	Movie posters

*I*NTERNET RESOURCE Programs to Download Usenet Binaries

```
http://jfm.bc.ca/psp.html
http://www.binaryboy.com/
http://www.pagesz.net/~mhare/ASP1-A3/
http://www.winfiles.com/apps/98/news.html
http://www.fiax.net/users/lololo/autopixs.htm
```

WHAT'S IN A NAME?

binaries

In general, there are two types of data. TEXT consists of characters such as the letters of the alphabet, numbers, punctuation, and so on. Anything else is called BINARY DATA. The distinction is obviously a technical one, and I won't get into the details, except to say binary data is processed as bits (which I mentioned in Chapter 3) rather than as characters.

A file that contains binary data is called a BINARY FILE or, in the argot of Usenet, a BINARY. Thus, the newsgroups devoted to nontext postings (such as pictures and sounds) all have the word **binaries** in their name.

Posting an Article

You can post a Usenet article either in reply to someone else's article (that is, a follow-up) or as a brand-new article of your own. The details vary from one newsreader to another. I'll show you how to get started with Outlook Express (Internet Explorer) and Collabra (Netscape), but generally speaking, posting an article is simple with all newsreaders.

Let's start with a follow-up. You are reading an article, and you decide to post a reply. You have a choice of either replying to the newsgroup (in which case everyone reads your reply) or replying directly to the author of the article (in which case your reply is private). Most of the time you will reply to the newsgroup, so your article will become part of the discussion.

Within Outlook Express, click on the "Reply to Group" button. The newsreader will set up an article for you in a separate window. All you need to do is type your reply.

Within Collabra, click on the Reply button, and then choose "Reply to Group".

When your newsreader sets up your reply, the **Subject:** line will be filled in for you. To show that your article is a reply, the letters **Re:** will be inserted at the beginning of this line. For example, say you reply to an article with a subject of:

I need a Tuna and Grapefruit Recipe

The subject of your article will be:

Re: I need a Tuna and Grapefruit Recipe

Creating a brand new article is just as easy. The simplest way to do it is to open the newsgroup to which you want to post. Then tell your newsreader you want to compose a new article. (Within Outlook Express, click on the "Compose Message" button. Within Collabra, click on the "New Msg" button.)

Your newsreader will set up a new article for you in a separate window. All you need to do is type the subject and the body of the article. When you are finished, click on the Post button (Outlook Express) or the Send button (Collabra).

hint

To send a picture as part of your article, you simply attach a file that contains the picture, just as you do with a mail message. (See Chapter 5.) To do so, start composing an article, then:

Within Outlook Express, pull down the Insert menu, select "File Attachment", and specify the name of the file.

Within Collabra, click on the Attach button, select "File", and specify the name of the file.

When you reply to an article, it is customary to include part of the article in your reply, so people will know what you are talking about (just like when you reply to an email message). Your newsreader makes this easy by including the previous article within your reply.

When you include part of an article in this way, we say that you QUOTE it. To indicate which part of your message is quoted, your newsreader will insert a special character at the beginning of each line that is quoted. Traditionally, this character is a **>** (greater-than) sign. You can see this in Figures 12-6 and 12-7 earlier in the chapter. The article in Figure 12-7 is a reply to the article in 12-6.

hint

When you reply to a Usenet article, it is considered polite to keep the reply short by quoting only the relevant parts of the original article.

As you compose your reply, take a moment to delete all the unnecessary lines. As a general rule, the parts you quote should be shorter than the new lines you add. This makes your reply easier to read, which increases the chances that people will read it.

If you have never posted an article before, or if you are using a new newsreader, you may want to run a test. If so, it is considered bad manners to post a test article to a regular newsgroup. Instead, there are several groups just for test messages. You can post a message to one of these groups, and then take a look to see whether your message came through okay.

The test groups are shown in Figure 12-12. It is okay to send anything you want to these groups—that's what they are for. If you want to test posting a message to a moderated group, use `misc.test.moderated`.

Figure 12-12: Usenet groups to which you can send test messages

```
alt.test
bit.test
biz.test
comp.test
k12.test
misc.test
misc.test.moderated
news.test
```

To conclude this section, I would like to mention a few ideas for you to think about as you post articles to Usenet. Following these guidelines will help smooth your way in the Usenet community.

- Most people on Usenet are nice, but there are some idiots. If someone writes something that makes you mad, ignore him. Flaming someone is generally a waste of time, and all it does is ruin your mood. As you get older, one of the great lessons you will learn about life is that you can ignore people you don't like.
- If a newsgroup has a FAQ, read it before you post an article to that group.
- If you include a signature, keep it short.
- Some newsreaders allow you to include rich text (HTML) within your articles. Do not do so. HTML belongs on Web pages, not in Usenet articles. There are many

different newsreaders in use, and what looks good on your screen will probably not look good to other people. For a longer discussion of rich text and why you should avoid it, see Chapter 6.

● Do not type using all capital letters. Within a Usenet article, using all capital letters means YOU ARE SHOUTING.

● Once you post an article, there is no effective way to cancel it. Your article will remain on news servers around the world for several days to several weeks. In addition, it will be archived by the Usenet search engines (discussed in Chapter 9) and will be available to people indefinitely. So, as you compose an article, do your best to use good judgment, especially if you are angry or upset.

● As a general rule, you should post an article to one group only. If the article is relevant to more than one group, think carefully and pick the best one. On rare occasions, you might cross-post to two or three groups, but do not do so as a habit. The people you really want to read your article probably look at all the groups related to that topic, so cross-posting is almost always unnecessary. Some people do it, but they are not as intelligent and well-mannered as you and I.

Finding What You Want on Usenet

People often ask me for advice about how to use the Internet to find some information. If I think what they need will be on a Web page, I tell them to use a search engine. (See Chapter 9.) However, much of the time, I find myself telling people that the best way to get what they want is to send a question to the appropriate Usenet newsgroup and wait for someone to post an answer. This is especially true when you are looking for advice. Millions of people use Usenet, and many of them will be glad to help you.

The trick is, how do you find the right newsgroup? For example, say your baby has colic. Which newsgroup is the one to send a request for ideas and help? Or say you want to buy a camera. Where do the photography buffs hang out? Or suppose you want to talk about your favorite music group or writer or television show. Which group is the best one to read?

Sometimes you can guess what a group is for just by looking at its name. (For example, look at the newsgroups in Figure 12-5.) However, there are a huge number of newsgroups, and it is not an easy task to look through the entire list. Moreover, many of the names are obscure and won't make sense to you anyhow.

There is no easy answer to the question of how to find the newsgroup you want, but I can give you some good ideas. The best place to start is my Yellow Pages book, if you have it (*Harley Hahn's Internet & Web Yellow Pages*). In the book, I have thousands of items, organized into categories, and a lot of these items have Usenet newsgroups as well as Web sites. In many cases, the quickest way to find the newsgroup you want is to look up a related topic in the book.

Another way to find a group is to search for it on the Web. There are a variety of resources available. The best one I know of is the master list of Usenet groups that I maintain on my Web site. This list contains the names of all the non-bogus groups in the thirteen important hierarchies, about 7,000 groups in all. (See the discussion about hierarchies earlier in the chapter.)

For each group, I have written a short, one-line description, so it is easy to search for what you want. Conversely, if you see the name of a newsgroup somewhere and you are not sure what it means, you can use my master list to look up the description. This is the same list I use when I need to find a newsgroup quickly, so I am sure you will find it helpful.

*I*NTERNET RESOURCE Harley Hahn's Master List of Usenet Newsgroups

```
http://www.harley.com/usenet/
```

Aside from my master list, there are a number of other Web sites you can use. First, there are the Usenet search engines I described in Chapter 9. At these sites, you can not only look for newsgroups, you can search the archives of expired Usenet articles. Second, you can visit the Web sites that offer Web-based Usenet access (described earlier in this chapter). These sites allow various types of searches, and one of them may help you find what you need.

*I*NTERNET RESOURCE Places to Search for Usenet Newsgroups

```
http://www.talkway.com/
http://www.dejanews.com/
http://www.reference.com/
http://wren.supernews.com/
```

How Are Newsgroups Created?

Through the years, various procedures have been developed to create new Usenet groups. These procedures ensure that the process is handled in a thoughtful and practical manner. As I explained earlier, there are hundreds of Usenet hierarchies, the most important ones being the eight mainstream hierarchies and the five alternative hierarchies. The mainstream hierarchies have the most well-defined procedures for creating new groups, so let's start with those.

Within the **news** hierarchy, there are two groups that are used specifically for newsgroup creation, These groups are **news.announce.newgroups** and **news.groups**. **news.announce.newgroups** is a moderated group, and is used only for announcements relating to the creation of new groups. **news.groups** is an unmoderated group and is used for general discussion about new groups. Here is how it all works.

When the need arises for a new newsgroup, somebody will post an article to **news.announce.newgroups** proposing the creation of the group. This type of proposal is called an RFD ("request for discussion"). The moderator of **news.announce.newgroups** posts the RFD, at which time discussion begins in **news.groups**.

In most cases, the RFD will be discussed in other groups as well. For example, if the RFD proposes the creation of a new group related to bicycles, the discussion will take place not only in **news.groups**, but also in the various bicycle newsgroups. Thus, the people who would be most interested in the creation of a new group are the ones who discuss it. During the discussion, the people involved settle on a name for the group and create a CHARTER: a statement explaining the purpose of the group.

If, after several weeks of discussion, it is determined that there is a real need for the group, someone posts another article to **news.announce.newgroups** calling for a vote. This announcement specifies a specific voting period, which must be between 21 and 31 days. During this time, people vote by email for or against the creation of the new group. Anyone is allowed to vote, and each person may vote only once.

At the end of the voting period, the results are announced. For a new group to be created, it must receive at least two-thirds "yes" votes, and there must be at least 100 more "yes" votes than "no" votes. If this criterion is not met, the group is not created. If the criterion is met, the moderator of **news.announce.newgroups** will create the group.

The moderator creates a new group by using a special directive called a CONTROL MESSAGE. This is a short message that is transported throughout Usenet in the same way as a regular article. However, a control message has special header lines that are recognized by all news servers, and within these header lines are instructions to the news server telling it to perform a specific task.

To create a newsgroup, the moderator sends out a control message instructing all news servers to add the new group to their master list. (If it becomes necessary to delete a newsgroup, it is possible to send a different type of control message telling news servers to remove a specific group from their master list.)

As I mentioned earlier in the chapter, Usenet administration is distributed, not centralized, and each individual news administrator decides which newsgroups will be carried on his or her system. Thus, in order to create a new newsgroup, you not only have to send an appropriate control message to news servers throughout the world, you also have to get the news administrators to agree to accept the newsgroup on their systems.

Because all mainstream groups go through a careful and deliberate creation process, news administrators throughout the world will always honor a control message from the moderator of **news.announce.newgroups** requesting the creation of a new group.

In the other hierarchies, however, newsgroup creation is handled differently. Some hierarchies are controlled by one person, some by a group of people, and others by nobody. The most important of these other hierarchies is **alt**, which is, by far, the largest hierarchy in all of Usenet, so let's talk about how an **alt** group is created.

The **alt** hierarchy was established as an alternative to the original mainstream hierarchies. As such, the rules for establishing new **alt** groups are far more liberal than in the mainstream hierarchies. In particular, there is no formal voting procedure. Anybody who knows how to send a control message can create a new **alt** group.

Within the **alt** hierarchy, there is a special newsgroup, **alt.config**, that is used for discussion of new **alt** groups. Before someone creates a new **alt** group, it is considered proper to post an article to **alt.config** describing the new group and asking for comments. Before actually creating the group, a person should wait at least a week to see what other people have to say.

Remember, in order to successfully create a new group, it is necessary for the news administrators around the world to agree to create the group. If the group has not been previously discussed in **alt.config**, many news administrators will not create it. In fact, in such situations, it is common to see other people send out control messages canceling the group.

Some news administrators, however, will honor all newsgroup creation requests, and, as a result, you will see many frivolous **alt** groups with silly names. Still, the **alt** hierarchy does have a huge number of useful and active newsgroups, and the freedom that it offers is important to Usenet as a whole.

You will probably never need to create a new Usenet group, but if you ever decide to do so, make sure to wait until you have a fair amount of experience with Usenet. Wait until you understand how Usenet works and how groups are named and organized, and, before you move forward with your idea, discuss it in the related groups to see what other people have to say. Within the mainstream hierarchies, new groups usually arise as a consensus among a number of people. This is not necessary for **alt** groups, but having a discussion beforehand does make for better results. For more detailed information about newsgroup creation, check out the following resources.

(In the following lists, you will notice that I have specified the names of several newsgroups as URLs. The format is **news:** followed by the name of the group. I discuss this type of URL earlier in the chapter.)

*I*NTERNET RESOURCE Creating a Mainstream Newsgroup

`news:news.groups`

`news:news.announce.newgroups`

`http://www.faqs.org/faqs/usenet/creating-newsgroups/`

*I*NTERNET RESOURCE Creating an alt Newsgroup

`news:alt.config`

`http://www.cis.ohio-state.edu/~barr/alt-creation-guide.html`

`http://www.cs.ubc.ca/spider/edmonds/usenet/good-newgroup.html`

Mailing Lists

For many years—even before Usenet, and long before there was a Web—people have been using mailing lists to hold discussions. In fact, mailing lists are almost as old as the Internet itself.

Today, there are a vast number of mailing lists, even more than the number of Usenet groups. Many of these lists are open to anyone, and it is easy to participate: If you know how to use mail, you already know most of what you need to know. In this chapter, I will explain how mailing lists work, how to join them, and how to find the ones that interest you.

The Basic Ideas

A MAILING LIST is a facility that allows people to participate in an ongoing discussion via email. There are tens of thousands of mailing lists on the Internet. Many of them are private (and probably of no interest to you or me), but a large number of the mailing lists are—like Usenet discussion groups—open to anyone. When you join a mailing list (which is free), we say you SUBSCRIBE to the list. When you quit the list, we say you UNSUBSCRIBE.

Within a mailing list, messages are circulated by mail. The idea is simple: Each time someone sends a message, a copy of that message is sent to everyone who has subscribed to that list. Thus, to participate in a discussion about a particular topic, all you have to do is subscribe to a mailing list devoted to that topic. From then on, a copy of every message that anyone sends to the list will be sent to your mailbox automatically. When you unsubscribe from the list, you will stop receiving messages.

Every mailing list is controlled by a person referred to as the LIST OWNER. In most cases, the owner is the person who started the list or, perhaps, inherited the job from someone else. The duties of the owner of the mailing list are minimal, because, as I will explain in a moment, most of the work is done by an automated program.

The basic job of the list owner is to monitor the messages and sort out any problems that may arise. The owner also creates a document, called a WELCOME MESSAGE, that is sent to each person who subscribes to the list. The welcome message contains general information about the list, including its purpose, any rules regarding the discussion, and a description of any special features. The welcome message also contains instructions on how to unsubscribe to the list.

Some mailing lists are MODERATED, which means that a person, called the MODERATOR, decides which messages are sent out. In most cases, the moderator is the list owner, although it can be a different person.

Most lists are not moderated, and when you send a message, everyone sees it. With a moderated list, the message is first sent to the moderator. The moderator reads all the incoming messages and decides which ones should be sent to the list.

The main advantage of a moderated list is that the discussion stays more focused than with an unmoderated list. However, with a busy list, moderating can require a lot of time, and it is necessary to find someone willing to volunteer the hours.

We use the terms TRAFFIC or VOLUME to refer to the average number of messages sent to a particular list. Some mailing lists have low traffic, and you may not see more than a few messages in a week, or even in a month. Other mailing lists, however, have a lot of traffic, and a busy list can fill up your mailbox quickly. It is not uncommon, for example, to go away for a week's vacation and come back to find your mailbox overflowing with a lot of messages from your favorite mailing list. For this reason, some mailing lists provide a way to stop the messages temporarily when you know you are going to be away for a while. (I will show you how later in the chapter.)

When a list has a lot of traffic, it can be inconvenient to have your mailbox filled with many separate messages. Some mailing lists offer an alternative. Instead of receiving separate messages, you can choose to have all the messages for each day collected and sent to you as one large message, called a DIGEST.

How Are Mailing Lists Different from Usenet Newsgroups?

In some respects, mailing lists are similar to Usenet newsgroups (which I discuss in Chapter 12). They both cover a large variety of topics, discussed by people all over the world. There are, however, important differences.

The articles in a Usenet newsgroup are stored on various news servers around the Internet. When you post an article to a newsgroup, the article starts from your news server, and makes its way around the world by being copied from one server to another. Mailing lists are different. Each mailing list is managed by a MAILING LIST PROGRAM (sometimes called a LIST SERVER) running on a specific computer. When you send a message to a list, the mailing list program receives the message and sends a copy to everyone who is subscribed to the list.

To read the articles in a Usenet newsgroup, you have to use a special program, called a newsreader, to connect to a news server. To participate in a mailing list, all you need is a regular mail program.

This means that, when you subscribe to a mailing list, all the messages from that list are sent to your mailbox automatically. You do not pick and choose what you want to read (although you can always delete messages without reading them). With Usenet, you need only look at a newsgroup when you feel like it, and it is easy to browse from one group to another.

Thus, Usenet lends itself to exploring and skimming. Once you learn how to use your newsreader, it is simple to take a peek at any newsgroup you want, whenever you want. With a mailing list, you must subscribe and then wait for new messages to arrive in your mailbox.

For this reason, people are more selective about which mailing lists they subscribe to, compared to which newsgroups they read. This leads to a mailing list culture in which you see more serious, and longer, discussions than on Usenet. For example, many mailing lists are used by researchers and students for scholarly collaboration, something that is more difficult to maintain on Usenet. In fact, it is common to find mailing lists in which the participants have been talking together for months or even years. As such, these lists develop a community spirit. Although some Usenet newsgroups do develop this type of spirit, most groups are more like open forums, with people tending to drift in and out.

Like Usenet, mailing lists offer a lot of variety. There are lists for just about any topic you can imagine, and, in fact, there are a lot more mailing lists than Usenet news-groups. However, mailing lists tend to have more wheat and less chaff. In particular, there is virtually no spam—the unsolicited advertising that plagues Usenet.

The final difference I want to mention relates to names. Usenet newsgroups have names that consist of more than one part, such as:

alt.celebrities
biz.marketplace.international
rec.parks.theme

The first part of each name shows the hierarchy (in this case, **alt**, **biz**, and **rec**).

Since every mailing list is run from a particular computer, there is no need for a standardized naming system. All that is needed is a name that uniquely identifies the list on its own computer. Thus, mailing lists use simple, one-word names. I will show you how the system works in the next section. For now, here are a few examples:

Mailing List	Description
artist	Student artists
cinema-l	Movies
couples-l	Relationship stuff
games-l	Computer games
humor	Humor and jokes

WHAT'S IN A NAME?

*list-***1**

One of the oldest networks to support a large number of mailing lists was called Bitnet. (I will talk about Bitnet later in the chapter.) Within Bitnet, it was necessary to differentiate between a user name and a mailing list name. For this reason, people used the convention that all mailing list names would end with the characters **-1** (a hyphen followed by a lowercase "L"). For example, the Bitnet mailing list devoted to travel was called **travel-1**.

Today, Bitnet has been replaced by the Internet, but many of the Bitnet mailing lists still exist. Moreover, some people still use the **-1** naming convention. For these reasons, you will see many mailing lists with this type of name.

When you talk about such names, there are several ways to pronounce the **-1** characters. Many people pronounce the "el" but not the **-** character. Thus, you might hear someone say, "I subscribed to the "travel el" list."

Technical Unix people are more likely to pronounce the **-** character as "minus", because that is the custom with Unix. So a Unix person would talk about subscribing to the "travel minus el" list.

Mailing List Programs: Listserv, Listproc and Majordomo

As I mentioned earlier, every mailing list is managed automatically by a mailing list program. This program handles the details associated with running a list: processing subscription requests, making sure that messages are distributed to everyone on the list, creating digests, and so on. There are three common mailing list programs you will encounter on the Internet: LISTSERV, LISTPROC and MAJORDOMO.

A mailing list program has two jobs. First, there is the basic job of distributing the messages. The mailing list program receives every message sent to the list and sends a copy of the message to each person who has subscribed to the list. (If the list is moderated, every message is first sent to the moderator. The moderator then tells the program which messages to distribute.)

The second job performed by a mailing list program is to carry out various administrative commands. Anyone can issue such commands to a mailing list program by sending it a message with a particular format (which I will explain later in the chapter). When your message arrives, the program reads it and carries out your commands.

For example, to join a mailing list, you send a message to the mailing list program that administers that list. Within the message, you put a **subscribe** command. To quit a list, you send a message containing an **unsubscribe** command. Although there are a number of different commands you can send to any mailing list program, you really need to know only a few of them.

Thus, a mailing list program receives two types of mail: administrative messages that contain commands to be carried out, and regular messages that are to be distributed to everyone on the list. To keep things straight, each mailing list has two different addresses. The SUBSCRIPTION ADDRESS is the one to which you send commands. The LIST ADDRESS is the one to which you send messages. Here is an example.

In the last section, I mentioned a mailing list called **artist**. (This list, devoted to student artists, is owned by my chief researcher, Wendy Murdock.) The list address is:

artist@qnet.com

This is the address to which you would send regular messages. Anything sent to this address will be distributed to everyone on the list.

The subscription address is:

majordomo@qnet.com

This is the address to which you would send administrative commands, for example, to subscribe or unsubscribe to the list.

In most cases, a single mailing list program handles all the mailing lists on a particular computer. For example, the Majordomo program on **qnet.com** manages all the mailing lists on **qnet.com**. Thus, the subscription address will be the same for every mailing list on the same computer.

Figure 13-1 contains a few more examples, showing the subscription addresses and list addresses of the mailing lists I mentioned in the previous section.

Figure 13-1: Examples of mailing lists

Mailing List	Subscription Address	List Address
artist	majordomo@qnet.com	artist@qnet.com
cinema-1	listserv@american.edu	cinema-1@american.edu
couples-1	listproc@cornell.edu	couples-1@cornell.edu
games-1	listserv@brownvm.brown.edu	games-1@brownvm.brown.edu
humor	listserv@uga.cc.uga.edu	humor@uga.cc.uga.edu

WHAT'S IN A NAME?

Listserv
Listproc
Majordomo

Listserv, Listproc and Majordomo are all mailing list programs. Listserv is the oldest. It was originally developed by Eric Thomas, in 1986, for IBM mainframe computers on the Bitnet network (which I discuss later in the chapter). Later, Listserv was converted to run on other Bitnet computers, particularly DEC's VMS systems. The name Listserv stands for "List Server".

As the Internet became popular, Listproc was created to be the equivalent of Listserv for Unix computers on the Internet. Listproc was developed by an organization called CREN (Corporation for Research and Educational Networking), the successor to Bitnet. The name Listproc stands for "List Processor".

Majordomo was developed in 1992 by Brent Chapman, also to run under Unix. Majordomo is written in Perl (don't worry if that doesn't mean anything to you). Although it can do the basic job, Majordomo does not have as many features as Listserv and Listproc. The name Majordomo is taken from the term "majordomo", used to describe the chief steward in a large household, such as a palace. Within such a household, the majordomo is the servant with the most responsibility, the one who coordinates the activities of the other servants while performing the most important jobs.

Subscribing and Unsubscribing to a Mailing List

Subscribing to a mailing list is easy. All you need to do is mail a short message to the subscription address. The subject of the message can be anything you want (it is ignored). In the body of the message, put a single line containing a **subscribe** command. The format is as follows:

For Listproc and Listserv:
- The word **subscribe**
- The name of the mailing list
- Your first and last names

For Majordomo:
- The word **subscribe**
- The name of the mailing list

(The only difference for Majordomo is that you do not need to specify your first and last names.)

Here is an example that illustrates how to subscribe to a Listserv or Listproc mailing list. Let's say your name is Warren Peese, and you want to subscribe to the **humor** mailing list I mentioned in Figure 13-1. To do so, send the following message:

```
To: listserv@uga.cc.uga.edu
Subject: subscribe humor

subscribe humor Warren Peese
```

The next example shows a subscription command sent to a Majordomo list. The main difference is you do not put your first and last names:

```
To: majordomo@qnet.com
Subject: subscribe artist

subscribe artist
```

Notice that, in both cases, you do not have to specify your mail address. The mailing list program will pick up your address automatically from the header of your message.

To unsubscribe from a mailing list, send a message to the subscription address. In the body of the message, put a single line containing an **unsubscribe** command. The format is as follows:

- The word **unsubscribe**
- The name of the mailing list

Here is an example:

```
To: listserv@uga.cc.uga.edu
Subject: unsubscribe humor

unsubscribe humor
```

When you send commands to a mailing list program, it doesn't matter what you put in the **Subject** line. I always put something descriptive to make it easier to recognize the message when I see it in my outbox.

As a summary, Figure 13-2 shows the general format for subscribing and unsubscribing to a mailing list.

Figure 13-2: Subscribing and unsubscribing to a mailing list

Subscribing: Listserv or Listproc

> **To:** *subscription-address*
> **Subject:** *anything*
>
> **subscribe** *list-name your-first-name your-last-name*

Subscribing: Majordomo

> **To:** *subscription-address*
> **Subject:** *anything*
>
> **subscribe** *list-name*

Unsubscribing: Listserv, Listproc, or Majordomo

> **To:** *subscription-address*
> **Subject:** *anything*
>
> **unsubscribe** *list-name*

Note: With Listserv, you will sometimes see a **signoff** *command used as a synonym for* **unsubscribe***. The word "signoff" comes from the days of the old IBM mainframe computers, which were the original home of the Listserv mailing lists.*

When you subscribe to a mailing list, the mailing list program will send you a copy of the welcome message for that list. Save this message, as it will have information that may come in handy later. In particular, the welcome message will contain instructions for unsubscribing to the list.

If you subscribe to more than one list, an easy way to store the welcome messages is to use Windows Explorer to create a folder (directory) called **Mailing-lists**. Each time you get a welcome message, save it in this folder under the name of the list. For example, if you subscribe to the **artist** mailing list, you would save the welcome message in a file named **artist**. In this way, you can find any welcome message just by looking in your **Mailing-lists** folder.

hint

If you are new to mailing lists, you may be tempted to subscribe to several at the same time. My advice is to start with only one list. Wait a week and see how much traffic the list generates before you subscribe to another list.

If you subscribe to several high-traffic mailing lists at the same time, you will receive a lot of mail within a short time, and you may find it difficult to sort out the various messages.

Keeping the Addresses Straight

As you know, a mail address has the following format:

name @ *hostname*

where *hostname* is the name of a computer. Mailing lists use two different addresses:

- Subscription address (to which you send commands)
- List address (to which you send messages for the list)

The *name* in a subscription address will be the same as the name of the mailing list program: either **listserv**, **listproc** or **majordomo**. The *name* in a list address will be the name of the mailing list itself.

Here is an example. Consider a Majordomo mailing list named **artist** on the computer **qnet.com**. The two addresses are as follows:

- Subscription address: **majordomo@qnet.com**
- List address: **artist@qnet.com**

It is important to keep these addresses straight. You should use the list address only to send regular messages. For everything else, use the subscription address.

hint

It is common for beginners to send an unsubscribe request to the list address, rather than to the subscription address. Not only will this not work, but a copy of the message may go to all the people on the list, annoying everyone.

When it is time to unsubscribe, send the request to the subscription address.

Mailing List Commands

One of the jobs of a mailing list program is to carry out commands. To send such commands, mail a message to the subscription address of the list. Within the body of the message, you can put as many commands as you want, one per line. The subject of the message can be anything you want (it is ignored).

When your message is received, the mailing list program will process it, one line at a time. So far, I have described only two commands (**subscribe** and **unsubscribe**). However, there are others, the exact details of which vary depending on what type of mailing list program is being used.

In Figures 13-3, 13-4 and 13-5, I have summarized the basic commands for the three main mailing list programs: Listserv, Listproc and Majordomo. Most of the time, you will have to use only the **subscribe** and **unsubscribe** commands, but the others are there if you need them. My suggestion is to send for general help information to get a full list of commands. You can then ask for more specific instructions if you need them.

For example, to request general information from a Listserv program, you would use the **help** command. Here is a message that does just that:

```
To: listserv@uga.cc.uga.edu
Subject: help information request

help
```

When the Listserv program receives this request, it will send you the help information by return mail.

If you want to send more than one command, remember to put each one on a separate line. (The **info ?** command requests a list of all the help topics. See Figure 13-3.)

```
To: listserv@uga.cc.uga.edu
Subject: help information request

help
info ?
```

When you mail these types of messages, there is a potential problem I want you to be aware of. The mailing list program reads your message and processes it one line at a time. If the message happens to have any lines after the last command, the program will try to interpret them as commands, which will result in error messages.

This will happen if you have set your mail program to append a signature to the end of each message (see Chapter 5). It will also happen if you are using a free email facility that puts an advertisement at the end of each message.

To avoid such problems, put a single line with the word **end** after the last command. This tells the mailing list program to stop processing commands. Here is an example:

```
To: listserv@uga.cc.uga.edu
Subject: help information request

help
info ?
end

These lines will be ignored by the
mailing list program.
```

Figure 13-3: Summary of important Listserv commands

Subscribing and Unsubscribing

subscribe *list-name your-first-name your-last-name*
unsubscribe *list-name*
signoff *list-name* [same as **unsubscribe**]

Information About Lists

lists global/*keyword* [send list names containing the specified keyword]
review *list-name* [send information about the specified list]

Help Information

help [send general help information]
info ? [send a list of help topics]
info *topic* [send information about the specified topic]

Temporarily Turn Off Mail from the List

set *list-name* **nomail**

Turn Mail from the List Back On

set *list-name* **mail**

Request Messages to Be Sent in Digest Format

set *list-name* **digests**

Change Back to Normal (Non-Digest) Format

set *list-name* **mail**

Figure 13-4: Summary of important Listproc commands

Subscribing and Unsubscribing

   subscribe *list-name your-first-name your-last-name*
   unsubscribe *list-name*

Information About Lists

   info *list-name* [send information about the specified list]

Help Information

   help [send general help information]

   help *topic* [send information about the specified topic]

Temporarily Turn Off Mail from the List

   set *list-name* **mail postpone**

Turn Mail from the List Back On

   set *list-name* **mail**

Request Messages to Be Sent in Digest Format

   set *list-name* **mail digest**

Change Back to Normal (Non-Digest) Format

   set *list-name* **mail**

Figure 13-5: Summary of important Majordomo commands

Subscribing and Unsubscribing

    subscribe *list-name*
    unsubscribe *list-name*

Information About Lists

    info *list-name* [send information about the specified list]
    lists [send summary of all lists on that computer]

Help Information

    help [send summary of commands]

Finding Mailing Lists

There is no central directory of mailing lists, so when you are searching for a list devoted to a particular topic, there is no single place to look. I do, however, have two suggestions.

First, my Yellow Pages book (*Harley Hahn's Internet & Web Yellow Pages*) is an excellent place to start. In the book, I have thousands of different items, and many of them have mailing list information (along with Web sites and Usenet groups). Just look up the topic you want, and there is a good chance you will find an appropriate mailing list.

The second place to look for mailing lists is on the Web, where there are a number of well-maintained Web sites devoted to collecting and categorizing mailing list information. These sites contain information on a huge number of lists, so, with a little work, you will probably be able to find what you want. These Web sites are independent of one another, so my suggestion is to search them all before you make a final selection.

INTERNET RESOURCE Lists of Mailing Lists

    `http://www.liszt.com/`
    `http://www.lsoft.com/lists/listref.html`
    `http://www.neosoft.com/internet/paml/indexes.html`
    `http://catalog.com/vivian/interest-group-search.html`

Starting Your Own Mailing List

There are two ways to start your own mailing list. First, you can find a place that runs a mailing list program (Listserv, Listproc or Majordomo) and see whether someone will agree to create a list for you.

The best place to start is with your ISP. Many ISPs will set up mailing lists for their customers, either for free or for a fee. If you work or study at a university, you can probably get one of the system administrators to start a mailing list for you. Ask around to see what the local policy is.

As an alternative, there are a number of companies on the Web that provide "free" Web-based mailing lists. These services allow you to send and receive messages via your Web browser, as well as by regular mail. The interface for these lists is also designed to be used over the Web, and it is usually easy to subscribe and unsubscribe.

Of course, such services are not really free. Everyone who subscribes to your mailing list will have to look at advertisements, either at the Web site or inserted into the actual messages. Moreover, reading messages via a Web browser is a lot slower (and a lot more frustrating) than using your own mail program.

For this reason, these services are not my first choice. However, they do provide a practical alternative if you do not want to pay a fee, and you can't get your ISP or anyone else to give you a list for free. This is especially true if you want a small mailing list for a very specific purpose. For example, many people set up a free Web-based mailing list to keep in touch with the members of their family. What could be more cool than having your own family mailing list?

*I*NTERNET RESOURCE Web-Based Mailing Lists

```
http://www.listbot.com/
http://www.onelist.com/
http://www.coollist.com/
http://www.findmail.com/
http://zebu.addr.com/mail/
```

Mailing List Gateways

Although there are important differences between mailing lists and Usenet newsgroups, they both contain the same sort of information: messages (or articles) sent in by various people. Because of this similarity, it is possible to arrange for a mailing list to have a corresponding Usenet newsgroup. This means that every message sent to the mailing list is automatically posted to the newsgroup, and every article posted to the newsgroup is automatically sent to the mailing list. In such cases, you can participate by subscribing to the list or by reading the corresponding Usenet newsgroup. Either way, the content will be the same.

This type of facility requires a special program called a GATEWAY. The job of a gateway is to provide an automatic connection between two different types of information systems. In this case, we are talking about a Usenet/mailing list gateway. (We sometimes use the word "gateway" as a verb. For example, I might say that a mailing list is gatewayed to a particular Usenet group.)

The reason I mention all of this is because there is a well-known set of mailing lists that are gatewayed to an entire Usenet hierarchy. These mailing lists used to belong to a network called BITNET, and, some years ago, it was felt that some of them should be available via Usenet as well. To make this happen, a Usenet/mailing list gateway was created along with a set of newsgroups, one for each mailing list. All of these newsgroups are in the **bit** hierarchy.

Bitnet was started as an academic network in 1981 and grew so much that, by 1992, it connected about 1,400 organizations (mostly universities and research institutions) in 49 countries and supported several thousand mailing lists. Since then, however, the Internet has become the global network of choice. By the end of 1996, the Internet had absorbed most of what used to be Bitnet. Still, a large number of the mailing lists exist to this day, and some of them are gatewayed to Usenet newsgroups within the **bit** hierarchy.

The Listserv mailing list program was originally developed to run on Bitnet, and it is this program that supported the Bitnet mailing lists for so many years. For this reason, many of the **bit** Usenet groups have the word **listserv** in their name. You can see this in Figure 13-6, which shows a few examples of Bitnet mailing lists along with their corresponding Usenet newsgroups.

Figure 13-6: Examples of gatewayed Bitnet mailing lists

Mailing List	Newsgroup	Description
Blues-1	bit.listserv.blues-1	Blues music
Games-1	bit.listserv.games-1	Computer games
railroad	bit.listserv.railroad	Railroads and trains
museum-1	bit.listserv.museum-1	Museums
scuba-1	bit.listserv.scuba-1	Scuba diving
travel-1	bit.listserv.travel-1	Travel

WHAT'S IN A NAME?

Bitnet

Bitnet was started in the days when many universities had large IBM mainframe computers. In 1981, two researchers, Ira Fuchs at City University of New York and Greydon Freeman at Yale University, were discussing the Network Job Entry (NJE) protocol that was available for IBM mainframes. They decided that NJE could be used to connect computers over a leased telephone line, and they figured out a way to do so. Although they didn't know it at the time, this tiny two-computer network became the nucleus for what was to become the largest academic network in the world.

In other words, Fuchs and Freeman created the connection because they happened to have NJE. So, for this reason, they named their network BITNET, meaning "Because It's There Network". Later, this was changed to "Because It's Time Network".

Talking on the Net

Why do so many of us have computers, and why do we spend so much time using the Internet?

I don't know that we can ever answer these questions entirely, but I do know that all the time and effort we spend on the Internet has more to do with our nature than with making money and selling advertising. Human beings need to connect to one another, and that is why we have built so many tools to talk on the Net.

In previous chapters, we have discussed electronic mail, Web sites, Usenet discussion groups and mailing lists. All of these are important, but they do not allow you to carry on a real conversation. In this chapter, I will explain how to use the Internet to talk to other people. People all over the world are already talking on the Net, and, in a short time, you will be one of them.

The Basic Ideas

The term REAL-TIME refers to a process in which you sense and respond to something as it is happening. For example, talking on the telephone is a real-time experience, because you hear the other person's words as he says them. On the other hand, sending email is not real-time communication, because you do not see the messages as they are typed. Instead, you have to wait until a message is delivered before you can read it.

On the Internet, the word TALK refers to all types of real-time communication. For instance, let's say you and a friend are having a conversation by using a program that allows you to type messages back and forth. Even though you are typing (and not speaking), we say that you are talking. We often refer to this type of talking as CHATTING.

Most of the talking on the Internet is done by typing. However, there are other ways: you can talk by voice (as you do on a telephone), and you can also use real-time video (like people in the future). We will discuss all of these facilities—chatting, voice and video—in this chapter.

Talking on the Internet can be a lot different than talking in regular life. For example, it is common to talk with people on the Net whom you have never met face to face and probably never will. In addition, it is perfectly acceptable to start a conversation with someone you don't know. As a matter of fact, most people use anonymous nicknames, and, much of the time, there is no way to know whom you are talking to.

This makes for an interesting type of communication in which your mind communicates directly with another person's mind, with no voice, physical cues or other knowledge to distract you. As you might imagine, this type of talking has its own nuances and considerations (which we will discuss later in the chapter).

When you talk in person or over the telephone, you hear the other person's voice instantly. On the Net, however, there is sometimes a delay. As you type back and forth, it may take a few moments for the messages to be transmitted. Similarly, when you are talking via voice, there may be a short delay between the time you say something and when the other person hears it. This delay is referred to as LAG.

When the lag is small—as is often the case—the conversation flows smoothly and easily. If the lag becomes significant, however, it can make the conversation disjointed. Still, a bit of lag now and then is a normal phenomenon, and, after a while, you will find yourself adjusting to subtle changes without even noticing. Indeed, some people are so used to the lag that they routinely carry on several conversations at the same time, using the brief waiting periods to jump from one conversation to another.

To access a talk facility, you use a program called a TALK CLIENT. There are many different talk facilities available on the Internet for free. The particular client you use depends on which talk facility you want to access.

When you use the Web to talk, your browser can act as your talk client. Most of the non-Web talk facilities use a proprietary design which requires you to use a specific talk client. A few talk facilities allow you a choice of clients. In particular, this is the case for IRC, muds and most voice systems (all of which I will discuss later in the chapter).

In broad terms, there are two kinds of talk facilities.

The first kind uses a TALK SERVER as a central way station. When you use such a system, everything you type first goes to the server. The server then sends the information to all the other people taking part in the conversation.

The second kind of system uses a direct connection. Your talk client connects to the other person's talk client, and, as you type, your words are sent from your computer to the other person's computer without going through a central server.

Each of these systems has advantages. With a central server, it is possible to support a large number of people and a large number of simultaneous conversations. An example of this is IRC (Internet Relay Chat). When you connect to an IRC server, you will usually find hundreds of different conversations involving thousands of people from all over the world. Such systems are great places to hang out, because there is always someone to talk to.

Direct connections do not offer the same type of access. Since you are connected to, at most, a few people, you do not get the feeling of being in an international gathering place. However, you do have more privacy and control over your environment. Moreover, since your messages do not go through a central server, there is usually less lag, which makes it easier to carry on a more focused conversation.

Some talk clients will ask you to register before you can use the client. To register, you will have to give your name and mail address. My advice is to protect your privacy. Do not use your real name. Using a nickname is not only common, but perfectly acceptable. For advice on how to protect your mail address, see Chapter 6.

hint

On the Internet, people care about your ideas and what you have to say. Who you are and where you live are less important.

When you register with a particular talk facility, the information you specify is sent to a central server that acts as a public repository of names and addresses. The job of this server is to act as a directory for all the people who use the system. This is true even for systems that use direct connections, because you may still need a way to look up someone's name and address.

As you will see, the Internet offers a wide variety of ways to talk to other people. Throughout this chapter, I will discuss the various types of systems, and give you the information you need to get started. You can then experiment with the different talk facilities and see which ones you like best.

To start, let's talk about the simplest type of talk facility: Web chat rooms.

Web Chat Rooms

A WEB CHAT ROOM, or CHAT ROOM, is a talk facility that is offered via a Web site. Each chat room supports one multiperson conversation. There are many Web sites that offer public chat rooms.

When you visit such a Web site, think of yourself as being at a party in a large house with many different rooms. In each room there are a number of people talking. You can move from room to room, and listen or take part in the various conversations.

Some chat rooms are set up for general conversation. Others are devoted to particular topics or particular groups of people. For example, you might find a chat room where people talk about a popular television show, or a chat room just for teenagers.

Using a Web chat room is easy, because you do not need to install a special client program. All you need is a browser. There are two different ways in which this might work.

First, the chat room Web site may send your browser a Java applet to act as your talk client. (See Chapter 8 for a discussion of Java.) If so, your browser will run the applet automatically. You can see such a program in Figure 14-1.

FIGURE 14-1
A Web chat room using
a Java talk client

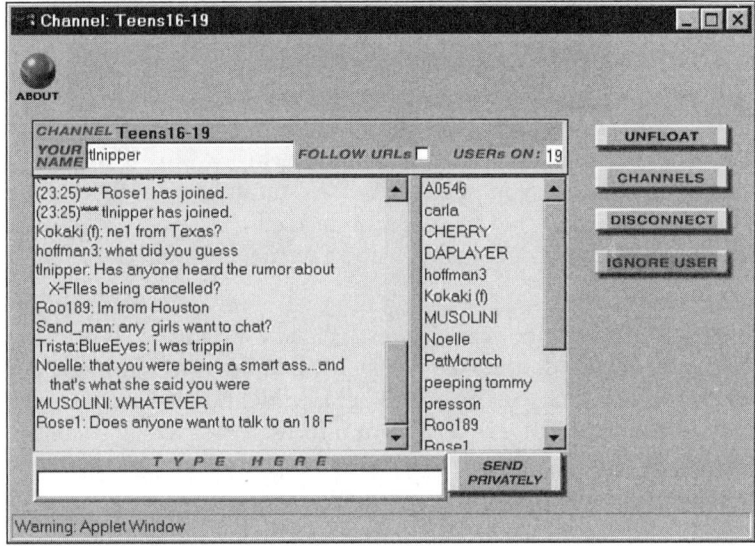

The other possibility is that you will use your browser as a talk client. You can see this in Figure 14-2. When you use a browser as a talk client, you are displaying regular Web pages that do not change. Thus, you must reload the Web page in order to see any new messages. You can do this by clicking the reload button. For convenience, most Web chat rooms are set up to cause your browser to reload the Web page automatically at regular intervals.

FIGURE 14-2
A Web chat room using
a browser as a talk
client

A Web chat room works by having a central server that acts as a way station. Everything you type is sent to the server, which then relays the information to the various client programs. Thus, all messages must pass through a server; they do not go directly from one person to another.

Web chat rooms are popular because they are readily available and do not require special software. If you have a browser running, you are ready to join a chat room. However, much of the conversation in Web chat rooms is transient and superficial. This is not the place for deep conversation or meaningful relationships.

Most Web chat rooms use only plain text. A few chat rooms enable you to display a picture along with your messages. This allows you to choose an image that illustrates your personality and makes it easy for people to recognize you. Other Web sites offer chat rooms with a specific visual environment. For example, while you are talking, it may look as if you are in a cave, or a forest, or a palace.

A few Web chat rooms are even more elaborate: They create artificial environments that you visit as you talk. You can move around from one place to another, and talk to the people you encounter. Within such systems, each person is represented by an AVATAR: a small picture or figure that moves and talks on your behalf. You control the appearance and actions of your avatar, which allows you to exhibit some of your own personality. Figure 14-3 shows people using avatars within an imaginary environment.

FIGURE 14-3
A Web chat room with avatars

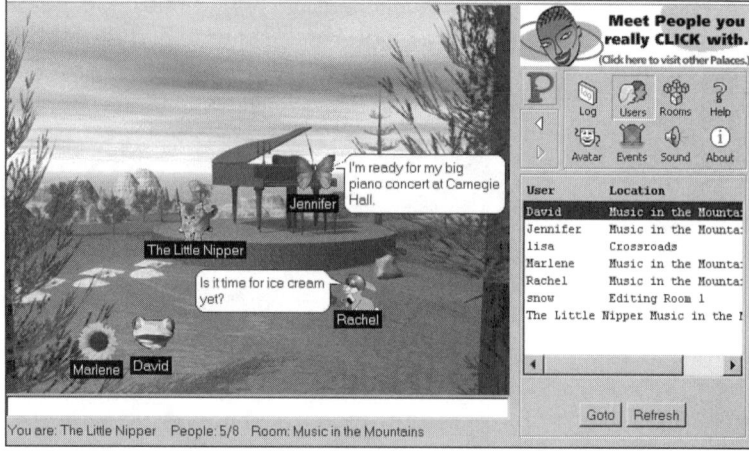

*I*NTERNET RESOURCE Web Chat Rooms

```
http://www.wbs.net/
http://chat.yahoo.com/
http://www.chatting.com/
http://www.talkcity.com/
http://chat.earthweb.com/
http://www.chatalyst.com/
http://www.cyber-beach.com/gateway.html
```

*I*NTERNET RESOURCE Avatar-Based Chat Rooms

```
http://www.net-world.com/
http://www.colonycity.com/
http://www.activeworlds.com/
http://www.palacespace.com/sites/
http://www.realtime.net/furcadia/
http://www.microsoft.com/ie/chat/vchatmain.htm
```

Direct Connections

As I explained earlier, some talk facilities use a central server as a relay station. When you use such a system, everything you type must first pass through the server. This is the case for the Web chat rooms we discussed in the last section, as well as with IRC and muds, which we will discuss later in the chapter. However, many of the Internet talk facilities use a direct connection in which your talk client communicates directly with the other person's talk client.

With a direct connection, your messages are transmitted faster because they do not go through a server. This means there is less lag, which makes it easier to carry on a conversation. In addition, your conversations are completely private. You may like to visit Web chat rooms to meet people and to make friends, but, once you do, you will find it more convenient and more comfortable to talk using a direct connection.

These types of talk facilities all require their own talk client, which you must download and install on your computer. Such clients are sophisticated programs. Not only can they send and receive messages, they can also perform a variety of other tasks. Each program has its own features, but there are two that are especially useful:

- **File transfer**: You can send files from your computer to the other person's computer. You may find it easier to transfer a file this way than to attach it to a mail message (see Chapter 5).

- **Web browsing**: With this feature, one person can control the other person's browser. This is handy when you want to show someone specific Web sites while you talk.

Even though these types of talk facilities use a direct connection, they still make use of a central server to act as a repository for names and addresses. Each time you start your talk client, it contacts this server and lets it know you are online. Thus, the server not only keeps track of who is registered with the system, it also knows, at any particular time, who is online and available for talking.

To help you keep track of the people with whom you like to talk, your client maintains a personal name and address list, sometimes referred to as a BUDDY LIST or a FRIENDS LIST. By checking with the central server, your client can tell you which of the people on your list are available for talking.

All of this makes it simple and easy to talk with someone. Just select a name from your personal list, and if the person is available, your talk client will establish a connection. For this reason, you will see this type of talk facility described as INSTANT MESSAGING.

In the following Internet Resource lists, I have listed a number of talk facilities for you to try. I have organized them into two groups. Here is why.

Some of the larger Internet companies offer a variety of free services, such as Web-based email, personalized news, chat rooms, and so on. These companies also offer instant messaging. Since the instant messaging is part of a larger system, I have kept these separate. Among these companies that offer free instant messaging are AOL, Excite, Infoseek and Yahoo. (Of course, the reason they offer these services is to make money by getting you to look at their ads.)

In order to use any of the direct connection programs, you will need to register. If you are concerned about your privacy, do not use your real name or mail address. For information on how to keep your mail address private, see the discussion in Chapter 6.

Some talk facilities are not part of these integrated systems. This group is shown in the second Internet Resource list. The most popular such service is ICQ (the name is a pun, "I seek you"). ICQ is used by a vast number of people all over the world. Figure 14-4 shows two people talking via ICQ.

FIGURE 14-4
A direct connection
using ICQ

*I*NTERNET RESOURCE Direct Connection Talk Facilities: Part of a Larger System

```
http://www.aol.com/aim/
http://pager.yahoo.com/jpager/
http://www.peoplelink.com/v1/down_infoseek/
http://talk.excite.com/communities/excite/pal/
```

*I*NTERNET RESOURCE Direct Connection Talk Facilities: Independent

```
http://www.icq.com/
http://www.powwow.com/
http://www.lolchat.com/
http://www.chchat.co.za/
```

Abbreviations Used While Talking

When you first start to talk on the Net, it is easy to feel a bit confused. If you are visiting a Web chat room or an IRC channel (discussed later in the chapter) where a number of people are talking at the same time, it may take a while to learn how to make sense out of what is happening. However, it won't be long before you start to feel the rhythm, and everything falls into place.

People who talk on the Net use a lot of abbreviations. This is because talking involves typing, and typing is slow. To help you get started, Figure 14-5 shows the most important abbreviations used while talking on the Net. You will find a more extensive list in Appendix C.

For the most part, the abbreviations are straightforward. However, there is one I want to discuss for a moment: the smiley. A SMILEY is a tiny representation of a smiling face:

`:-)`

(To see the smiling face, tilt your head sideways to the left.)

From time to time, you will find yourself typing something you mean as a joke, but which could be taken as being offensive. When this happens, you use a smiley to tell the other person not to be offended. The smiley means "just kidding".

For example, say you are talking about UFOs, and someone is describing how he was kidnapped the other night by a bunch of aliens dressed as Supreme Court justices. You might say:

```
I do find that hard to believe, but the next time
I see the Tooth Fairy, I'll ask her what she thinks :-)
```

Sometimes, you will see **<G>** or **<g>** ("grin") used instead of a smiley.

Figure 14-5: Abbreviations used while talking on the Net

Abbreviation	Meaning
:-)	smiley
;-)	winking smiley
<G>	grin (same as a smiley)
AFK	away from keyboard
BBL	be back later
BF	boyfriend
BRB	be right back
BTW	by the way
CUL8R	see you later
CYA	see ya (good-bye)
F2F	face to face (in person)
FYI	for your information
GF	girlfriend
IC	I see
IMHO	in my humble opinion
J/K	just kidding
L8R	(see you) later
LDR	long distance relationship
LOL	laughing out loud
OIC	oh, I see
PAW	parents are watching
PDA	public display of affection
RL	real life
ROFL	rolling on the floor laughing
SO	significant other
TTFN	ta-ta for now (good-bye)
TTYL	talk to you later

hint

When you talk on the Net, using all caps (all capital letters) means you are shouting. For example:

I WON THE LOTTERY!

Unless you really mean to shout, do not type in all caps. It is considered rude.

Voice and Video on the Net

Most of the talk on the Internet involves typing messages back and forth. This is the case with the Web chat rooms and direct connections we have discussed so far, and with IRC and muds, which we will talk about later in the chapter. However, it is possible to talk over the Net using voice and even video.

To do so, you need to have the appropriate equipment on your computer. For voice, you need a microphone and speakers (although headphones will also work). For video, you need either a special camera that connects to your computer, or an adapter that can connect a regular camera to a computer.

Voice communication over the Net is sometimes referred to as INTERNET PHONE. An Internet phone system is a lot like the direct connection facilities I described earlier in the chapter, except you use voice instead of typing. You initiate a connection by using your talk client. Once the connection is made, you talk by using your microphone and speakers, just as if they were a telephone.

The biggest advantage of using an Internet phone system is the cost. There is no special fee for making calls over the Internet, so, aside from anything you might have to pay for hardware or software, you can talk as long as you want for free. Much of the time, the connection works just fine, and you will have the satisfying experience of talking to someone without paying a long distance fee.

So why doesn't everyone use the Internet for all their telephone calls? There are several reasons.

In general, the regular telephone system is a lot more reliable and offers higher quality. With an Internet phone program, you can't always connect perfectly whenever you want. Moreover, the voice quality can vary. Most of the time it is okay, but sometimes there is a noticeable lag or an echo, which can quickly take the fun out of a free connection.

Another advantage to the telephone system is that everyone already has access to a phone. You can't use an Internet phone system unless the other person has Internet access, a computer with a microphone and speakers, and the appropriate software. In addition, you both have to be running the phone program at the same time in order to make the connection.

My feeling is that you are better off using the regular telephone system almost all of the time, especially if you live in a country like the United States, where long distance rates are low. However, there are two situations in which it makes sense to use an Internet phone system.

First, if you like playing on the Net and meeting strangers, it can be fun to talk to random people around the world for free. The companies that create Internet phone systems maintain directories, and, whenever you feel like it, you can search the directory for someone to call. You can also put your name in the directory and invite people to call you.

Using voice to talk to people you don't know can be fun for a while, but, most likely, you will get tired of it and go back to chatting in the regular manner. Moreover, you will find that many people will decline to talk to people they don't already know.

However, there are times when using an Internet phone program really pays off. If you have a relationship with someone that involves extremely long phone calls, you can save money by talking over the Net. For example, an Internet phone program is the ideal way to talk to your boyfriend in Australia.

In the business world, there are companies that use the Net instead of the telephone system for regularly scheduled phone calls, such as daily marketing conferences with their overseas offices. In such cases, an Internet phone system can save you a *lot* of money.

hint

Many people generate huge long distance bills having phone sex with a significant other. If this is an important factor in your life, try using an Internet phone program. In a few weeks, you will save so much money that you will be able to visit your significant other in person (with enough cash left over to buy a copy of this book for all your friends).

Some of the Internet phone programs offer video as well as voice. To receive video, you do not need special hardware. To send video, however, you need a video camera that is designed to connect to your computer.

Video over the Internet can be fun to play with, but you should realize that it is not the high resolution, full motion video you see on your television. Although you see images, they are updated intermittently, not continuously. To tell you the truth, although the idea of free video over the Net sounds cool, it's really not that big a deal.

hint

One of the big advantages to talking to someone over the Internet (or over the telephone) is that you do not have to look at each other while you are having a conversation.

If you would like to try using voice or video, the following Internet Resource will help you get started. My advice is to try the various programs and see which one you like best.

In some cases, you will get the best results if both people are using the same Internet phone program. However, this is not a requirement. An international standard called H.323 defines how voice and video work over the Internet. As long as you are using an H.323-compliant program, you can talk to anyone else using an H.323-compliant program.

Most of these programs offer other features besides the basic voice (or video) connection. While you are talking, you can also:

- Type messages back and forth
- Transfer files
- Control the other person's browser
- Collaborate by drawing within a shared window (called a WHITEBOARD)

Microsoft NetMeeting has another useful feature. You can have more than one person controlling a program that is running on one of the computers. This feature, called APPLICATION SHARING, allows you to work together with another person on just about anything you want. (However, it can be slow.)

Both Microsoft and Netscape offer free Internet phone programs. The Microsoft program (NetMeeting) can be downloaded independently of Internet Explorer. The Netscape program (Conference) is part of the Communicator suite, and must be downloaded and installed along with the rest of the Netscape software.

*I*NTERNET RESOURCE Voice and Video Communication

```
http://www.freetel.com/
http://cu-seeme.cornell.edu/
http://www.intel.com/cpc/videophone/
http://www.microsoft.com/netmeeting/
http://home.netscape.com/communicator/conference/
```

IRC (Internet Relay Chat)

IRC (Internet Relay Chat) is the largest of the Internet talk systems. The first version of IRC was created in 1988 by a Finnish programmer named Jarkko Oikarinen. Since then, IRC has grown enormously.

To use IRC, you must first download and install an IRC CLIENT on your computer. Once you have an IRC client, you use it to connect to one of the IRC NETWORKS. You can then talk to anyone else who is connected to the same network. IRC is so popular that, no matter when you connect, there will be many people for you to talk with.

There are more than 50 different IRC networks, each one using its own group of IRC SERVERS. The larger networks have dozens of servers around the world; the smaller networks have only a few servers. To use a particular IRC network, all you need to do is tell your IRC client to connect to any server on the network. Once you are connected, you have access to the entire network.

WHAT'S IN A NAME?

EFnet
Undernet
DALnet
IRCnet

Through the years, many IRC networks have been formed with varying degrees of success. Today, there are more than 50 different networks, the largest of which are EFnet, Undernet, DALnet and IRCnet.

IRC was started in 1988. By 1990, the original network had grown to encompass a number of servers around the world. The people in charge had intense philosophical disagreements over the design of the network. As a result, one group of people and the server they ran were banished from the network. The server was a computer named **eris.berkeley.edu**. This group formed their own network, but eventually it died out. In the meantime, what was left of the original network became known as the "Eris-free Network" or EFnet. Since then, EFnet has grown enormously, and, to this day, it is still the largest of the IRC networks.

By 1993, EFnet was becoming large and cumbersome, and another group of people decided to start an alternative network, which they named Undernet. The name was chosen as a whimsical description of an "underground network", hidden from the main network.

In 1995, another group of EFnet people created a network called DALnet as an alternative to EFnet and Undernet. The name comes from one of the members of the group, Sven Nielsen, whose nickname was "Dalvenjah FoxFire".

In 1996, the last of the large IRC networks, IRCnet, was started by yet another group of people who broke away from EFnet.

IRC is a mature, complex system, and there is a lot for you to learn. To get you started, I will explain the basic terminology, and show you where to get the software and the information you need. Once you have read this section, you can start by downloading and installing your own IRC client. You will then be able to connect to a server and start talking.

Each IRC network has a number of CHANNELS, each of which supports a different conversation. Once you have connected to an IRC server, you can JOIN one of the channels. This allows you to participate in that particular conversation. When you are tired of that conversation, you can LEAVE the channel.

All networks have a variety of channels; a large network may have thousands. Channels are dynamic: Anyone can create a channel at any time. Once the last person leaves, the channel is automatically deleted. Some channels are so popular, however, that they have existed continuously for years.

When someone creates a channel, he specifies a name for it. He can also specify an optional short description called a TOPIC. The purpose of the topic is to let people know what the channel is being used for. Some channels are created to discuss a specific subject, while others are used for more general conversation. As you use IRC, you can join and leave channels whenever you want, and you can be in more than one at the same time.

Channel names start with the **#** (number sign) character. Here are some examples:

```
#hottub
#beginner
#help
#IRCaddicts
#Wasteland
```

When you type a channel name, you can use either upper- or lowercase letters. Although some names are created with uppercase letters, it is easier to use all lowercase when you type.

The person who creates a channel becomes the CHANNEL OPERATOR or OP. The op has special control over that particular channel. He decides whether the channel will be open to the public, or whether it will be private (in which case, people may join by invitation only or by entering a password). If someone in the channel is a troublemaker, the op can kick him off the channel or even ban him permanently. The op can share power by allowing someone else to also become an op (for that channel).

People on IRC do not use their real names. Instead, each person uses a NICKNAME or NICK. You can use any nick you want (and you can change it whenever you want), as long as no one else on the network is already using the same name.

Most IRC clients put each channel in a separate window to help you keep the various conversations separate. You can then follow the conversation just by looking at the window. Every time anyone sends a message, it will be broadcast to everyone who has joined that channel. As you watch a channel, you will see messages appear near the bottom of the window and scroll up. At the very bottom of the window, there is an area that you use to type your own messages. When you do, they will be sent to the server which will broadcast them to everyone in the channel.

Figure 14-6 shows a typical IRC session. Within this session, I have joined three different channels, each of which has its own conversation. In addition to these windows, there is a fourth window showing various status messages.

FIGURE 14-6

A typical IRC session

As you watch the window for a particular channel, you will see two types of messages in the window. First, you will see the regular messages that people type back and forth. These messages will have the form:

<*nickname*> *message*

For example, here are two messages sent by a person using the nickname **carrie**:

```
<carrie> It takes a lot of energy to be so cute.
<carrie> But I manage :-)
```

Aside from conversation, you will also see system messages, generated by the IRC server. These messages give you information about the channel itself. For instance, every time someone joins or leaves a channel, you will see such a system message. All system messages start with the characters *******. For example:

*** carrie (amish@undependable.com) has joined #hottub

In a busy channel, the messages will fly by quickly, and you may be confused. Don't worry. Once you get used to IRC, your mind will notice what it needs to notice and will ignore everything else. In no time at all, you will be able to keep track of several different channels, while carrying on several conversations at the same time.

To control your IRC session, you use IRC commands. All of the commands start with a **/** (slash) character, in order to distinguish them from regular messages. For example, the command to join a channel is **/join** followed by the name of the channel. Thus, to join the **#hottub** channel, you would type:

/join #hottub

To leave a channel, you use the **/leave** command:

/leave #hottub

Figure 14-7 contains a summary of the most important IRC commands.

In order to get used to IRC, take some time to experiment with the various commands. As you do, don't forget to type a **/** character at the beginning of each command. Otherwise, your command will be interpreted as a message, and it will be broadcast to everyone in the channel. Consider this example.

The command to send a private message is:

/msg *nickname message*

Thus, to send a private message to the person using the nick **carrie**, you would type:

/msg carrie Did you get the secret letter I sent you?

What happens if you inadvertently leave out the **/** character?

msg carrie Did you get the secret letter I sent you?

The IRC server will interpret what you typed as a regular message and show it to everyone in the channel.

Figure 14-7: Important IRC commands

Command	Description
/dcc chat *nickname*	Start or accept a direct talk connection
/dcc send *nickname files*	Send files to the specified person
/help	Display help information
/help *command*	Display help about the specified command
/join *#channel*	Join the specified channel
/leave *#channel*	Leave the specified channel (same as **/part**)
/list	Display a list of all channels
/list *#channel*	Display information about the specified channel
/list -max *n*	Display channels that have no more than *n* people
/list -min *n*	Display channels that have at least *n* people
/me *action*	Emote (show) the specified action to current channel
/mode *#channel* **+pi**	Make the specified channel completely private
/msg *nicknames text*	Send a private message to specified people
/nick *nickname*	Change your nickname to specified name
/part *#channel*	Leave the specified channel (same as **/leave**)
/ping *nickname*	See how long it takes to get to specified person and back
/query *nicknames*	Open private message window to talk to specified people
/quit	Disconnect from the server
/who *	Show basic information about everyone in current channel
/who *nickname*	Show basic information about the specified person
/whois *nickname*	Show all available information about the specified person

hint

For a good time, join a crowded channel, and, after waiting a few minutes, enter the following command:

`msg hotlips I would love to meet you (and the whipped cream)`

(Be sure you do *not* type a **/** character at the beginning of the command.)

Aside from channels, IRC also supports a facility called DCC (which stands for "Direct Client to Client connection"). DCC allows you to establish a direct connection with another person. Once you establish such a connection, you can talk in private, as well as transfer files back and forth. The basic DCC commands are listed in Figure 14-7. DCC is useful to know, so when you get a chance, see if you can find someone to help you practice the commands.

hint

For security reasons, never accept a program or a script via DCC to run on your computer. It is not uncommon for people to offer programs that can cause harm to your system. One of my friends, who shall remain nameless (Martin Rivers), once got into trouble in just that way.

He was talking to someone via DCC, and the person offered him a batch file (a type of script). Martin accepted the file and ran it. The batch file then proceeded to delete some important Windows files from his computer. As a result, Martin had to reformat his hard disk, which wiped out all his files.

The next idea I want to mention is that of a BOT. A bot is a program that performs actions automatically in a specific IRC channel. (The name stands for "robot".) A bot can be programmed to respond to different types of input, to generate output, and to carry out various tasks. For example, a bot can be used to keep a channel open permanently, even when there are no people in it. Although bots can be helpful, many people have used them to cause trouble and abuse the system. For this reason, some IRC networks ban bots altogether. Other networks allow them, but with restrictions.

To finish this section, I would like to leave you with some resources to help you get started. First, you need to download and install an IRC client. The clients I have suggested here are particularly good ones. If you need more help, you can either look at the help system within your client program, or check with the help resources on the Web. Once you have an IRC client, connect to a server and join a channel. If you need more information, check with some of the following resources.

*I*NTERNET RESOURCE IRC Clients

```
http://www.mirc.com/
http://www.bcpl.lib.md.us/~frappa/pirch.html
```

*I*NTERNET RESOURCE IRC Help Information

```
http://www.irchelp.org/
http://www.newircusers.com/
http://wkweb5.cableinet.co.uk/DANDEB/ircmg.htm
```

Muds

A MUD is an elaborate, text-based imaginary environment. Although muds are used for talking, they offer a lot more: You can have adventures, explore exotic places and solve puzzles. You can also take part in group events, such as going on a quest or attending a wedding.

Muds are fantasy role-playing environments in which each person becomes a character. For example, you might be a magician, a druid, a thief, a warrior or a pirate. As you use the mud, your character interacts with other characters and with the mud itself. You move around from place to place, and as you do, things happen. For instance, you may be exploring a cave and happen upon an evil magician who tries to kill you. Or you may encounter a young warrior who asks you to join her on a quest to save a city from a hungry dragon.

Participating in a mud is a long-term experience. Every mud has regular users who form a large, extended family. Once you join a mud (which is free), you can create your own character and use it every time you visit that mud. It is common for people to return to a mud over and over, for months or even years. Each time you return, you will meet some of the same people, and over time, you will develop long-term friendships.

Muds provide a rich experience, because they offer a detailed environment that changes as you move from one place to another. Since muds are text-based, there are no pictures, only words to describe what you see. However, words are more compelling than pictures, and the imaginary world of a mud will, over time, become as real to you as the setting of a novel or story.

Each mud has a geography that is created by the people who administer the mud. Every mud is different. One mud might have villages and towns with stores, houses, and so on. Another mud might have a large series of rooms to explore. Figure 14-8 shows a typical description of a setting within a mud.

Figure 14-8: An imaginary setting within a mud

```
You are in the Heart's Haven Square.

This is the central gathering place for people
traveling in and out of the city. Heart's Haven
is a coastal city, with the ocean located to the
southeast. To the northeast, the city rises up a
gentle-sloping hillside, and to the northwest you
see a massive rock face. In any direction you look,
you can see interesting shops and beautiful places
to wander. You feel very welcome here. A tall,
black obelisk decorates the center of the town
square. The bustle and commotion of a thriving town
surround you.

There are four obvious exits:
east, north, south and west.
```

WHAT'S IN A NAME?

mud
mudder

The first mud dates back to a role-playing program developed in 1978 by Richard Bartle and Roy Trubshaw. At the time, they used the acronym MUD to stand for "Multi-User Dungeons" (as in Dungeons and Dragons). Later, people started to use "Multi-User Dimension", but eventually the name "mud" became a full-fledged word on its own (which is why I write it in lowercase letters).

The word "mud" can also be used as a verb. For example, "I have to finish my homework, so I can go mud" or "Monica fell asleep during the President's speech, because she was tired from mudding all night."

A person who uses a mud is sometimes called a MUDDER.

Broadly speaking, there are two types of muds: social muds and adventure muds.

Social muds are used primarily for chatting and socializing. They do have an imaginary geography, and people do adopt character roles, but mostly, these muds are for talking. Unlike Web chat rooms and IRC, muds provide an enduring social setting. People tend to stay longer, return more often, and take time to learn how things work. Once you start to spend time on a mud, you will make friends who will become an important part of your life. In fact, it is common for people on muds to have friendships that last for years.

hint

You will see social muds referred to by a variety of names: TinyMUDs, MUSHs, MUCKs, MUSEs, and MOOs. The distinction between the various subcategories is not important. Just remember that all muds of these types are for talking.

Adventure muds have two purposes. They are for talking and for role-playing adventures. The examples I previously described, including the one in Figure 14-8, are taken from adventure muds. Every adventure mud has a complex environment based on a particular theme. For example, there are adventure muds based on medieval fantasy, gothic horror, science fiction settings, and futuristic techno-cultures. I myself sponsor an adventure mud named Zhing. To give you an idea of what these muds are like, here is a brief description of Zhing.

Zhing was planned and developed by a group of people who have years of mudding experience. These people have created a rich and engaging environment based on a medieval fantasy theme. Like all adventure muds, you can spend time talking with other people, but there are also a great many places to explore. Zhing has five continents, one of which is an archipelago. There are coastlines, mountains, forests, streams, caves, cliffs (which you can climb), castles, beaches, docks (where you can catch fish to eat), parks, an underground cavern, a maze, roads, and cities that have restaurants, pubs, hospitals, armories, and various types of shops. Within Zhing, there are a lot of activities to keep you busy, either alone or in the company of other people, so there is always something to do.

hint

Muds are magical places. There is nothing else like them, on or off the Net.

So how do you access a mud? Muds use a client/server system, so, to start, you must download and install a mud client. Once your client is up and running, you can have it connect to any mud you want.

In order to connect to a mud, you need to know two pieces of information. First, you need to know the address of the mud. This is a regular Internet address that identifies the host (that is, the computer) on which the mud resides. For example, the host for Zhing is `zhing.com`.

The second thing you need to know is the PORT NUMBER used by the mud. Port numbers work as follows.

Because Internet computers can provide a variety of services, a client must be able to tell a server exactly what type of service is being requested. To do this, the client uses a port number. All Internet client/server systems use port numbers, but, in most cases, you don't have to worry about them, because your client takes care of the details automatically. For example, the basic Internet services, such as mail and Usenet and the Web, all use standard port numbers. When you access one of these services, your client automatically sends the appropriate port number to the server.

Muds, however, do not use standard port numbers. For this reason, in order to access a mud, you must specify a port number as well as an address. In general, people who design muds choose port numbers that are easy to remember. For example, the port number for Zhing is **4000**.

In case you were wondering about other port numbers, Figure 14-9 shows some of the standard numbers used on the Internet. Except for muds, you don't really need to know any of this, so don't worry if you don't recognize some of the technical terms. Your client programs know what to do.

Figure 14-9: Standard port numbers used on the Internet

Service	Port Number
DNS	53
FTP	20, 21
IRC	194
Mail	25 (SMTP), 110 (POP), 143 (IMAP)
Telnet	23
Usenet	119 (NNTP)
Web	80 (HTTP), 443 (HTTPS), 8080 (HTTP, sometimes)

To start mudding, begin by downloading and installing a mud client on your computer. Then take a few minutes and read some of the basic information to make sure you get started properly. To help you, I have put an introduction to muds on my Web site. The address is:

`http://www.harley.com/mud/`

When you need more information, you can take a look at the following FAQs (frequently asked question lists) and tutorials. Once you are ready to start mudding, check out the lists of muds for one that looks intriguing. (Your mud client will also come with its own list of muds.) If you would like to visit the Zhing mud, you can connect by using the following information:

> <u>Zhing mud</u>
> host = **zhing.com**
> port = **4000**

*I*NTERNET RESOURCE Mud Clients

```
http://www.chaco.com/pueblo/
http://www.zuggsoft.com/zmud/zmudinfo.htm
```

*I*NTERNET RESOURCE Mud FAQs and Tutorials

```
http://www.harley.com/mud/
http://www.godlike.com/muds/
http://lucien.berkeley.edu/moo.html
http://www.imaginary.com/LPMud/lpmud_faq.html
http://www.faqs.org/faqs/games/mud-faq/part1/
```

*I*NTERNET RESOURCE Lists of Muds

```
http://moolist.yeehaw.com/
http://www.chaco.com/lists/
http://www.mudconnector.com/
http://mudlist.eorbit.net/~mudlist/
http://www.godlike.com/muds/extended.html
```

Expectations and Reality

Isn't it amazing that you can sit in front of your computer and, just by clicking your mouse and typing on your keyboard, talk to people all over the world?

Talking on the Net is a pleasant way to pass the time, but it can be much more. The Internet is a part of our mainstream culture, and meeting people on the Net is considered a normal, legitimate way to make friends. Many people use the Net every day to meet with their friends and to develop relationships. Some relationships are brief; others last for months and years. Some relationships are casual; others are deeply passionate and enduring.

You may hear someone talk about the Internet as if it were different from "real life", but, for a great many people, the Net is a part of real life. The friends they have on the Net are just as real as their job, their home and their family.

And why not? When you talk on the Net, you are communicating directly with other people's minds. By bypassing the limitations of appearance and physical presence, you learn to judge people by their ideas and by how they express themselves. All this makes for a culture in which *what* you are matters a whole lot more than *who* you are. However, the Internet is different from other parts of life. To be successful, you need to develop new skills and new ways of looking at other people.

To start, you need to be persistent. When you begin to talk on the Net, it is easy to feel confused and overwhelmed. As you watch the conversation in a Web chat room or an IRC channel or a mud, you will see people coming and going. Moreover, the messages move fast, and it can be hard to understand what is happening.

Don't worry. All the people who look as if they are so confident were, at one time, beginners just like you. Human beings are flexible and adaptable, and it won't be long before you know what you are doing and you will feel right at home. Whatever happens, don't allow yourself to be intimidated by other people. Not everyone on the Net is polite, and a few people take particular delight in being mean to newcomers. All they are doing is demonstrating their own insecurities, so don't let such people hurt your feelings.

To help you get off to a good start, I have two suggestions. First, recognize that the Internet talk facilities have been around for some time and have all developed their own cultures. (This is especially true of IRC and the muds.) Thus, your first steps should be to learn how things are done, just as you would if you moved to a foreign country.

At the beginning, it is a good idea to listen more than you talk. Do your best to learn the new words and to understand the behaviors that are expected of you. Each type of talk facility has a rhythm of its own, which you will absorb. After all, there are thousands of people using the Internet to talk right now, and most of them aren't nearly as smart as you.

My second suggestion is to put some effort into improving your typing. The better you type, the faster you will communicate, and the more likely people will respond to what you have to say. Remember, people judge you by what they see, and, on the Net, all they can see is your words. In my experience, the easiest way to learn to type quickly is to spend lots of time talking on the Net. When your mind wants to say something, your fingers will figure out what to do.

hint

On the Internet, typing well is more important than dressing well.

As a rule, people who talk on the Net use nicknames to remain anonymous. As a result, the Internet has developed a wonderful freedom of expression in which people are comfortable saying whatever they want. There are a lot of advantages to such an environment. After all, the Internet is the largest open forum in the world and people should feel free to express themselves however they want. As you talk on the Net, you are in an environment where people's ideas and personalities matter more than who they are or where they live.

For this reason, you must realize that many people are not who they seem to be. People can present themselves in any way they want: They can tell the truth, they can lie, and they can exaggerate. For example, it is common for people to misrepresent their age, their weight, and even their sex. This does not mean that you always need to be distrustful and suspicious. Rather, you must learn to accept people based on their ideas. Do not depend on what anyone says about himself, unless you have a way to verify it independently.

If you are talking with someone and your intuition tells you that something is not right, be prudent and break off the conversation. Be polite, but don't worry about hurting someone else's feelings. There are plenty of other people to talk to.

Just as important, be sure to protect your own privacy. As a general rule, do not tell anyone your real name, your phone number or your street address. If you get to know someone well, you may want to give him some personal information, but please, make sure you really do know him well, and use your discretion.

hint for parents

Before you let your children talk on the Net, teach them that they must never give out any type of personal information without your permission.

If your children are young, you can find places for them where they will be talking with other children. To make sure you feel comfortable, you may want to watch as they talk.

Once you start to make friends, the time may come when you want to meet someone in person. Such meetings can work out well, and many satisfying relationships have started on the Internet. However, you should realize that it is possible to develop a deep bond with people, even to the point of intimacy, and still not really understand who they are.

On the Internet, people can present themselves in any way they want, and it is human nature for all of us to dwell on our strengths and downplay our weaknesses. When you talk to someone in person, you can see what he looks like, his body language and his mannerisms. You can also see how he reacts to you, and how you feel being with him.

All this is missing when you talk over the Net. So, when you are going to meet somebody in person for the first time, do not take anything for granted. Arrange to meet the person in a public place and, if possible, take a friend with you. The friend will be more than a chaperone. Although you may have talked to someone for hundreds of hours, meeting him or her in person is bound to generate a lot of pressure and some awkwardness. Having a friend with you will make the meeting more relaxed and a lot more comfortable.

The last point I want to make has to do with developing a sense of perspective. Talking on the Net is fun, and making friends is certainly rewarding, but you must never forget that there is more to life than the Internet. Many people get so wrapped up with their Internet friends or with their muds that they neglect other aspects of life.

It is important for your health and your sense of well-being to maintain a balance in your life. You are a human being, so don't forget you need fresh air, exercise and face-to-face relationships that involve normal responsibilities and obligations.

hint

Go outside. The Net will be there when you get back.

Net Sex

Warning: The following section contains material for mature audiences only, so do not read it unless you are an adult or unless your parents are not in the room.

NET SEX refers to an activity in which two people type erotic messages back and forth in order to achieve a state of sexual arousal leading to physical resolution. For the most part, Net sex takes place between two consenting people in a private place within some type of talk facility. Frequently, the people having Net sex are masturbating at the same time. There is nothing wrong with this; after all, it is a private activity. However, if you choose to engage in Net sex, I do want you to understand what is probably happening at the other end. Net sex is safe in a physical way, because there is no actual contact. However, there are a few important considerations.

Net sex involves real feelings and real sensations. Within the anonymity of the Internet, it may be easy to forget your inhibitions, but you must remember that you are interacting with another person. People have feelings, so don't forget to be nice.

If you ever meet a Net sex partner in person, do not have any expectations. Do not assume that, just because someone had Net sex with you, he or she will want to have real sex. Nor should you assume that you have a deep relationship with someone just because you have had Net sex. For many people, Net sex is a way to experiment or to release sexual tension. Chances are, there is not much meaning beyond the obvious.

You should be aware that most talk programs have a way to save the transcript of a conversation. Although you may think your encounter is completely private, your partner may be recording everything. For this reason, some people will have Net sex only with people they know well.

Finally, you must remember that the Internet is based on anonymity and voluntary standards of behavior. When you meet someone on the Internet, there is no way to know who they really are or if they are telling the truth, so please use discretion and judgment. (But don't forget to have fun.)

hint

Net sex requires you to use your imagination, and there is no doubt that experiences that fulfill your fantasies can be highly satisfying.

However, imagine your disappointment if you were to find out that the blonde, 21-year-old college girl who likes to be tied up and ravished is really a balding, 55-year-old accountant named Marvin from Fargo, North Dakota.

Creating Your Own Web Site

There is a lot involved in making your own Web site. Creating even a simple Web site can require you to understand a fair bit of detail. However, with the right tools and a bit of practice, the job becomes a lot easier.

In this chapter, I will explain the important ideas and show you where to find the resources you need. Before we start, I want to make sure you are familiar with the following sections from previous chapters. Please take a few minutes now to review this material, as it will make our job easier later on.

Chapter 4 Internet Addresses

- URLs
- File Names and Extensions
- Directories and Subdirectories
- Pathnames
- What a ~ (Tilde) Means in a Pathname

Chapter 7 The Web

- The Basic Ideas
- Entering a URL

hint

Before you start to build your Web site, I want you to give some thought as to what you are going to put on it.

My suggestion is to devote your Web site to an area of life you find fascinating. Do you like to collect trading cards? Do you enjoy knitting or needlework? Are you a history buff? Do you write stories or draw cartoons?

Look within yourself and ask, "What do I love to do or make or collect or think about so much that I would do it all day long if I didn't have to work?"

That should be the theme of your Web page. Share your passion with the world.

HTML

When you look at a Web page, you see text, pictures and other objects. It is important to understand how these components are put together into a single page.

Each Web page is stored as a file on a Web server. This file contains the text that will be on the page, along with special instructions called TAGS. When your browser reads the file, it uses the tags as guidelines. The tags specify which components are to be used and how they should be displayed on the page.

The tags are written according to a set of specifications called HTML (Hypertext Markup Language). Thus, to create a Web page, you need to make a file containing the text of the page along with the appropriate HTML tags. You can put in the tags yourself, or you can have a program do it for you. When you create such a file, it will be stored with a name that ends with the extension **html** or **htm**, for example, **harley.html** or **harley.htm**.

hint

We use the term HTML in two ways. First, it is the name of the system used to define the appearance and structure of Web pages. Thus, we might say, "Every Web page has an HTML file that contains the text of the page along with the tags that describe that page."

Informally, we often use the term HTML to refer to the contents of such a file. For example, you might hear someone say, "Don't get rid of that file. It contains the HTML for the main page of my Web site."

HTML tags have a special format, so they won't be confused with regular text. Each tag starts with a **<** (less-than) character and ends with a **>** (greater-than) character. To explain what I mean, I will show you a few examples. You don't have to memorize the details. I just want you to get a feeling for what HTML tags look like.

Let's start with one of the tags used for text formatting, the **
** tag. When a browser displays text, it ignores extra spaces and blank lines. All the words are formatted as a continuous stream. The browser breaks the lines in such a way as to make them fit within the width of the page.

However, there may be times when you want to force your browser to break a line at a particular place. To do so, you put a **
** tag at that place. For instance, when the following text is displayed, the browser will jump to a new line after the word **lamb:**

**Mary had a little lamb
 Its fleece was white as snow.**

Here is another example of an HTML tag. The **<img>** (image) tag tells the browser to display a picture:

<img src="cat.gif">

In this case, the picture to be displayed is stored in the file **cat.gif**. (The term **src** means "source".)

Many HTML tags work in pairs. For instance, to display words in italic, you use a "start-italic" tag **<i>** and an "end-italic" tag **</i>**. As an example, the tags in the following line tell the browser to display the word **best** in italic:

This is the <i>best</i> Web site in the world.

Here is another example of tags used in a pair. To create a link to another page, you use:

<a> to indicate the beginning of the link

</a> to indicate the end of the link

(The letter **a** stands for "anchor", an HTML technical term.)

Let's say you are designing a Web page containing the following sentence:

Visit my cat's Web page.

Within this sentence, you want the words **my cat's** to be a link. When someone clicks on this link, you want their browser to jump to the file **fluffy.html**. To do so, you use the **<a>** and **</a>** tags to define the link as follows:

Visit <a href="fluffy.html"> my cat's </a> Web page.

(The term **href** means "hypertext reference".)

WHAT'S IN A NAME?

HTML

When you embed tags within text, we say that you MARK UP the text. Thus, we can explain the name HTML—Hypertext Markup Language—as follows:

- Hypertext refers to text that contains links.
- Markup shows that there are tags embedded in the text.
- Language sounds cool even though HTML isn't really a language.

As you might imagine, the HTML system has a lot of details. There are many tags, and it can take a long time to learn how to use them well. However, it is not necessary to understand HTML to create Web pages. Instead, you can use a program called a Web page editor to handle all the details. All you need to do is lay out the page the way you want, and the editor will create the HTML file for you. (We will talk about Web page editors later in the chapter.)

Does this mean you do not have to learn HTML? For most people, the answer is yes, you do not need to learn HTML. However, if you are the type of person who likes to control every little detail of your work, having an understanding of HTML allows you to read and modify the file generated by your Web page editor.

If you know enough HTML, you can create a Web page from scratch, writing all the tags yourself without the help of a program. I often do this myself. In fact, this is how all Web pages used to be created in the olden days (the mid-1990s).

To show you what HTML looks like, Figure 15-1 contains the specifications for a small Web page. The Web page itself is shown in Figure 15-2 on page 329. This is a simple example, but it does give you the flavor of HTML. (Note: All the lines that begin with **<!--** are descriptive comments that are ignored by the browser. The comments are there to make the HTML easy to read.)

If you want to look at more complex examples, your browser can help you. Go to any Web page, pull down the View menu and select "Source" (Internet Explorer) or "Page Source" (Netscape). Your browser will open a new window and show you the HTML for the page you are looking at. For some good examples, visit the pages on my Web site:

http://www.harley.com/

You will find it interesting to compare the HTML tags with what you see on your screen.

If the time comes that you want to learn more about HTML, the following resources will help you. For reference, Figure 15-3 on page 330 contains a list of the most important HTML tags and what they do.

*I*NTERNET RESOURCE HTML Tutorials

    http://www.quadzilla.com/

    http://www.tips-tricks.com/

    http://www.werbach.com/barebones/

    http://www.htmlgoodies.com/tutors.html

    http://www.hotwired.com/webmonkey/teachingtool/

    http://www.ncsa.uiuc.edu/General/Internet/WWW/HTMLPrimer.html

The Components of a Web Page

Web pages are built out of eight different types of components. They are:

- Text
- Links
- Pictures
- Sounds
- Tables
- Forms
- Frames
- Programs

Figure 15–1: HTML for a simple Web page

```
<!-- Sample Web Page: Copyright 1998, The Little Nipper -->

<!-- Start of the page -->
  <html>

<!-- Head -->
  <head>
    <title>The Little Nipper's Web Page</title>
  </head>

<!-- Start of the body -->
  <body>

<!-- Picture of The Little Nipper -->
  <center>
    <img src="nipper.jpg">
    <p>
    <font size="5" face="Arial">
      I am The Little Nipper
    </font>
  </center>
  <p>

<!-- A Message from The Little Nipper -->
  <font size="4" face="Arial">
    I was born in Southern California, on April 6, 1991.
    Since then, I've lived a life made up of one part
    hard work (chasing things and being a good companion)
    and two parts leisure (eating, sleeping and sitting
    in the sun).
    <p>
    <center>
      Check out this cool Web site:
      <a
      href="http://www.harley.com/">
        Harley Hahn's Web Site</a>
    </center>
  </font>

<!-- End of the body -->
  </body>

<!-- End of the page -->
  </html>
```

FIGURE 15–2
A simple Web page

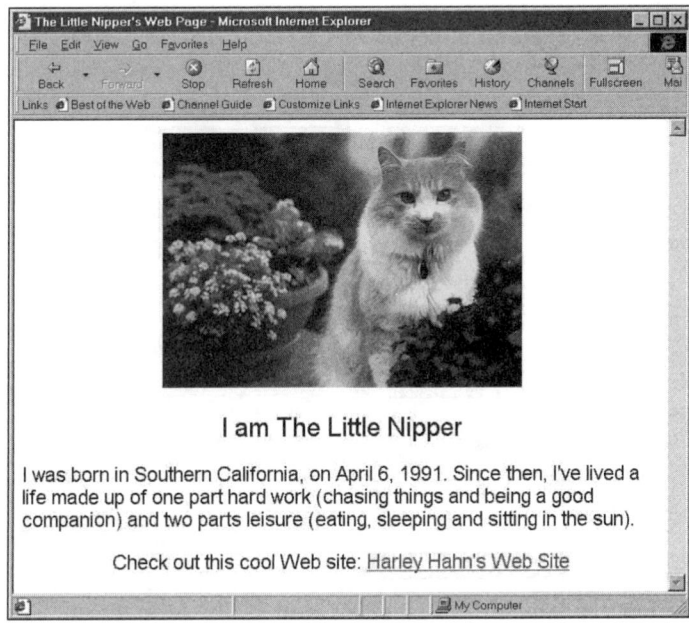

Let's take a moment and discuss each of these building blocks in turn.

Text: A Web page can contain any text you want. The text is stored in the HTML file along with the tags for that page. You have some degree of control over how the text is to be displayed. For instance, you can use italic or boldface, and you can specify that the text should be a particular font (typeface). You can also make text wrap around pictures, line up in columns, or be formatted into a list.

Most of the time, it is best to use plain, ordinary text broken into paragraphs. When a browser displays the page, it will automatically format the paragraphs to fit within the size of the browser window.

Links: The links on your page are what turns the text into hypertext. A link points to a specific Internet resource such as a Web page, a picture, a sound, a mail address, or a Usenet group. When you click on a link, your browser does whatever is necessary to follow that link. In most cases, this means fetching and displaying another Web page.

You can attach links to either words or pictures. One special type of picture is an image map. Within an image map, various parts of the picture correspond to different links. Image maps are often used as navigation aids.

Figure 15–3: The most important HTML tags

HTML Tag	Purpose
`<!-- text -->`	a comment (ignored by browser)
`<a href="URL"> text </a>`	define link text to URL
`<b> text </b>`	display text in boldface
`<body>…</body>`	define the body of the Web page
` `	break text onto a new line
`<center> text </center>`	center text
`<font>…</font>`	change the color, style or size of the font (typeface)
`<form>…</form>`	create a form
`<frame>…</frame>`	define an individual frame
`<frameset>…</frameset>`	define a set of frames
`<head>…</head>`	define the head of the Web page
`<h1> text </h1>`	display text in heading 1 style
`<hr>`	display a straight line (horizontal rule)
`<html>…</html>`	define the beginning and end of the Web page
`<i> text </i>`	display text as italic
`<img…>`	display a picture (image)
`<map>…</map>`	create an image map
`<meta>`	information for the Web server or a search engine
`<ol>…</ol>`	create an ordered (numbered) list
`<p>`	start a new paragraph
`<table>…</table>`	create a table
`<title> text </title>`	specify the title of the Web page
`<u> text </u>`	underline text
`<ul>…</ul>`	create an unordered (non-numbered) list

Pictures: You can use various types of pictures on your Web pages: drawings, icons, photographs, and so on. Each picture is stored in a separate file. As a general rule, photographs are stored using a format called JPEG, while all other pictures are stored using a format called GIF. You can tell the format of a picture by looking at the extension of the file name. For example, a file containing a photograph of a car might be called **car.jpg**; a file containing a drawing of a box might be called **box.gif**.

? WHAT'S IN A NAME?

JPEG
GIF

The JPEG format is used to store photographs. The name comes from the organization that developed the standard: the Joint Photographic Experts Group.

The GIF format is used to store all other types of images, especially drawings, cartoons and icons. The GIF format was developed by a company named CompuServe, which used to own an online service. (The service was bought by AOL.) The original GIF format was developed so CompuServe's users would have a way to store and exchange pictures. The name GIF stands for "Graphics Interchange Format".

You will often see people use the terms JPEG and GIF to refer to pictures that use these formats. For example, let's say you are at a Web page party, and you overhear two people talking in the hallway:

Person 1: I'm almost finished building my new Web site. I already put in a bunch of JPEGs of my family. Now all I need is some small drawings to fill in the empty spaces.

Person 2: I have some drawings of space aliens talking to Elvis that will look great on your page. I'll send you the GIFs in the morning.

Person 1: Thank you, Person 2. You sure are a good friend.

One particular type of GIF you will encounter is an ANIMATED GIF. This type of GIF consists of one file that contains a sequence of pictures. When a browser encounters an animated GIF, it displays the pictures one after another, creating a simple animation. To make an animated GIF, you must first create the separate pictures. You then use a special tool that puts the pictures together into a GIF file using the animated GIF format.

Sounds: It is possible to put sounds on a Web page. Like pictures, each sound is stored in its own file. The most common way to use sounds is to create a link to a sound file. When you click on the link, your browser retrieves the sound file and plays its contents.

There are a number of different file formats used to store sounds. The most common is the WAV format, which is stored in files with the extension **wav**. For instance, you might have a file named **moo.wav** that contains the sound of a cow.

Other common types of sound files are used for streaming audio (see Chapter 10) and for music. The most common streaming audio format is RealAudio, which uses files with the extensions **ra** and **ram**. There are a number of formats used for music, the most common being MIDI, which uses files with an extension of **mid**.

WHAT'S IN A NAME?

WAV
MIDI

The WAV format for storing sound in computer files was developed by Microsoft. The name stands for "waveform data". (A sound can be thought of as a wave that travels through the air.)

The MIDI format was originally developed in 1982 to allow musicians to connect one synthesizer to another. Today, a modern version of the MIDI format is used to store and manipulate music on computers, synthesizers, keyboards, and other electronic music devices. The name MIDI stands for "Musical Instrument Digital Interface".

Tables: A table is a structure that contains information in rows and columns. When you create a table, your Web page editor generates HTML tags that describe the size of the table and its contents. Figure 15-4 shows a Web page that contains a table.

Forms: A form contains specific areas into which you can type information as you are reading a Web page. Once a form is filled out, you click on a button. The browser then sends the information to the Web server, where it is processed by a separate program. Figure 15-5 shows a Web page that contains a form.

Using forms on a Web page requires special facilities. First, you need to write (or find) a program to process the information that will come from the form. Next, you need to place the program in the appropriate directory on the Web server. I won't go into the details, as they are too complex. I will, however, mention a common technical term associated with forms, so you will recognize it when you see it.

When you write a form-handling program, the information is passed between the server and the program using a system called the Common Gateway Interface, or CGI. Thus, the term "CGI programming" refers to creating a program that processes data from a Web page form.

Frames: It is sometimes convenient to design a Web page that contains other, smaller Web pages. This is done by using a facility called FRAMES. A frame is a specific area of a Web page that can contain data from another page.

When you create frames with your Web page editor, it generates the appropriate HTML tags to specify the size and contents of each frame. When your browser encounters such tags, it creates the frames and fills them with the appropriate content.

Frames are useful when you want to have a Web page that consists of several independent components. For example, let's say you are designing a picture gallery.

FIGURE 15–4
A Web page containing
a table

FIGURE 15–5
A Web page containing
a form

You might use one frame to display the names of all the pictures that are available for viewing. When someone clicks on a name, the actual picture is displayed in a second frame. Figure 15-6 shows a Web page that contains frames.

Programs: Using a program as part of a Web page enables you to utilize many different types of features on your Web site. There are a variety of tools and programming languages available for working with Web pages. However, they are all complex, and the details are well beyond the scope of this book.

If you can't program, don't worry. Programming is not necessary for building most types of Web pages. In fact, HTML was designed so that people would be able to create Web pages without programming.

For reference, here are the names of the most common Web programming tools, so, if you see them, you will at least know what they are. (For a discussion of Java and ActiveX, see Chapter 8.)

- Java
- ActiveX
- JavaScript
- JScript
- VBScript
- Visual Basic
- Perl
- C++
- C

FIGURE 15–6

A Web page containing frames

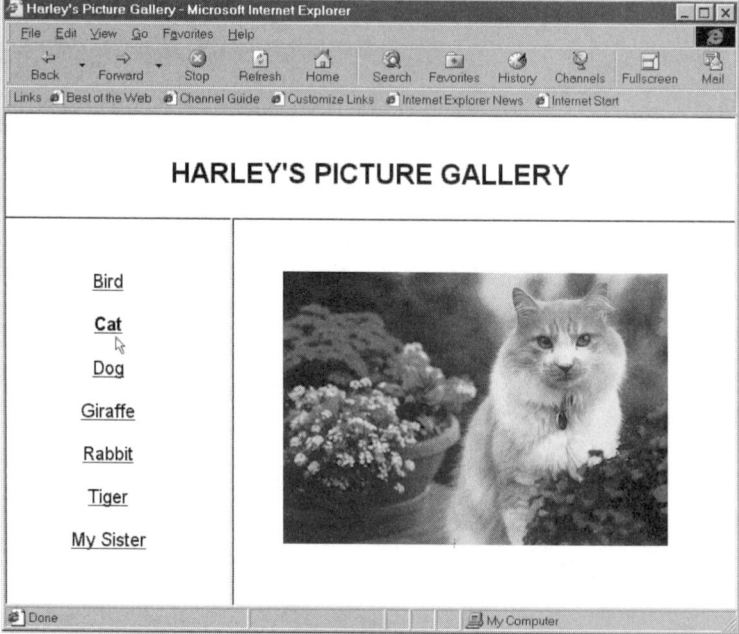

By the way, although the names Java and JavaScript look similar, they have nothing to do with each other. JavaScript was created by Netscape. For marketing reasons, they chose a name that sounded like Java.

Web Page Editors

A WEB PAGE EDITOR is a program used to create, modify and maintain Web pages. Some Web page editors also have tools that make it easy to send your files to the Web server and to manage large Web sites consisting of many pages.

There are two basic types of Web page editors. The first type is called a WYSIWYG EDITOR. The name "wysiwyg" (pronounced "whiz-ee-whig") stands for "what you see is what you get". With a wysiwyg editor, you work directly with the elements on your Web page: text, pictures, tables, and so on. You create and arrange them however you want. Behind the scenes, the editor generates the HTML for you and saves it in a file. Wysiwyg editors are easy to use because you never need to look at the actual HTML.

Some people would rather write the HTML themselves. These people use an HTML EDITOR. This type of editor allows you to work directly with the HTML tags. You can immerse yourself in as much detail as you want, with complete control over the final product. (I often use an HTML editor myself.)

Once you have created a Web page, all you have to do is copy it to a Web server and the page is on the Internet. (I will discuss how to find a Web server later in the chapter.) When you copy a Web page to a server, we say that you PUBLISH the page. More formally, you upload the page from your computer to the Web server. (Remember, "upload" means to copy data from your computer to the Internet; "download" means to copy data from the Internet to your computer.)

Wysiwyg editors have a built-in feature that makes it easy to publish your Web pages. Some HTML editors do not have such a feature, and you have to upload the pages yourself using FTP (see Chapter 2). If you use such an editor, you will need an FTP client program to do the uploading for you.

All Web page editors are complex programs that take time to master. My suggestion is to start with a wysiwyg editor and spend some time learning how to use it well. As you become more advanced, you can try an HTML editor if you want.

Both Microsoft and Netscape offer free wysiwyg editors to complement their Web browsers. The Microsoft editor is called FRONTPAGE EXPRESS. In order to use FrontPage Express, you must have Internet Explorer.

You can get the editor in one of two ways. First, when you install Internet Explorer, specify that you want the "full installation". This will install FrontPage Express along with a number of other tools. Alternatively, if you have already installed Internet

Explorer without FrontPage Express, start the browser, pull down the Help menu and select "Product Updates". This will take you to a Microsoft Web page where you can download various programs, including FrontPage Express.

Once you have FrontPage Express, you can start it as a separate program or within Internet Explorer. Within the browser, pull down the Edit menu and select "Page".

If you like FrontPage Express a lot, Microsoft has a more powerful version you may want to use. The more powerful program is called FrontPage (without the "Express"). Unlike FrontPage Express, however, FrontPage costs money.

hint

Within a Microsoft product name, the word "Express" identifies the less powerful version of the product. The Express product is free; the other product costs money. For example:

- FrontPage and FrontPage Express (Web page editors)
- Outlook and Outlook Express (mail programs)

The Netscape Web page editor is called COMPOSER. Composer is free: It comes as part of the Netscape Communicator suite. To use Composer, you need to download and install Communicator. Once you have Composer, you can start it as a separate program or from within the Netscape browser. Within the browser, pull down the Communicator menu and select "Page Composer".

*I*NTERNET RESOURCE Free Web Page Editors

```
http://home.netscape.com/download/
http://www.microsoft.com/ie/download/
```

*I*NTERNET RESOURCE Web Page Editors

```
http://cws.internet.com/32html.html
http://www.tucows.agis.net/htmledit95.html
http://tucows.tierranet.com/htmlbeginner95.html
```

*I*NTERNET RESOURCE FTP Client Programs

`http://cws.internet.com/32ftp.html`

`http://tucows.lauderdale.net/ftp95.html`

Pictures and Sounds

For variety, you may want to use some non-textual components to enhance your Web pages. For example, you can put photographs on your Web site as well as decorate the pages by using drawings, icons, buttons, and other types of graphics. You can even set the background to be a color or a particular design. Finally, you might want to put some sounds on your page (although this is a resource that should be used sparingly).

So where do you get such components? You can either make them yourself or find them for free on the Net. Let's start with photographs.

To use a photograph, it must be stored in a file, usually a JPEG file. There are several ways you can turn your own photos into JPEGs.

First, you can use a digital camera. A digital camera stores photographs as computer files, rather than using regular negatives. Such a camera will come with an interface to connect to a PC, along with whatever software you need to transfer the files to your computer. If you have a video camcorder, you can buy an adapter called a VIDEO CAPTURE BOARD, which you install in your computer. Once you connect your camcorder to the board, you can create copies of individual video frames and store them as image files on your computer.

Alternatively, you can take regular pictures and use them to create JPEGs. The best way to do this is to use a SCANNER, a device that you connect to your computer. A scanner processes an image on paper and creates a computer file containing that image. (We say that the scanner DIGITIZES or SCANS the image.) Scanners, of course, cost money. If you want to digitize a lot of photos, you may want to buy your own scanner. Otherwise, you may be able to find a place—such as a copy shop—where you can pay to use a scanner whenever you need one.

There is another way to get JPEGs from regular photos. Some film processing companies will develop regular film and create not only prints or slides, but computer files. The computer files will be stored on a floppy disk or CD. Some companies have a service where you can send in your film and download the finished files from the company's Web site.

hint

Once you have photos stored as computer files, it is easy to share them with your friends. To share a photo stored as a JPEG, all you need to do is attach it to a mail message (see Chapter 5).

In addition to your own photographs, you can also make use of photos that are available for public use. There are many such photos on the Internet. If you are looking for a particular type of image, the following Internet Resource will help you find what you need.

INTERNET RESOURCE Photographs

```
http://ipix.yahoo.com/
http://www.lycos.com/picturethis/
http://www.internet-stuff.com/multimedia_gallery/
```

You may or may not want to use photographs on your Web site, but you will probably want to use other types of pictures. For example, you can use buttons to act as links, or drawings to illustrate the text. As with photographs, you can either make your own pictures or use ones that are ready-made.

If you want to make your own pictures, you can use a GRAPHICS PROGRAM. There are lots of different programs, ranging from easy-to-use utilities to complex, sophisticated tools used by graphic artists. Using such programs, you can create your own pictures, modify existing pictures, and make image maps, animated GIFs, and so on.

However, you do not need to be an artist to use pictures on your Web site. There are a huge number of pictures available for free on the Internet. There are also a lot of backgrounds available for free.

When you are using the Web and you see an image you like, it is easy to save a copy to a file. Simply right-click on the image. Then select "Save Picture As" (with Internet Explorer) or "Save Image As" (with Netscape). Obviously, it is easy to steal pictures on the Web. However, if you are going to use a picture on your Web site, be sure to ask permission first. (Send mail to the person who runs the site.)

INTERNET RESOURCE Buttons, Graphics and Backgrounds

```
http://www.pambytes.com/
http://www.animfactory.com/
http://www.coolgraphics.com/
http://www.grapholina.com/Graphics/
http://www.coolarchive.com/index.cfm
http://www.thefreesite.com/freegraphics.htm
```

INTERNET RESOURCE Clip Art

```
http://www.clipart.com/
http://www.barrysclipart.com/
http://www.webplaces.com/html/clipart.htm
http://www.microsoft.com/clipgallerylive/default.asp
```

INTERNET RESOURCE Image Editors

```
http://cws.internet.com/32webimg.html
http://tucows.jefnet.com/imgedit95.html
```

Aside from pictures, you may also want to use sound on your Web site. If so, there are many sounds available for free on the Web. In addition, if your computer has a microphone, you can record your own sounds and save them as WAV files. To do so, you can use the Sound Recorder program that comes free with Windows.

To find the Sound Recorder program, click on the Start button. Select "Programs", then "Accessories", then "Multimedia" (Windows 95) or "Entertainment" (Windows 98). To start the program, click on "Sound Recorder".

*I*NTERNET RESOURCE   Sounds

```
http://www.dailywav.com/
http://www.wavcentral.com/
http://www.cartoonwavs.com/
http://www.midiarchive.com/
http://www.soundamerica.com/
http://www.webthumper.com/midi/
```

Web Page Design Tips

To help you develop your Web page design skills, here are a few tips.

When you finish your Web pages, you should look them over carefully before you upload them to your Web server. As you do, it is important to realize that not everyone uses the same browser. Thus, what you see on your computer, with your monitor and your browser, will not be the same as what other people see.

Professional Web designers always look at their designs on a variety of systems, using a number of different browsers and monitors. They strive for a design that will look good and behave correctly on a variety of configurations. You don't have to be that picky, but, at the very least, I want you to look at your Web pages with both major browsers: Internet Explorer and Netscape. You probably already use one of these, but you will need to install the other one for testing purposes.

Such tests are especially important when you use the Microsoft or Netscape Web page editors. FrontPage and FrontPage Express are designed to work with Internet Explorer, and Composer is designed to work with Netscape. When you use these editors, it is common to end up with small features that do not work right on the other company's browser. Thus, before you upload your Web pages, you always need to look at them with both browsers.

Let's move on now to some specific design points. As you explore the Web, you will see many sites—especially corporate sites—that use elaborate graphics. In my opinion, such graphics are not that important. In fact, a graphics-laden site will irritate many people, because the pictures take a long time to download if you are using a modem.

Remember, most people who use the Web are looking for information, not pictures. Strive to make your Web site easy to read, well-organized, and pleasant to look at. There is no need to make your Web pages look like an avant-garde magazine (unless you are an avant-garde magazine).

Here are some practical guidelines. First, follow your heart and your passions. Use your Web site to develop and share information about the areas of life that are important and interesting to you. Your goal should be to attract the right people to your site: the people who care about the same things as you.

There are too many Web sites out there that have nothing to say. How much time do you spend looking at other people's family photos and personal information? As one of my readers, I know you are a melting pot of intelligence, creativity, imagination and good taste. Let your Web site celebrate what is special about you: Share your interests and your expertise with the world.

The next guideline has to do with how you organize your Web site. Build a home page that acts as a central gateway for the whole site. This home page will often be the first thing people see when they visit your site, so choose a simple title that shows the theme of your site. Make sure this page has links to all the major features of your site, to make it easy for people to find what they want.

Remember, though, there is no way to force people to use the home page to enter your site. For example, someone might find your site via a search engine, and there is no guarantee that the search engine will point to your home page. It is altogether possible that people will jump right into the middle of the site.

Thus, you need to design your pages so that people can navigate through the entire site from any one of the pages. To do so, put some navigation aids on every page. For example, you might use a set of links at the top or bottom of the page. The links should point to the home page, as well as the other major features of your site. The goal is that, no matter where someone starts, he or she should be able to get to your home page with a single click.

I won't go on and on about Web page design. I have faith that, with a bit of practice, you will be able to create an interesting, well-organized Web site. However, I do want to offer one last piece of advice. There are a number of design techniques I want you to avoid—things that do not work well on the Web:

- It is possible to make words blink off and on. Do not do so. Anything that blinks, flashes or changes will keep catching the eye of your reader and irritate him.
- Avoid bright or complex backgrounds for your pages. Use a simple, low-contrast background. Otherwise, your pages will be too hard to read, and people will just skip them.
- Never make your Web site play music automatically: It is too annoying. If you want to put music on your pages, set it up so the visitor must press a button to start the music.
- Do not make your page create new browser windows. When you create a new window automatically, it forces the person to close it later, which is a bother. If someone wants a new browser window, he can create one himself whenever he wants by pressing the **Ctrl-N** key.

- If you use frames on your Web site, do not set them up so that a person going to another Web site will find himself trapped in one of your frames. You do not need to make it convenient for people to return after leaving your site. If someone wants to return, he will press the Back button.

- Test your Web pages after you upload them to the Web server. Do not assume they work properly just because they worked on your computer.

- If you link to other sites from your Web pages, test the links regularly (at least every month) to make sure they still work.

- Finally, never, ever use a notice that your Web site is "Under Construction". All good Web sites are always under construction. The metaphor was cute for a short time in 1994, and that time has long since passed. If your Web site is not ready, do not show it to people. If your Web site is ready, it is not necessary to advertise the general idea that you will be improving the pages from time to time.

Finding a Server to Host Your Web Site

In order to have a Web site, you need to arrange for the use of a Web server that is connected to the Internet. Once you upload your Web pages to such a server, they will be available to anyone on the Net. When someone provides this service for you, we say that they HOST your Web site.

When you look for a Web site host, you want a server that runs 24 hours a day and has a high-speed Internet connection. However, there is no reason why your Web site needs to be on a computer near you. A Web site can be hosted anywhere on the Internet, even in another country.

There are a great many Web site hosting services on the Internet, so you have a lot of choice. Start your search by checking with your ISP (Internet service provider). Many ISPs offer free or low-cost Web hosting to their customers.

If your ISP does not provide this service—or you want more choice—you can turn to one of the commercial providers. Some commercial providers charge money, others offer Web hosting for free.

Now, free sounds like a good deal, but I want you to think twice before you sign up. These services are free because they subject your visitors to a lot of advertising. For example, the Web hosting service will put ads on your Web pages, and there is nothing you can do about it. In addition, when someone visits one of your Web pages, the server may cause a new browser window to open on that person's computer. Inside this window will be an advertisement. The person will have to stop what he is doing (that is, reading your Web page) in order to close the window.

Some people say, "Well, what's so bad about a few advertisements? Isn't it worth it if I can have my Web site hosted for free?" My opinion is, no. Remember, you are not the one who has to look at the ads. The people who visit your Web site are the ones being imposed upon. If you want to attract people to your site, you should make it as pleasant as possible.

Suppose some company were to offer you free local telephone service with the condition that, every time someone called you, that person would have to listen to a short commercial before they could connect to your phone. Would you agree to such a service? I hope not. So think twice before you subject your Web visitors to a similar imposition.

The Web hosting business is extremely competitive, and it is not hard to find a reasonable price. However, like many other services on the Internet, you get what you pay for. If you are creating a Web site for a business, don't even think about using a free service. You need the support (and the ad-free environment) of a regular commercial provider.

When you investigate Web hosting services, look for the following:

- **Price**: Get a flat rate, so you know what you will be paying. Many Web hosting services have different plans. Check how the prices will change if you need to move from one plan to another.

- **Disk space**: How much disk space do you get to store your files? How much does it cost for extra space should you need it?

- **Connectivity**: Does the provider have reliable high-speed access? To find out for yourself, connect to several Web sites hosted by the same provider and see how fast they load. Be sure to try this experiment at different times of the day, as the demand can vary: Almost everything looks fast in the middle of the night.

- **Technical support**: When you have a problem, it is important to be able to reach a live person. Is such support available? What are the hours? Realistically, you can't expect anyone to spend a lot of time helping you design a Web page. However, you should be able to get assistance if you have a logistical problem, such as trouble sending files to their server.

- **FrontPage support**: One of the most popular Web page editors is Microsoft's FrontPage. (See the discussion on Web page editors earlier in the chapter.) Some Web hosting services use Web servers that have special built-in support for FrontPage. These services are referred to as "FrontPage Extensions". If you use FrontPage for your Web page editor, find a hosting service that offers such support.

If you have a business (or if you are an extra-cool person), you may want to get your own domain name to use with your Web site. For example, here is a typical Web site address you might have with an ISP:

```
http://www.undependable.com/users/harley
```

With your own domain name, you can use an address like:

`http://www.harley.com/`

If this is important to you, you need to find a Web hosting company that supports personalized domain names. (This service may cost extra.) For more information about getting your own domain name, see Chapter 16.

To investigate free Web hosting services, check out the Internet Resource below. To find regular pay-for-service companies, use a search engine to look for **Web hosting**. You will find a lot of choices. (I talk about search engines in Chapter 9.)

hint

Many schools provide free Web site hosting for their students. Remember, though, your Web site will be available only while you are at the school. When you leave, you will have to find another host. If you want a permanent place for your Web site, you should use a commercial provider.

INTERNET RESOURCE Free Web Site Hosting

`http://www.xoom.com/`
`http://www.tripod.com/`
`http://www.geocities.com/`
`http://www.angelfire.com/`

Promoting Your Web Site

Once your Web site is ready, you will want to share it with other people. One way to do this is to get your site listed with various search engines. (I discuss search engines in Chapter 9.) Many search engines have a form you can fill out to submit your Web site for inclusion in their database.

In addition, here are some tools that can help you find good ways to promote your Web site.

*I*NTERNET RESOURCE Promoting Your Web Site

```
http://www.addme.com/
http://www.rankthis.com/
http://www.sitelaunch.net/
http://www.siteowner.com/free.cfm
http://www.mmgco.com/top100.html
http://www.promotionworld.com/free.shtml
```

Getting Your Own Domain Name

The time may come when you want to have your own domain name. For example, if you run a business, you may want an address that is easy to remember, such as **fun-things.com**. Or, if you use the Net just for fun, you may want to have a personal domain just because it seems like a cool thing to do (which it is).

In this section, I will explain what you need to do to acquire and use your own domain name.

How to Get Your Own Domain Name

A domain name works only if the rest of the world has a way to translate your hostnames into IP addresses (see Chapter 4). This means you need to arrange for your domain to be serviced by DNS (the domain name system).

The easiest way to do this is to find an ISP (Internet service provider) to help you. The ISP will arrange two things. First, they will register your domain name with the appropriate authority. Second, the ISP will provide DNS service for your name by adding it to their name server. In addition, the ISP can also arrange to handle mail for your new address, and host a Web site for you.

Let's consider an example.

Say that your name is Elmo and you want to use the domain name **fun-things.com**. To start, you find an ISP and arrange for them to register the name **fun-things.com** for you. At the same time, they put this domain name in their name server. Your domain is now accessible to anyone on the Net.

Next, your ISP arranges to accept mail on your behalf. This allows people to send mail to an address like:

elmo@fun-things.com

When messages are sent to this address, they are received by your ISP's mail server, and stored until you are ready to read them. If necessary, your ISP can also set up other mail addresses within the same domain, such as:

susie@fun-things.com
ogbert@fun-things.com
sales@fun-things.com

Finally, you might have your ISP set up a Web site for you under the name **www.fun-things.com**. Once this is done, anyone on the Net can access this site by using the URL:

http://www.fun-things.com/

Thus, having your own domain name means arranging for four separate services:

- Registering your domain name with the appropriate authority
- Setting up DNS service for your domain name
- Arranging for mail service using your domain name
- Hosting a Web site using your domain name

As you saw in our example, it is common for ISPs to provide all four of these services. Be aware, however, that each of these services costs money, so it is a good idea to shop around. You do not need to buy all four of these services from the same ISP, although it is certainly easier to do so.

Registering a Domain Name

In Chapter 4, we discussed how there are two types of top-level domains: organizational domains (**com**, **edu**, **gov**, **int**, **mil**, **org** and **net**) used mostly—but not exclusively—within the United States, and geographical domains (such as **au**, **ca**, **fr**, **jp** and **uk**) used widely outside the U.S. Each top-level domain is administered by a specific organization called a REGISTRAR.

For geographical domains, each country has a registrar charged with the responsibility of managing the top-level domain for that country. For example, the **ca** (Canadian) domain is managed by a Canadian registrar, the **fr** (French) domain is managed by a French registrar, and so on.

The organizational domains, which are more generic, are handled differently. The three domains that are open to general usage: **com**, **org** and **net** are managed by an organization called the INTERNIC (Internet Network Information Center).

If you want your own domain name, either you or your ISP must register that name with the appropriate organization. This is done by submitting a form via email. For a geographical domain, you must work with the appropriate organization in your country. For one of the public organizational domains (**com**, **org** or **net**), you register with the Internic.

Depending on the domain name you want, there may or may not be a cost for registering it. Some countries register geographical-based names for free, while others charge for the service. With the preceding organizational domain names discussed, there is always a fee: $35 U.S. per year, with the first two years being paid in advance. Thus, it costs $70 up front to register a new name.

hint

The yearly domain name registration fee covers only the cost of establishing and maintaining the domain name. There are other costs to consider.

You will still have to pay your ISP for DNS service, mail service, and Web site hosting. In addition, most ISPs charge an extra fee if they send in the domain name registration for you (on top of the money you must pay the registrar).

Thus, it is a good idea to shop around and compare ISP fees. They can vary significantly.

INTERNET RESOURCE Domain Name Registries

```
http://www.corenic.org/
http://www.uninett.no/navn/domreg.html
http://www.internic.net/rs-internic.html
```

Choosing a Domain Name

The first step in choosing a domain name is to decide which top-level domain you want to use. If you are in the U.S., you probably want to use the **com** domain. If you are outside the U.S., you can choose either a geographical domain or an organizational domain. However, unless you have a good reason to do otherwise, you should probably use the geographical domain for your country.

Next, you need to decide what domain name you want. With an organizational domain, the format will be:

`name.domain`

For example, if you have a company named Fun Things, you might choose the name:

`fun-things.com`

If you are using a geographical domain, visit the Web site of the registrar and look for their rules. These will vary from country to country. As an example, here is a typical name you might use for a company in England:

`fun-things.co.uk`

(The **co** means "commercial".)

When it comes to picking a name, there are only a few rules you must follow. A name must:

- Contain no more than 22 characters
- Contain only letters, numbers and hyphens
- Start with a letter
- End with a letter or a number

Using Whois to Check a Domain Name

Once you know what domain name you want, you must check to see whether it is available. To do so, you use a service called WHOIS (pronounced "who is").

Each registrar runs a whois server for the domains they manage (although they may call it by a different name). You can use the whois server to check whether a domain name is already in use. If the name is available, you can register it for yourself. Otherwise, you will have to choose a different name.

hint

To find the whois server for a particular top-level domain, go to the Web site of the registrar for that domain.

If a domain name is in use, the whois server will display a summary of the registration information for that name. This is a good way to find out information about who controls a particular domain name. For fun, I have shown the whois information for a typical domain name in Figure 16-1.

Figure 16-1: Whois information for a typical domain name

```
Microsoft Corporation (MICROSOFT-DOM)
   One Microsoft Way
   Redmond, WA 98052
   US

   Domain Name: MICROSOFT.COM

   Administrative Contact:
      MSN Hostmaster  (MH37-ORG)  msnhst@MICROSOFT.COM
      tel.: 206 882 8080  fax.: 206 703 2641

   Technical Contact, Zone Contact:
      MSN NOC  (MN5-ORG)  msnnoc@MICROSOFT.COM
      206 882 8080
   Billing Contact:
      MSN Domain Billing  (MDB-ORG)  msnbill@MICROSOFT.COM
      206 882 8080

   Record last updated on 08-Jul-97.
   Record created on 02-May-91.
   Database last updated on 23-Mar-98 03:55:44 EDT.

   Domain servers in listed order:
   ATBD.MICROSOFT.COM              131.107.1.7
   DNS1.MICROSOFT.COM              131.107.1.240
   DNS3.NWNET.NET                  192.220.250.7
   DNS4.NWNET.NET                  192.220.251.7
```

Specifying Contact Names When You Register a Domain Name

You register a domain name by filling out a form and emailing it to a registrar. To fill out the form, you will have to specify certain information. The forms differ from one registrar to another, but you will often be asked to specify the names of three people: a technical contact, an administrative contact, and a billing contact.

The technical contact is the person who will be contacted if a technical problem arises with the domain name. Normally, this contact would be your ISP. The administrative contact is the person who administers the domain name, and the billing contact is the person to whom the invoices will be sent.

My advice is to make sure that *you* are named as both the administrative and billing contact. In addition, make sure that you, not the ISP, are listed as the owner of the name. Here is why.

Once a domain name is established, the registrar will not let just anyone make changes. After all, you don't want some malevolent person to be able to send in a form by email and steal other people's domains. The only people allowed to make changes are the technical and administrative contacts. When you first register, you specify email addresses for these contacts, and only mail that comes from one of these addresses will be accepted when a change is requested.

It is common for ISPs to put their address down for all three contacts. However, if you ever decide to move your domain name to a different ISP, you will have to get the old ISP to send in the change for you.

Don't let this happen. If your ISP sends in the form for you, insist that *you* be the administrative contact. That way, no matter what happens, you will have control over your own domain name. (After all, you are paying for it.) Take my word for it: This small precaution can save you a lot of trouble.

Also, when it comes to paying the bills, you want to make sure you are the billing contact to ensure that the invoices go right to you. If your ISP is the billing contact, they may forget to pass along the bill, and if you don't pay it, you will lose your domain name.

Remember, it's your domain name, so stay in control.

hint

When the going gets tough, the tough get their own domain names.

Top-Level
Internet Domains

In Chapter 4, I discuss Internet addresses in detail. All Internet addresses end with a domain name, which consists of a number of sub-domain names, separated by . (period) characters. The rightmost sub-domain is called a top-level domain. For example, in the following URL (Web address), the domain is **www.royal.gov.uk**, and the top-level domain is **uk**.

`http://www.royal.gov.uk/`

In the following mail address, the domain is **microsoft.com**, and the top-level domain is **com**.

`billg@microsoft.com`

There are two types of top-level domains. Organizational domains represent a particular category, and geographical domains are assigned to a particular country or region of the world.

This appendix contains a full list of all the organizational and geographical top-level domains in current use. In a few places, where it is not obvious how the domain name was derived, I have included a short explanatory note in square brackets.

Organizational Top-Level Domains

Domain	Description
com	commercial
edu	U.S. universities [educational]
gov	U.S. federal government
int	international
mil	U.S. military
net	network providers
org	miscellaneous organizations

Geographical Top-Level Domains

Domain	Description
ac	Ascension Island
ad	Andorra
ae	United Arab Emirates
af	Afghanistan
ag	Antigua and Barbuda
ai	Anguilla
al	Albania
am	Armenia
an	Netherlands Antilles
ao	Angola
aq	Antarctica
ar	Argentina
as	American Samoa
at	Austria
au	Australia
aw	Aruba
az	Azerbaijan
ba	Bosnia-Herzegovina
bb	Barbados
bt	Bhutan
bd	Bangladesh
be	Belgium
bf	Burkina Faso
bg	Bulgaria
bh	Bahrain
bi	Burundi
bj	Benin
bm	Bermuda
bn	Brunei Darussalam
bo	Bolivia
br	Brazil
bs	Bahamas
bv	Bouvet Island
bw	Botswana
by	Belarus
bz	Belize
ca	Canada

Domain	Description
cc	Cocos Islands [Keeling Islands]
cd	Congo [Democratic People's Republic]
cf	Central African Republic
cg	Congo [Republic of]
ch	Switzerland [*Confoederatio Helvetica*]
ci	Ivory Coast [*Cote D'Ivoire*]
ck	Cook Islands
cl	Chile
cm	Cameroon
cn	China
co	Colombia
cr	Costa Rica
cu	Cuba
cv	Cape Verde
cx	Christmas Island
cy	Cyprus
cz	Czech Republic
de	Germany [*Deutschland*]
dj	Djibouti
dk	Denmark
dm	Dominica
do	Dominican Republic
dz	Algeria [*Al Djazair*]
ec	Ecuador
ee	Estonia
eg	Egypt
er	Eritrea
es	Spain [*España*]
et	Ethiopia
fi	Finland
fj	Fiji
fk	Falkland Islands [Malvinas Islands]
fm	Micronesia [Federated States of]
fo	Faroe Islands
fr	France
ga	Gabon
gb	Great Britain: England, Scotland, Wales
gd	Grenada
ge	Georgia

Domain	Description
gf	French Guiana
gg	Guernsey
gh	Ghana
gi	Gibraltar
gl	Greenland
gm	Gambia
gn	Guinea
gp	Guadeloupe
gq	Equatorial Guinea
gr	Greece
gs	South Georgia and South Sandwich Islands
gt	Guatemala
gu	Guam
gw	Guinea-Bissau
gy	Guyana
hk	Hong Kong
hm	Heard and McDonald Islands
hn	Honduras
hr	Croatia [*Hrvatska*]
ht	Haiti
hu	Hungary
id	Indonesia
ie	Ireland
il	Israel
im	Isle of Man
in	India
io	British Indian Ocean Territory
iq	Iraq
ir	Iran
is	Iceland
it	Italy
je	Jersey
jm	Jamaica
jo	Jordan
jp	Japan
ke	Kenya
kg	Kyrgyzstan
kh	Cambodia [formerly Khmer Republic]
ki	Kiribati

Domain	Description
kn	Saint Kitts and Nevis
kr	South Korea
kw	Kuwait
ky	Cayman Islands
kz	Kazakhstan
la	Laos
lb	Lebanon
lc	Saint Lucia
li	Liechtenstein
lk	Sri Lanka
lr	Liberia
ls	Lesotho
lt	Lithuania
lu	Luxembourg
lv	Latvia
ly	Libya
ma	Morocco
mc	Monaco
md	Moldova
mg	Madagascar
mh	Marshall Islands
mk	Macedonia [*Makedoniya*]
ml	Mali
mm	Myanmar
mn	Mongolia
mo	Macau
mp	Northern Mariana Islands
mq	Martinique
mr	Mauritania
ms	Montserrat
mt	Malta
mu	Mauritius
mv	Maldives
mw	Malawi
mx	Mexico
my	Malaysia
mz	Mozambique
na	Namibia
nc	New Caledonia

Domain	Description
ne	Niger
nf	Norfolk Island
ng	Nigeria
ni	Nicaragua
nl	Netherlands
no	Norway
np	Nepal
nu	Niue
nz	New Zealand
om	Oman
pa	Panama
pe	Peru
pf	French Polynesia
pg	Papua New Guinea
ph	Philippines
pk	Pakistan
pl	Poland
pm	St. Pierre and Miquelon
pn	Pitcairn Island
pr	Puerto Rico
pt	Portugal
pw	Palau
py	Paraguay
qa	Qatar
re	Réunion
ro	Romania
ru	Russia
rw	Rwanda
sa	Saudi Arabia
sb	Solomon Islands
sc	Seychelles
sd	Sudan
se	Sweden
sg	Singapore
si	Slovenia
sj	Svalbard and Jan Mayen Islands
sk	Slovakia
sh	St. Helena
sl	Sierra Leone

Domain	Description
sm	San Marino
sn	Senegal
so	Somalia
sr	Suriname
st	Sao Tome and Principe
sv	El Salvador
sy	Syria
sz	Swaziland
tc	Turks and Ciacos Islands
td	Chad [*Tchad*]
tf	French Southern Territories
tg	Togo
th	Thailand
tj	Tajikistan
tk	Tokelau
tm	Turkmenistan
tn	Tunisia
to	Tonga
tp	East Timor [Portuguese Timor]
tr	Turkey
tt	Trinidad and Tobago
tv	Tuvalu
tw	Taiwan
tz	Tanzania
ua	Ukraine [*Ukraina*]
ug	Uganda
uk	United Kingdom: England, Scotland, Wales, Northern Ireland
um	U.S. Minor Outlying Islands
us	United States
uy	Uruguay
uz	Uzbekistan
va	Vatican City State
ve	Venezuela
vc	St. Vincent and the Grenadines
vg	British Virgin Islands
vi	U.S. Virgin Islands
vn	Vietnam
vu	Vanuatu
wf	Wallis and Futuna

Domain	Description
ws	Western Samoa
ye	Yemen
yt	Mayotte
yu	Yugoslavia
za	South Africa
zm	Zambia
zr	Zaire
zw	Zimbabwe

Time Zones on the Internet

The Internet is used around the world, and times must be expressed carefully, especially within the headers of mail messages and Usenet articles. In general, the Internet uses a 24-hour clock. For example, within a header, you will see 20:50 instead of 8:50 PM. (If you are not used to a 24-hour clock, use the conversion information in Figure B–1.)

Aside from the actual time, it is also important to know the time zone. This information is usually expressed in one of three ways. First, you might see the local time along with the local time zone. For example, the following header line specifies a time of 8:50 PM, Pacific Daylight Time (PDT):

Date: Wed, 8 Apr 1998 20:50:17 PDT

Another way you might see this same information is with the time converted to GMT (Greenwich Mean Time), also referred to as UT (Universal Time) or UTC (Coordinated Universal Time). You will see GMT/UT/UTC times even when a mail message or Usenet article did not originate in that time zone. The conversion is done automatically by the software. Here is the same time as previously specified as GMT:

Date: Thu, 9 Apr 1998 03:50:17 GMT

Notice how, in this example, the GMT time is 3:50 AM one day later. This is because GMT is 7 hours ahead of PDT. For reference, Figure B–2 summarizes the time zones used in the U.S. and how they compare to GMT.

One last way in which you may see time specified within a header is a local time followed by the number of hours difference from GMT:

Date: Wed, 8 Apr 1998 20:50:17 -0700

This header line shows the same time, 8:50 PM, and indicates that the local time zone is -7 hours different from GMT.

Figure B–1: The 24-hour time system compared to the AM/PM system

On the Internet, time is often specified using a 24-hour clock. The following table shows the 24-hour values and their equivalent AM/PM times.

```
12 midnight = 00:00        12 noon = 12:00
     1:00 AM = 01:00        1:00 PM = 13:00
     2:00 AM = 02:00        2:00 PM = 14:00
     3:00 AM = 03:00        3:00 PM = 15:00
     4:00 AM = 04:00        4:00 PM = 16:00
     5:00 AM = 05:00        5:00 PM = 17:00
     6:00 AM = 06:00        6:00 PM = 18:00
     7:00 AM = 07:00        7:00 PM = 19:00
     8:00 AM = 08:00        8:00 PM = 20:00
     9:00 AM = 09:00        9:00 PM = 21:00
    10:00 AM = 10:00       10:00 PM = 22:00
    11:00 AM = 11:00       11:00 PM = 23:00
```

Figure B–2: U.S. time zones compared to GMT

Abbreviation	Time Zone	Difference from GMT
GMT	Greenwich Mean Time	0
UT	Universal Time	same as GMT
UTC	Coordinated Universal Time	same as GMT
EST	Eastern Standard Time	-5 hours
EDT	Eastern Daylight Time	-4 hours
CST	Central Standard Time	-6 hours
CDT	Central Daylight Time	-5 hours
MST	Mountain Standard Time	-7 hours
MDT	Mountain Daylight Time	-6 hours
PST	Pacific Standard Time	-8 hours
PDT	Pacific Daylight Time	-7 hours

WHAT'S IN A NAME?

GMT, UT, UTC

Greenwich (pronounced "Gren-itch"), a borough of London, was the home of the Royal Observatory from 1675-1985. It was at this observatory that our modern system of timekeeping and longitude was developed. For this reason, the imaginary north-south line that runs through the observatory is designated as 0 degrees longitude.

In 1884, the time at Greenwich was adopted as the global standard used to determine all the time zones around the world. This global standard time is called Greenwich Mean Time or GMT. (In this context, the word "mean" refers to "average".) GMT is used widely on the Internet, and is sometimes referred to by the newer, more official name of UT (Universal Time).

In addition to UT, you may see another name, UTC (Coordinated Universal Time). UTC is the official value of Universal Time as calculated by the U.S. National Bureau of Standards and the U.S. Naval Observatory.

By the way, you might wonder why the abbreviation for Coordinated Universal Time is UTC, not CUT. Here is why:

UTC was adopted as an official international standard in 1970. The work was done by a group of experts within the International Telecommunications Union. When it came time to name the new standard, the group had a problem. In English, the abbreviation for Coordinated Universal Time would be CUT. But in French, the name is Temps Universel Coordiné and the abbreviation would be TUC. The group wanted the same abbreviation to be used everywhere, but they couldn't agree on whether it should be CUT or TUC. The compromise was to use UTC. Although the abbreviation is inexact in both English and French, it had the enormous advantage of keeping the peace.

(Not too many people know that, but now you do.)

Abbreviations Used When Talking on the Net

A great deal of the communication on the Internet consists of people typing text to one another—in mail messages and Usenet articles, and while talking to other people using IRC, chat rooms, talk facilities and muds.

To save time and effort, there are a number of common abbreviations and acronyms used while communicating on the Net. I have collected the most important ones in Figure C–1.

Some of the abbreviations are used only in certain contexts. For example, you will generally see **Objoke** only in Usenet humor groups (where a person posting a message has included an "obligatory joke"), while **BRB** would be used when two people are chatting and one tells the other he must leave for a moment, but will "be right back".

(Note to parents and teachers: You will notice that a few of the words in Figure C-1 are swear words. I have included them for two reasons. First, people really do talk like this on the Net, so don't get excited; second, I want you to know what your kids mean when they use these abbreviations.)

Aside from abbreviations and acronyms, you will commonly see people use a smiley. This indicates that what the person is saying should be taken as being inoffensive. Here are the three most common smileys:

```
:-)     :)     ;-)
```

(To see the smiling faces, tilt your head sideways to the left. Notice that the rightmost smiley is winking.)

You will sometimes see **<grin>** or **<g>** used instead of a smiley. Thus, all of the following examples have the same meaning:

```
Don't worry, we can't all be smart and good-looking :-)

Don't worry, we can't all be smart and good-looking :)

Don't worry, we can't all be smart and good-looking ;-)

Don't worry, we can't all be smart and good-looking <grin>

Don't worry, we can't all be smart and good-looking <g>
```

hint

There is a convention that, while talking on the Net, you put words that describe an emotion within angled brackets < > in order to set the words off from regular text. For example, say you are in a Web chat room talking with someone at work about the new artichoke crop in Venezuela. All of a sudden, the boss walks into your friend's office, so your friend types:

```
BRB, boss <grumble>
```

You may also see asterisk characters * * used instead of < >. For instance, when your friend gets back to the keyboard, he types:

```
Gotta leave *sigh*. I have to go collate 1000 copies of the
company's "Employee Guidelines for Proper Internet Usage".
```

To which you reply:

```
ROFL!
```

(As you can see, regular abbreviations and acronyms are written without the < > or * * characters.)

Figure C–1: Abbreviations used while talking on the Net

Abbreviation	Meaning
:-)	smiley
:)	smiley
;-)	winking smiley
:-O	surprised smiley
:-P	disgusted smiley (with tongue sticking out)
:-P	excited smiley (with tongue sticking out)
AFAIK	as far as I know
AFK	away from keyboard
BBL	be back later
BF	boyfriend
BFD	big fuckin' deal
BG	big grin
BRB	be right back
BTW	by the way
CU	see you
CUL	see you later

Abbreviation	Meaning
CUL8R	see you later
CYA	see ya (good-bye)
F2F	face to face (in person)
FAQ	frequently asked question list
FRP	fantasy role playing
FUBAR	fucked up beyond all recognition
FWIW	for what it's worth
FYI	for your information
<G>	grin (same as a smiley)
GAL	get a life
GD&R	grinning, ducking and running
GF	girlfriend
<GRIN>	grin (same as a smiley)
HTH	I hope this helps
IANAL	I am not a lawyer
IC	I see
IC	in character (while role playing)
ICWUM	I see what you mean
IMHO	in my humble opinion
IMNSHO	in my not so humble opinion
IMO	in my opinion
IOW	in other words
IRL	in real life
J/K	just kidding
LDR	long distance relationship
L8R	(see you) later
LOL	laughing out loud
MOTAS	member of the appropriate sex
MOTOS	member of the opposite sex
MOTSS	member of the same sex
NP	no problem
Ob-	(as a prefix) obligatory
Objoke	obligatory joke
OIC	oh, I see
OMG	oh, my God!
OOC	out of character (while role playing)
OS	operating system
OTOH	on the other hand
PAW	parents are watching

Abbreviation	Meaning
PDA	public display of affection
POV	point of view
PM	private message
RL	real life
ROFL	rolling on the floor laughing
ROTFL	rolling on the floor laughing
ROTFLMAO	rolling on the floor laughing my ass off
RPG	role playing game
RTFM	read the fuckin' manual (before asking a question)
SO	significant other
THX	thanks
TTFN	ta-ta for now (good-bye)
TTYL	talk to you later
TYVM	thank you very much
WTF	who the fuck?/what the fuck?/why the fuck?
WU?	what's up?
WUF?	where are you from?

*I*NTERNET RESOURCE Lists of Smileys

```
http://www.pop.at/smileys/
http://www.czweb.com/smilies.htm
http://www.eff.org/papers/eegtti/eeg_286.html
```

Glossary

note

[X] indicates the chapter or appendix in which the term is defined.

16-bit: With respect to Windows software, describes a program that is designed to run under the older Windows 3.*x* operating systems. Compare to **32-bit**. [11]

32-bit: With respect to Windows software, describes a program that is designed to run under the Windows 95, Windows 98 or Windows NT operating systems. Compare to **16-bit**. [11]

active channel: Microsoft's name for a Web-based channel. [7]

active desktop: An enhancement to Windows, created by Microsoft, that allows you to display active elements, such as channels, on your desktop. The Active Desktop also allows you to use a similar interface to access all resources, whether they are on your computer or on the Web. [7]

ActiveX: A programming system, developed by Microsoft and promoted as a richer and more powerful alternative to Java. Unlike Java applets, ActiveX programs do not run within a controlled environment. [8]

address:

1) A specification describing the exact name of a computer, person or resource on the Internet. [2]

2) Informally, a synonym for either a mail address or a URL (Web address). [4, 5]

address bar: Within a browser, an area in the browser window that displays the URL of the current Web page, and into which you can type a specific URL when you want to load a different page. [7]

address book: Within a mail program, a facility for storing names and addresses along with other related information. [5]

ADSL: (Asymmetric Digital Subscriber Line) A technology that allows high-speed Internet connections over a telephone line. See also **DSL**. [3]

alias: A name, within a mail address book, that represents a list of addresses. [6]

all caps: Describes words that are typed in uppercase (all capital letters). [6]

Altavista: A particular search engine having an emphasis on archiving the content of the Web, which can then be referenced by searching for all the Web sites that contain specific words. [9]

alternative hierarchy: Within Usenet, one of five hierarchies, distributed around the world, which do not use standardized procedures for creating new groups. The mainstream hierarchies are **alt**, **bionet**, **bit**, **biz** and **k12**. [12]

analog: Describes a quantity that can vary continuously from one value to another. [3]

animated GIF: A type of GIF file that, when displayed, creates a simple animation. [15]

Anonymous FTP: An Internet service that allows people to download files without having an account on the computer on which the files are stored. [2, 11]

antivirus program: A program used to search out, identify and, when possible, neutralize such viruses as may be present in the memory or the file system of a computer. [8]

AOL: A large ISP that offers extra content and services along with Internet access. In the U.S., the name AOL stands for America Online. [3]

applet: A small program, designed to be embedded within a larger system and run within a controlled environment. [8]

application sharing: Within a talk facility, a feature that allows people to collaborate by having joint control over a program running on one person's computer. [14]

archive: A single file that contains a collection of one or more compressed files. Programs to be downloaded are stored as archives to make the downloading process faster and simpler. After an archive is downloaded, it must be unpacked. [11]

ARPA: (Advanced Research Projects Agency) An agency that used to be part of the U.S. Department of Defense. [1]

Arpanet: An early computer network, the ancestor of the Internet. The Arpanet was funded by ARPA. [1]

article: Within Usenet, a message sent to a discussion group. Same as a **posting**. [2, 12]

asymmetric: Describes an Internet connection in which the available bandwidth is allotted unevenly between downstream and upstream transmissions, usually with more bandwidth for downstream. [3]

attach: To combine a file with a mail message such that the file is sent to the recipient along with the message. [2, 5]

attachment: A file that is combined with a mail message such that the file is sent to the recipient along with the message. [2, 5]

AutoComplete: In a browser, as you are typing a URL, a facility that guesses which URL you want by looking at what you have already typed and comparing it to URLs you have used previously. [7]

avatar: Within a talk facility, a small picture or figure that moves and talks on your behalf. [14]

B-channel: In an ISDN system, one of two channels that carry computer and voice data with a bandwidth of up to 64K bps (a total of 128K bps for both B-channels). The designation "B" stands for "bearer", because B-channels bear (transport) the data. Compare to **D-channel**. [3]

backup: A copy of a file or a set of files, maintained as a safeguard in case the original data needs to be restored. [7]

bandwidth: The capacity to transmit data. On the Internet, bandwidth is measured in bits per second. [3]

binary: Within Usenet, slang for a binary file. [12]

binary data: Any data that is not text. [12]

binary file: A file that contains binary data. [12]

binary system: A mathematical system, based on powers of 2 (such as 1, 2, 4, 8, 16, 32, and so on), used by computer scientists and programmers to work with computer memory. [3]

bit: The smallest unit of data storage; there are 8 bits in 1 byte. Mathematically, bits are represented by quantities that can have a value of either 0 or 1. The name "bit" stands for "binary digit". [3]

Bitnet: A large, defunct academic network, now absorbed by the Internet, that at one time supported several thousand mailing lists. [13]

bits per second: The unit of measurement used to describe the speed of an Internet connection. Abbreviated as bps. [3]

blacklist: As used by filtering software, a list of Web sites to which the software will block access. [8]

blind copy: A secret copy of a mail message sent to one or more recipients. Within the header of the message, the recipients who are to receive a blind copy are specified on the **Bcc** line. [5]

body: The main part of a mail message or Usenet article, containing the text of the message/article. [5, 12]

bogus: Describes a newsgroup that does not really exist or is not used in a meaningful way. [12]

Bookmarks list: Within Netscape, a list of items used to store URLs for later recall. In Internet Explorer, this is called the Favorites list. [7]

bot: Within IRC, a program that, within a channel, performs certain actions automatically. (The name comes from the word "robot".) [14]

bounce: After sending a mail message, to have that message returned as undeliverable. [5]

bps: Abbreviation for "bits per second". The unit of measurement used to describe the speed of an Internet connection. [3]

browser: A client program, such as Internet Explorer or Netscape, used to access the Web as well as other Internet facilities, such as mail, Usenet and Anonymous FTP. For most people, a browser acts as the primary interface to the Internet. [2, 7]

buddy list: With respect to a talk facility, a personal list containing the names and addresses of people to whom you may want to talk. Same as a **friends list**. [14]

bundled: Describes a product that is included, for no extra cost, when you purchase another product. For example, most new PCs come bundled with a variety of software. [3]

byte: Within a computer, a unit of data storage consisting of 8 bits. Each byte can store a single character. [3]

cache: Within a browser, a temporary storage area used to hold the contents of recently viewed Web pages. [7]

carbon copy: A paper copy produced on a typewriter by using carbon paper on top of an extra piece of paper. [5]

case sensitive: Describes a name in which the difference between lower- and uppercase letters is significant. [4]

CD-ROM drive: A long-term storage device that reads data on CDs (compact discs). The term "ROM" stands for "read-only memory", and indicates that the drive can read the CD, but not change what is on it. [3]

censorware: A pejorative term for filtering software, used by people who believe that such software is unnecessarily restrictive. [8]

certificate: The name used by Netscape for a file containing a private/public key pair, as well as other information, for use with an encryption system. (Microsoft uses the name "digital ID".) [6]

CGI: (Common Gateway Interface) A system used to pass data between a Web server and a program designed to process the data. [15]

channel:

1) On the Web, an information source that can send information to your computer automatically according to a predetermined schedule. [2, 7]

2) On IRC, a facility supporting a single multiuser conversation. [2, 4]

3) Within an ISDN system, one of three separate parts, each of which furnishes a specific amount of bandwidth. ISDN uses two B-channels and one D-channel. [3]

channel op: Within an IRC channel, a person who has certain privileges allowing him or her to control the channel in various ways. Same as **op**. [14]

charter: With respect to a Usenet newsgroup, the description and purpose of the group as written by the people who created the group. [12]

chat: To talk by typing messages back and forth in real time. [14]

chat room: On the Web, a facility allowing a group of people to talk by typing messages. Same as **Web chat room**. [2, 14]

click: To press the left button of a mouse. [7]

client: A program that requests a service. On the Internet, you use client programs to access various services from servers. [1]

clipboard: An invisible storage area maintained by Windows to allow you to copy or move data from one place to another, even between windows. [6]

close button: On a window, a small button with a picture of an "X", in the top-right corner of the window, that, when pressed, closes the window permanently. [7]

coaxial cable: The type of cable used for cable TV services and for cable Internet access. [3]

Collabra: Part of the Netscape Communicator suite of Internet software, a Usenet newsreader. [12]

Composer: A free wysiwyg Web page editor, distributed by Netscape to complement the Netscape browser. [15]

compression utility: Any program that provides the service of creating and unpacking archives, in particular, zip file programs. [11]

content advisor: Within Internet Explorer, a facility that allows you to control access to Web sites based on a rating system. [8]

context menu: Within Windows, when you right-click on an object, a menu that is displayed containing selections relevant to that object. [7]

control: A self-contained program, designed to provide a specific function, that can be used as a component within other programs or on Web pages. [10]

cookie: Data sent by a Web server and stored in a file on your computer by your browser. [8]

copy [to the clipboard]: To copy selected data to the clipboard without changing the original data. [6]

cross-post: On Usenet, to post an article to more than one newsgroup. [12]

cut [to the clipboard]: To move selected data to the clipboard while deleting the original data. [6]

cyberspace: A deprecated term used to refer to the Internet. Note: Use of this word will instantly mark you as a person who does not know what he is talking about. [1]

D-channel: In an ISDN system, a channel that carries internal control information with a bandwidth of up to 16K bps. The designation "D" stands for "data", although it is the B-channels that carry the actual computer and voice data. Compare to **B-channel**. [3]

DALnet: One of the large IRC networks. The others are EFnet, Undernet and IRCnet. [14]

data: Information that is stored on a computer. [1]

DCC: (Direct Client to Client connection) Within IRC, a facility that allows you to establish a direct connection with another person, either for chatting or for transferring files. [14]

decrypt: To decode encrypted data in order to restore it to its original format. [6]

demodulation: The process used by a modem to convert analog data to digital data. [3]

desktop: Within Windows, the background of your display area; what you see when you have no open windows. [7]

dialog box: A window, displayed by a program, in which you are asked to enter information or choose from a selection of choices. [7]

dialup connection: A means of connecting to the Internet using a modem and a regular phone line. [3]

digest: With respect to a mailing list, a format in which individual messages are collected and sent out at intervals as one single message. [13]

digital: Describes a quantity that can take on only specific, discrete values. [3]

digital ID: The name used by Microsoft for a file containing a private/public key pair, as well as other information, for use with an encryption system. (Netscape uses the name "certificate".) [6]

digitize: With respect to a scanner, to process an image on paper and create a computer file containing that image. Same as **scan**. [15]

directory: Within a file system, an entity that contains files and other directories. Same as **folder**. [4]

DNS: (domain name system) The system used to organize all the hostnames on the Internet, and to translate a hostname into an IP address. [4]

DNS server: A server, maintained by an ISP for the use of its customers, that handles DNS requests (such as the translation of a hostname into an IP address). [4]

domain: A set of hostnames that have the rightmost part of their names in common. For example, all the hostnames that end in **edu** belong to the **edu** domain. [4]

domain name system: Same as **DNS**. [4]

double-click: To press a mouse button twice in a row. [7]

down: Describes a computer or communication link that is currently not working. [1]

download: To copy a file from another computer to your computer. [2, 11]

downstream: Describes the transmission of data from the Internet to your computer. [3]

drag: To use a mouse to move an object from one location to another, by pointing to the object, pressing a mouse button, and moving the mouse while holding down the button. [7]

DSL: (Digital Subscriber Line)

1) A family of technologies that allows high-speed Internet connections over a telephone line. The DSL family includes ADSL (Asymmetric DSL), HDSL (High-bit-rate DSL), RADSL (Rate Adaptive Asymmetric DSL), SDSL (Symmetric DSL) and VDSL (Very high-bit-rate DSL). [3]

2) In common parlance, "DSL" is often used as a synonym for ADSL. [3]

EFnet: One of the large IRC networks. The others are Undernet, DALnet and IRCnet. [14]

electronic mail: Same as **mail, email.** [2]

email:

1) A system for sending and receiving messages from one Internet address to another. [2, 5]

2) A message that has been sent via this system. [2]

3) [verb] To send a message. Same as **mail.** [2]

email virus: A type of virus that, supposedly, can cause damage to a computer merely by opening or reading a mail message. There are no email viruses—the belief that they exist is a virus hoax. [8]

emulate: The action of a program that makes a computer act like a different type of device. For example, a telnet client is a program that emulates a terminal. [2]

encrypt: To encode data in such a way that it cannot be read or used until it is decrypted. [6]

Ethernet: A technology used to connect computers to a local network. [3]

Ethernet port: In a PC, a socket you can use to connect your PC to a network. [3]

execute [a program]: To have a computer follow the instructions in a program. Same as **run** (a program). [1]

expire: With respect to a Usenet article, to delete that article after it has been stored on a news server for a particular amount of time. [12]

extension: Within a file name, the last part of the name, indicating the type of data contained in the file. For example, in the file name **index.html**, the extension **html** indicates that the file contains a Web page (hypertext). [4]

FAQ: (frequently asked questions list) A list of questions and answers about a particular topic, written for people who are new to that topic. [9, 12]

Favorites list: Within Internet Explorer, a list of items used to store URLs for later recall. In Netscape, this is called the Bookmarks list. [7]

file: A collection of data stored under a specific name. [2, 4]

File Manager: The program used to manage files and directories within Windows 3.*x*. [4]

filter: Within a mail program, a facility that scans incoming mail and performs a particular action whenever an incoming message meets specified criteria. [6]

filtering software: Any of a number of programs used to control access to Web sites based on specific criteria, such as blacklists and whitelists. [8]

flame:

> **1)** Within Usenet, an article in which someone criticizes another person or complains vociferously (that is, a real stinker). [12]
>
> **2)** [verb] To post such an article. [12]

flame war: A situation in which a group of people flame one another repeatedly. [12]

floppy: Same as **floppy disk**. [3]

floppy disk: A small, plastic-encased, portable data storage device. The most common type of floppy disk can store up to 1.44MB of data. [3]

floppy disk drive: A long-term storage device that reads and writes data on a removable floppy disk. [3]

focus: The attribute of a window that makes it the active window, the one currently controlled by the keyboard. [7]

folder:

> **1)** Within a file system, an entity that contains files and other directories. Same as **directory**. [4]
>
> **2)** Within a mail system, one of several containers for messages stored on your computer. [5]
>
> **3)** Within a Favorites or Bookmarks list, a collection of items and/or other folders. [7]

follow: While looking at a Web page, to use a link by clicking on it with your mouse. [2, 7]

follow-up: On Usenet, an article that is written in reply to a previous article. [12]

form: Within a Web page, a component that contains specific areas into which the user can type information. This information is then sent to the Web server to be processed. [15]

forward: After receiving a mail message from someone, to send a copy of that message to a third person. [5]

frame: Within a Web page, a specific area that can contain data from another page. [7, 15]

freeware: Software that can be distributed and used for free. [11]

friends list: With respect to a talk facility, a personal list containing the names and addresses of people to whom you may want to talk. Same as a **buddy list**. [14]

FrontPage Express: A free wysiwyg Web page editor, distributed by Microsoft to complement the Internet Explorer browser. [15]

FTP:

> **1)** An Internet service that allows you to copy files from one computer to another. [2, 11]
>
> **2)** [verb] To copy files by using the FTP service. [2]

FTP client: A program used to copy files to or from an FTP server. [2]

FTP server: A server to which (or from which) you can copy files using FTP. [2]

gateway: A program that provides an automatic connection between two different types of information systems, such as between a mailing list and a Usenet newsgroup. [13]

GB: Abbreviation for **gigabyte**. [3]

geek: A nerd who is cool. [1]

geographical domain: A two-letter top-level domain that is assigned to a particular country or region. See Appendix B for a full list. [4]

GIF: (Graphics Interchange Format)
1) A file format commonly used to store non-photo pictures, such as drawings, cartoons and icons. Compare to **JPEG**. [15]
2) Informally, a file containing a picture in GIF format. For example, "My friend sent me a GIF of Mickey Mouse." [15]

gigabyte: A unit of measurement used for computer memory and data storage, 1,073,741,824 (2^{30}) bytes. Informally, a gigabyte is about 1,000,000,000 (a billion) bytes. Abbreviated as GB. [3]

GMT: (Greenwich Mean Time) The time zone based on the location of the Royal Observatory in Greenwich (a borough of London, England), used as an international standard. Equivalent to UT and UTC. [B]

graphics: Data consisting of pictures (such as drawings, photographs, and illustrations) or other visual elements. [2]

graphics program: A program used to create, manipulate and modify pictures. [15]

H.323: An international standard that describes Internet voice and video talk systems. [14]

hard disk: A long-term storage device in which data is stored on several hard disc-shaped plates. [3]

hardware: The physical parts of a computer. [1]

header: Within a mail message or Usenet article, a standard section at the beginning of every message that contains technical information such as the **From**, **To**, **Date** and **Subject** lines. [5, 12]

header line: A single line within the header of a mail message or Usenet article. [5, 12]

helper application: A program used to enhance the capabilities of a browser. Unlike a plug-in, a helper application is a completely separate program that usually (but not always) does its work in a separate window. [10]

hierarchy: Within Usenet, one of the top-level categories into which newsgroups are organized. The first part of a newsgroup name shows the hierarchy to which the newsgroup belongs. For example, the newsgroup **rec.humor** is in the **rec** hierarchy. [12]

history list: Within a browser, a list of the URLs of Web pages you have visited recently. [7]

home directory: In Unix, a directory that is assigned to a particular user for his exclusive use, within which he can create files and subdirectories as he sees fit. [4]

home page:
1) Within a browser, the Web page that is loaded automatically each time the browser starts. [7]
2) On a Web site, the main Web page, designed as the starting place for users of that site. [7]

horizontal scroll bar: A scroll bar at the bottom of a window, used to scroll the contents of the window to the left and right. [7]

host:
> **1)** When using telnet, the computer to which you log in. [2]
>
> **2)** Any computer connected to the Internet. [4]
>
> **3)** [verb] To provide the service of maintaining a Web server used by people to make their Web sites available to the public. [15]

hostname: The unique name given to an Internet computer. [4]

HTML: (Hypertext Markup Language)
> **1)** The system of specifications used to define the appearance and structure of Web pages. [7, 15]
>
> **2)** Informally, the contents of an HTML file. For example, "Don't get rid of that file. It contains the HTML for the main page of my Web site." [15]

HTML editor: A Web page editor designed to help people create Web pages by composing HTML. Compare to **wysiwyg editor**. [15]

HTTP: (Hypertext Transfer Protocol) The protocol used to transfer data between Web servers and Web clients (browsers). [7]

hypertext: Data that contains links to other data or to resources. On the Web, hypertext is displayed on Web pages. [2, 7]

icon: A small picture that represents a resource of some type. [7]

ICQ: An Internet service that allows direct communication connections between users. The name ICQ is a pun ("I seek you"). [2]

IETF: (Internet Engineering Task Force) An organization that forms working groups to study problems and to create solutions related to the technology used to run the Internet, particularly the various Internet protocols. [1]

image map: Within a Web page, a picture in which various parts correspond to different links. [7]

IMAP: (Internet Message Access Protocol) A protocol used by a mail client program to receive incoming messages from a mail server. With IMAP, messages remain on the server until they are deliberately deleted by the user. Compare to the **POP** protocol. [5]

IMAP server: A server to which a mail client program can connect to receive incoming mail via the IMAP protocol. [5]

information superhighway: A deprecated term used to refer to the Internet. Note: Use of this word will instantly mark you as a person who does not know what he is talking about. [1]

installation program: A program that, when run, performs all the tasks that are necessary to make a specific piece of software ready to run on your computer. [11]

instant messaging: A talk facility that makes it easy to establish a direct connection with another person. [14]

[the] Internet: The worldwide, general-purpose, communication and information system. Same as **Net**. [1]

Internet appliance: A special-purpose computer used primarily to access the Internet. [3]

Internet Engineering Task Force: Same as **IETF**. [1]

Internet Explorer: A browser developed by Microsoft. [2, 7]

Internet phone: Any system that uses a direct connection between you and another person to enable you to talk over the Internet by using voice. [14]

Internet Relay Chat: An Internet service that allows people all over the Net to have multiple, multiuser conversations, each one on a separate "channel". Same as **IRC**. [2]

Internet service provider: A company that provides Internet access to the public. Same as **ISP**. [3]

[the] **Internic**: (Internet Network Information Center) An organization that, among other jobs, manages some of the organizational top-level domains (in particular, **com**, **net** and **org**). [16]

IP: (Internet Protocol) The protocol, used along with TCP, to send data over the Internet. IP sends the data packets. TCP manages the flow and ensures that the data arrives intact without errors. [1]

IP address: A unique, four-part number, identifying a specific Internet computer. For example, the IP address of **www.harley.com** is **207.155.37.136**. Same as **IP number**. [4]

IP number: Same as **IP address**. [4]

IRC: (Internet Relay Chat) An Internet service that allows people all over the Net to have multiple, multiuser conversations, each one in a separate "channel". [2, 14]

IRC client: A client used to access the IRC system. [2, 14]

IRC network: A system in which various IRC servers are connected so as to allow anyone connected to one server to talk to anyone connected to any of the other servers. The four largest IRC networks are EFnet, Undernet, DALnet and IRCnet. [14]

IRC server: A server used to provide IRC services. [2, 14]

IRCnet: One of the large IRC networks. The others are EFnet, Undernet and DALnet. [14]

ISDN: (Integrated Services Digital Network) A service, offered by a telephone company, that allows you to connect to an ISP using all-digital technology. [3]

ISP: (Internet service provider) A company that provides Internet access to the public. [3]

item: Within a Favorites or Bookmarks list, an object with a name and other properties, used to store a particular URL. [7]

Java: A set of specifications, developed by Sun Microsystems, used to create programs (called applets) that can be embedded within Web pages, and run within a controlled environment (the Java virtual machine), thereby ensuring a measure of safety to the computer on which the applet is running. [8]

Java virtual machine: A controlled environment, designed for safety, within which Java applets must run. [8]

join: Within IRC, to become a participant in a channel. [14]

JPEG: (Joint Photographic Experts Group)
1) A file format commonly used to store photographs. Compare to **GIF**. [15]
2) Informally, a file containing a photograph in JPEG format. For example, "My friend sent me a JPEG of his cat playing the piano." [15]

K56Flex: One of two obsolete standards used by 56K bps modems to send and receive data, the other such standard being X2. Both K56Flex and X2 have been replaced by V.90. [3]

KB: Abbreviation for **kilobyte**. [3]

key: A unique pattern of bits used to encrypt or decrypt data. [6]

kilobyte: A unit of measurement used for computer memory and data storage, 1,024 (2^{10}) bytes. Informally, a kilobyte is about 1,000 bytes. Abbreviated as KB. [3]

leave: Within IRC, to stop being a participant in a channel. [14]

link: Within hypertext (on a Web page), an item that, when selected, causes a jump to another Web page, to more information, or to another resource on the Net. [2, 7]

links bar: Within Internet Explorer, a bar that can be customized with buttons that point to whatever URLs you want. [7]

list address: With respect to a mailing list, the address to which you send messages that are to be distributed to all the people who have subscribed to the list. [13]

list owner: The person who is in charge of a mailing list. [13]

list server: Same as **mailing list program**. [13]

Listproc: A type of mailing list program. [13]

Listserv: A type of mailing list program. [13]

log in: To initiate a work session with a host computer by typing a user name and password. [2]

lowercase: Describes the small letters of the alphabet (a, b, c, d…). Compare to **uppercase**. [4]

mail:

1) A system for sending and receiving messages from one Internet address to another. Same as **email**. [2, 5]

2) [verb] To send a message. [2]

3) A message that has been sent via this system. [5]

mail address: A unique identifier used to send mail to someone. [4]

mail program: A client used to send and receive mail. [2, 5]

mail server: A server that receives and stores incoming mail. [2, 5]

mailing list: A facility used for group discussion in which the messages are sent by mail to the members of the group. [2, 13]

mailing list program: A program that automatically performs the routine tasks needed to support a mailing list. [13]

mainstream hierarchy: Within Usenet, one of eight hierarchies, distributed around the world, that are subject to well-defined procedures for the creation of new groups. The mainstream hierarchies are **comp**, **humanities**, **misc**, **news**, **rec**, **sci**, **soc** and **talk**. [12]

Majordomo: A type of mailing list program. [13]

mark up: To insert HTML tags into text. [15]

maximize: To change the size of a window to be as large as possible. [7]

maximize button: On a window, a small button near the top-right corner of the window. When the maximize button has a picture of a single square, pressing the button changes the size of the window to be as large as possible. When the button has a picture of two overlapping rectangles, pressing the button restores the window to its original size. [7]

MB: Abbreviation for **megabyte**. [3]

megabyte: A unit of measurement used for computer memory and data storage, 1,048,576 (2^{20}) bytes. Informally, a megabyte is about 1,000,000 (a million) bytes. Abbreviated as MB. [3]

megahertz: The unit of measurement used to describe the speed of a processor. Megahertz means millions of cycles per second. Abbreviated as MHz. [3]

Messenger: Part of the Netscape Communicator suite of Internet software, a mail program. [5]

MHz: Abbreviation for "megahertz", the unit of measurement used to describe the speed of a processor. Megahertz means millions of cycles per second. [3]

MIDI: (Musical Instrument Digital Interface) A file format used to store and manipulate music on computers, synthesizers, keyboards, and other electronic music devices. [15]

minimize: To make a window disappear without closing it permanently, and without stopping the program that is currently running in the window. [7]

minimize button: On a window, a small button with a picture of a single line, near the top-right corner of the window, that, when pressed, makes the window disappear without closing it permanently, and without stopping the program that is currently running in the window. [7]

modem: A device that provides an interface between a computer and a communication line, such as a phone line or cable. The name "modem" stands for "modulator/ demodulator". [3]

moderated: Describes a newsgroup or mailing list in which a person, called the moderator, controls which articles (messages) are allowed to be sent to the group (list). [12, 13]

moderator: A person who controls which articles or messages are allowed to be sent to a particular Usenet newsgroup or mailing list. Such a newsgroup or mailing list is said to be moderated. [12, 13]

modulation: The process used by a modem to convert digital data to analog data. [3]

motherboard: In a PC, the main circuit board. [3]

mud: An elaborate, multiuser, text-based imaginary environment, used for talking and role-playing, often based on a fantasy, gothic or science fiction theme. [2, 14]

mud client: A client used to access a mud. [2]

multimedia: Data consisting of sounds, animation, or video. [2]

name server: A computer that provides DNS information on behalf of all the hostnames in a particular domain. [4]

navigate: On the Web, changing from one Web page to another. [7]

nerd:
>   **1)** A person who spends large amounts of time engaged in an activity in which he is particularly knowledgeable. [1]
>   **2)** An Internet expert. [1]

[the] **Net**: The worldwide, general-purpose, communication and information system. Same as the **Internet**. [1]

Net sex: An activity in which two people type erotic messages back and forth in order to achieve a state of sexual arousal leading to physical resolution. [14]

Netcaster: Part of the Netscape Communicator suite of Internet software, a program used to access Web channels. [2, 7]

Netnews: Same as **Usenet**. [2, 12]

Netscape: An informal term for any of the browsers (Navigator, Communicator) created by the Netscape Communications company. [2, 7]

network: Two or more computers connected together in order to share resources or information. [1]

newbie: A person who is new to the Internet. Note: Don't use this word. It makes you look like a goof. [1]

[the] **News**: Same as **Usenet**. [2, 12]

news server: A server that stores Usenet articles and makes them available via newsreaders (Usenet client programs). [2, 12]

newsfeed: The service offered by a news server. [12]

newsgroup: A Usenet discussion group. [2, 12]

newsreader: A client program used to access the Usenet system of discussion groups. [2, 12]

nick: Within IRC, an anonymous name chosen by a person. Same as **nickname**. [14]

nickname: Within IRC, an anonymous name chosen by a person. Same as **nick**. [14]

NNTP: (Network News Transfer Protocol) The protocol used to distribute Usenet articles. [12]

NNTP server: Same as a **news server**. [12]

on (the Net): Being connected to the Internet. [1]

online:
>   **1)** Describes a person or computer currently connected to the Net. [1]
>   **2)** Describes a service on the Net that is currently available. [1]

op: Within an IRC channel, a person who has certain privileges allowing him or her to control the channel in various ways. Same as **channel op**. [14]

Opera: A browser, designed to be small, fast, and easy to use. [7]

operating system: The master control program that runs a computer. The most widely used operating system for PCs is Microsoft Windows. [3]

options: Within Internet Explorer, a setting that contains configuration information or that allows you to control some aspect of the operation of the browser. [7]

organizational domain: A top-level domain that represents a particular category. See Appendix A for a full list. [4]

organizational hierarchy: Within Usenet, a hierarchy in which the newsgroups are of interest primarily to people with an interest in a particular organization, for example, a university or a company. [12]

Outlook Express: Part of the Microsoft Internet Explorer suite of Internet software, a mail program, and a Usenet newsreader. [5, 12]

packet: On the Internet, a small amount of data, sent as an intact unit from one computer to another. When a computer needs to send data, it divides the data into packets which are sent to the destination computer. The destination computer reassembles the packets into the original data. [1]

page icon: Within Internet Explorer, an icon, just to the left of the address bar, that represents the URL of the current Web page. [7]

page proxy icon: Within Netscape, an icon, just to the left of the address bar, that represents the URL of the current Web page. [7]

parent directory: A directory that contains another directory. (The other directory is referred to as a subdirectory.) [4]

paste [from the clipboard]: To copy the entire contents of the clipboard to a specified location within a window. [6]

path: Same as **pathname**. [4]

pathname: The specific description of the location of a file or directory, consisting of a series of directory names, separated by slash (/) characters, possibly ending with a file name. [4]

PCT: (Private Communications Technology) A protocol, developed in part by Microsoft, used to provide secure connections over the Internet. [8]

personal toolbar: Within Netscape, a bar that can be customized with buttons that point to whatever URLs you want. [7]

PICS: (Platform for Internet Content Selection) A set of specifications used to create rating systems for Internet resources. [8]

plug-in: A program designed to enhance the capabilities of a browser by processing a particular type of data that the browser cannot handle on its own. [10]

point to: With respect to a URL, to refer to a particular resource. [4]

POP:

1) (point of presence) An access point provided by an ISP (Internet service provider). A POP is usually accessed by dialing a telephone number. [3]

2) (Post Office Protocol) A protocol used by a mail client program to receive incoming messages from a mail server. With POP, messages are deleted from the server once they are sent to the client. Compare to the **IMAP** protocol. [5]

POP server: A server to which a mail client program can connect to receive incoming mail via the POP protocol. [5]

portal: A Web site, offering a variety of services, designed to act as a generalized starting point for using the Internet. [7]

post: To send an article to a Usenet newsgroup. [12]

posting: Within Usenet, a message sent to a discussion group. Same as an **article**. [2, 12]

preferences: Within Netscape, a setting that contains configuration information or that allows you to control some aspect of the operation of the browser. [7]

private key: A key that can be used to decrypt data that has been encrypted by using a corresponding public key. [6]

processor: In a PC, the main chip that carries out the instructions within a program; informally, the "brain" of the computer. [3]

program: A list of instructions that, when carried out by a computer, makes the computer act in a certain way. [1]

protocol: A specification (set of technical rules) used by client and server programs to communicate with one another. [1]

public key: A key that can be used to encrypt data such that it can be decrypted only by using a corresponding private key. [6]

publish: With respect to a Web page, to upload the page from your computer to a Web server. [15]

push: The system used to support channels, in which information is sent to your computer automatically according to a pre-determined schedule. [7]

push client: A client program which you run on your computer in order to give you access to channels. [7]

quote: To include all or part of an original mail message or Usenet article within a reply. [5, 12]

RAM: The working memory inside a PC, measured in MB (megabytes). The name RAM stands for "random access memory", a term used for historical reasons. [3]

readme file: A file, included within an archive, containing important information about the other files in the archive. If the archive holds a program, the readme file will usually contain information about installing and using the program. [11]

real-time: Describes a process in which you sense and respond to something as it is happening. [14]

regional hierarchy: Within Usenet, a hierarchy in which the newsgroups are of interest primarily to people in a particular country, city or other region. [12]

registrar: An organization charged with the responsibility of managing the registration of domain names within one or more top-level domains. [16]

reply:
> **1)** A mail message sent in response to a previous message. [5]
> **2)** [verb] To send such a message. [5]

resize: To change the size of a window. Same as **size**. [7]

rich text: Within a mail message, text written in HTML that can contain elements such as italic, boldface, various typefaces, pictures, links to Web sites, and so on, as well as regular text. [5]

right-click: To press the right button of a mouse. [7]

ringmaster: A person who administers a Web ring. [9]

root name server: One of a number of special computers that maintain a list of those name servers that handle the various top-level domains. [4]

run (a program): To have a computer follow the instructions in a program. Same as **execute** (a program). [1]

scan: With respect to a scanner, to process an image on paper and create a computer file containing that image. Same as **digitize**. [15]

scanner: A device, connected to a computer, that processes an image on paper and creates a computer file containing that image. [15]

scheme: Within a URL, the first part of the URL. The scheme describes the type of resource being identified. For example, in the URL **http://www.harley.com/**, the scheme is **http**. [4]

scroll: To move the contents of a window in a particular direction, either up and down, or left and right. [7]

scroll bar: Within a window, a bar at the far right or at the bottom of the window, used to scroll the contents of the window. [7]

search engine: A program that can search a large database for specific information. More specifically, a facility that allows you to search a database with information about the contents of the Web. [9]

second-level domain: The set of all hostnames that have the two rightmost parts of their names in common. For example, all the hostnames that end with **mit.edu** belong to the **mit.edu** second-level domain. [4]

secure connection: A facility, used to transmit data, in which the data is encrypted as it is sent and decrypted as it is received. [8]

security: Issues related to protecting yourself and your computer against problems that might arise as you use the Internet to interact with the outside world. [8]

security certificate: An electronic confirmation, offered by a Web site and recognized by Internet Explorer, indicating that the Web site is "secure and genuine". [8]

security level: Within the Internet Explorer security system, a description of those security features that are to be applied to particular Web sites. [8]

server: A program or computer that provides a service. On the Internet, all services are accessed by client programs that communicate with servers. [1]

shareware: Software that can be distributed and evaluated for free, but which you must pay for if you want to use after the evaluation period. [11]

shortcut: An icon that points to a particular resource, such as a URL. [7]

signature: A small amount of information, stored in a signature file, that is automatically appended to the end of outgoing mail messages or Usenet articles. Typically, a signature will contain information such as a name, mail address, street address, phone number, Web site address, and so on. [5, 12]

signature file: A file, containing a signature, whose contents are automatically appended to the end of outgoing mail messages or Usenet articles. [5, 12]

signing authority: An organization that issues digital IDs or certificates to use for encrypting and decrypting data. [6]

size: To change the size of a window. Same as **resize**. [7]

smiley: A series of characters, such as **:-)** or **:)**, that looks like a sideways face, indicating that what you are saying should be taken as being inoffensive. [6, 12, 14]

S/MIME: (Secure Multipurpose Internet Mail Extensions) A protocol used to encrypt and decrypt data on the Internet, especially mail messages. [6]

SMTP: (Simple Mail Transfer Protocol) The protocol used to send messages to a mail server. [5]

SMTP server: A server to which a mail client program can send outgoing mail via the SMTP protocol. [5]

snail mail: Regular post office mail. On the Net, the word "mail" always refers to email. [2]

software: Computer programs. [1]

spam: Unsolicited advertisements or inappropriate messages sent by email or posted to Usenet newsgroups. [2, 6, 12]

spammer: A person or company that sends spam. [2, 6]

SSL: (Secure Sockets Layer) A protocol, developed by Netscape, used to provide secure connections over the Internet. [8]

status bar: Within a browser, an area at the bottom of the browser window in which URLs and various informative messages are displayed. [7]

streaming: Describes a system used to transmit audio or video, in which data is played in real time as it arrives. Streaming is what makes continuous broadcasting possible over the Internet. [10]

subdirectory: A directory that is contained within another directory. (The other directory is referred to as the parent directory.) [4]

sub-domain: A domain that belongs to a more specific domain. For example, **pacbell.net** is a sub-domain of the **net** domain; **mail.pacbell.net** is a sub-domain of the **pacbell.net** domain. [4]

subscribe:
1) With respect to a channel, to indicate to your push client that you want to start receiving information from that channel. [7]
2) Within Usenet, to indicate to your newsreader that it should put a specific newsgroup on the list of groups you read. [12]
3) With respect to a mailing list, to tell a mailing list program that your address should receive copies of all messages sent to the list. [13]

subscription address: With respect to a mailing list, the address to which you mail commands to the mailing list program. This is the address to which you send mail to subscribe or unsubscribe to the list. [13]

suite: A collection of related computer programs, sold as a unit. [3]

surf: A deprecated term meaning "to use the Internet". Note: Use of this word will instantly mark you as a person who does not know what he is talking about. [1]

table: Within a Web page, a component that presents information in rows and columns. [15]

tag: An HTML command. All tags are contained within < (less-than) and > (greater-than) characters, for example, **
**. [15]

talk:
>**1)** To send data from one computer to another. [1]
>**2)** To have a real-time conversation with someone over the Internet, either by typing messages back and forth, or by voice. [2]

talk client: A program used to talk on the Internet. [14]

talk server: A server used to maintain a talk connection. [14]

taskbar: Within Windows, a long bar, displayed at one edge of the desktop, that contains the Start button as well as other buttons, each of which represents a program that is currently running. [7]

TB: Abbreviation for **terabyte**. [3]

TCP: (Transmission Control Protocol) The protocol, used along with IP, to send data over the Internet. IP sends the data packets. TCP manages the flow and ensures that the data arrives intact without errors. [1]

TCP/IP: The family of protocols used to run the Internet. (TCP/IP is pronounced as five separate letters, "T-C-P-I-P".) [1]

telnet: A service that allows you to connect to a remote computer, log in, and run programs on that computer. [2]

telnet client: A program that allows you to use telnet to access a remote host. The telnet client connects to the remote host and then begins to act like (emulate) a terminal. [2]

terabyte: A unit of measurement used for computer memory and data storage, 1,099,511,627,776 (2^{40}) bytes. Informally, a terabyte is about 1,000,000,000,000 (a trillion) bytes. Abbreviated as TB. [3]

terminal: The hardware used to access a remote host via telnet. In the olden days, people would use terminals that had a keyboard, a screen, and possibly a mouse. Today, we use a PC to run a program (called a telnet client) that makes the PC act like (emulate) an old-fashioned terminal. [2]

text: Data consisting of characters such as the letters of the alphabet, numbers, punctuation, and so on. [2, 12]

thread:
>**1)** With respect to email, a sequence of mail messages relating to the same subject, such that each message (except the first) is a reply to one of the previous messages. [5]
>**2)** On Usenet, a sequence of related articles consisting of an original article, replies to that article, as well as all subsequent replies. [12]

tilde: The ~ character (pronounced "til-duh"), used within a Unix pathname to indicate the home directory of a particular user. [4]

title bar: Within a window, a bar at the top of the window that contains descriptive information about the contents of the window. [7]

top-level domain: The most general domains—**com**, **edu**, **au**, **ca**, and so on—comprising the organizational domains and the geographical domains. [4]

topic: Within an IRC channel, a short description of the purpose of that channel. [14]

traffic: A measure of the average number of messages sent to a mailing list. Same as **volume**. [13]

Undernet: One of the large IRC networks. The others are EFnet, DALnet and IRCnet. [14]

uniform resource locator: Same as **URL**. [4]

uninstall: To follow a specific procedure in order to remove an installed program from your computer. [11]

unpack: To process an archive so as to reconstruct the original files stored within the archive. [11]

unsubscribe:

1) With respect to a channel, to indicate to your push client that you want to stop receiving information from that channel. [7]

2) Within Usenet, to indicate to your newsreader that it should remove a specific newsgroup from the list of groups you read. [12]

3) With respect to a mailing list, to tell a mailing list program that you no longer want to receive copies of messages sent to the list. [13]

unzip: To unpack a zip file. [11]

up: Describes a computer or communication link that is currently working. [1]

upload: To copy a file from your computer to another computer. [2]

uppercase: Describes the capital letters of the alphabet (A, B, C, D...). Compare to **lowercase**. [4]

upstream: Describes the transmission of data from your computer to the Internet. [3]

URL: (uniform resource locator) A formal specification used to identify specific Internet resources. In particular, URLs are used to identify Web pages. [4]

Usenet: A worldwide system of discussion groups. Same as **the News**, **Netnews**. [2, 12]

Usenet search engine: A search engine devoted to searching a database in which the contents of all the Usenet newsgroups are archived. [9]

UT: (Universal Time) One name for the principal time zone used as an international standard. Equivalent to UTC and GMT. [B]

UTC: (Coordinated Universal Time) One name for the principal time zone used as an international standard. Equivalent to UT and GMT. [B]

V.90: The current standard used by 56K bps modems to send and receive data. V.90 replaced two older, obsolete standards: K56Flex and X2. Pronounced "vee-dot-90". [3]

vCard: An electronic business card that can be attached to outgoing mail messages. Pronounced "vee-card". [5]

vertical scroll bar: A scroll bar at the far right of a window, used to scroll the contents of the window up and down. [7]

video capture board: An adapter that, when installed in your computer and connected to a video camcorder, allows you to create copies of individual video frames and store them as image files on your computer. [15]

virtual: Describes objects and experiences that exist only on the Net or on your computer. [2, 10]

virus: A small program, designed to insert itself into a file containing another program, becoming active when that program runs. [8]

virus hoax: An erroneous belief or rumor that a particular virus, perhaps nonexistent, is a potential source of trouble. Virus hoaxes spread by mail and on Usenet discussion groups when well-meaning people warn other people about nonexistent problems. [8]

volume: A measure of the average number of messages sent to a mailing list. Same as **traffic**. [13]

VRML: (Virtual Reality Modeling Language) A set of tools used to create 3-D, virtual, multiuser environments. (VRML is pronounced either as four separate letters, "V-R-M-L", or as a single word, "vermal".) [2, 10]

VRML world: A 3-D, multiuser, virtual environment based on VRML. [2, 10]

WAV: A file format used to store sounds. [15]

[the] **Web**: Part of the Internet, a global information delivery system used to display various types of data and to provide access to a variety of services. To access the Web, you use a client program called a **browser**. [2, 7]

Web chat room: On the Web, a facility allowing a group of people to talk by typing messages. Same as **chat room**. [2, 14]

Web page: On the Web, the information that is displayed from a file containing hypertext. [2, 7]

Web page editor: A program used to create, modify and maintain Web pages. [15]

Web ring: A collection of Web sites organized into a loop such that, from any Web site in the ring, you can follow links to move forward or backward so as to traverse the entire ring. [9]

Web server: A computer that stores Web pages and makes them available to anyone with access to that computer. [2, 7]

Web site: A group of related Web pages, maintained by a person or organization. [2, 7]

website: Same as **Web site**. [2, 7]

welcome message: A message that is sent to all new subscribers of a mailing list. [13]

whiteboard: Within a talk facility, a feature that allows people to collaborate by drawing within a shared window. [14]

whitelist: As used by filtering software, a list of Web sites to which the software will allow access. [8]

whois: A service, provided by a registrar, that allows you to look at some of the registration information related to a particular domain name. You can use whois to see whether a particular domain name has been registered. [16]

Windows: An operating system (master control program) used to run PCs. Windows is made by Microsoft. [3]

Windows Explorer: The program used to manage files and directories within Windows 95 and Windows 98. [4]

[the] **World Wide Web**: An old system that was the ancestor of the Web. [2]

wysiwyg editor: A Web page editor that allows you to work directly with the elements of a Web page—text, pictures, tables, and so on—without having to worry about HTML. The name "wysiwyg" (pronounced "whiz-ee-whig") stands for "what you see is what you get". Compare to **HTML editor**. [15]

X2: One of two obsolete standards used by 56K bps modems to send and receive data, the other such standard being K56Flex. Both X2 and K56Flex have been replaced by V.90. [3]

Yahoo: A particular search engine having an emphasis on organizing the content of the Web according to categories. [9]

zip file: An archive using the "zip" format. Zip files have an extension of `zip`, for example, `harley.zip`, and must be unpacked by a special program called a zip file program. [11]

zip file program: A program that provides the service of unpacking zip files. [11]

zone: Within the Internet Explorer security system, one of several categories into which you can classify Web sites. [8]

Index

Symbols

\ (backslash), in pathnames, 89

<!...> HTML tag (comments), 327, 330

> (greater-than symbol), HTML tags, 325

< (less-than symbol), HTML tags, 325

(number sign), IRC channels, 308

? (question mark), searches directly from browsers, 209-211

/ (slash)
    IRC commands, 310
    in URLs, 89-90

~ (tilde), in pathnames, 92-93

3-D. See VRML (Virtual Reality Modeling Language)

16-bit programs, 235

24-hour clock, equivalent AM/PM times, 366

32-bit programs, 235

56K modems, 53

360-degree photo plug-ins, 230

A

<a> HTML tag (anchors), 326, 330

abbreviations
    Internet communications, 370-373
    in mail messages, 126-127
    talk facilities, 302-304
    Usenet, 263-264

abuse mail address (for ISP customer complaints), 82

accounts, multiple, 60

acknowledgments, xxi-xxv

acquiring domain names, 348-349

active channels (Internet Explorer), 176

Active Desktop, 177-178

Active Server Pages (ASP), 86

ActiveX, 189-190
    Internet Explorer security settings, 190

ActiveX controls, 224-225
    installing, 227

address bar in browsers, 151
    searches directly from, 209-211

address books
    aliases, 134
    mail, 114-115

addresses
    list address (mailing lists), 280, 284
    subscription address (mailing lists), 280, 284

addresses, domain names, 74-75, 356. See also DNS (Domain Name System)
    acquiring, 348-349
    checking availability of, 351-352
    contact information, 352-353
    registering, 349-350
    second-level, 75
    selecting, 350-351
    sub-domains, 75
    top-level, 68-74, 356-363

addresses, hostnames, 68
    deciphering, 72-74
    uppercase/lowercase letters, 69
    URLs in, 83

addresses, IP, 75-77
    translating hostnames to, 77-78
addresses, mail, 19, 80-82, 96
    disguising, 256
    finding, 134-136
    privacy, 139
addresses, URLs (Uniform Resource
    Locators), 82-85
    ~ (tilde) in, 92-93
    abbreviations when typing, 89-91,
        152-153
    case sensitivity, 91-92
    https, 184
    in mail messages, 130-131
    pathnames, 88-89
    saving, 166-172
    sending in mail messages, 172-173
    troubleshooting, 158-159
    typing, 151-152
addressing mail messages, 112-114
    to groups, 133-134
Adkins, James, xxiii
administration of the Internet, 11-13
ADSL (Asymmetric Digital Subscriber
    Line), 57
adventure muds, 315
advertisements on Web pages, blocking,
    149-150
advertising. See also promoting
    spam (junk mail), 26-27
    on the Web, 26
aliases for mail addresses, 134
Altavista (search engine), 203-204
alternative hierarchies (Usenet), 251
    creating newsgroups, 273
America Online (AOL), 64-65
analog, compared to digital, 51
anchors (<a> HTML tag), 326, 330
animated GIF, 331
Anonymous FTP, 28-30, 237-238
antivirus programs, 43-44, 193-194
AOL (America Online), 64-65

applets (Java), 189
application sharing with
    NetMeeting, 306
applications. See also programs; software
    16-bit, 235
    32-bit, 235
    antivirus programs, 43-44
    bundled with PCs, 43
    clients, 5-6
    distribution with anonymous FTP,
        28-30
    freeware, 235
    installing, 238-240
    mail, 19, 96, 100-102
    mailing list programs, 279-281, 284-288
    operating systems, 42
    requirements for Internet connections,
        38, 44-45, 65
    servers, 5-6
    shareware, 235
    suites, 43
    uninstalling, 241
    in Web pages, 334-335
    word processors, 43
applications, downloading, 234
    anonymous FTP, 237-238
    directories for saving files, 236-237
    overview, 234-235
    Usenet binaries, 267
archives, 234
    executable programs, 238
    unpacking, 234
    Usenet, 207
    zip files, 239-240
Armbruster, Rob, xxiii
Arpanet
    history of the Internet, 2
    history of telnet, 34
articles (Usenet), 25, 244
    cross-posting, 265
    distribution, 244-245
    finding, 271
    flames, 265
    follow-up, 265

format of, 258-260
freedom of speech, 245-246
posting, 267-270
reading, 256-259
spoilers, 265
threads, 265
time zones, 366-367
ASP (Active Server Pages), 86
asymmetric bandwidth, 56
Asymmetric Digital Subscriber Line
(ADSL), 57
attachments
articles (Usenet), 268
mail messages, 19, 102, 109
audio. *See* sound
autocomplete feature (browsers), 153
availability of domain names, checking,
351-352
avatars, 298

B

<b> HTML tag (bold), 330
B-channels (ISDN), 54-55
Babin, Len, xxii
quotation of, xxi
Back button (browsers), 155
backing up
Bookmarks list (Netscape), 172
Favorites list (Internet Explorer), 169
backslash (\), in pathnames, 89
bandwidth, 50
asymmetric, 56
Bcc: line (mail messages), 112-114
Berners-Lee, Tim (history of World Wide
Web), 21
Bess, Ginny, xxiv
quotation of, xxi
binaries (Usenet), 266-267
binary system, 40
Bitnet, 290-291
bits, 49-50

bits per second (bps), 50
blacklist, filtering software, 198
blind copies (mail messages), 112-114
blocking advertisements on Web pages,
149-150
blocking software, 198-200
body
articles (Usenet), 260
mail messages, 102, 108
<body> HTML tag, 330
bogus newsgroups (Usenet), 254
boldface (<b> HTML tag), 330
Bookmarks list (Netscape), 166, 169-172
bots (IRC), 312
bounced mail messages, 119-120
Bowen, Julie, xxv
quotation of, xxi
bps (bits per second), 50

 HTML tag (line breaks), 325, 330
Brady, James, xxii
quotation of, xxi
browser plug-ins, 222-224, 228
360-degree photos, 230
finding, 231
installing, 225-226
multimedia, 229
music, 230
streaming audio/video, 228
VRML, 33, 229
browser windows
management of, 160-162
opening, 162-163
browsers, 22-23, 44-45, 145-147. *See also*
Internet Explorer; Netscape
abbreviations when typing URLs,
90-91, 152-153
ActiveX controls, 224-225, 227
address bar, 151
advertisements, blocking, 149-150
autocomplete feature, 153
Back/Forward buttons, 155
cache, 163-164

channels, 23-24
complexity of, 144-145
default home pages, 175
file extensions, 220-222
FTP clients, 29
graphics, viewing/hiding, 149-150
help, 151
history list, 155
home page, setting, 173-175
mail programs with, 100
newsreaders, 25
Opera, 146-147
options/preferences, 147, 149
programs, installing automatically, 240
saving URLs, 166-172
scroll bars, 155
search engines, accessing quickly,
  208-209
searches, directly from address bar,
  209-211
status bar, 154
as talk clients, 297
typing URLs, 151-152
URLs for newsgroups, 257
warning messages, 182-183
Web pages, designing, 340
Web sites for, 147
Web-based mail services, 99-100
buddy lists, 300
bulleted lists (<ul> HTML tag), 330
bundled software, 43
business cards. *See* **vCards**
buttons of mouse, reversing, 158. *See also*
  custom buttons
buying PCs
cost, 46-47
type to buy, 45-46
bytes, 39, 50

C

cable connections, 57-59
cache (browsers), 163-164

**Caillau, Robert (history of World Wide
  Web), 21**
cameras, digital, 337
Campbell, Carrie, xxiii
carbon copies (mail messages), 112-114
cards (business). *See* **vCards**
case sensitivity
hostnames, 69
pathnames, 91-92
Cc: line (mail)
headers, 105
messages, 112-114
CD-ROM drives, 41
censorship of the Internet, 14-16
<center> HTML tag, 330
center of the Internet, 13-14
central processing units (CPUs), 38-39
speed, 45
certificates
mail encryption, 141-142
security certificates, 191
CGI (Common Gateway Interface), 332
channel guides, Web sites for, 177
channel operators (IRC), 308
channels, 167, 175-177
IRC, 30, 308-309
ISDN, 54-55
Web, 23-24
charters (Usenet), 272
chat rooms, 30. *See also* **talk facilities**
abbreviations, 370-373
on Web, 296-299
**children, safety precautions on Internet,
  195-197**
filtering software, 198-200
choosing
domain names, 350-351
ISPs, 61-63
mail programs, 100-102
theme of Web page, 324, 341
Web site hosts, 342-344

clicking, 157
   double-clicking, 157
   right-clicking, 157-158
client/server networks, 4-6
clients, 5-6
   FTP, 29, 337
   IRC, 30, 307, 312
   mail, selecting, 100-102
   mud, 32, 317
   push, 175-177
   talk facilities, 295
   telnet, 34
   types of, 35
clip art, Web sites for, 339
clipboard (Windows), 131-132
closing windows, 161
coaxial cable, 57
Collabra (newsreader), 246
   configuring, 256
   posting articles, 267
   reading articles, 258
   signature files, 260
   starting, 256
   subscribing to newsgroups, 257
com top-level domain, exceptions to usage, 71-72
comics Web sites, 162
commands
   IRC, 310-312
   mailing lists, 284-288
comments (<!...>) HTML tag, 327, 330
commercial newsfeeds, 248-249
commercial Web site hosting, compared to free Web site hosting, 342-343
Common Gateway Interface (CGI), 332
communications. *See also* **mail;**
   talk facilities
   abbreviations, 263-264, 370-373
   censorship of the Internet, 14-16
   digital, compared to analog, 51
   packets, 6-7
   protocols, 7-8
   real-time, 294

   spread of information on the Internet, 13-14
   upstream/downstream speed, 56
Composer, 336
compression of archives, 234
compression utilities, 239
computer viruses, 192-194
   antivirus programs, 43-44, 193-194
   hoaxes, 194-195
   mail, 193
   mail messages about, 118
computers (PCs), 38
   alternatives to, 47-48
   cost, 46-47
   disks, 41-42
   memory, 39-40
   operating systems, 42
   processors, 38-39
   software, 43-45
   type to buy, 45-46
configuring newsreaders, 255-256
connections (Internet)
   alternatives to PCs, 47-48
   AOL, 64-65
   cable, 57-59
   dialup, 53-54
   DSL, 56-57
   finding ISPs, 60-61
   hardware requirements, 45-46
   ISDN, 54-55
   local compared to long distance phone
      calls, 63-64
   modems, 52
   multiple accounts, 60
   port numbers, 315-316
   requirements, 38, 65
   secure connections, 183-184
   selecting ISPs, 61-63
   services available, 59-60
   software requirements, 44-45
   speed, 3-4, 49-50
   telnet, 33-34
   types of, 48-49
   upstream/downstream speed, 56

contact information, registering domain names, 352-353

Content Advisor (Internet Explorer), 199

content filters, 198-200

context menus, 157-158

control messages (Usenet), 272

controls, 224

converting photographs to JPEG file format, 337-338

cookies, 184-186
    Internet Explorer settings, 186-187
    Netscape settings, 187

Coordinated Universal Time (UTC), 366-367

copies of Web pages, sending, 173

copying
    Bookmarks list (Netscape), 172
    data (Windows clipboard), 131-132
    Favorites list (Internet Explorer), 169

cost
    ISPs, 61
    PCs, 46-47

CPUs (central processing units), 38-39
    speed, 45

Cragg, Noel, xxiii

creating
    shortcuts to Web pages, 164-166
    Usenet newsgroups, 271-274

cross-posting articles (Usenet), 265

custom buttons in browsers, creating, 208

cutting data (Windows clipboard), 131-132

cyberspace, 10-11

D

D-channel (ISDN), 54-55

daily comics Web sites, 162

DALnet (IRC), 307

data, 4
    transmission, upstream/downstream speed, 56
    types of, 21

date/time on message headers, 105, 366-367

Date: line (mail headers), 105

DCC (Direct Client to Client connection), 312

default home pages (browsers), 175

delay (talk facilities), 295

deleting
    cookies in browsers, 187
    icons, 239
    mail messages, 112
    shortcuts, 166

descriptions in URLs, 84-85
    pathnames, 88-89

designing Web pages, 340-342

desktop, 164
    Active Desktop, 177-178
    icons, deleting, 239

dialog boxes, 152

dialup connections, 53-54
    local compared to long distance phone calls, 63-64

digests (mailing lists), 277

digital, compared to analog, 51

digital cameras, 337

digital Ids (mail encryption), 141-142

Digital Subscriber Line (DSL), 56-57

Direct Client to Client connection (DCC), 312

direct connections (talk facilities), 295, 299-301

directories, 86-87
    home directories, 92
    pathnames, 88-89
    saving files when downloading programs, 236-237

discussion groups. *See* Usenet

disks, 41-42

DNS (Domain Name System), 8, 75-78
    access to, 78-79
    name servers, 78

documents (HTML). *See* Web pages

domain names, 74-75, 356. *See also* DNS (Domain Name System); top-level

domains
acquiring, 348-349
checking availability of, 351-352
obtaining, 343-344
registering, 349-350, 352-353
second-level, 75
selecting, 350-351
sub-domains, 75
double-clicking, 157
downloading, 335
data, security issues, 188-189
files with FTP, 28-30
Usenet binaries, programs for, 267
downloading programs, 234
anonymous FTP, 237-238
directories for saving files, 236-237
overview, 234-235
downstream/upstream data transmission, 56
dragging, 155
Dragushan, Ron, xxiii
quotation of, xxi
DSL (Digital Subscriber Line), 56-57

E

Echard, Maribeth, xxiv
editing
images, Web sites for, 339
mail messages, 123-124
Web pages, 335-337
EFnet (IRC), 307
electronic commerce, secure connections, 183-184
Elias, Isidor, xxii
quotation of, xxi
email, 19-20. *See also* **mail**
emoticons. *See* **smileys**
emptying Trash folder (mail messages), 112
encryption for mail messages, 140-142
end command (mailing list programs), 285

entering searches directly in browsers, 209-211
entering URLs, 151-152
abbreviations for, 152-153
for newsgroups, 257
errors
mail messages, 119-120
URLs, troubleshooting, 158-159
Essig, Don, xxiv
quotation of, xxi
Ethernet, 46
executable programs as archives, 238
expiration of articles (Usenet), 248
extensions (file names), 85-86, 220-222

F

F1 key (help), 151
fantasy (muds), 32-33, 313-317
FAQs (Frequently Asked Questions), 212-215, 261-262
Favorites list (Internet Explorer), 166-169
figures, list of, ix-xi
file attachments
articles (Usenet), 268
mail messages, 19, 102, 109
file extensions, 85-86, 220-222
file formats
images on Web pages, 330-331
sound files, 331-332
File Manager, 87
file names, 85-86
File Transfer Protocol (FTP), 8, 28-30
anonymous FTP, 237-238
clients, 29, 337
servers, 29
files, 28
archives, 234
downloading with FTP, 28-30
organizing, 86-87
readme, 238
saving, when downloading programs, 236-237

uploading with FTP, 28-30
zip, 239-240
filtering
mail messages, 139-140
software, 198-200
finding. *See also* **search engines; searches**
ISPs, 60-61
mail addresses, 134-136
mailing lists, 288
newsgroups, 270-271
plug-ins, 231
flame wars, 265
flames, 265
floppy disks, 41
focus (windows), 156
folders, 86-87
mail messages, 111-112
follow-up articles (Usenet), 265
`<font>` **HTML tag, 330**
`<form>` **HTML tag, 330**
formats
images on Web pages, 330-331
sound files, 331-332
forms (Web pages), 332-333
Forward button (browsers), 155
forwarding mail messages, 117-119
`<frame>` **HTML tag, 330**
frames (Web pages), 156-157, 332, 334
`<frameset>` **HTML tag, 330**
free Web site hosting
compared to commercial Web site
hosting, 342-343
Web sites for information, 344
freedom of speech on the Internet, 14-16
Usenet, 245-246
freeware, 235
**Frequently Asked Questions (FAQs),
212-215, 261-262**
friends lists, 300
`From:` **line (mail headers), 104**
FrontPage Express, 335-336

FTP (File Transfer Protocol), 8, 28-30
anonymous FTP, 237-238
clients, 29, 337
servers, 29
`ftp`, **in hostnames, 73**

G

Garstang, Marlene, xxiii
gateways (mailing lists), 289-291
geeks, 10
**geographical top-level domains, 70-71,
357-363**
Ghens, Michael, xxiii
GIF image format, 331
gigabytes, 39-40
glossary, 375-396
GMT (Greenwich Mean Time), 366-367
graphics, 22, 145. *See also* **images**
icons, 154
programs, 338
Web pages, viewing/hiding, 149-150
greater-than symbol (>), HTML tags, 325
Greenwich Mean Time (GMT), 366-367
**groups, sending mail messages to,
133-134**

H

**H.323 standard (voice/video
communications), 306**
`<h1>` **HTML tag (headings), 330**
Hahn, Harley
acknowledgments, xxi-xxv
personal note from, i-ii
Web site, 175, 327
hard disks, 41
hardware, 4
alternatives to PCs, 47-48
disks, 41-42
memory, 39-40
modems, 52-54

processors, 38-39
requirements for Internet connections, 38, 45-46, 65

Harley Hahn's Internet & Web Yellow Pages, 197, 202, 270, 288

Hayes, Tom, xxiv
quotation of, xxi

HDSL (High-bit-rate Digital Subscriber Line), 57

<head> HTML tag, 330

headers for articles (Usenet), 258-259

headers for mail messages, 102-108
Cc: line, 105
Date: line, 105
From: line, 104
Message-Id: line, 107
Organization: line, 108
Received: line, 106-107
Reply-To: line, 107
Subject: line, 104-105
time zones, 105, 366-367
To: line, 104
X-Mailer: line, 108

headings (**<h1>** HTML tag), 330

help, 151. *See also* **troubleshooting**

help command (mailing list programs), 285

helper applications, 224

hiding graphics on Web pages, 149-150

hierarchy (Usenet), 249-255
creating newsgroups, 271-274

High-bit-rate Digital Subscriber Line (HDSL), 57

history
Internet, 2-3
telnet, 34
Usenet, 24
Web, 21

history list (browsers), 155

hoaxes (viruses), 194-195

Holzschlag, Molly, xxiii

home directories, 92

home pages in browsers, setting, 173-175

horizontal rule (**<hr>** HTML tag), 330

horizontal scroll bars, 155

hosting Web sites, 342-344

hostnames, 68
acquiring, 348-349
checking availability of, 351-352
deciphering, 72-74
domains. *See* domains
registering, 349-350, 352-353
relationship with domains, 74-75
selecting, 350-351
translating to IP addresses, 77-78
uppercase/lowercase letters, 69
URLs in, 83

hosts, 34

Hougland, Lunaea
quotation of, xxi
Web site, xxii

<hr> HTML tag (horizontal rule), 330

HTML (Hypertext Markup Language), 146, 325
documents. *See* Web pages
editors, 335
Web sites for tutorials, 327

HTML tags, 324-330
<a> (anchors), 326, 330
<b> (bold), 330
<body>, 330
**
** (line break), 325, 330
<center>, 330
comments (**<!...>**), 327, 330
<font>, 330
<form>, 330
<frame>, 330
<frameset>, 330
<h1> (headings), 330
<head>, 330
<hr> (horizontal rule), 330
<html>, 330
<i> (italics), 325, 330
<img> (image), 325, 330
<map> (image maps), 330
<meta>, 330
<ol> (ordered lists), 330
<p> (paragraphs), 330

`<table>`, 330
`<title>`, 330
`<u>` (underline), 330
`<ul>` (unordered lists), 330
`<html>` HTML tag, 330
HTTP (Hypertext Transfer Protocol), 8, 146
hyperlinks, 20-21, 145
  `<a>` HTML tag, 326, 330
  following, 20, 145
  identifying, 154
  image maps, 154
  navigating Web pages, 154
  shortcuts, creating, 165
  Web pages, 329
hypertext, 20-22, 145-146
Hypertext Markup Language. *See* HTML

I

`<i>` HTML tag (italics), 325, 330
icons, 154. *See also* shortcuts
  deleting, 239
  page icons, 165
ICQ (talk facility), 31, 300
IETF (Internet Engineering Task Force), 7
image editors, Web sites for, 339
image maps, 154, 329
  `<map>` HTML tag, 330
images. *See also* graphics; photographs
  graphics programs, 338
  `<img>` HTML tag, 325, 330
  Usenet, 266-267
  Web sites for, 339
images on Web pages, 330-331, 337-339
  designing, 340
  saving from, 338
imaginary environments
  muds, 32-33, 313-317
  VRML (Virtual Reality Modeling Language), 33, 229
IMAP (Internet Message Access Protocol), 8, 98

`<img>` HTML tag (images), 325, 330
imported bookmarks (Internet Explorer), 168
`info ?` command (mailing list programs), 285
information superhighway, 10-11
installation programs, 234
installing
  Active Desktop, 178
  ActiveX controls, 227
  FrontPage Express, 335
  plug-ins, 225-226
  programs, 238-240
instant messaging, 300
Integrated Services Digital Network (ISDN), 54-55
Internet, 2
  administration of, 11-13
  censorship of, 14-16
  client/server system, 4-6, 35
  history of, 2-3
  spread of information on, 13-14
  terminology, 9-11
  uses for, 18-19
Internet appliances, 47
Internet connections
  alternatives to PCs, 47-48
  AOL, 64-65
  cable, 57-59
  dialup, 53-54
  DSL, 56-57
  finding ISPs, 60-61
  hardware requirements, 45-46
  ISDN, 54-55
  local compared to long distance phone calls, 63-64
  modems, 52
  multiple accounts, 60
  port numbers, 315-316
  requirements, 38, 65
  secure connections, 183-184
  selecting ISPs, 61-63
  services available, 59-60
  software requirements, 44-45

speed, 3-4, 49-50
types of, 48-49
upstream/downstream speed, 56
Internet Engineering Task Force (IETF), 7
Internet Explorer, 22-23, 145
active channels, 176
Active Desktop, 177-178
ActiveX controls, 224-225, 227
cache settings, 164
Content Advisor, 199
cookies, settings, 186-187
custom buttons, creating, 208
Favorites list, 166-169
file extensions, master list of, 222
FrontPage Express, installing, 335
graphics, viewing/hiding, 150
history list, 155
home page, setting, 173
options, setting, 147, 149
Outlook Express, 101
page icons, 165
plug-ins, installing, 226
reloading Web pages, 164
screen elements, 148
secure connections, 184
security warning messages, 182
security zones, 190-192
sending copies of Web pages via mail, 173
sending URLs in mail messages, 172
shortcuts for typing URLs, 153
software included, 45
windows, opening new, 162
Internet Explorer, newsreader for, 246
configuring, 256
posting articles, 267
reading articles, 259
signature files, 260
starting, 256
subscribing to newsgroups, 257
Internet Message Access Protocol (IMAP), 8, 98
Internet phone, 304

Internet Protocol (IP), 8, 76
Internet Relay Chat (IRC), 30, 307-313
Internet resources, 22, 145
360-degree photo plug-ins, 230
advertisement blocking software, 150
antivirus programs, 194
avatar-based chat rooms, 299
browsers, downloading, 147
channel guides, 177
for children, 197
clip art, 339
comics, 162
commercial newsfeeds, 249
connecting to DNS servers, 78-79
creating Usenet newsgroups, 274
default home pages, 175
direct connection talk facilities, 301
domain names, obtaining, 343-344
downloading Usenet binaries, 267
FAQs (Frequently Asked Questions), 215
filtering software, 198-200
free Web hosting, 344
FTP clients, 337
Harley Hahn, 175, 327
hosting, 342-344
hostnames, deciphering, 73
HTML tutorials, 327
image editors, 339
images, 339
Internet Explorer security zones, 190-191
IRC clients, 312
IRC help, 313
ISPs, lists of, 63
list of, xii-xiii
Lunaea Hougland, xxii
mail address directories, 135
mail programs, 102
mailing lists, finding, 288
Movielink, 185
mud clients, 317
mud FAQs, 317
muds, list of, 317

multimedia plug-ins, 230
music plug-ins, 230
newsreaders, 247
organizational/regional hierarchies
   (Usenet), 253
organizing, 341
photographs, 338
plug-ins, finding, 231
portals, 174
promoting, 344-345
push clients, 177
rating systems, 199
registries for domain names, 350
smileys, 373
software repositories, 235
sounds, 340
streaming audio/video plug-ins, 229
Usenet searches, 208, 271
virus hoaxes, 195
voice/video communications, 306
VRML plug-ins, 229
Web chat rooms, 299
Web page editors, 336
Web rings, 215-216
Web-based mail services, 100
Web-based mailing lists, 289
Web-based newsreaders, 247
Wendy Murdock, xxii, 151
zip file programs, 240
Internet service providers. *See* **ISPs**
Internet zone (Internet Explorer), 191
Internic, registering domain names, 349
IP (Internet Protocol), 8, 76
IP addresses, 75-77
   translating hostnames to, 77-78
IRC (Internet Relay Chat), 30, 307-313
IRCnet (IRC), 307
**ISDN (Integrated Services Digital
   Network), 54-55**
ISPs (Internet service providers), 48, 342
   abuse mail address (for customer
      complaints), 82
   AOL, 64-65
   dialup connections, local compared to
      long distance phone calls, 63-64

DNS server access, 78-79
domain names, acquiring, 348-349
finding, 60-61
multiple accounts, 60
selecting, 61-63
services available, 59-60
italics (`<i>` HTML tag), 325, 330

J-K

Jackson, Cheryl, xxiv
   quotation of, xxi
Java, 189, 225, 335
Java virtual machine, 189
JavaScript, 335
JPEG image format, 331
   converting photographs to, 337-338
judgment, viewing Web sites, 15
**junk mail messages (spam), 26-27,
   136-138**
Jurkowski, Zbigniew, xxiii
   quotation of, xxi

Kennedy, Scott, xxiii
Keramaris, Terry, xxiii
keyboard shortcuts
   Back/Forward buttons (browsers), 155
   closing windows, 161
   F1 key (help), 151
   Internet Explorer, typing URLs, 153
   Netscape, adding/editing
      bookmarks, 171
   opening new windows, 162
   reloading Web pages, 164
   restoring minimized windows, 161
   right-clicking, 158
   scrolling in windows, 156
   URLs, typing, 152
kilobytes, 39-40

L

lag (talk facilities), 295
**LDAP (Lightweight Directory Access
   Protocol), 8, 135-136**

Leon, Gil, xxiii

less-than symbol (<), HTML tags, 325

Lewis, Ruth, xxiv

line breaks (`<br>` HTML tag), 325, 330

links, 20-21, 145
    `<a>` HTML tag, 326, 330
    following, 20, 145
    identifying, 154
    image maps, 154
    navigating Web pages, 154
    shortcuts, creating, 165
    Web pages, 329

Linstruth, Chris, xxiii

Linstruth, Patrick, xxiii

list address (mailing lists), 280, 284

list owners (mailing lists), 276

list servers, 277

Listproc (mailing list program), 279-281
    commands, 287
    subscribe command, 281-282

lists. *See* mailing lists

lists on Web pages
    `<ol>` HTML tag (ordered lists), 330
    `<ul>` HTML tag (unordered lists), 330

Listserv (mailing list program), 279-281
    commands, 286
    subscribe command, 281-282

Literary Machines, 21

Local Intranet zone (Internet Explorer), 191

local phone calls (dialup connections), compared to long distance calls, 63-64

locating. *See* finding

logging in to terminals, 34

long distance phone calls (dialup connections), compared to local calls, 63-64

long-term storage. *See* disks

lowercase letters in hostnames, 69

Lumpkin, James, xxiii

M

mail
    address books, 114-115, 134
    attachments, 19
    definition, 19-20
    overview, 96-97
    spam (junk mail), 26-27, 136-138
    virus hoaxes, 194
    viruses, 193
    Web-based services, 99-100

`mail`, in hostnames, 73

mail addresses, 19, 80-82, 96
    disguising, 256
    finding, 134-136
    privacy, 139

mail messages
    abbreviations, 126-127
    addressing, 112-114
    attachments, 102, 109
    body, 102, 108
    conventions, 122, 125
    encryption, 140-142
    errors, 119-120
    filtering, 139-140
    folders, 111-112
    forwarding, 117-119
    headers, 102-108
    inappropriate uses for, 124-125
    parts of, 102-103
    personal names/titles in, 126
    privacy issues, 127-129
    replying to, 115-117
    rich text, 108, 129-130
    sending copies of Web pages, 173
    sending to groups, 133-134
    sending URLs in, 172-173
    shouting in, 126
    signatures, 102, 109-110
    smileys, 125-126
    spam, 136-138
    spelling/punctuation/paragraph breaks, 123-124
    threads, 117

time zones, 105, 366-367
URLs in, 130-131
vCards, 102-103, 110
mail programs, 19, 96
selecting, 100-102
mail servers, 19, 96
IMAP, 98
POP, 97-98
SMTP, 97-98
mailing lists, 276
commands, 284-288
compared to Usenet, 25-26, 277-279
finding, 288
gateways, 289-291
list address/subscription address, 284
mailing list programs, 277-281
overview, 276-277
starting your own, 289
subscribing to, 281-283
unsubscribing from, 282-283
`mailto` **URLs, 84**
mainstream hierarchies (Usenet), 251
creating newsgroups, 271-273
Majordomo (mailing list program), 279-281
commands, 288
subscribe command, 281-282
managing browser windows, 160-162
`<map>` **HTML tag (image maps), 330**
maximizing windows, 160-161
megabytes, 39-40
megahertz (MHz), 39
memory, 39-40
long-term storage, 41-42
`Message-Id:` **line (mail headers), 107**
messages
IRC, 309-310
mail. *See* mail messages
mailing lists, volume of, 277
Usenet. *See* articles (Usenet)
Messenger (Netscape mail program), 101
`<meta>` **HTML tag, 330**
MHz (megahertz), 39

Microsoft ActiveX, 189-190
Internet Explorer security settings, 190
Microsoft ActiveX controls, 224-225
installing, 227
Microsoft FrontPage Express, 335-336
Microsoft Internet Explorer, 22-23, 145
active channels, 176
Active Desktop, 177-178
ActiveX controls, 224-225, 227
cache settings, 164
Content Advisor, 199
cookies, settings, 186-187
custom buttons, creating, 208
Favorites list, 166-169
file extensions, master list of, 222
FrontPage Express, installing, 335
graphics, viewing/hiding, 150
history list, 155
home page, setting, 173
options, setting, 147, 149
Outlook Express, 101
page icons, 165
plug-ins, installing, 226
reloading Web pages, 164
screen elements, 148
secure connections, 184
security warning messages, 182
security zones, 190-192
sending copies of Web pages via mail, 173
sending URLs in mail messages, 172
shortcuts for typing URLs, 153
software included, 45
windows, opening new, 162
MIDI (Musical Instrument Digital Interface) sound format, 331-332
Miller, Eric S., xxiv
MIME (Multipurpose Internet Mail Extensions), 8
minimizing windows, 161
modems, 52-54
moderated mailing lists, 276
moderated newsgroups, 260-261
moderators (mailing lists), 276

Montgomery, Marcy, xxiii
Morgan, Lori, xxiv
  quotation of, xxi
motherboards, 38
mouse
  dragging, 155
  reversing buttons, 158
  right-clicking, 157-158
Movielink Web site, 185
moving
  between Web pages, 153-155
  shortcuts, 166
  windows, 162
mud clients, 32
muds, 32-33, 313-317
multimedia, 22, 145
  plug-ins, 229
multiple accounts, 60
multiple recipients, sending mail
  messages to, 133-134
Multipurpose Internet Mail Extensions
  (MIME), 8
Murdock, Wendy
  quotation of, xxi
  Web site, xxii, 151
Murphy, Eldrice, xxiii
music
  file formats for, 331
  plug-ins, 230
Musical Instrument Digital Interface
  (MIDI) sound format, 331-332

N

name servers, 78
naming
  files, 85-86
  mailing lists, 278-279
  Usenet hierarchy, 249-255
navigation
  Web pages, 153-155
  Web site organization, 341
nerds, 10

Nesbitt, Kenn, xxiii
Net, 2. *See also* Internet
Net sex, 320-321
net top-level domain, exceptions to usage,
  71-72
Netcaster, 176
NetMeeting, 306
Netnews, 24, 244. *See also* Usenet
Netscape, 23, 145
  Bookmarks list, 166, 169-172
  cache settings, 164
  cookies, settings, 187
  custom buttons, creating, 208
  displaying list of plug-ins, 227-228
  file extensions, master list of, 222
  graphics, viewing/hiding, 150
  history list, 155
  home page, setting, 173
  installing plug-ins, 226
  Netcaster, 176
  page proxy icons, 165
  plug-ins, 222-224
  preferences, setting, 147-149
  reloading Web pages, 164
  screen elements, 149
  secure connections, 184
  security settings, 192
  security warning messages, 183
  sending copies of Web pages via
    mail, 173
  software included, 45
  URLs, typing, 152
  windows, opening new, 162
Netscape Collabra (newsreader), 246
  configuring, 256
  posting articles, 267
  reading articles, 258
  signature files, 260
  starting, 256
  subscribing to newsgroups, 257
Netscape Composer, 336
Network News Transfer Protocol (NNTP),
  8, 248

networks
administration of the Internet, 11-13
client/server, 4-6
Ethernet, 46
history of the Internet, 2
IRC, 307
packets, 6-7
protocols, 7-8
Neuromancer, **11**
newbies, 11
news servers, 25, 244, 247-249
Usenet article distribution, 244-245
newsfeeds, 248
commercial, 248-249
newsgroups. *See* **Usenet**
newsreaders, 25, 244, 246-247
articles (Usenet), reading, 256-259
configuring, 255-256
nicknames (IRC), 308
NNTP (Network News Transfer Protocol),
8, 248
number sign (#), IRC channels, 308

O

<ol> HTML tag (ordered lists), 330
online, 9
opening browser windows, 162-163
Opera (browser), 146-147
operating systems
Unix, 91-92
Windows, 42
ops (IRC), 308
options on browsers, setting, 147-149
ordered lists (<ol> HTML tag), 330
org top-level domain, exceptions to usage,
71-72
Organization: line (mail headers), 108
organizational hierarchies (Usenet), 252
organizational top-level domains, 69,
71, 356

organizing
files, 86-87
mail messages, 111-112
Web sites, 341
welcome messages (mailing lists), 283
Outlook Express, 101, 246
configuring, 256
posting articles, 267
reading articles, 259
signature files, 260
starting, 256
subscribing to newsgroups, 257
owners (mailing lists), 276

P

<p> HTML tag (paragraphs), 330
packets, 6-7
page icons, 165
page proxy icons, 165
pages (Web), 22, 145. *See also* **Web sites**
advertisements, blocking, 149-150
cache, 163-164
components of, 327, 329
design tips, 340-342
editors, 335-337
elements of, 145-146
file extensions, 86, 220-222
forms, 332-333
frames, 156-157, 332, 334
graphics, viewing/hiding, 149-150
home page, setting in browser, 173-175
HTML (Hypertext Markup
Language), 146
HTML tags, 324-330
hypertext, 22
images, 330-331, 337-339
links, 154, 329
navigating, 153-155
programs in, 334-335
publishing, 335
reading, 155-157
selecting theme of, 324, 341
sending copies of, 173

shortcuts, creating, 164-166
sound, 331-332, 339-340
source code, viewing, 327
tables, 332-333
text, 329
URLs. *See* URLs
pairs (HTML tags), 325
paragraph breaks in mail messages, 123-124
paragraphs (<p> HTML tag), 330
parent directories, 87
parental control software, 198-200
pasting data (Windows clipboard), 131-132
pathnames, 88-89
~ (tilde) in, 92-93
case sensitivity, 91-92
PCs (personal computers), 38
alternatives to, 47-48
cost, 46-47
disks, 41-42
memory, 39-40
operating systems, 42
processors, 38-39
software, 43-45
type to buy, 45-46
PCT (Private Communications Technology), 184
performance (speed)
cable connections, 58-59
Internet connections, 3-4, 49-50
modems, 53-54
processors, 39, 45
upstream/downstream, 56
personal information, security of sending over the Web, 180-182
personal names in mail messages, 126
personal note from Harley Hahn, i-ii
personal toolbar (Netscape), 172
phone, voice communications over Internet, 304-306
photographs
360-degree photo plug-ins, 230
converting to JPEG file format, 337-338
Web sites for, 338

PICS (Platform for Internet Content Selection), 199
pictures. *See* images; photographs
Pierce, John, xxiv
quotation of, xxi
plug-ins, 222-224, 228
360-degree photos, 230
finding, 231
installing, 225-226
multimedia, 229
music, 230
Netscape, displaying list of, 227-228
streaming audio/video, 228
VRML, 33, 229
Point of Presence (POP), 62
Point-to-Point Protocol (PPP), 8
Polly, Jean Armor, xxiii
POP (Point of Presence), 62
POP (Post Office Protocol), 8, 97-98
pornography, 14
port numbers, 315-316
portals, 174
ports, Ethernet, 46
Post Office Protocol (POP), 8, 97-98
posting articles (Usenet), 267-270
postmaster mail addresses, 81
pound sign (#), IRC channels, 308
PPP (Point-to-Point Protocol), 8
preferences for browsers, setting, 147-149
price
ISPs, 61
PCs, 46-47
privacy. *See also* security
mail addresses, 139, 256
mail messages, 118-119, 127-129
talk facilities, 318-320
Private Communications Technology (PCT), 184
private keys (encryption), 140
problems, troubleshooting. *See also* help
bounced mail messages, 119-120
URLs, 158-159

processors, 38-39
   speed, 45
programs, 4-5. *See also* **applications;**
   software
   16-bit, 235
   32-bit, 235
   clients, 5-6
   freeware, 235
   installing, 238-240
   mail, 19, 96, 100-102
   mailing list programs, 279-281, 284-288
   servers, 5-6
   shareware, 235
   uninstalling, 241
   in Web pages, 334-335
programs, downloading, 234
   anonymous FTP, 237-238
   directories for saving files, 236-237
   overview, 234-235
   Usenet binaries, 267
promoting Web sites, 344-345
protocols, 7-8
   FTP (File Transfer Protocol). *See* FTP
   HTTP (Hypertext Transfer Protocol),
      8, 146
   IMAP (Internet Message Access
      Protocol), 8, 98
   LDAP (Lightweight Directory Access
      Protocol), 8, 135-136
   NNTP (Network News Transfer
      Protocol), 8, 248
   PCT (Private Communications
      Technology), 184
   POP (Post Office Protocol), 8, 97-98
   S/MIME (Secure Multipurpose Internet
      Mail Extensions), 8, 140
   SMTP (Simple Mail Transfer Protocol), 8,
      97-98
   SSL (Secure Sockets Layer), 184
public keys (encryption), 140
publishing Web pages, 335
punctuation, checking in mail messages,
   123-124

purchasing PCs
   cost, 46-47
   type to buy, 45-46
push clients, 175-177

Q-R

question mark (?), searches directly from
   browsers, 209-211
quotations in acknowledgments
   section, xxi
quoting
   articles (Usenet), 268
   mail messages, 116

RADSL (Rate Adaptive Asymmetric
   Digital Subscriber Line), 57
RAM (random-access memory), 39-40
rating systems (Web sites), 198-200
reading
   articles (Usenet), 256-259
   Web pages, 155-157
readme files, 238
real-time, 294
RealAudio, 223, 331
`Received:` **line (mail headers), 106-107**
recording sound, 339
Red, Michael, xxiii
regional hierarchies (Usenet), 252
registering domain names, 349-350
   contact information, 352-353
Reinisch, Karen, xxiv
reloading Web pages from cache,
   163-164
remote access (telnet), 33-34
renaming shortcuts, 166
`Reply-To:` **line (mail headers), 107**
replying to mail messages, 115-117
request for discussion (RFD), 272
requirements for Internet connections,
   38, 65
   hardware, 45-46
   software, 44-45

resizing windows, 161

restoring minimized windows, 161

Restricted Sites zone (Internet Explorer), 191

reversing mouse buttons, 158

RFD (request for discussion), 272

rich text in mail messages, 108, 129-130

right-clicking, 157-158

ringmasters, 216

rings (Web), 215-216

risks. *See* security

Rivers, Martin, xxiii
    quotation of, xxi

role-playing, 32-33, 313-317

root name servers, 78

Russo, Rich, xxiii

S

S/MIME (Secure Multipurpose Internet Mail Extensions), 8, 140

safety. *See* security

saving
    files when downloading programs, 236-237
    images from Web pages, 338

saving URLs, 166-167
    Bookmarks list (Netscape), 169-172
    Favorites list (Internet Explorer), 167-169

scanners, 337

schemes (URLs), 83

scroll bars, 155

scrolling in windows, 155-156

SDSL (Symmetric Digital Subscriber Line), 57

Search button (browsers), 208

search engines, 202-204
    accessing quickly, 208-209
    tips for using, 204-206
    Usenet, 206-208
    Web sites, promoting, 344-345

searches. *See also* search engines
    directly from browsers, 209-211
    for mail addresses, 134-136
    starting, 202
    tips for, 216-218
    Usenet, 270-271
    Web rings, 215-216

second-level domains, 75

secure connections, 183-184

Secure Multipurpose Internet Mail Extensions (S/MIME), 8, 140

Secure Sockets Layer (SSL), 184

security. *See also* privacy
    ActiveX, 189-190
    children, safety precautions on Internet, 195-200
    cookies, 184-187
    DCC (Direct Client to Client connection), 312
    downloading data, 188-189
    encryption (mail messages), 140-142
    filtering software, 198-200
    Internet connections, 183-184
    Internet Explorer security zones, 190-192
    Java, 189
    Netscape settings, 192
    personal information, sending over the Web, 180-182
    viruses, 192-195
    warning messages, 182-183

security certificates, 191

selecting
    domain names, 350-351
    ISPs, 61-63
    mail programs, 100-102
    theme of Web page, 324, 341
    Web site hosts, 342-344

self-control (Internet usage), 15

sending
    articles (Usenet), 267-270
    copies of Web pages, 173
    mail messages to groups, 133-134

personal information over the Web, security of, 180-182

URLs in mail messages, 172-173

servers, 5-6

DNS, access to, 78-79

FTP, 29

hosting Web sites, 342-344

IRC, 30, 307

list servers, 277

mail servers, 19, 96-98

name servers, 78

news servers, 25, 244-249

talk facilities, 295

types of, 35

Web servers, 22, 145

whois servers, checking availability of domain names, 351-352

sex

Net sex, 320-321

pornography, 14

shareware, 235

sharing Web pages, 172-173

shortcuts to Web pages, creating, 164-166. *See also* **keyboard shortcuts**

shouting in mail messages, 126

signatures

articles (Usenet), 260

mail messages, 102, 109-110

signing authorities, 141

Simple Mail Transfer Protocol (SMTP), 8, 97-98

sites (Web), 22, 145. *See also* **Web pages**

360-degree photo plug-ins, 230

advertisement blocking software, 150

antivirus programs, 194

avatar-based chat rooms, 299

browsers, downloading, 147

channel guides, 177

for children, 197

clip art, 339

comics, 162

commercial newsfeeds, 249

connecting to DNS servers, 78-79

creating Usenet newsgroups, 274

default home pages, 175

direct connection talk facilities, 301

domain names, obtaining, 343-344

downloading Usenet binaries, 267

FAQs (Frequently Asked Questions), 215

filtering software, 198-200

free Web hosting, 344

FTP clients, 337

Harley Hahn, 175, 327

hosting, 342-344

hostnames, deciphering, 73

HTML tutorials, 327

image editors, 339

images, 339

Internet Explorer security zones, 190-191

IRC clients, 312

IRC help, 313

ISPs, lists of, 63

list of, xii-xiii

Lunaea Hougland, xxii

mail address directories, 135

mail programs, 102

mailing lists, finding, 288

Movielink, 185

mud clients, 317

mud FAQs, 317

muds, list of, 317

multimedia plug-ins, 230

music plug-ins, 230

newsreaders, 247

organizational/regional hierarchies (Usenet), 253

organizing, 341

photographs, 338

plug-ins, finding, 231

portals, 174

promoting, 344-345

push clients, 177

rating systems, 199

registries for domain names, 350

smileys, 373

software repositories, 235

sounds, 340

streaming audio/video plug-ins, 229

Usenet searches, 208, 271

virus hoaxes, 195
voice/video communications, 306
VRML plug-ins, 229
Web chat rooms, 299
Web page editors, 336
Web rings, 215-216
Web-based mail services, 100
Web-based mailing lists, 289
Web-based newsreaders, 247
Wendy Murdock, xxii, 151
zip file programs, 240
sizing windows, 161
slang (Usenet), 262-265
slash (/)
   IRC commands, 310
   in URLs, 89-90
smileys, 125-126, 263-264, 302, 370
   Web sites for, 373
Smith, Sossity, xxiv
SMTP (Simple Mail Transfer Protocol), 8, 97-98
snail mail, 19
Snyder, Keith, xxiii
social muds, 314-315
software, 4-5, 43-45. *See also* **applications; programs**
   antivirus programs, 43-44
   bundled with PCs, 43
   distribution with anonymous FTP, 28-30
   operating systems, 42
   requirements for Internet connections, 38, 44-45, 65
   suites, 43
   word processors, 43
software repository Web sites, 235
software, downloading, 234
   anonymous FTP, 237-238
   directories for saving files, 236-237
   overview, 234-235
   Usenet binaries, 267
sound
   music plug-ins, 230
   RealAudio, 223

   streaming audio, 223, 228, 331
   Web pages, 331-332, 339-340
Sound Recorder program, 339
source code (Web pages), viewing, 327
spam, 26-27, 136-138
   avoiding, 255-256
   Usenet, 248-249
speed
   cable connections, 58-59
   Internet connections, 3-4, 49-50
   modems, 53-54
   processors, 39, 45
   upstream/downstream, 56
spell-checking mail messages, 123-124
spoilers, 265
SSL (Secure Sockets Layer), 184
starting
   mailing lists, 289
   newsreaders, 256
   searches, 202
status bar (browsers), 154
stopping download of graphics on Web pages, 149-150
streaming audio, 223, 331
   plug-ins, 228
sub-domains, 75
subdirectories, 86-87
Subject: line (mail headers), 104-105
subscribing to
   channels, 175-177
   mailing lists, 276, 281-283
   newsgroups, 257
subscription address (mailing lists), 280, 284
suffixes (file extensions), 85-86, 220-222
suites (software), 43
surf, 10-11
switching mouse buttons, 158
Symmetric Digital Subscriber Line (SDSL), 57
system messages (IRC), 310

T

<table> HTML tag, 330

tables (Web pages), 332-333

tags (HTML), 324-330
  <a> (anchors), 326, 330
  <b> (bold), 330
  <body>, 330

 (line break), 325, 330
  <center>, 330
  comments (<!...>), 327, 330
  <font>, 330
  <form>, 330
  <frame>, 330
  <frameset>, 330
  <h1> (headings), 330
  <head>, 330
  <hr> (horizontal rule), 330
  <html>, 330
  <i> (italics), 325, 330
  <img> (image), 325, 330
  <map> (image maps), 330
  <meta>, 330
  <ol> (ordered lists), 330
  <p> (paragraphs), 330
  <table>, 330
  <title>, 330
  <u> (underline), 330
  <ul> (unordered lists), 330

talk facilities, 30-32
  abbreviations, 302-304, 370-373
  chat rooms, 30
  clients, 295
  direct connections, 295, 299-301
  expectations compared to reality,
    317-320
  ICQ, 31
  IRC (Internet Relay Chat), 30, 307-313
  lag, 295
  muds, 313-317
  Net sex, 320-321
  overview, 294-296
  servers, 295
  voice/video communications, 31, 304-306
  Web chat rooms, 296-299

taskbar, 161

TCP (Transmission Control Protocol), 8

TCP/IP protocols, 7-8

technical support (ISPs), 62

telephone, voice communications over
  Internet, 304-306

telnet, 8, 33-34

terabytes, 39-40

terminal emulation, 34

terminals, 34

terminology of Internet usage, 9-10
  words to avoid, 10-11

testing posting of articles (Usenet), 269

text, 22, 145
  Web pages, 329

theme of Web page, selecting, 324, 341

threads
  articles (Usenet), 265
  mail messages, 117

tilde (~), in pathnames, 92-93

time zones, 366-367

time/date on message headers, 105,
  366-367

title bar, 161

<title> HTML tag, 330

titles in mail messages, 126

To: line (mail messages), 104, 112-114

tolerance, viewing Web sites, 15

top-level domains, 68, 71, 74, 356
  exceptions to usage, 71-72
  geographical, 70, 357-363
  organizational, 69, 356

topics, IRC channels, 308

tracking Web usage with cookies,
  184-186

traffic, mailing lists, 277

Transmission Control Protocol (TCP), 8

Trash folder (mail messages),
  emptying, 112

trolling, 138

troubleshooting. *See also* help
  bounced mail messages, 119-120
  URLs, 158-159

Trusted Sites zone (Internet Explorer), 191

Tyndall, Sylvia, xxiii

Tyndall, Timothy, xxiii

typing searches directly in browsers, 209-211

typing URLs, 151-152
  abbreviations for, 152-153
  for newsgroups, 257

U

<u> HTML tag (underline), 330

<ul> HTML tag (unordered lists), 330

underline (<u> HTML tag), 330

Undernet (IRC), 307

Uniform Resource Locators. *See* URLs

uninstalling programs, 241

United States, top-level domains, 70-71

universal broadcasting, 13

Universal Time (UT), 366-367

Unix operating system, 91
  home directories, 92

unordered lists (<ul> HTML tag), 330

unpacking archives, 234

unsubscribing from mailing lists, 276, 282-283

unzipping zip files, 239

updating channels. *See* subscribing to channels

uploading, 335
  files with FTP, 28-30

uppercase letters
  hostnames, 69
  shouting in mail messages, 126

upstream/downstream data transmission, 56

URLs (Uniform Resource Locators), 82-85
  ~ (tilde) in pathnames, 92-93
  abbreviations when typing, 89-91, 152-153

case sensitivity of pathnames, 91-92
  http, 146
  https, 184
  in mail messages, 130-131
  for newsgroups, typing in browsers, 257
  pathnames, 88-89
  saving, 166-172
  sending in mail messages, 172-173
  shortcuts, creating, 164-166
  troubleshooting, 158-159
  typing, 151-152

Usenet, 24-25, 244
  abbreviations, 263-264
  compared to mailing lists, 25-26, 277-279
  creating newsgroups, 271-274
  FAQs (Frequently Asked Questions), 261-262
  finding newsgroups, 270-271
  flames, 265
  freedom of speech, 245-246
  gateways with mailing lists, 289-291
  hierarchy, 249-255
  history of, 24
  moderated newsgroups, 260-261
  news servers, 244, 247-249
  newsreaders, 244-247, 255-256
  number of newsgroups, 254-255
  overview, 244
  pictures, 266-267
  search engines, 206-208
  slang, 262-265
  spam, 26-27, 248-249
  spoilers, 265
  time zones, 366-367
  URLs, 84

Usenet articles, 25, 244
  cross-posting, 265
  distribution, 244-245
  follow-up, 265
  format of, 258-260
  posting, 267-270
  reading, 256-259
  threads, 265

UT (Universal Time), 366-367
UTC (Coordinated Universal Time), 366-367

V

vCards (mail messages), 102-103, 110
VDSL (Very high-bit-rate Digital Subscriber Line), 57
vertical scroll bars, 155
video
    capture boards, 337
    communications over Internet, 304-306
    conferencing, 31
    streaming audio/video plug-ins, 228
viewing
    graphics on Web pages, 149-150
    plug-ins list (Netscape), 227-228
    source code for Web pages, 327
    Web pages, 155-157
Virtual Reality Modeling Language (VRML), 33, 229
viruses, 192-194
    antivirus programs, 43-44, 193-194
    hoaxes, 194-195
    mail, 193
    mail messages about, 118
voice communications, 31
    over Internet, 304-306
volume (mailing lists), 277
VRML (Virtual Reality Modeling Language), 33, 229

W

warning messages (security), 182-183
WAV sound format, 331-332
Web
    ActiveX, 189-190
    advertising on, 26
    channels, 23-24, 175-177
    chat rooms, 30, 296-299
    complexity of, 144-145
    downloading data, security issues, 188-189
    help, 151
    Java, 189
    overview of, 20-21, 145-149
    security, sending personal information, 180-182
    tracking usage with cookies, 184-186
Web browsers, 22-23, 44-45, 145-147. *See also* Internet Explorer; Netscape
    abbreviations when typing URLs, 90-91, 152-153
    ActiveX controls, 224-225, 227
    address bar, 151
    advertisements, blocking, 149-150
    autocomplete feature, 153
    Back/Forward buttons, 155
    cache, 163-164
    channels, 23-24
    complexity of, 144-145
    default home pages, 175
    file extensions, 220-222
    FTP clients, 29
    graphics, viewing/hiding, 149-150
    help, 151
    history list, 155
    home page, setting, 173-175
    mail programs with, 100
    newsreaders, 25
    Opera, 146-147
    options/preferences, 147, 149
    programs, installing automatically, 240
    saving URLs, 166-172
    scroll bars, 155
    search engines, accessing quickly, 208-209
    searches, directly from address bar, 209-211
    status bar, 154
    as talk clients, 297
    typing URLs, 151-152
    URLs for newsgroups, 257
    warning messages, 182-183
    Web pages, designing, 340
    Web sites for, 147
    Web-based mail services, 99-100

Web pages, 22, 145. *See also* **Web sites**
advertisements, blocking, 149-150
cache, 163-164
components of, 327, 329
design tips, 340-342
editors, 335-337
elements of, 145-146
file extensions, 86, 220-222
forms, 332-333
frames, 156-157, 332, 334
graphics, viewing/hiding, 149-150
home page, setting in browser, 173-175
HTML (Hypertext Markup
  Language), 146
HTML tags, 324-330
hypertext, 22
images, 330-331, 337-339
links, 154, 329
navigating, 153-155
programs in, 334-335
publishing, 335
reading, 155-157
selecting theme of, 324, 341
sending copies of, 173
shortcuts, creating, 164-166
sound, 331-332, 339-340
source code, viewing, 327
tables, 332-333
text, 329
URLs. *See* URLs
Web rings, 215-216
Web servers, 22, 145
hosting Web sites, 342-344
Web site searches
accessing search engines quickly,
  208-209
directly from browsers, 209-211
search engines, 202-204
starting, 202
tips for, 204-206, 216-218
Web sites, 22, 145. *See also* **Web pages**
360-degree photo plug-ins, 230
advertisement blocking software, 150
antivirus programs, 194
avatar-based chat rooms, 299

browsers, downloading, 147
channel guides, 177
for children, 197
clip art, 339
comics, 162
commercial newsfeeds, 249
connecting to DNS servers, 78-79
creating Usenet newsgroups, 274
default home pages, 175
direct connection talk facilities, 301
domain names, obtaining, 343-344
downloading Usenet binaries, 267
FAQs (Frequently Asked
  Questions), 215
filtering software, 198-200
free Web hosting, 344
FTP clients, 337
Harley Hahn, 175, 327
hosting, 342-344
hostnames, deciphering, 73
HTML tutorials, 327
image editors, 339
images, 339
Internet Explorer security zones,
  190-191
IRC clients, 312
IRC help, 313
ISPs, lists of, 63
list of, xii-xiii
Lunaea Hougland, xxii
mail address directories, 135
mail programs, 102
mailing lists, finding, 288
Movielink, 185
mud clients, 317
mud FAQs, 317
muds, list of, 317
multimedia plug-ins, 230
music plug-ins, 230
newsreaders, 247
organizational/regional hierarchies
  (Usenet), 253
organizing, 341
photographs, 338
plug-ins, finding, 231

portals, 174
promoting, 344-345
push clients, 177
rating systems, 199
registries for domain names, 350
smileys, 373
software repositories, 235
sounds, 340
streaming audio/video plug-ins, 229
Usenet searches, 208, 271
virus hoaxes, 195
voice/video communications, 306
VRML plug-ins, 229
Web chat rooms, 299
Web page editors, 336
Web rings, 215-216
Web-based mail services, 100
Web-based mailing lists, 289
Web-based newsreaders, 247
Wendy Murdock, xxii, 151
zip file programs, 240

Web-based mail services, 99-100

Web-based mailing lists, 289

Web-based newsreaders, 247

WebTV, 47

welcome messages (mailing lists), 276
organizing, 283

whiteboard, 306

whitelist (filtering software), 198

whois servers, checking availability of domain names, 351-352

Windows, 42

windows
closing, 161
focus, 156
maximizing, 160-161
minimizing, 161
moving, 162
opening new, 162-163
resizing, 161
scrolling in, 155-156

Windows clipboard, 131-132

Windows Explorer, 87

word processing software, 43

working memory, RAM (random-access memory), 39-40

World Wide Web (WWW). *See also* **Web browsers; Web pages; Web sites**
ActiveX, 189-190
advertising on, 26
channels, 23-24, 175-177
chat rooms, 30, 296-299
complexity of, 144-145
downloading data, security issues, 188-189
help, 151
Java, 189
overview of, 20-21, 145-149
security, sending personal information, 180-182
tracking usage with cookies, 184-186

www, in hostnames, 73

wysiwyg editors, 335

X-Z

X-Mailer: line (mail headers), 108

Yahoo (search engine), 203

Zhing (adventure mud), 315

zip file programs, 239

zip files, 239-240

zones (security), Internet Explorer, 190-191